MASTERS

OF

ANCIENT

COMEDY

By Lionel Casson:

THE ANCIENT MARINERS

Seafarers and Sea Fighters of the Mediterranean in Ancient Times

MASTERS OF ANCIENT COMEDY

Selections from Aristophanes, Menander, Plautus, and Terence

Selections from

Aristophanes

MASTERS

Menander

OF

Plautus

ANCIENT

Terence

COMEDY

Edited and Translated by LIONEL CASSON

Minerva Press

Library of Congress catalog card number: 60-13140

First paperbound edition published in 1967, by arrangement with The Macmillan Company.

Funk & Wagnalls, *A Division of* Reader's Digest Books, Inc.

TO

MY

PARENTS

Preface

Masters of Ancient Comedy is not only the first anthology of its kind in English but the first book to include an English translation of Menander's recently discovered play *The Grouch.* In a sense these two "firsts" are interlocked: it was the discovery of Menander's play that to a great extent made the anthology possible.

Ancient comedy had three great periods: Greek Old Comedy, in the fifth century B.C., Greek New Comedy in the late fourth and early third, and Roman Comedy in the late third and early second. Until 1905 only the first and third periods were available to the modern world—the one represented by the plays of Aristophanes, the other by those of Plautus and Terence—and the disparity between the two was so great there was little point in combining them between the covers of one book. Nothing was extant to represent Greek New Comedy, which not only bridged the gap but had a profound effect upon the two great Romans and, through them, upon the whole future of comedy in the Western world. In 1905 some fragments of plays by Menander, the star of New Comedy, came to light. Then, in 1959, a complete play from his hand was published (it had been found a few years earlier), and for the first time the materials were at hand to illustrate all three periods of Greek and Roman comedy.

So little is left of Menander that I felt it necessary to include all the extended portions preserved of his work, three fragmentary plays as well as the new one. From the eleven extant plays of Aristophanes I have selected one of the gayest and most representative; from the twenty by Plautus, one example of his pure farce and one of his more romantic style; from the six of Terence, his two acknowledged masterpieces. The result is a varied program that runs the gamut from the topical satire of Aristophanes through the comedy of manners of Menander and Terence to the slapstick of Plautus.

All Greek and Roman drama was in verse. Moreover, Aristophanes and Plautus were both, in a sense, writing musical comedy: a considerable portion of their plays is not dialogue to be spoken but lyrics to be sung. These by their very nature called for translation in verse. Everywhere else I have used prose.

The usual purpose of a verse translation is to retain the style and spirit of the original at the expense, if necessary, of literal accuracy; and, of a prose translation, precisely the opposite. What I have done is to reverse this usual state of affairs: I have chosen prose in order to retain the spirit, if not the style, of the original, and my prose is, if anything, more free than many a translation in verse.

There have been many periods in the history of drama when verse was the only accepted vehicle for comedy. Today, of course, playwrights writing in the vein of Menander or Plautus use normal colloquial speech. My aim was to make these ancient plays sound as much like contemporary comedy as I could—and still remain a translator and not an adapter. That meant not only using prose, but a prose that reflected the vocabulary and rhythms of contemporary speech. Every line I translated I subjected to a simple test: I read it aloud and asked myself whether it sounded the way a person would express himself in the given situation today. Frequently the original lent itself to a rendering that satisfied this requirement and was at the same time a close translation; more often, close translation was impossible and I rendered the general sense of a passage with no attempt to reproduce the meaning of the individual words; at times I frankly paraphrased. All references that would make sense only to ancient audiences or modern scholars I replaced with some sort of current equivalent. For the ubiquitous oaths and exclamations that invoke the names of ancient deities I substituted modern expressions; I converted drachmas and talents into dollars (allowing for current inflation has made my figures considerably higher than those in earlier translations); I replaced ancient geographical names with modern equivalents: I doctored the jokes, where necessary, to make them intelligible to today's audiences. Moreover, in line with my aim to make living theater of these plays, I added full stage directions, just as a modern playwright would.

My renderings in verse of the lyric portions reproduce in a very general way the metrical patterns of the originals, which are extremely fluid and flexible, characterized by lines of unequal length and by frequent changes of meter.

Three people kindly went through the manuscript of this book and made suggestions from which I have profited greatly. My largest debt is, as always, to my father: every page has felt the improving touch of his fine feeling for clarity and accuracy in language. Mr. Alfred Hart's keen critical eye and practical experience in the theater have been responsible for a multitude of changes that have added flavor and pace to the dialogue. And many a particularly apt turn of phrase was contributed by my wife.

It was the practice of the ancient comic writers to conclude with a plea for approval. I must conclude with a plea for indulgence.

Rome
January, 1960

Contents

Greek Old Comedy

/

Aristophanes' The Acharnians

The Origin of Comedy

Among the many intellectual gifts with which the ancient Greeks were blessed was that particularly ingratiating one, a sense of humor. It gleams brightly in the earliest of their preserved literature, the poems of Homer; it flashes in the works of such early poets as Archilochus and Anacreon; and it made possible for Greece the shining distinction of having created comedy.

As a matter of fact, the Greeks are responsible not only for comedy but for practically every other aspect of the theater of the Western world as well: tragedy, melodrama, mime, ballet, the art of acting, costume design, stage machinery, the theater building itself. It is exasperating that the origin of something so significant should be so obscure: no one knows for certain under what circumstances or precisely when the Greeks got the brilliant idea of having men impersonate imaginary characters, and thereby created drama. All we can say definitely is that drama came into being sometime during the sixth century B.C.; that its roots lay in religion, in particular the festivals in honor of the wine-god Dionysus, source of the fertility that caused the grapes to grow and of the joy the wine gave; and that the city of Athens played the leading role in its development. In 534 B.C., as part of the program at the festival of the Greater Dionysia in Athens, a man named Thespis led a troupe into a primitive theater—and the Western world's first formal dramatic performance was under way.

What Thespis presented on that memorable day was an embryonic form of tragedy. What of comedy? Where did it originate?

Crude comic performances that formed part of rustic festivals very likely go back to society's earliest history. But the first formal produc-

3

tions we have any real knowledge of, the earliest that have been preserved, are the plays put on by the people of Athens in the fifth century B.C. as part of their festivals honoring Dionysus—Old Comedy, as it has come to be known. And within these plays we find some clues to the source of Greek comedy, certain distinctive features that are best explained as vestigial remains of that from which it originally sprang.

The first such feature is the key role played by a chorus. The simplest way to account for this is to assume that the performances evolved from some sort of procession of singers and dancers. A second feature is the fact that the actors wore the phallic symbol conspicuously displayed; the procession, then, must have been part of the fertility rites connected with the worship of Dionysus. A third is the curious section, found in most of the plays, called the *parabasis:* the action stops, the chorus steps forward and, in an address that has a rigidly fixed structure—a passage in anapestic meter, another in trochaic meter (*epirrhema*), a song (the "ode"), then a responsive second trochaic passage (*antepirrhema*) and song (the "antode")—speaks directly to the audience on whatever topics its heart (or, rather, the playwright's heart) desires; it then steps back and the action gets under way again. Such a curious, formal, nondramatic element must be a remnant of old ritual left embedded in the plays, perhaps a carry-over of the moment when the chief revelers of the procession made an address to all present at the festival.

From the religious observance out of which it grew comedy inherited, then, among other things, actors adorned with the phallic symbol and a chorus that sang and danced and, at the appropriate moment, interrupted the action to deliver its peculiar direct address to the audience. On this trunk the Athenian comic writers grafted whatever they found useful: some elements from contemporary tragedy, and some from various forms of farce that were flourishing in other Greek states. In 486 B.C., at the Greater Dionysia, comedies were for the first time included in the program. The brilliant career of Athenian Old Comedy had been launched.

Producing a Play in Fifth-Century Athens

In Athens of the fifth century B.C., drama was far from pure entertainment: it was something special, run by the state as the principal feature of an important religious event, a festival dedicated to Dionysus. What is more, it was part of a contest: the plays were judged and prizes awarded to the best comedy and tragedy.

There were two such festivals that quickly came to the fore as occasions for the presenting of plays. The more important has already been mentioned, the Greater Dionysia. It took place at the end of March or the beginning of April. Three days were given over to the dramatic competitions. During the period of particular concern to us, the last quarter of the fifth century B.C., three playwrights took part in the contest for tragedy, and three in that for comedy. Each tragedian put on a trilogy, a group of three plays, in the morning, and each comic writer one comedy in the afternoon. Comedies, as indicated above, were first included in this festival in 486 B.C., and they continued to be part of it for at least the next three hundred and fifty years.

The second festival was the Lenaea, which occurred at the end of January or the beginning of February. Here the emphasis was on comedy. Three comic writers competed, each with one play; three tragedians also took part, but with only two plays instead of the trilogy allowed at the Greater Dionysia. The Lenaea was the younger of the two festivals; comedy was not introduced until 442 B.C. and tragedy not until 432. Comedies formed part of the program for at least three hundred years.

The production of plays at either the Lenaea or the Greater Dionysia was entirely in the hands of the state. Athens had two annually elected officials called archons who, although titular heads of the government, had for the most part purely formal duties. One such was to preside over the two festivals, an archon in charge of each. Any interested playwright submitted a script, or scripts if his field was tragedy, to the appropriate archon, who selected from those offered the number he needed. The scripts were all in verse, for both ancient tragedy and comedy eschewed prose. Most of the scenes were written in iambic lines of six feet each which the actors delivered in ordinary speech; some were in more complex meters, and for these the actors used a sort of recitative to flute accompaniment; then there were a considerable number of lyric passages that were sung to the accompaniment of flute or lyre.

The state underwrote, directly or indirectly, all expenses. The biggest of these was the chorus. Old Comedies are, in a way, more like our musical than our "legitimate" comedies: they contain certain set pieces which the chorus sang and danced (what the music sounded like or the dances looked like we have no idea; no records of either have survived). When the chorus engaged in dialogue with an actor, its leader delivered the lines by himself, and in ordinary speech or recitative, as the meter demanded; but the whole body could, at any moment, break into brief bursts of song. There were twenty-four people in a comedy chorus and they had to be paid, costumed, provided with a dancing master and a flute player, and trained with exacting care. Since the cost of all this was too much for the state to assume directly, the archon assigned to each playwright a *choregus,* "chorus handler," a wealthy Athenian who, as part of his obligations to the government, put up all the money required for the chorus.

The second largest expense was the actors. In the early days of Greek drama, the playwright himself appeared in the leading role; but this practice was soon abandoned, and the professional actor came into being. The archon selected the number of leading men required for his festival and assigned them by lot, one to each playwright. The leading men, too, were involved in a contest: a prize was awarded to the best tragic and best comic actor. The state assumed all their costs directly. And the state also supplied, assigned, and paid for all the other performers, actors and supernumeraries, that were required. For reasons not exactly clear (perhaps cost was one), the Athenians had the curious custom of limiting a playwright to three speaking actors, the one involved in the actors' contest who generally played the chief role exclusively, and two others who divided the remaining roles between them. In tragedy the number never exceeded three; in comedy supernumeraries were occasionally assigned a few lines; in both any number of mute walk-ons was permitted. As in Shakespeare's day, men took all the parts. The playing of multiple roles was made possible, and the use of males in female roles made easier, by the fact that all performers wore masks. These were of linen stiffened with clay, and covered the whole head, resting on the shoulders. The actors of comedy, in addition, were grotesquely padded about the belly and buttocks, and, of course, wore the phallic symbol. Most of the time the actors delivered lines in ordinary speech or recitative, but they could join the chorus in a song or another actor in a duet, and, on occasion, could even render a solo.

When the day for the contests arrived, people began to flock to the theater early in the morning. They brought lunch and cushions with them, for the program went on until late afternoon and the seats were hard. The state charged admission in order to cover the costs of keeping the theater in repair and of cleaning it once the festival was over. But since the plays were part of a festival of the people, given by the people and for the people, the state could not in good conscience deny entrance to any citizen. It solved the problem by setting up a "seeing fund" which furnished the price of admission to those too poor to afford it. The first rows were reserved for dignitaries: priests, the archons, foreign ambassadors, and so on. The best seat in the house, first row center, belonged, understandably enough, to the priest of Dionysus.

After the last play was over there came that tense moment when the awards were announced. A panel of ten judges issued four lists containing, respectively, the order in which they rated the tragic playwrights, comic playwrights, tragic leading actors, and comic leading actors. The victors—and that meant those who topped the lists; only first place really counted—were crowned with ivy, and the choregi hurried off to arrange farewell banquets for their casts. The last act in this drama of putting on dramas was the inscribing on imperishable stone of a record of what had taken place: the names and order of rating of the playwrights, plays, leading actors, and choregi—these last shared all honors equally with the others and took just as much pride in them.

Thus the Athenian theatergoer was in a far different position from his modern counterpart. We can go to the theater every day of the year for our personal entertainment, and can see anything from an early Greek tragedy to the latest *avant-garde* piece. The Athenian saw plays, by and large, on only two occasions during a year, and both were great events, public religious holidays when the whole town turned out for the dramatic contests, and for three days everyone lived and breathed nothing but drama—it must have been somewhat like a combination of Easter and the World Series. Moreover, all the plays he saw were new; it was only on rare occasions that special circumstances permitted the presenting of a revival. And let us not forget that, if he couldn't afford it, he got his ticket free.

All the plays, comedies and tragedies, during the fifth century B.C. were put on in the Theater of Dionysus on the south slope of the Acropolis. The remains the tourist sees today are of a great stone edifice. It had a much different look when Aeschylus or Sophocles or Aristophanes put on their works: there was no stage then, and the construction was for the most part of wood. The seats, enough to accommodate fourteen thousand people, were set in tiers in the curve of a hollow in the steep hillside and came down to a wide level expanse. Here the first row embraced half of a great circle, about eighty-five feet in diameter. Within it lay a somewhat smaller one, about sixty-five feet in diameter; this was the area in which the chorus performed its dances. Back of this circle, standing free, was a building—the "scene building" as the Greeks called it—that served as backdrop and housed the actors' dressing rooms. It was a long, two-story structure flanked by two short wings projecting toward the circle, the whole forming a shallow U with a wide mouth. The oblong area in the embrace of the U, bounded by the circle in front, the façade of the building behind, and the wings on either side, was where the play was staged: it offered an area approximately fifty feet long and twelve deep. The backdrop had three doors that could be used for entrances and exits, and the spaces that, on either side of the circle, separated the scene building from the seating area provided side entrances.

Like Shakespeare's, this theater demanded much more from the spectator than is demanded today. Since the action had to go on in front of the façade of the scene building, the dramatist generally set the scene in a street or a palace court; when, however, he did otherwise, his hearers simply had to imagine the backdrop away. The plays went on under Greece's bright sun and blue skies; if the plot at any time called for darkness, the viewer had to create the illusion for himself. Since interior scenes were impossible, all action had to take place outdoors; but this probably made little difference to an audience of ancient Greeks, who carried on far more of their lives in the open than we. There was no curtain and there were no act divisions or intermissions; the plays were very short—they generally run for an hour or a little more—and, when breaks in the action were necessary, the playwright had the chorus take over for a brief song and dance. And, though the natural acoustics were fairly good, a pair of leather lungs did a lot to help an actor in his career.

Aristophanes (ca. 450–ca. 387 B.C.)

Each year the playwrights submitted their scripts to the archons, badgered the choregi for the best in dancers, costumes, and musicians, and, above all, listened intently as the judges announced the winners. For, in addition to kudos, victory automatically meant a place on the program the following year. As time went on, certain names began to appear regularly year after year. In tragedy it was first Aeschylus, followed soon by Sophocles and Euripides. In comedy it was Aristophanes.

Aristophanes was only one of a number of talented writers of Old Comedy. He had rivals who as often as not snatched the prize from him.

But after his death his reputation outstripped all the others. The only examples of Old Comedy that have survived are from his hand; of some forty plays that he wrote, eleven are extant.

The prime purpose of a Greek play, forming as it did the main feature of a religious festival, was to educate as well as entertain, and this is as true of Aristophanes' bawdiest comedy as it is of Aeschylus' loftiest tragedy. What differed was not the end but the means. Aristophanes used humor and satire and invective to achieve an objective as worthy as any sought by the tragedians: the inculcating of the idea of good citizenship. He wanted to drive out cant and hypocrisy and pretense from the Athenian way of life, to point up the unhappiness, both large-scale and small, that these caused, and he pursued this goal unflaggingly all his life. At the same time it must be admitted that he was no saint, that he had his own set of prejudices. He came from a family of wealth and standing, and his aristocratic and conservative up-bringing made him hostile in politics to the leaders of Athens' popular party and their aims; he tended to see cant and hypocrisy and pretense more readily there than in the opposing camp.

In a very real sense, all of Aristophanes' plays are variations on three themes: politics and the war with Sparta, a war that had begun when Aristophanes was a young man and lasted most of his lifetime; literature, in particular the writings of that *avant-garde* tragedian Euripides; and education, in particular the teachings of the sophists, a group whose curriculum and educational ends were diametrically opposed to what Aristophanes believed in. It can be seen immediately from this that practically every line he wrote was necessarily topical. That is why he must be presented to the modern world accompanied by a long intro-duction and a sheaf of notes. Today's readers of *The Acharnians* are somewhat in the position of a man from Mars who is asked to appreci-ate a play that satirizes the relations between the United States and Latin America, gives pungent advice to the West on how to deal with the Soviet Union, throws a few brickbats at progressive education, and includes a parody of the stylistic oddities of James Joyce—and is studded with choral passages for which neither music nor dance no-tation is provided, but merely bare lyrics.

The Acharnians

In 427 B.C. the youthful Aristophanes for the first time was "granted a chorus," as the Greeks put it: the archon accepted his play *The*

Banqueters for presentation at the Lenaea. He had arrived. The following year his *Babylonians* was on the program of the Greater Dionysia and, in 425, *The Acharnians*, the earliest preserved comedy in Western literature, was put on at the Lenaea. It received first prize, probably the playwright's first victory.

Although *The Acharnians* is not generally listed among Aristophanes' greatest plays, it is a close runner-up. Moreover, it offers what none of the others do, a cross-section of his interests. The opening scene satirizes the political situation at Athens, another pokes fun at Euripides, and the whole is a powerful plea for peace. He was later to devote an entire play, *The Knights,* to the first of these topics, two, *The Thesmophoriazusae* and *The Frogs,* to the second, and two, *The Peace* and *Lysistrata,* to the third.

In 431 B.C. Athens was the greatest nation of the Greek world. Her destiny was being guided by that renowned statesman Pericles. She had the most powerful fleet afloat. She headed an empire that encompassed most of the Greek states of the Aegean area; she referred to them as "allies," and called the money and services they provided "contributions" but nobody was fooled: they were subjects and their payments were tribute.

But when Aristophanes wrote *The Acharnians,* Pericles had been dead for four years and Athens was locked in a life-and-death struggle with the other leading power of Greece, Sparta, who had behind her not only her own matchless army but the resources of many of the states of mainland Greece. The war had been raging for six years, and significant changes had taken place in Athens during that time.

The city showed all the signs of a nation at war: soldiers strutted through the streets, the brass hats were riding high, tempers were short —and so was food; the farms of Athens had been devasted and supplies had to come from overseas under the watchful eye of the navy.

The government was engaged in frantic diplomatic activity: both Athens and Sparta were sending embassies to the Persian king to get him—and his ample treasury—on their side, and Athens was trying to coax the semibarbaric Thracians—and their hard-bitten troops—into joining her as allies.

Politics was marked by partisanship and hypocrisy. There were two bitterly opposed parties, one anxious to negotiate a peace, the other dedicated to carrying on the fighting. The peace party was made up, for the most part, of the wealthy and the aristocratic, the "knights," as the Athenians called them, who bore the bulk of the financial burden. But at the moment the pro-war, popular party was in the saddle. It was led by a violent but extremely capable man, Cleon, who had succeeded Pericles as the dominant politician in Athens. Cleon had one clear-cut advantage over his opposition: the farm vote. Since, thanks to the navy, the city could be fed on supplies from overseas, the farmers in the out-lying areas—including Acharnae, a district seven miles to the north— had been evacuated and brought within the city walls. For six years they had looked on helplessly as the Spartan army laid waste their orchards and vineyards. They could think of nothing but evening the score, and those too old for military duty made a convenient, ever-present voting bloc to jam through Cleon's pro-war measures. Moreover, all who had anything selfish to gain from the fighting were behind Cleon: professional soldiers, armorers, demagogues, and above all the informers, the self-appointed, self-important reporters of "subversive" activity.

Such was the state of affairs that winter day in 425 B.C. when *The Acharnians* was presented.

The Acharnians

1

DRAMATIS PERSONAE

Dicaeopolis "Honest Citizen," an Athenian farmer
Clerk of the Athenian Assembly
Amphitheus "Godly," a messenger of the gods
Athenian envoy to the Persian Court
Pseudartabas "Shortweight," a member of the Persian secret service
Theorus, Athenian envoy to the court of Sitalces in Thrace
Chorus of old men of Acharnae
Daughter of Dicaeopolis
Cephisophon, friend and associate of Euripides
Euripides
Lamachus, a general in the Athenian army
A man from Megara
Two young girls, his daughters
An informer
A man from Boeotia
Nicarchus, an informer
Servant of Lamachus
An Athenian farmer
A best man
A bridesmaid

13

An army orderly

A messenger

Another messenger

SCENE   The action of the first scene is in the meeting place of the
Athenian assembly. The rest of the action takes place in front of Dicaeopolis' house or nearby. The backdrop shows three house fronts: in the
center is Dicaeopolis', on one side is Euripides', on the other Lamachus'.

(*Wooden benches have been set in place in the open space before
the three house fronts to represent the Pnyx, the meeting place of
Athens' political assembly. One group is clustered behind a little dais
that serves as a speaker's platform; these are for the* prytaneis, *the members of the committee that presides over the meetings. Another group,
in front of the dais, is for the citizens. In the first row thereof sits a
lone figure—Dicaeopolis.*

*Dicaeopolis, "Honest Citizen," is a sturdy forthright chap in his
early forties. Like so many of his fellow citizens, he had been pulled
off his farm six years earlier and forced to live in the city, where, since
he is still of military age, he takes his turn doing guard duty at the
lookout posts on the city walls.*

*He has been sitting by himself for quite some time: the meeting was
scheduled to start early in the morning and by now it is almost noon.*)

DICAEOPOLIS (*brooding to himself*)   The things that have been eating
    my heart out—such a load of them! And my pleasures? A hand-
    ful. Just a handful, four maybe. But my woes! I reckon them by
    the sand-dune-grain-count. Let's see, what have I enjoyed,
    what was worth getting out of the dumps for? (*Brightening*) Oh,
    I know: it warmed the cockles of my heart when I saw how the
    Knights made Cleon cough up all those bribes. That cheered
    me. Knights, I love you for that piece of work, (*quoting a line
    from Euripides*) "For it was good for Greece." (*Turning glum
    again*) But then I had a woe to cancel it out, a tragic one. There
    I was at the theater, practically drooling with pleasure as I
    waited for a play by Aeschylus—and the announcer says, "The
    next number on the program is by Theognis."[1] You can imagine

---

[1] Instead of a play by Aeschylus, the Athenian Shakespeare as it were,
Dicaeopolis had to sit through one by Theognis, a second-rate writer whose works
were so lifeless and cold he was nicknamed "Snow."

what a shock *that* gave me. But then a pleasure to balance it out: after Moschus,[1] Dexitheus[1] came on to sing a dramatic song. But then, this year, we had Chaeris,[1] with that crouch of his, for the war-song. I took one look, blacked out—and practically passed out. (*Working himself up*) But never, never since I was a little shaver, have I been so cut, so cut to the—chin, as today. Here it is assembly day, we're supposed to meet at dawn —and the place is deserted. Everybody's jabbering in the marketplace and running every which way to get away from the red rope.[2] Even the chairman and his committee aren't here yet. They'll come hours late and spill into the place in a mob, shoving each other to get the front row seats. Wait'll you see. (*Shaking his head ruefully*) But how to get peace—that they don't care about one bit. (*Heaving a sigh*) Oh, Athens, Athens!

(*Falls silent; then, more calmly*) I'm always the first to get to these meetings. I take a seat and, since I'm all by myself, I gripe, I yawn, I fart, fidget, stretch, scratch, scribble, figure my bills—and look out over the fields, yearning for peace to come back. I hate the city. I want my own village where you never hear things like (*imitating an Athenian street-hawker*) "Charcoal for sale! Oil, vinegar for sale!" We made everything there for ourselves; we never had to be sold on the place.

(*Pauses, then grimly*) Today I'm here all set and ready to interrupt and shout down or heckle any speaker who talks on anything except peace. (*Suddenly a mob surges in, stage left, and a group makes a rush for the seats behind the speaker's platform.*) Well, look who's here, promptly at noon—the chairman and his committee! What'd I tell you? Just what I said would happen. It's every man for himself to get a front seat!

CLERK (*shouting*)　Step forward, everybody, step inside the official area!

(*A last-minute arrival, Amphitheus "Godly," suddenly dashes in and*

[1] Moschus was a lyre player as bad as Dexitheus was good. Chaeris was a singularly untalented Theban bagpiper who apparently affected a peculiar stance when playing.

[2] The Athenian police had an efficient system for rounding up a quorum for assembly meetings. A road led from one end of the market place to the Pnyx. The police stationed themselves in a line at the opposite end holding, stretched out, a rope daubed with fresh red paint. They then walked forward slowly— and anyone in the market place ended up either with a red smear and a fine, or in the Pnyx.

sinks into the seat alongside Dicaeopolis. He is dressed, not in ordinary clothes, but in the flowing garments worn by actors portraying gods on the Greek tragic stage.)

AMPHITHEUS *(excitedly, to Dicaeopolis)*   Has anyone asked for the floor yet?

CLERK   The meeting is now called to order. Does anyone wish the floor?

AMPHITHEUS *(rising)*   I do.

CLERK   Name, please.

AMPHITHEUS   Amphitheus.

CLERK *(looking up suspiciously)*   Are you mortal?

AMPHITHEUS   No, immortal *(Declaiming in tragic style, in imitation of the characters who serve as prologues in Euripides' plays and start things off with a lengthy pedigree)*

> The first of my name was child of Ceres and
> Triptolemus. Of him was Celeus born,
> Who wed Phaenarete, my grandmother.
> From her was sprung Lycinus, and I from him—

And so I'm immortal. Now, the gods have appointed me and me alone to arrange a peace with Sparta. But, gentlemen, although I am immortal, I haven't any money for travel expenses: the committee refuses to vote me any.

CLERK *(calling, and jerking his head significantly at Amphitheus)* Sergeants-at-arms!

(A pair of burly policemen appear and start hustling Amphitheus off.)

AMPHITHEUS *(in tragic style)*   Oh, Triptolemus and Celeus! Will you forsake me now?

DICAEOPOLIS *(rising to his feet, indignantly)*   Mr. Chairman! You are committing a violation of the procedure of this assembly in putting this man out. He wants to make peace for us so that we can sheath our swords.

CLERK   Silence! Be seated!

DICAEOPOLIS   I will not, by god! Not unless the committee commits itself to a debate about peace.

CLERK *(disregarding him, announcing)*   The envoys to the Court of the King.

DICAEOPOLIS (*muttering as he sits down*) Fine King! Envoys! I'm sick and tired of those fops and their swindling.

CLERK Silence!

(*The members of the Athenian diplomatic mission to the Court of the Persian King, the "Great King," enter and walk to the speaker's platform. They are dressed, not as they should be, in Athenian clothes, but in gorgeous Oriental costume.*)

DICAEOPOLIS (*aside*) Wow! Holy harem, look at those clothes!

ENVOY (*addressing the meeting*) You sent us to the Court of the Great King on an expense account of ten dollars per diem[1]—eleven years ago.

DICAEOPOLIS (*making a rapid mental calculation, aside*) That poor money!

ENVOY Well, first we had to cross the plains. It was exhausting. There we were, traveling in comfortable litters, lying at our ease, shaded by awnings. We had a terrible time.

DICAEOPOLIS (*aside*) And I sure had a fine time here—lying on straw at a lookout post.

ENVOY Whenever we were entertained, they *made* us drink. Out of gold-encrusted crystal. And only straight liquor.

DICAEOPOLIS (*aside, sadly*) Ah, my city of Athens, do you see how your envoys make a laughingstock of you?

ENVOY (*confidentially*) You know, with those foreigners, what makes a man is knowing how to put away the food and liquor.

DICAEOPOLIS (*aside*) And with us it's knowing how to go after the girls and boys.

ENVOY After four years we finally arrived at the King's Court. But we found out that he had taken the army and gone off—to go to the bathroom. We had to wait eight months until he got off the pot.

DICAEOPOLIS And how long did it take him to wipe himself?

ENVOY (*promptly*) A month. Then he came back to court and entertained us. Served us whole oxen en casserole.

DICAEOPOLIS (*aside*) Whole oxen en casserole? Who ever saw anything like that? How this man can lie!

ENVOY And he served us a bird that, I swear, was three times as big as Cleonymus.[2] They called it a yellow-bellied cheat.

[1] Two drachmas a day, a princely wage by Athenian standards, far greater actually than the rough equivalent here given.

[2] Cleonymus was one of Aristophanes' favorite targets. In play after play he jeers at the man's enormous bulk and his cowardice.

DICAEOPOLIS (*aside*) So that's why you had to cheat us out of ten dollars a day.

ENVOY And now we want to present to you the Right Honorable Shortweight, the King's Private Eye.

DICAEOPOLIS (*aside*) I'd like to see a crow poke out one of yours, Right Honorable Envoy.

CLERK (*announcing*) The King's Private Eye.

(*A member of the Persian secret service enters, flanked by two eunuchs. They walk gingerly toward the envoys. The king's representative is dressed in Oriental costume but his mask shows, instead of a face, one enormous eye with a beard below it. The eye bears a curious resemblance to an oarport of a war galley, and the beard to the leather covers that were lashed around the opening to keep out water when the seas were choppy.*)

DICAEOPOLIS (*aside*) My god! Man dear, are you trying for a naval look? What do you want to do, round a cape and find your way to a dock? You've even got a bag under your eye!

ENVOY (*to the Persian*) Honorable Shortweight, would you please tell the assembly the message the King sent you to deliver to the Athenians.

PERSIAN Iartaman exarx anapissonai satra.

ENVOY (*condescendingly*) Understand what he says?

DICAEOPOLIS God, no!

ENVOY He says the King's going to give you money. (*To the Persian*) Say the word "money" louder and clearer.

PERSIAN You fat-ass Greek. No get money.

DICAEOPOLIS Heaven help us, *that's* clear enough!

ENVOY (*pretending not to have understood*) What's he saying?

DICAEOPOLIS He says the Greeks are a bunch of fatheads if they expect any money from Persia.

ENVOY No! He says we're going to get barrels of money.

DICAEOPOLIS What do you mean, "barrels"? You're as big a crook as they come! Move away, I'm going to cross-examine him myself. (*To the Persian*) Now listen, you, and speak up, so I don't have to use this (*brandishing his fist*) and give you a blood bath. Is your King sending us any money? (*A vigorous shake of the head.*) Then our envoys are putting one over on us? (*A vigorous nod.*) These fellows say "yes" just the way we do in Greek. They must come from right around here. (*Looking closely at one of the two eunuchs*) I know who one of these eunuchs is—it's Cleisthenes![1] (*Parodying a line from Euripides and one from the poet Archilochus*)

> Oh, you of the hot-souled soft and shaven rump,
> You big baboon, who boasts no beard to shave,

so you've come here dressed as a eunuch, eh? And who's the other one? Of course—Straton![1]

CLERK Silence! Be seated! (*Turning to the Persian and the envoys*) The Senate cordially invites the King's Private Eye to dinner at City Hall. (*They leave.*)

DICAEOPOLIS (*aside*) It's enough to make a man hang himself! I spend my days here on guard duty—and they get the invitations; City Hall's never closed to *them*. (*Grimly*) I'm going to do something drastic, something big. Where's that Amphitheus?

(*Amphitheus appears from a side entrance.*)

AMPHITHEUS Here I am.

DICAEOPOLIS (*digging into a purse*) Take this money for your expenses and arrange a treaty with Sparta—for me, and me alone, just me and my family. (*To the Assembly*) Go ahead, kid yourselves; keep sending those embassies of yours!

(*Amphitheus hurries off, Dicaeopolis resumes his seat, and the clerk proceeds to introduce the next item on the agenda.*)

CLERK Will Theorus,[2] our envoy to the Court of Sitalces,[3] step forward, please.

THEORUS (*rising*) Right here.

DICAEOPOLIS (*aside*) Another crook.

THEORUS (*addressing the meeting*) We wouldn't have spent all that time in Thrace—

DICAEOPOLIS (*aside*) If you weren't being paid all that money.

THEORUS —if it hadn't snowed all over Thrace and the rivers hadn't frozen over. It was just about the time Theognis[4] was putting

[1] Cleisthenes, a beardless effeminate, was another of Aristophanes' favorite victims. Straton apparently was a kindred spirit.

[2] Theorus was one of Cleon's satellites.

[3] Sitalces was at this time king of a considerable empire in Thrace. He actually did conclude a treaty with Athens, and undertook a campaign in fulfillment of his obligations under its terms.

[4] See p. 14, n. 1.

on a tragedy here. I had to spend the whole time matching Sitalces drink for drink. It's unbelievable how pro-Athenian that man is. He really loves you. He's even had carved on all the trees, "Sitalces loves the Athenians." His son, the one you just made an honorary citizen, is so crazy about the Greek sausage you'll serve at his induction ceremony, that he's been begging his father to help his new fatherland. And Sitalces swore—over the drinks—that he'll come with so many soldiers you'll think it's a plague of locusts.

DICAEOPOLIS (*aside*) I'm damned if I believe a word of it—except the part about the plague and the locusts.

THEORUS (*triumphantly*) And he's sent ahead a crack unit of the Thracian army.

DICAEOPOLIS (*brightening, aside*) Now you're talking!

CLERK Will the Thracians that Theorus brought please step forward.

(*A dozen or so decrepit, half-starved figures shuffle forward. The phalli they are wearing are conspicuously circumcised.*)

DICAEOPOLIS What the devil's this?

THEORUS (*proudly*) The flower of the Thracian army!

DICAEOPOLIS The flower of the army? (*Standing up and moving closer to inspect them*) Tell me this: who sliced the flower of the army's tools this way?

THEORUS (*disregarding him*) They're light-armed troops—but they'll strong-arm all of Boeotia for you. For ten dollars per man per day.

DICAEOPOLIS Ten dollars for this bobtailed bunch? The navy, the safeguard of our state, isn't going to like that.[1] (*As he continues his inspection the bag containing his lunch comes temptingly close to the Thracians and one of them whips out a skinny arm and neatly empties it.*) Oh, my god! I'm ruined! One of the flowers just swiped my garlic! Give me that back, you! (*The garlic is passed along and each gobbles a bite.*)

THEORUS Hey, you poor fool! Don't go near 'em! They've had garlic![2]

DICAEOPOLIS (*turning to the chairman and his committee, indignantly*) Gentlemen! Are you going to let me be treated this way in my

---

[1] Rowers in the navy received a drachma a day, exactly half of what was being asked for these Thracian mercenaries.

[2] The joke derives from the popular Athenian sport of cockfighting. Cocks were supposed to fight better when primed with garlic.

own homeland? And by foreigners? All right. I hereby forbid this meeting from taking up the question of pay for the Thracians. (*Looking up into a sky that is clear and blue*) I wish to report that I've had a sign from heaven: I felt a drop of rain.

CLERK (*promptly*) The Thracians will kindly leave and return the day after tomorrow. The meeting is adjourned.

(*The clerk, the chairman, his committee, Theorus, the Thracians, and so on, file out stage right, taking benches and platform with them. Dicaeopolis is left standing alone.*)

DICAEOPOLIS (*to himself*) Damn! That was a good lunch I lost. (*Amphitheus races in, stage left.*) Look, here's Amphitheus back from Sparta. Hi, Amphitheus, how did it go?

AMPHITHEUS (*without stopping*) Go? I'm still going and I can't stop! The Acharnians are after me; I've got to get away from them!

DICAEOPOLIS (*forcibly holding him*) What's the matter?

AMPHITHEUS I was hurrying here to bring you the treaties when some old codgers got wind of it. They're from Acharnae, tough and rough old fellows, made of oak and maple, Marathon veterans.[1] They all hollered at me, "Damn you! The enemy's cut down our vineyards and you're making treaties!" Then they started to fill their pockets with stones. I turned and ran. But they came after me, yelling their heads off.

DICAEOPOLIS (*impatiently*) Let them yell. Have you got the treaties?

AMPHITHEUS Right here. Three samples, as a matter of fact. (*Pulling out a flask*) Here's one labeled "Five Years."[2] Try it.

DICAEOPOLIS (*sniffing and making a face*) Phew!

AMPHITHEUS What's the matter?

DICAEOPOLIS I don't like it. It smells of pitch and naval stores.[3]

AMPHITHEUS (*pulling out a second*) Try this. It's marked "Ten years."

[1] Marathon was the glorious battle (490 B.C., during the first Persian War) in which the Athenians, almost single-handed, drove back a Persian attempt to invade Attica and thereby saved from conquest not only themselves but the rest of Greece.

[2] The Greek word for "treaty" literally means "libations of wine" since such offerings were an essential part of any treaty ceremony. Here, as well as later in the play, Aristophanes puns on the two senses of the word.

[3] A five-year treaty was too short; it would provide just a breathing spell, giving both sides time to build up their naval strength and renew the fight. A ten-year treaty was not long enough either; it would give Athens time enough to reconsolidate her hold on her overseas subjects and tempt her into trying the fortunes of war again.

DICAEOPOLIS (*sniffing*) Sour—like the embassies that make the rounds of our allies, as if they're holding back.

AMPHITHEUS (*pulling out a third*) Here's one marked "Thirty Years. On Sea and Land."

DICAEOPOLIS (*sniffing rapturously*) Oh, Bacchus! A bouquet of nectar and ambrosia! No smell of the draft board about this one. Drink it and it tells you, "Go where you will." I'll take this treaty, I'll toast it, I'll enjoy it to the full—and to hell with the Acharnians. I'm going to hold a little celebration for my discharge from the war right now.

AMPHITHEUS And I'm going to get out of the way of those Acharnians right now.

(*Amphitheus hurries off, stage right, and Dicaeopolis enters his house.*

A second later the Chorus charges in, stage left, brandishing stones. They are a group of tough and spry oldsters from Acharnae, a country town seven miles north of Athens near the well-wooded slopes of Mount Parnes. The old men had spent their lives cutting the oak and maple from the hillsides and burning it into charcoal; this industry was their sole means of support. But, like Dicaeopolis, they had been evacuated from their farms and cooped up in Athens. In addition to disliking city life, since they are over military age, they have nothing to do with their time and must depend on their families for their support. Like any citizen they could, of course, pick up a few pennies by turning up for jury duty, and, during the war, they developed a voracious appetite for it.)

CHORUS This way, men! After him! Stop everybody you meet and ask which way he went. We've got to catch him; it's for the good of the nation. (*Turning and addressing the audience*) Hey, there, do any of you know where that fellow with the treaties made off to?

(*Feeling the effects of running at their age, they come to a halt and sing, puffing and wheezing.*)

> He's gone. He got away. Oh, damn,
> I'm just too old. Now back when I
> Was young, I used to keep right up
> With Phayllus, the Olympic champ—
> With a bag of charcoal on my back!

This treaty carrier wouldn't have made
It then. Loped off this way? Not then!

(*They start milling about again.*) But now my bones are stiff, and
Lacrateides here, his legs are old, so the fellow got away. After
him! We may be old, but no one's going to have the laugh on
us; no one's ever going to say he got away from the men of
Acharnae!

(*They halt and sing again, puffing and wheezing.*)
God damn it all! The man's made peace
With our enemies. They ruined my fields,
And I'll fight and fight this hated war
And not give up till I drive a stake
Through their hearts, a piercing pointed one,
To the hilt. I'll teach them not to trample
Upon my vines again, by god!

(*Milling about again*) I've got to find him. Look for him—and with
a stony look! Chase him from country to country, if need be,
until we catch him. Then I'll stone him until I get tired—which
will be never!

(*The door of Dicaeopolis' house opens.*)

DICAEOPOLIS (*from inside*)   Silence! The ceremony is about to begin.
CHORUS   Quiet everybody! Did you hear someone say "silence?" (*As
Dicaeopolis appears in the doorway*) There's the man we want!
Wait—everybody out of his way. I think he's coming out now
to hold a service.

(*The chorus moves off to the side. Dicaeopolis walks downstage, followed by his wife and daughter and two servants. Since he has just
concluded a one-family truce, he is about to hold a one-family celebration, a miniature version of the great festival in honor of Dionysus,
one of the two at which comedies were presented. He and his family
are carrying all the necessary equipment: basket, pot, sacramental cake,
and large phallic symbol.*)

DICAEOPOLIS   Silence! The ceremony is about to begin. (*To his
daughter*) Basket girl, you go ahead a little. (*To one of the
servants*) Xanthias, hold that phallus up straight. (*To the girl*)
Now put down the basket, dear, and we'll begin.
DAUGHTER (*putting down the basket and taking out the cake*)   Mother,
hand me the ladle and I'll pour the sauce on the cake.

DICAEOPOLIS (*viewing the activity with satisfaction*)   Fine, fine. (*Praying*) Oh, Lord Dionysus, may this procession and sacrifice that I and my family offer you so joyfully to mark my release from war, and our celebration of your rites, proceed with good omen. And may my treaty bring me thirty years of happiness. (*Turning to the girl*) Come, dear, look as if butter wouldn't melt in your mouth. (*As the girl picks up the basket*) Hold your basket sweetly, sweet. He'll be a lucky man, the one who marries you. And he'll give you a brood of sweet little chicks, just as sweet as you are—when you fart getting up in the morning. Now, go ahead—and watch out that someone doesn't make off with your jewelry in the crowd. (*To the servants*) Now you two walk behind the basket girl. And keep that phallus up straight. I'll bring up the rear and sing the phallic hymn. Wife, you go up on the roof and play spectator. Forward march!

(*The wife scuttles up to the roof of Dicaeopolis' house, the girl settles her basket, the slaves shoulder the phallus, Dicaeopolis picks up the pot, and the little procession gets under way.*)

DICAEOPOLIS (*marching and singing*)

> Oh, Phallus, fellow reveler
> Of Bacchus, nighttime wanderer,
> Adulterer and pederast,
> A hearty welcome. I've come home
> At last, after six long years away.
> For I have made a private peace.
> I'm free! From war, from woe, from fuss,
> From Major General Lamachus!
>
> Far more to my taste it is to find
> My neighbor's pink-cheeked slavey tres-
> Passing and stealing wood. I grab her waist,
> I pick her up, I throw her down—
> And then proceed to go to town.
>
> So join us, Phallus, as we drink,
> And if hung over, when morning comes
> Gulp down a bracing cup of peace.
> Hang up the swords, we've our release!

CHORUS (*rushing out and singing*)

> There he is! The man we want!
> Hit him, hit him, hit him hard!
> Smack the scoundrel, everybody!
> Don't hold back, men, don't hold back!

DICAEOPOLIS (*shielding himself with his pot*) God almighty, what's going on here? Watch out, you'll smash my pot!

CHORUS (*singing excitedly*)

> Damn you, it's you we'll smash. With these here stones.

DICAEOPOLIS Gentlemen! Gentlemen of Acharnae! What's the reason for this?

CHORUS (*singing excitedly*)

> The reason? Because I hate a man
> Without a sense of shame or honor,
> A traitor to his fatherland.
> The only one to treat for peace!
> How can you look me in the face?

DICAEOPOLIS You don't understand why I did it. You've got to listen to me.

CHORUS (*singing excitedly*)

> I'll do no listening now to you.
> To the grave! Burial to be with stones.

DICAEOPOLIS No, not until you hear me out. (*As they threaten to throw*) Please! Gentlemen! A little patience!

CHORUS (*singing excitedly*)

> I've got no patience left for you.
> And let's have none of your long speeches.
> I hate you even more than Cleon—
> Whose hide I'll tan and give the Knights
> For soles and heels.[1]

Listen to any long speeches from you? I'm going to get even with you, that's what. A man who made peace with Sparta!

---

[1] Cleon, the head of the pro-war party, was the object of the playwright's bitterest invective. At the Greater Dionysia of 426 B.C., Aristophanes presented *The Babylonians* (now lost), in which he attacked the politician fiercely. Cleon replied by bringing him up on charges before the Athenian Senate. The Senate backed up Aristophanes. Cleon was a tanner by trade and there are frequent scornful allusions to this fact in the plays.

DICAEOPOLIS   Gentlemen, leave the Spartans out of this. Just listen to me and decide whether or not I was right to make my treaty.

CHORUS   Don't talk to me about being right—not when you've made a treaty with people who don't know what it is to respect an oath or keep faith.

DICAEOPOLIS (*pointedly*)   But I happen to know that these Spartans, these people we're so terribly angry at, are not responsible for all our troubles.

CHORUS   Not responsible for all our troubles? Damn you, how dare you say that to my face! And you want me to spare you!

DICAEOPOLIS (*stubbornly*)   No, I tell you, not all. And I can prove to you right now that there have been lots of times when they've been the injured party.

CHORUS   What a thing to say! Enough to give a man a heart attack! You mean you have the nerve to argue in favor of our enemies?

DICAEOPOLIS (*grimly*)   What's more, I'm willing to put my head on the block while I speak, and, if what I say isn't true and I don't convince the people—(*He draws his finger across his neck.*)

CHORUS   Men of Acharnae! What are we waiting for? The stones! Let's work this fellow over until he's as bloody red as a Spartan uniform.

DICAEOPOLIS   Your mood is black and hot—like charcoal. Gentlemen of Acharnae, you're not going to listen? You're really not going to listen?

CHORUS   Our minds are made up. We're not going to listen.

DICAEOPOLIS   This is an outrage!

CHORUS   I'd sooner die than listen to you.

DICAEOPOLIS   Gentlemen! Don't talk that way!

CHORUS   You're going to die this minute.

DICAEOPOLIS (*suddenly switching from conciliation to defiance*)   Then I'm going to tear *your* hearts out. I'll kill your dearest friend. I'm holding him as hostage. I'm going to get him and slit his throat.

(*Dicaeopolis dashes into his house. The chorus stands disconcerted.*)

CHORUS   Men of Acharnae, what does this threat of his mean? He can't have one of our children locked in there, can he? What makes him so sure of himself?

(*Dicaeopolis bursts out of his door. He has a bag of charcoal cradled in his left arm; in his right hand he holds a knife pointed at the cord about its neck. He is parodying a scene from Euripides'* play Telephus, *in which Telephus, wounded incurably by Achilles and informed by an oracle that only the wounder himself could heal him, disguises himself as a beggar, sneaks into the Greek camp, snatches the infant Orestes from his cradle, and threatens to kill him unless the Greeks offer help.*)

DICAEOPOLIS (*glaring at them*) Go on, start throwing if you want. I'll destroy this on the spot. I'll find out soon enough which of you has any feelings—for charcoal.

CHORUS We're done for! A charcoal bag! Our dearest friend, our neighbor! Don't do it! (*As Dicaeopolis brings the knife closer*) No! No!

DICAEOPOLIS I'm going to kill it. Go on, yell your heads off. My mind's made up. I'm not going to listen.

CHORUS (*singing tragically*)
It's me you'll kill, the lover of those coals.

DICAEOPOLIS You didn't listen to me when I wanted to talk a minute ago.

CHORUS (*singing excitedly*)

But now I will. You want to talk?
You want to tell me how you love
The Spartans? Go ahead. I'll never
Betray my dear little charcoal bag.

DICAEOPOLIS First you drop those stones.

CHORUS (*singing*)

All gone. And you put down that knife!

DICAEOPOLIS Not yet. I think you've still got some in your pockets.

CHORUS (*singing*)

All shaken out. They're empty. See?
No more excuses—you put down
That knife. When I turned I shook them out.

DICAEOPOLIS Hah! You were all trying to shake a shout for help out! These coals almost met their death. And all because their devoted friends and neighbors have no sense. (*Suddenly holds the bag away from himself.*) And the poor bag got so scared it lost control and let go a squirt of coal dust all over me, like a squid. (*Glaring at the chorus*) It's incredible how sour men's minds

can be! They're willing to heave stones and holler, but not to
listen to a dose of good sense—not even when I'm willing to say
what I have to say about Sparta with my head on a block!
And yet I love life as well as the next man. (*He rushes into his
house.*)

CHORUS (*singing*)

Go ahead, bring out a block, and, damn you, then get started.
What's this big speech all about? I'm dying now to hear it!

(*As Dicaeopolis comes out with a chopping block*) Remember—
you set the terms. Put your head on that block and start talking.

DICAEOPOLIS (*setting the block in place*) See? Here's the block.
(*Taking his place behind it*) And here's the poor little speaker.
But don't worry; by god, I'm coming out fighting. I'm going to
speak my mind in favor of Sparta. And yet I know there are
a lot of things I should be afraid of. I know what our people
from the rural areas are like. Some crooked politico praises them
and the state to the skies and, right or wrong, they lap it up.
They never realize they're being sold down the river. And I
know what our old men are like. All they want is to serve on
juries and see to it that the poor defendants get stung. And I
know what Cleon's like; he let me have it because of my
comedy last year.[1] He haled me before the Senate, slandered
me with lies, gave me the rough side of his tongue, gurgled
and guggled away at me, washed his filthy linen on me—I was
just about asphyxiated, I was that mud-beslung. (*Moving away
from the block*) But first, before I begin my speech, let me change
my clothes and make myself look like the world's most pitiful
object.

CHORUS (*singing*)

What's this new twist? What're you up to? Come,
        no more delaying.
Put on the thatch Hieronymus[2] cultivates—better
        than Pluto's helmet!

[1] See p. 25, n. 1.
[2] One of the possessions of the God of the Underworld was a helmet that made
the wearer invisible. Hieronymus was a poet who, as members of the craft so
often do, went around with a shaggy unkempt mop of hair, vast enough, the
chorus implies, to hide a man as effectively as the famous mythological helmet.

Or open up Sisyphus' bag of tricks. This case is coming to trial; no more pretexts.

(Dicaeopolis looks toward the door of Euripides' house—the best place to find beggar's rags, from the inexhaustible collection of the playwright who specialized in characters down on their luck.)

DICAEOPOLIS *(to himself)* The moment has come. Be brave, my heart![1] I'd better go call on Euripides. *(Walking up to the door)* Hello in there!

(The door opens and Cephisophon, friend and associate of the playwright, takes his stand in the doorway.)

CEPHISOPHON Who is it?

DICAEOPOLIS Is Euripides in?

CEPHISOPHON *(imitating the philosophical, paradoxical style of Euripides)* He's in—and he isn't. If you can follow me.

DICAEOPOLIS *(shaking his head in admiration)* Euripides, you lucky man! Imagine having a servant who can give such clever answers! *(To Cephisophon)* Please call him.

CEPHISOPHON *(starting his reply with a typical Euripidean expression)* Oh, but that's impossible.

DICAEOPOLIS Oh, but you must. *(Cephisophon turns on his heel and slams the door behind him.)* Oh, but I'll just knock on the door; I'm not leaving. *(Calling)* Euripides! Euripides, old boy! If you've ever opened your door to anybody, open it to me now. I'm Dicaeopolis. My address is—

EURIPIDES *(from inside)* I'm busy!

DICAEOPOLIS Roll yourself out as you are.

EURIPIDES Oh, but that's impossible.

DICAEOPOLIS Oh, but you must.

EURIPIDES Oh, but—well, I'll roll myself out. But I'm too busy to come down.

(A little cart with Euripides, couch and all, on it is rolled out onto the roof over the first floor of the house. He is dressed in a flowing tragic costume that has clearly seen better days.)

---

[1] It is typical of Euripides to have his characters address their "heart" or their "soul."

DICAEOPOLIS Euripides—

EURIPIDES *(in tragic style)*

What is this cry you've uttered?

DICAEOPOLIS *(thoughtfully)* You work up there although you could
just as well down here. No wonder you write about cripples.
(Taking a good look at him) Look at those clothes! What do you
do, wear the rags from your tragedies? No wonder you write
about beggars. *(Pleadingly)* Euripides! I beg you, on my knees,
give me some rags from that old play of yours. I've got to make
a speech to the chorus, *(pointedly, since lengthy addresses were
a Euripidean specialty)* a long one. I've got to be good. If not,
it means my life.

EURIPIDES *(thinking aloud)* Now which set of rags would that be?
(Poking around in a pile beside him and pulling out a set) You
wouldn't mean these that poor old Oeneus[1] wore, would you?

DICAEOPOLIS No, not Oeneus. Somebody even worse off.

EURIPIDES How about Phoenix?[1] *(Hopefully)* He was blind.

DICAEOPOLIS No, not Phoenix. Someone even worse off than Phoenix.

EURIPIDES *(to himself)* What rags does this this fellow want, anyway?
(To Dicaeopolis) Maybe you mean the ones of that poor beggar
Philoctetes?[1]

DICAEOPOLIS *(scornfully)* No, from someone way more beggarish
than him.

EURIPIDES *(holding up a set)* Maybe these filthy tatters that Bellerophon[1] wore when he was crippled?

DICAEOPOLIS *(impatiently)* No, not Bellerophon. The fellow I mean
was crippled, all right, but he was a beggar. Talked a lot. Had
the gift of the gab.

EURIPIDES *(a light dawning)* I know—Telephus.

[1] The references are to those of Euripides' plays whose heroes ended up in
particularly unfortunate circumstances (none of the works mentioned, as it
happens, are extant today). Oeneus was a king who had been cast off his
throne by rascally nephews. Phoenix, because of some foul play, had been
blinded and driven out by his own father. Philoctetes had spent ten years as a
castaway on a barren island, suffering all the time from an incurable wound.
Bellerophon had tried to ride the winged horse Pegasus to heaven, had been
struck down by Zeus, and had ended up as a penniless cripple. Thyestes had
been stripped of his possessions and driven into exile by his brother, Agamemnon.
Ino, at one point in a checkered career, had been smuggled into a palace dis-
guised as a humble servant.

DICAEOPOLIS *(rapturously)* That's it—Telephus! Please, Euripides, give me the stuff he wore.

EURIPIDES *(calling to Cephisophon inside)* Hey! Give this fellow Telephus' rags. They're on top of Thyestes'.[1] Next to Ino's.[1]

CEPHISOPHON *(opening the door and handing a bundle to Dicaeopolis)* Here they are.

DICAEOPOLIS *(as he holds up a garment riddled with holes)* O Zeus, who sees all and sees through all, grant that I look like the world's most pitiful object. *(Puts on the rags.)* Euripides, since you've been nice enough to give me these rags, would you please give me the accessories? How about Telephus' hat? *(Quoting from the* Telephus)

> For I must play a beggar's part today—
> To be who I am, and yet to seem another.

The audience will know who I am, all right, but the chorus will stand around like a pack of fools while I screw them up with smart little phrases.

EURIPIDES *(handing it to him, in tragic style)*

> A gift to one who weaves such subtle schemes.

DICAEOPOLIS *(parodying a line from the* Telephus)

> My blessing on you. But on Telephus—

(He makes an expressive gesture. He then puts on the hat—and a rapturous expression comes over his face as he feels himself infused with the verbal agility of a Euripidean hero.) Wonderful! I'm full of smart little phrases already. But, Euripides, I need a crutch. The kind beggars use.

EURIPIDES *(tossing one down, in tragic style)*

> Here it is. Now get you gone from these marbled halls!

DICAEOPOLIS *(to himself)*

> My soul! You see how from this house I'm thrust?

And yet I still need a lot of stuff. Let's stick to him, keep after him, nag him. *(To Euripides)* Euripides, give me a little basket. One that's all charred from holding a lamp.

EURIPIDES

> You wretch! What need have you of such work of wicker?

[1] See p. 30, n. 1.

DICAEOPOLIS

Need have I none, but yet I wish to have it.

EURIPIDES (*tossing it down*)

You weary me. Go, get you from this house.

DICAEOPOLIS

May heaven reward you—as it has your mother![1]

EURIPIDES   Go!

DICAEOPOLIS   One more thing: a cup. One that's cracked around the rim.

EURIPIDES (*tossing it down*)   Take it and be damned! You're a plague upon my house.

DICAEOPOLIS (*parodying a line from Euripides*)

How blind to the evils you create yourself!

But, Euripides, good old Euripides, I need just one more thing. A little pot. And a sponge for a stopper.

EURIPIDES   Ye gods, man, you're taking a whole tragedy from me! (*Tossing it down*) Here. Now go!

DICAEOPOLIS   I'm going. (*Starts to leave, then stops; to himself*) What can I do? I need it, I'm lost without it. (*Turning back*) Euripides, good old Euripides, if you give me this one last thing I promise I'll go and never come back. Give me some dry leaves for the little basket.

EURIPIDES   You'll be the death of me! (*Tossing out a handful*) Here. There go all my plays!

DICAEOPOLIS   I'm done. I'm going now. (*Quoting from the* Telephus)

For I make myself a burden—
I was unaware the chieftains loathed me so.

(*Starts to go off again, then stops; to himself*) Oh, my god! I forgot the most important item! Everything depends upon it. (*Turning back*) Euripides, good old Euripides, dear old friend Euripides, may I die and rot in hell if I ever bother you again, but I need just one more thing, only one, one only. Will you ask your mother for some herbs for me?

EURIPIDES (*thundering*)

The man insults us! Close the gates of my house!

---

[1] Euripides' mother made her living—or so Aristophanes would have us believe—by peddling greens in the market place.

(Euripides is wheeled inside and Dicaeopolis starts walking back to his block.)

DICAEOPOLIS *(to himself)*   Oh, my soul, we must go without our herbs. Are you aware of the seriousness of the contest in which you contest today? We're going to talk in favor of Sparta! *(His soul reacts by stopping him dead in his tracks.)* Forward now, my soul, here's the starting line. You're holding back! You just had a good swig of Euripides straight, didn't you? *(Taking a step forward)* Bravo! Come now, poor heart, step up there, put your head down there and say whatever you feel is right. Courage! Come, let's go! *(Dashes the rest of the way and lays his head on the block.)* Good work, heart!

CHORUS *(singing)*

> What will you do? What will you say?
> By god, he *is* a man of brass
> And iron—to stake his neck to the state
> And stand alone and speak against
> Us all! He's not afraid one bit.
> Well, you wanted it this way. Now talk!

DICAEOPOLIS *(putting down staff and basket, and leaning on the block; he begins with a parody of Telephus' speech to the Greek chieftains)*

> Do not be angered, gentle audience,
> If a beggar dare address the men of Athens

about the state, and an actor in a comedy at that. Even comedy knows the difference between right and wrong. I'm going to say some terrible things—but they're true. This time Cleon can't accuse me of running down the state in the presence of strangers: it's the Lenaea;[1] we're by ourselves. There are no strangers in town yet; it's too early for the allies to send in their tribute and soldiers. We're by ourselves, winnowed clean of all the chaff—for the resident aliens belong here; if the citizens are the grain, they're the bran.

Now, I hate the Spartans and I hope Poseidon, God of Earth-

[1] *The Babylonians* (see p. 10) had been given at the Greater Dionysia, which took place in late March or early April, a time when the sailing season had opened and out-of-towners used to flock to Athens to see the plays. *The Acharnians* was presented at the Lenaea, which took place in late January or early February, before the sailing season had opened; the audience, consequently, was almost wholly local.

quakes, their own special god, brings every house in their town
down on their heads. My poor vines have been cut too. But—
I can talk openly, we're all friends here—why blame things
on the Spartans? Certain Athenians—I don't say the whole
state; mind you, I do *not* say the whole state—certain small-
minded troublemakers, worthless bad pennies, counterfeits, kept
denouncing as contraband the little coats Megara[1] used to export
to us. And they couldn't see a cucumber or a rabbit or a piglet
or a clove of garlic or a lump of salt but it had to be from Megara
and had to be confiscated and sold on the spot. Up to this point
it was just small potatoes, just our Athenian way of doing things.
But then some drunken playboys go to Megara and steal a whore
named Simaetha. The Megarians take it to heart, garlic themselves up, and get even by stealing a pair from Aspasia's house.[2]
And that's how war broke out all over Greece—on account of
three prostitutes. Because, you see, the next step was for our
Olympian Pericles to thunder and lightning in his wrath, throw
all Greece into an uproar, and pass that decree that sounds like
a beer song:

> No Megarians any more to be
> On land, in port, or on the sea.

Then Megara, since she was slowly starving to death, begged
the Spartans to get this whore-inspired decree revoked. They
begged us again and again, but we said No. And the next sound
to be heard was the rattling of swords.

[1] No state suffered from the war as much as Megara, a small neighbor of
Athens. Megara existed on trade, particularly the sale of the items Aristophanes
enumerates. In 432 B.C., Pericles decreed that all the ports in the Athenian
Empire were to be closed to her, a terrible blow to her economic life and one
of the immediate causes of the war. Then, in the very first year of the war,
a massive Athenian expedition did a thorough job of ravaging her fields—and
repeated the process twice yearly thereafter.
   Aristophanes hated no group in Athens more than the *sykophanteis*, "informers." These were citizens who, since the law encouraged it, took it upon
themselves to report and prosecute evildoing, and during wartime this meant
particularly any activity they considered enemy-inspired or tending to favor the
enemy. The verb *phainein* which means "show," "inform against," "denounce,"
I have taken the liberty of rendering "report subversive activity"; the Greek
term conjured up, I think, much the same feelings as the words I have used
to translate it do today.
[2] Aspasia, a beautiful and accomplished courtesan, was Pericles' mistress.
She was in no sense a madam, as Aristophanes mockingly implies.

You'll tell me Sparta shouldn't have done it. All right, tell me what she should have done? Suppose a Spartan sailed out in a skiff, took a puppy from your tiniest island, declared it contraband, and sold it off. Would you sit still and stay home? You would not! You'd order out a fleet of three hundred galleys on the spot. The city'd be in an uproar: soldiers shouting, paymasters jabbering, crowds jamming the market, commanding officers being besieged, rations being measured out, figureheads being gilded; and haggling—for oar covers, oarlocks, casks, garlic, oil, bags of onions, garlands, fish, streetwalkers; and black eyes; and the navy yard—oars being planed, pegs hammered, oarlocks fitted, time-beaters tootling, bos'ns piping, fifers trilling, whistlers whistling. That's what you'd do. I know it. Then why don't we figure Telephus[1] would do the same? Because we just have no sense.

(The chorus splits into two half-choruses; they face each other glaring.)

SEMICHORUS A   Is that so? Damn you, god damn you! What do you mean, you beggar, by talking to us like that? What's more, you've insulted every informer in Athens!

SEMICHORUS B   By god, every word he says is true. He hasn't lied once.

SEMICHORUS A   Even if it's true, why did he have to talk about it? He can't speak that way and get away with it! *(They make a rush for Dicaeopolis.)*

SEMICHORUS B   Hey you! Where are you running to? Stand where you are! If you lay a hand on that man, I'll heave you up—

(The two choruses start to scuffle; the anti-Dicaeopolites have the worst of it and start calling frantically for help.)

SEMICHORUS A *(singing)*

> Lamachus![2] Man of the lightning look,
> Man of the terribly plumed brass hat,
> Come to the rescue and save me! Come!
> Lamachus, neighbor and friend, please come!

[1] Dicaeopolis says "Telephus" instead of "Sparta" since he is quoting the exact words of a line from Euripides' play.

[2] Lamachus was an Athenian general whom Aristophanes has selected to represent the military mind. Actually he was a brave, conscientious soldier who ultimately was killed in action. After his death, in a later play, Aristophanes mentions him with the respect he deserves.

Is there an officer in the house?
Stormer of cities or colonel? Help!
Hurry and help me before I'm killed!

(The door of Lamachus' house opens and Lamachus bursts out dressed in breastplate and plumed helmet, and carrying a sword and a shield emblazoned with the Gorgon's head.)

LAMACHUS *(in tragic style)*

A cry of battle came to my ears. From where?
Where must I to the rescue and sow the seeds
Of war? Who has roused my sleeping sword from its scabbard?

DICAEOPOLIS   Lamachus, our hero! *(Covering his eyes)* Oh, those platoons and those plumes!

SEMICHORUS A *(pointing to Dicaeopolis)*   Lamachus! This fellow's been saying nasty things about the state.

LAMACHUS *(eyeing Dicaeopolis' get-up)*   How can a beggar like you have the nerve to say such things?

DICAEOPOLIS   Lamachus, our hero, please excuse it. It was just a poor beggar's ramblings.

LAMACHUS   What did you say to them? Speak up!

DICAEOPOLIS *(covering his eyes and swaying unsteadily)*   I can't tell you: I'm so scared at the sight of those weapons, I'm dizzy. *(Pointing to the Gorgon's head emblazoned on the shield)* Please! Take that bogeyman away!

LAMACHUS *(lowering the shield)*   All right.

DICAEOPOLIS   Now put it on the ground. Face down.

LAMACHUS *(doing so)*   There.

DICAEOPOLIS   Now give me one of the feathers from your helmet.

LAMACHUS *(plucking out an enormous plume)*   Here, take this tuft.

DICAEOPOLIS *(not yet taking it and bending his head over)*   Now hold my head. I'm going to vomit. I hate those plumes so much they turn my stomach. *(Takes the plume and starts to stick it down his throat.)*

LAMACHUS   Hey, you! What're you going to do? Use that tuft to make you vomit?

DICAEOPOLIS *(eyeing the plume)*   Tuft is it? What bird does this "tuft" come from? The Great Boastard?

LAMACHUS   I'll kill you!

DICAEOPOLIS (*unperturbed*) Not a chance, Lamachus. You're not that
strong. But maybe you're strong enough to slice off my foreskin.
You've got the tools.

LAMACHUS Is that the way you talk to an officer of the Athenian
army, you beggar?

DICAEOPOLIS So I'm a beggar, am I?

LAMACHUS What are you then?

DICAEOPOLIS (*throwing off the rags*) What am I? A decent citizen—
and not a member of the Ancient Order of Wardheelers. And,
ever since this war began, a member of the Ancient Order of
Fighting Soldiers. And you? Since the war began, a member of
the Ancient Order of Pocket Liners.

LAMACHUS (*blustering*) I was elected—

DICAEOPOLIS (*interrupting*) Sure, by a bunch of cuckoos. It's just
because I hate all that sort of thing that I made my treaty. I
can't stand seeing men with gray hairs fighting in the ranks while
youngsters like you go running off on diplomatic missions. There
are the Tisamenophenippuses[1] and the Scoundrelipparchideses
pocketing their fifteen dollars per day in Thrace, another gang
with General Chares, the Geretotheodores and the Diomirascals
in Epirus, still another gang in Sicily—at Camerina, Messina,
Filthymessina.

LAMACHUS (*superciliously*) Of course. They were all elected.

DICAEOPOLIS How come you people somehow or other always get on
the public payroll and (*gesturing toward the chorus*) these
fellows never do? (*Turning to the chorus*) How about it,
Marilades? You're old and gray; have you ever served as an
envoy? (*To Lamachus*) He says no. And yet he's a good man
and a hard worker. (*Turning back to the chorus*) Dracyllus!
Euphorides! Prinides! How about it? Any of you ever seen
Persia or Epirus? (*To Lamachus*) They say no. But Coesyra's[1]
son and Lamachus, *they* get away on missions. Why? Because
of all the money they owe their families and creditors—I mean
used to owe. When their friends gave them advice it sounded

[1] The names in this and the following lines are combinations made up from
the names of some families in Athens that had wealth, position, and power—and
worthless members. The first blends the names Tisamenus and Phaenippus; the
second includes the name Hipparchides; the third blends Geres and Theodorus.
Coesyra was a name borne by many of the women in the Alcmaeonid family,
the noblest and proudest house in Athens.

like the people throwing slops out of the window at night: "Get
away! Get away!"

LAMACHUS (*throwing up his hands*)   Oh, Democracy! Must a man put
up with this?

DICAEOPOLIS   No, he mustn't—once the name "Lamachus" leaves the
public payroll.

LAMACHUS (*shouting*)   I'll wage war against every man in the Peloponnese with all my might. I'll shatter them everywhere, on land
and sea!

DICAEOPOLIS   And I'll issue an invitation to every man in the Peloponnese and in Megara and in Boeotia to come and trade with me.
But not Lamachus. No, sir!

(*Lamachus and Dicaeopolis enter their houses. The chorus now
prepares to deliver the parabasis.*)

CHORUS   The man's the winner of the debate. He's changing the
People's mind about his truce. It's time for the anapests. Ready
—step forward!

ANAPESTS

Not once since our playwright turned his mind to the choruses
of comedy has he ever stepped forward to use this address of ours
to tell you what a great man he is. But his enemies have been
slandering him before the Athenian people—and they are notori-
ously quick to jump to conclusions. He writes comedies against
the state, it's alleged, he jeers at the People. So he feels he
must reply before the Athenian People—who can be equally
quick to change their minds.

He claims that you should shower honors on the playwright
who cured you of being so taken in by fancy speeches from
strangers, of loving it when you're flattered, of being, in short,
solid-headed citizens. Before this, whenever foreign envoys
wanted to take you in, the first thing they did was to refer to
Athens as "the garden spot of Greece"; the minute anyone said
that, just because of this garden nonsense, you sat right up on the
tips of your tails. And if anyone flattered you by referring to
"fair and shining Athens," just because of this "shining" nonsense, something he could have said about sardines in oil, he
got whatever he was after. You should shower honors on the

playwright not only for accomplishing all this, but also for showing the people of our allied democracies what rule by *our* democracy is like. That's why, from now on, our allies are going to flock here—bringing their tribute with them, of course—: they're dying to see this best of all playwrights, the man who dared to tell the truth to the People of Athens. Why, his reputation for frank speaking has made its way abroad, even to Persia. When the Great King was interrogating a diplomatic mission from Sparta, after asking which of the two rivals had the stronger navy, he asked which of the two had this playwright who spoke so openly whenever wrong was done. Because, the King explained, the people who have an adviser like that not only have become much better men, but will be sure to win the war. That's why Sparta is suing for peace—and demanding to get Aegina.[1] They're not interested in the island; they just want to take this playwright from you. But don't you give him up. He'll go on writing comedies that tell the truth. He gives his word he'll go on teaching you what's right and good, to bring you happiness. He'll never fawn, never bribe, never cheat, never swindle, never pander—no, he'll do nothing but teach you the best things in life. (*With increasing warmth*) Cleon will answer by scheming, by working every trick in the book against me. Let him! I have the good on my side. Right is my ally. That coward! That seducer of the state! Catch me in such a role? Never!

(*Singing*)   ODE

Muse of the Acharnians, fiery flame-tempered violent
    muse, come to me here,
Quick as the spark you see dart from the fire-hot embers
    aglow from the fanning,
Just when the fire is ready for frying, and the fish have
    been laid in a row,
And the sauce has been whipped up, glistening and tart,
    and the basting's about to begin.
Come to me, come to your neighbor; bring me a tune
    of the country, a rousing
Clear-pitched melodious tune.

[1] Aegina was an island state off the coast of Attica, which Athens had conquered and settled with her own people. Aristophanes either had been born there or was somehow connected by blood with the original population.

Epirrhema

We oldtimers have a complaint against the state. We once
fought your battles on the sea. And now do we get from you
the old-age benefits we've earned? We're treated abominably!
Old as we are, you bring us up on charges and let some smart
young lawyer make a laughingstock of us. After all, at our age,
we're nothing, we're dumb, we're like a flute with a broken
reed; the only thing we have to support us, our only anchor to
windward, are these canes. We take our stand before the bench,
mumbling toothlessly. We can't see a thing—except the blind-
ness of justice. But your youngster, after rushing around to get
himself appointed to the case, dashes in and opens fire by dis-
charging his rhetoric at us. Then he drags us up, baits his verbal
traps, and cross-examines us. He claws and gnaws at some old
Tithonus,[1] he addles the poor man's aged brains. The old fellow
mumbles through his gums, hears a verdict pronounced against
him, and leaves, brokenhearted and in tears, to tell his friends
that the money he had saved for his funeral is now to go for
his fine.

(*Singing*)   Antode

How is it right to destroy at the so-called bar of justice
  a gray-headed oldster,
A man who has suffered and fought at your side, a man
  who's a man, a hero in battle,
Who sweated and fought in the swelter at Marathon?
  We were at Marathon then,
And *we* did the chasing that day. But now we're the
  quarry, the victims of unbearded youngsters,
Rascally shysters, who hound us, who sue us, who hale
  us to trial—and we're trapped.
Marpsias![2] What about that!

---

[1] Tithonus is a mythological figure who represented for the Greeks what
Methusaleh does for us.

[2] Marpsias may have been a politician who had opposed some measure introduced to bring relief to needy veterans. The name means "snatcher."

ANTEPIRRHEMA

What sort of justice is it when poor, bent old Thucydides[1] is destroyed grappling with Cephisodemus,[1] that fast-talking public prosecutor, that foreigner who's as wild as the steppes where he was born. It brings tears of pity to my eyes to see that ex-slave cop make mincemeat of the old fellow. When he was the Thucydides of old, by god, he wouldn't have put up with any nonsense from god himself; he'd have pinned to the mat a dozen Euathluses,[1] he'd have hooted and shouted down three thousand cops—and he'd have gone to the country this particular one came from and shot every relative he had. Well, if you won't leave us oldtimers in peace, at least pass a law for the allocation of lawsuits: let the old men face some old and toothless prosecutor, and the young men some fast-talking pansy like Alcibiades. Hereafter, in trials for banishment, or, if a man's already fled, for fines, let it be old against old, young against young.

(*The parabasis is now over and the chorus steps back. A moment later Dicaeopolis appears carrying some stones and three whips.*)

DICAEOPOLIS (*as he sets the stones in various spots, to himself*) Here are the boundaries of my market. Here every man in the Peloponnese and Megara and Boeotia can come to trade with me. But not Lamachus! No, sir! And I'm appointing these three whips of Tanners-town leather to be Commissioners of the Market; they've been officially elected. Positively no informers allowed— or any other type of skunk. I'll go in now and get the official copy of the treaty and post it in my market where everyone can see it.

(*Dicaeopolis reenters his house. As he does, a Megarian comes on stage, a scrawny, emaciated figure, lugging a large empty sack. After him trot his two little daughters looking every bit as starved as he. The Megarian speaks in the dialect of his region.*)

MEGARIAN (*to himself*) Well, howdy, market in Athens! Megara is right glad to see ya. I've missed ya more'n my own mother.

---

[1] This is not the famous historian Thucydides but a prominent statesman who had once been the political rival of the mighty Pericles himself. Late in life he was brought up on some charges by the young advocates Cephisodemus and Euathlus. The former apparently had a strain of barbaric Scythian blood in his

(*Turning to the two girls*) Ya pore li'l' things, yo're as bad off
as yore pore old daddy. Come along, mebbe ya'll find some
scraps o' black bread. Now listen, both of ya—and those bellies
of yours too. D'ya want me to sell ya, or are ya a-hankerin' to
go hongry?

DAUGHTERS   Sell us!

MEGARIAN   Thet's whut I reckon, too. (*Shaking his head dolefully*)
But who's a-goin' to be crazy enough to fall fer sich a bad bargain? Well, I've got a Megarian trick up the old sleeve. I'll fix
ya up, and tell 'em I got a pair o' pigs fer sale. (*Handing each
a pair of boots shaped like hoofs*) Put on these here pig's feet
so's you'll look like ya come from a prize sow. Because, by damn,
effen I don't sell ya and ya go back home ya'll find out fer real
whut it is to be hongry! (*Handing them a pair of false snouts*)
And put on these here snouts. Now jump into this here sack.
(*They jump in. The sack has a hole at each end; their snouts
stick out of one and hoofs out of the other.*) Now, remember to
grunt and squeal. Sound like them pigs they use on the altar.
I'll call Dicaeopolis. (*Shouting*) Dicaeopolis! Ya wanna buy
some pigs?

DICAEOPOLIS   (*as he comes out of his house*) Well, Mr. Megarian,
what's up?

MEGARIAN   Come to do a little sellin'.

DICAEOPOLIS   How are things back home?

MEGARIAN   Well, we bin a-standin' round the fire—

DICAEOPOLIS   (*interrupting jovially*) Mighty nice way to pass the time,
especially if there's a little music around.

MEGARIAN   —and starvin'.

DICAEOPOLIS   What else is going on at Megara?

MEGARIAN   Nothin' much. When I left thar, town council was a-
figurin' out the fastest and best way fer all of us to die off.

DICAEOPOLIS   (*grimly*) Well, you'll get out of your troubles, all right.

MEGARIAN   Yo're plumb right.

DICAEOPOLIS   What else is doing at Megara? How's wheat selling?

MEGARIAN   Sky high, god knows!

---

veins; he was, of course, neither foreign-born nor an ex-policeman (the Athenian
police force was made up of slaves from Scythia, a primitive area on the shores of
the Black Sea). Euathlus was a particularly skilled debater; Aristophanes uses a
metaphor from wrestling, since the literal meaning of the man's name is "athletic."

DICAEOPOLIS   Got any salt for sale?

MEGARIAN (*bitterly*)   It's all in yore people's hands now, hain't it?

DICAEOPOLIS   How about garlic?

MEGARIAN   What d'ya mean, garlic? Every year yore people come a-raidin' our fields and ya don't leave a single solitary clove. Yo're as bad as field mice.

DICAEOPOLIS   What *have* you got to sell, then?

MEGARIAN   Pigs. Best grade, good enough fer use on the altar.

DICAEOPOLIS   Fine, fine, let's see them.

MEGARIAN   Fine pigs, these here. Pick 'em up, effen ya want. Plenty of fat on them bones.

DICAEOPOLIS (*picking up one of the "pigs"*)   What's going on here? What *is* this?

MEGARIAN   Dern it, it's a pig![1]

DICAEOPOLIS (*suspiciously*)   Where does this pig come from?

MEGARIAN   Megara. It's a pig, I tell ya.

DICAEOPOLIS   It doesn't look like it to me.

MEGARIAN   What a nerve! Did ya ever see anybody as suspicious as this here feller? He allows as how this hain't no pig. Come on, betcha a pound o' yore best salt this is whut we call pig in Greek.

DICAEOPOLIS   Sure. But it's human pig.

MEGARIAN   Dern tootin' it is. Bred it myself. Whose did ya think it was, anyway? Ya wanna hear whut it sounds like?

DICAEOPOLIS   I sure do.

MEGARIAN   Come on, piggie, make a sound. Quick! (*No sound is forthcoming.*) Whut's the matter? Make a sound, blast ya, or, by damn, I'll haul ya off back home!

DAUGHTERS (*promptly*)   Wee wee!

MEGARIAN   Now is thet a pig or hain't it?

DICAEOPOLIS   It sounds like a pig now. But five years from now, when it grows up, it'll be a pussy.

MEGARIAN   Believe me, it'll be jist like its mother.

DICAEOPOLIS   But it's not good enough for use on the altar.

MEGARIAN   Whut d'ya mean? Why hain't it good enough fer use on the altar?

DICAEOPOLIS   No tail.

---

[1] The jokes in the next twenty-five-odd lines are based on the fact that the Greek word for "pig" also means "female genitalia."

MEGARIAN It's young yet. Wait'll it grows to pighood. Then ya'll have a fine piece o' tail. (*Pointing to the other*) Effen ya'll jist be willin' to raise it, ya'll have a fine bit o' pig here.

DICAEOPOLIS It looks exactly like the other one.

MEGARIAN They're both from the same litter. Effen ya'll jist wait fer it to fatten up and grow some curly bristle, ya'll have a fine bit o' pig to put on the altar fer Aphrodite.

DICAEOPOLIS But we don't offer pig to Aphrodite.

MEGARIAN Don't offer pig to Aphrodite? She's the only one in heaven ya do offer it to! These pigs got the sweetest flesh ya ever did taste. Jist run a spit through 'em.

DICAEOPOLIS Are they old enough to eat without the mother?

MEGARIAN (*promptly*) God, yes! And without the father too.

DICAEOPOLIS Piggie!

FIRST DAUGHTER Wee wee!

DICAEOPOLIS Do you like peas?[1]

FIRST DAUGHTER Wee wee wee!

DICAEOPOLIS How about figs from Phibalis?[1]

FIRST DAUGHTER Wee wee!

DICAEOPOLIS (*to the other*) How about you? You like them?

SECOND DAUGHTER Wee wee wee!

DICAEOPOLIS Listen to the way they squealed when I said "figs"! (*Calling to his servants*) One of you inside there! Bring some figs for these pigs. (*A servant rushes out with a handful and Dicaeopolis starts feeding them to the girls.*) Will they eat them? Wow! Good god, look at those jaws go! These aren't pigs, they're gobblers, if you ask me.

MEGARIAN (*aside, as he puts a fig in his mouth*) They didn't eat 'em all; here's one I helped myself to.

DICAEOPOLIS Say, these are darn cute little animals. How much you want for them?

MEGARIAN Bunch of garlic fer one, pound o' salt fer t'other.

DICAEOPOLIS I'll buy them. Wait here. (*Turns to go into his house.*)

MEGARIAN It's a deal. (*As Dicaeopolis goes into the house, to himself*) Good god, wish I could sell the wife and my mother at the same price!

---

[1] The reference to peas involves a *double-entendre*: the Greek word for "chick-pea" also means "penis." Very likely the same sort of thing is involved in the mention of figs. Phibalis was a district of Megara that, before the war, was noted for its fine figs.

(At this moment an informer enters.)

INFORMER   Hey you! Where are you from?

MEGARIAN   Megara. I'm sellin' pigs.

INFORMER   I hereby accuse you and your pigs of subversive activity. You're both enemies of the state!

MEGARIAN   *(to himself, helplessly)*   Here it comes again. Same old thing thet started all our troubles!

INFORMER   A Megarian fellow traveler, eh? You'll pay for it! *(Making a grab at the sack)* Let go of that sack!

MEGARIAN   *(shouting)*   Dicaeopolis! Help! An informer!

DICAEOPOLIS   *(rushing out with his three whips in his hand)*   An informer after you? Who? *(Addressing the whips)* Commissioners of the Market! You're not keeping informers out of my market! *(To the informer, sarcastically)* Doesn't even have a light and look what a bright boy he is!

INFORMER   I'm doing my duty. I'm reporting subversive elements in the state.

DICAEOPOLIS   *(raising the whips)*   Now get going and find your subversives somewhere else or you'll be sorry. *(The informer runs.)*

MEGARIAN   *(shaking his head commiseratingly)*   What a curse you Athenians have to put up with!

DICAEOPOLIS   *(handing him two parcels)*   Never mind, friend Megarian. Now give me the pigs and take your salt and garlic. And good luck to you!

MEGARIAN   *(bitterly)*   There's precious little o' that fer us.

DICAEOPOLIS   Sorry. Well, I can use it if you can't.

MEGARIAN   Piggies, now thet yore daddy's gone, remember to put salt on yore bread yoreselves—effen ya get any!

(Dicaeopolis takes the "pigs" into his house and the Megarian leaves.)

CHORUS   *(singing)*

> Now there's a lucky and happy man. You haven't
>   heard what happened?
> His scheme for a market's a great success. He'll sit
>   and count his profits.
> If Ctesias[1] the informer,
> Or others of that ilk,
> Come anywhere near the spot,
> They'll wish they had not!

[1] See p. 46, n. 1.

There's no one there to get you sore by beating you
    to the bargains.
No Prepis[1] or Cleonymus will rub his ass against you
And filthy all your clothes;
You'll safely wear your best.
And Hyperbolus[1] won't dare
Subpoena you there!

Cratinus[1] won't accost you there, all shaved and
    curled and made up,
No "Artemon[2] in a litter borne" he, but "Artemon
    for the gallows" born.
He writes—and his songs are foul,
And so's the smell from his armpits.
His father's stink made us run—
Like father, like son.

And Pauson[1] won't insult you there, that crook,
    that utter scoundrel.
And neither will Lysistratus,[1] that disgrace to all
    his neighbors,
A villain double-dyed,
A beggar, a panhandler.
He shivers and starves—a freak!—
Eight days every week.

(*A man from Boeotia enters. Boeotia and its chief city, Thebes,
had suffered very little during the war, and the Boeotian, consequently,
offers a striking contrast to the poor Megarian. He is fat and jovial and
arrives loaded down with things to sell. He heads a small entourage:
behind him is a well-fed servant, equally loaded down, and, behind
him, a group of Boeotia's famous bagpipers; the Boeotian, in a word, is
all set for a gay peacetime market day. He speaks in the same dialect
as the Megarian.*)

[1] Nothing more is known about Ctesias other than that, as Aristophanes' words
indicate, he was an informer. Prepis was an effeminate. For Cleonymus see
p. 17, n. 2. Hyperbolus was one of the playwright's prime targets, a successful
shyster who, when Cleon died, succeeded him as head of the pro-war party.
Cratinus was an effeminate dandy. Pauson was a painter who was chronically
broke, and Lysistratus obviously was a victim of the same affliction.

[2] There were two Artemons who were "litter-borne." The first, who lived
two centuries earlier, had been immortalized in a well-known poem by Anacreon;
he was a scoundrel who made so much money he had himself carried about
everywhere instead of walking. The second was one of Pericles' military engineers
who, having been lamed during some attack, had to be carried about thereafter
on a litter.

BOEOTIAN (*slinging down his bag with a sigh of relief*) By damn, this here shoulder of mine is plumb wore out! (*To the servant*) Ismenias, my boy, put down thet thar sack o' mint. Easy, boy, easy! (*To the bagpipers*) All you pipers from Thebes! Start a-blowin' on them thar sticks and dog-ass bags o' yourn!

(*The music reaches Dicaeopolis' ears inside and, not being a Boeotian and a born bagpipe lover, he comes racing out.*)

DICAEOPOLIS Quiet! What's this, a swarm of wasps? Get the hell away from my door! How did these damn buzzpipes get to my house, anyway? They sound like Chaeris.[1]

BOEOTIAN (*quick to agree with a potential customer*) Mister, yo're derned tootin' right. They bin a-blowin' behind me all the way from Thebes. Knocked all the blossoms offen my mint too. Now, how'd you like to buy some of these here animals? Got 'em two-legged or four-footed.

DICAEOPOLIS Greetings, old sourdough from Boeotia! Now, what have you got?

BOEOTIAN Jist about all the goodies Boeotia kin offer: marjoram, mint, mats, wicks, ducks, daws, francolins, coots, plovers, divers—

DICAEOPOLIS Looks like you're bringing fowl weather to my market.

BOEOTIAN —geese, rabbits, foxes, moles, hedgehogs, cats, weasels, easels, otters, eels from Lake Copais—

DICAEOPOLIS (*roused by the mention of Athens' greatest delicacy to interrupt in tragic style*)

O bearer of the sweetest morsel known
To man, if you speak true and do bring eels,
May I give them proper greeting, bid them welcome?

BOEOTIAN (*parodying a line from a play by Aeschylus, to the sack of fish*)

O first among the fifty maids of Copais,
Come out, give ear to the gentleman's welcoming words.

DICAEOPOLIS (*like a lover in tragedy addressing a long-lost sweetheart*)

O dearest eels, how long have I yearned for you!
At last you've come! My prayers, my chorus'[2] prayers,

---

[1] See p. 15, n. 1.
[2] The chorus was always invited to a farewell banquet after the play was over.

And those of Morychus[1] have been fulfilled.
Servants! Bring out the grill, bring out the bellows,
And turn your eyes upon her, this matchless eel
Who, six long years away, has returned unto
Her yearning lover. Greet her, lads! I'll spread
A couch of charcoal to serve our charming guest.
Unwrap her now. Until the day I die,
I'll keep you by my side—en casserole!

BOEOTIAN (*seeing his prize piece of merchandise disappear*)   Hey!
Who's a-goin' to pay me fer thet eel?

DICAEOPOLIS (*airily*)   Oh, I'm taking it for your market entry fee. Now,
how about these other things? Are they for sale?

BOEOTIAN   You bet. Everythin' goes.

DICAEOPOLIS   How much are you asking? Or will you swap for a load
from here?

BOEOTIAN   Sure thing. I'm willin' to take anythin' ya have here that
we don't have back home.

DICAEOPOLIS   Want to buy some of our local sardines? Some pottery
maybe?

BOEOTIAN (*scornfully*)   Sardines? Pottery? Got 'em back home. How
about somethin' we hain't got back home that you fellers got a
surplus of?

DICAEOPOLIS (*triumphantly*)   I've got it! An informer! We'll pack one
up like a pot and you can take him back with you.

BOEOTIAN   By damn, yo're right. I could take him, exhibit him like a
monkey full o' dirty tricks, and make a mint o' money.

(*A small man enters, stage right, and walks rapidly toward them.*)

DICAEOPOLIS   Here's one coming right now. Nicarchus. He wants to
report you.

BOEOTIAN (*dubiously*)   He's purty small.

DICAEOPOLIS (*reassuringly*)   But pure evil, every inch.

NICARCHUS (*pointing to the Boeotian's wares*)   Who owns this?

BOEOTIAN   By damn, it belongs to this feller right here, me. Brought
it from Thebes.

NICARCHUS   Well, this fellow right here is hereby reporting it for subversive activity. All this stuff is contraband.

BOEOTIAN   What the devil are ya' doin'? Makin' war on these pore
li'l' birds?

[1] Morychus was a well-known epicure.

NICARCHUS   I'm reporting them *and* you.

BOEOTIAN   What'd I do wrong?

NICARCHUS   I'll tell you; I want everyone here to hear it. You're smuggling in lampwicks from the enemy!

DICAEOPOLIS   So he's a subversive because of a lampwick, eh?

NICARCHUS   Certainly. One lampwick could burn up our navy yard.

DICAEOPOLIS   Oh, my god! A lampwick burn the navy yard? How?

NICARCHUS   Some Boeotian could mount it on a waterbug, wait until the wind was just right, from the north, light it, and set the bug floating down a sewer toward the navy yard. Then, if the flame once touched any of our ships, they'd all go right up in smoke.

DICAEOPOLIS   Damn you to hell! Go up in smoke because of a bug and a lampwick, eh? (*Advances on him and grabs him.*)

NICARCHUS (*shrieking*)   I'll sue you!

DICAEOPOLIS (*holding him tightly, to the Boeotian*)   Stop his mouth! (*Shouting to the servants in his house*) Bring me some straw! I want to pack him up like a pot so's he won't break in transit.

(*A servant rushes out with straw, and Dicaeopolis and the Boeotian begin packing the informer up.*)

CHORUS (*singing*)

> My dear sir, pack with care
> This merchandise, so that
> He'll get it back
> Without a crack.

DICAEOPOLIS (*having finished packing the informer, strikes the package as if testing a jug, and hears, instead of a ring, the cries and threats of the contents; singing*)

> Oh, I'll take care of that.
> But listen to that sound!
> It won't ring true!
> It's god damned, too.

CHORUS   What good's this pot?

DICAEOPOLIS   This pot? A lot.
> A bowl for storing woe,
> A vase for shyster briefs,
> A cup to mix
> A scoundrel's tricks.

CHORUS
                But can a person dare
                To keep around the house
                And use this thing?
                You heard it ring!

DICAEOPOLIS (*turning the package upside down preparatory to shoving it in the Boeotian's sack.*)

                This pot's so strong, my friend,
                That it will never break.
                But hang it so:
                Feet up, head low.

(*He shoves the package into the sack.*)

CHORUS (*to the Boeotian*)

                It's packed just fine.

BOEOTIAN   It'll be a gold mine!

CHORUS   My friend, go where you will,
                Go make your pile with this
                All-purpose jug,
                Informer-mug.

DICAEOPOLIS (*to the Boeotian*) I had a hard time packing up the damn thing. Here you are; pick up your pot, my Boeotian friend.

BOEOTIAN (*to his servant*) Ismenias, let's go. Bend down and lemme git this on yore shoulder.

DICAEOPOLIS Now, handle it carefully on the way back. You're carrying something that's rotten through and through, but, well— (*shrugs.*) If you get it home and make money out of it, you'll be a happy man because, of all things, informers!

(*The Boeotian, the servant carrying the informer, and the bagpipers leave, stage left. As they do, a servant emerges from Lamachus' house.*)

SERVANT (*like a sergeant shouting to his men*) Dicaeopolis!

DICAEOPOLIS Who is it? And what are you shouting at me for?

SERVANT Orders from Lamachus. Here's five dollars; you're to give him some of your thrushes. And here's fifteen dollars; you're to give him one of the eels from Lake Copais. It's for the Pitcher Feast.

DICAEOPOLIS And just who's this Lamachus who wants an eel?

SERVANT (*awesomely*) Lamachus the terrible, man of the mighty hide, wielder of the Gorgon shield, brandisher of the triple long-shadowing crest!

DICAEOPOLIS The answer is absolutely *No!* Not even if he offered me that shield of his. Let him brandish his crest over his army rations. And if he makes any fuss, I'll call my Commissioners of the Market. (*Picking up the rest of his purchases from the Boeotian*) I'm taking all this stuff for myself and I'm going in (*quoting a line from an old song*)

'neath wings of thrush and blackbird.

(*He enters his house.*)

CHORUS (*singing*)

What a sight, what a sight!
All of you, look at this brilliant, superintelligent
man.
He signed his own treaty and now he can traffic in
all the world's goods,
Things one can use for the household,
Things one can warm for the table.
Every good thing automatically comes to his door.

I'll never invite to my house the terrible God of War.
He'll never sit at my table or join in the merriment
there.
For he is a drunkard who staggered in tipsy when we
were enjoying
All of the good things of life. He broke things, he
spilled things, he brawled,
He brought on us all kinds of woe. When we begged
him to stop, when we said,
"Please have a seat. Now a toast altogether to
brotherly love,"
He answered by piling even higher than ever our
vines on his fires,
And spilling, to spite us, the wine in our vines, all
the wine in our vines.

What a sight, what a sight!
Look at him! Ready to swoop on his banquet, elated
and proud.

To show how he lives now he's scattered these
  feathers in front of his door.
O Peace, sister to the lovely
Goddess of Love and the Graces,
Never till now have I known how full fair was
  your face.

Would that some Eros, crowned with a garland of
  flowers
Just as he's drawn in his picture,[1] might lead you,
  O Peace, to my side.
Or maybe you think I'm a little too old? Yet if you'd
  be my bride,
Three things would I promise you. First, I would set
  out some sweet little vines,
All in a row. Next, figs would I carefully place by
  their side,
Tender new shoots. And, third, I would plant us a
  vine for the house.
Yes, old as I am. And a full belt of olives would
  circle our farm
To furnish the oil for anointing us both when the
  new moon shines forth.

*(A herald enters. The day happens to be the day of the Pitcher
Feast and everyone, including Dicaeopolis and Lamachus, is busy with
preparations, particularly cooking. For, at this festival, all partakers
supplied their own provisions. The high point of the day was a drinking competition in which a prize, a full wineskin, was given to the man
who first downed a three-quart pitcher of wine.)*

HERALD   Hear Ye! Hear Ye! In accordance with our ancient practice,
         when the trumpet gives the signal, all of you will empty your
         pitchers. First one to finish gets the skin—of Ctesiphon.[2]

*(The announcement rouses Dicaeopolis, and he rushes out carrying
a fistful of thrushes. Some servants are at his heels. He turns and shouts
to others inside.)*

---

[1] A famous painting by Zeuxis in the Temple of Aphrodite at Athens represented Eros as a lovely boy wearing a wreath of roses.
[2] Ctesiphon was enormously fat; his hide would make a gratifyingly large
wineskin.

DICAEOPOLIS Boys! Girls! Didn't you hear? What are you doing? Didn't
you hear the announcement? Hurry and get the rabbits stewed,
roasted, browned on both sides, and off the fire! And get the
garlands ready! And bring me the spits to put through the
thrushes!

CHORUS (*drooling at what they see and hear and smell, singing*)

> I envy your sagacity—
> But even more all this good cheer!

DICAEOPOLIS (*preparing to roast the thrushes on the spit before them*)
Ah, but what will you say when you see these thrushes roasting
on the spit?

CHORUS Right. You've got a good point there.

DICAEOPOLIS Boy! Stir up the fire!

CHORUS (*singing*)

> You hear? He'll cook it by himself!
> He's chef and gourmet all in one.

(*A farmer enters, stage left, giving all the signs of being in the throes
of despair. His farm happens to be at Phyle, near the border between
Boeotia and Attica, and hence an easy target for raiders from across the
line.*)

FARMER (*moaning*) Oh, my god, my god!

DICAEOPOLIS Good god, who are you?

FARMER An unhappy man.

DICAEOPOLIS Then stay away from me. It's catching.

FARMER My dear friend, you're the only one who stocks peace. Let
me have some, please. Just a five-year supply will do.

DICAEOPOLIS What happened to you?

FARMER I'm ruined. I lost my team of oxen.

DICAEOPOLIS Where?

FARMER At Phyle. The Boeotians took them.

DICAEOPOLIS You poor fellow! You should be dressed in black.

FARMER I swear to you, that team was my livelihood. I had god's
plenty—of dung.

DICAEOPOLIS Well, what do you want?

FARMER I've cried both my eyes out over that team. Now, if you have
any feelings for good old Dercetes of Phyle, hurry and rub some
peace lotion on my eyes.

DICAEOPOLIS I know you're in a bad way, but I don't practice medicine.

FARMER Please, I beg you. Maybe then I can find my team.

DICAEOPOLIS I can't do a thing. But go tell your hard-luck story to Pittalus.[1]

FARMER Please! Just one drop of peace! Just a dropful in this little tube!

DICAEOPOLIS Not the teenchy weenchiest bit. Go do your crying somewhere else.

FARMER (*as he departs, stage left*) This is awful! Oh, my poor sweet little team of oxen, the farmer's friend!

CHORUS (*singing*)

> He finds the taste of peace is sweet.
> There'll be no share for others, I think.

DICAEOPOLIS (*to the servants*) Pour out the honey for the sausage. And fry the squid.

CHORUS Listen to the way he shouts orders!

DICAEOPOLIS And roast those slices of eel!

CHORUS (*singing*)

> This smell! These orders that you shout!
> You'll kill me! Your famished neighbors too.

DICAEOPOLIS Roast these things and make sure they're well browned!

(*A best man, fresh from a wedding, enters, stage right.*)

BEST MAN Dicaeopolis!

DICAEOPOLIS (*somewhat annoyed by this second interruption*) Now who are you?

BEST MAN (*handing him a package*) A bridegroom sends you this meat from his wedding banquet.

DICAEOPOLIS Mighty nice of him, whoever he is.

BEST MAN And in return he wants you to pour a cupful of peace into this little jar so's he won't have to join the army and can go on making love to his bride.

DICAEOPOLIS Now, you just take your meat and go. I don't want it. I wouldn't pour out any of my peace for a million dollars! (*At this moment a bridesmaid from the wedding enters.*) Now, who's this?

---

[1] Pittalus was no doubt a well known doctor.

BEST MAN A bridesmaid. She's got something to tell you in private from the bride.

DICAEOPOLIS (*to the bridesmaid, impatiently*) All right, what have you got to tell me? (*The girl whispers in his ear.*) Oh, lord, this is a riot, this request from the bride! She's desperately anxious to keep her husband's penis out of the army and in the house. (*To the servants in his house*) Bring out the treaty! Hers is the only request I'll grant, because she's a woman and not equal to the rigors of the war. (*To the bridesmaid as he prepares to "pour" out some "peace" for her*) Now, my girl, hold your little jar down here. (*He "pours" some in.*) You know how to use it? Tell the bride that, the minute they start calling up recruits, she's to rub this on her husband's penis nightly. (*The best man and bridesmaid leave, stage right.*)

DICAEOPOLIS (*to the servants*) Take the treaty back and bring me my ladle. I want to fill the wine cups.

(*An army orderly comes racing in, stage left.*)

CHORUS (*in tragic style*)

> But who is this with brow so deeply furrowed,
> Who hastens like a messenger of woe?

ORDERLY (*knocking on Lamachus' door, in tragic style*)

> It's war! O Lamachus, come back to us!

LAMACHUS (*rushing out of his house, in tragic style*)

> Who makes this noise before my bronze-clad halls?

ORDERLY Orders from the high command to take your platoons and plumes, leave for the front immediately, and stand guard in the snow against any enemy attempt to break through. We've received intelligence that Boeotian raiders intend to attack during the Pitcher Feast.

LAMACHUS The high command! Long on heads and short on brains. This is awful: they're not even letting me stay here for the holiday!

DICAEOPOLIS Ah, war! So dramatic and Lamachic!

LAMACHUS What I have to put up with! What's this? Are *you* making fun of *me*?

DICAEOPOLIS (*brandishing four feathers from the birds he's been pre-*

paring for the spit)   How'd you like to fight with a four-winged Geryon?[1]

LAMACHUS   Oh, oh, what a message this orderly has brought me!

(A messenger races in, stage right.)

DICAEOPOLIS   Oh, oh, what message does this fellow bring me?

MESSENGER   Dicaeopolis!

DICAEOPOLIS   What?

MESSENGER   Take your picnic basket and pitcher and leave for the banquet immediately. The priest of Dionysus[2] sent me to get you. But hurry! You've been holding up dinner all this time. Everything else is ready: tables, couches, cushions, covers, garlands, myrrh, candy, whores, honey cakes, seed cakes, biscuits, cookies, and pretty dancing girls—*(parodying a phrase from a popular song)* "the darlings of Harmodius."[3] Hurry! Don't waste a minute.

LAMACHUS   *(forlornly)*   And look at me!

DICAEOPOLIS   Of course. You signed up for a hitch with that big Gorgon of yours. *(To the servants)* Lock up the house. Pack up the dinner.

(In the following lines, the orders from Lamachus and Dicaeopolis are shouted to their servants inside. After each, a servant rushes out with the item called for.)

LAMACHUS   Boy! Bring out my knapsack.

DICAEOPOLIS   Boy! Bring out my picnic basket.

LAMACHUS   Salt and onions, boy.

DICAEOPOLIS   Fish steak for me, please. I can't stand onions.

LAMACHUS   Some of that smelly salt fish, boy. Wrap it in a fig leaf.

DICAEOPOLIS   And a luscious stuffed fig leaf for me; I'll cook it at the feast.

LAMACHUS   Hand me the two feathers for my helmet.

DICAEOPOLIS   Hand me the wild pigeons and the thrushes.

[1] Geryon was one of the monsters Heracles had to cope with. It had three heads, three bodies, six hands, six feet and, what is more to the point, a pair of wings.

[2] The priest of Dionysus, the key figure at the festival during which this play was being given, was seated right in the center of the first row.

[3] Harmodius was one of the Athenians' most beloved heroes of the past, and the subject of one of their favorite drinking songs. He was not the most moral of men, and Aristophanes gibes at this fact by changing the opening words of the song in his honor "O dearest Harmodius" to "the darlings of Harmodius."

LAMACHUS   This ostrich plume is nice and white.

DICAEOPOLIS   This pigeon breast is nice and browned.

LAMACHUS   Listen, you. Stop making fun of my armor.

DICAEOPOLIS   Listen, you. Stop staring at my thrushes.

LAMACHUS   Bring me the crate with my three plumes.

DICAEOPOLIS   Bring me the plate with my rabbit meat.

LAMACHUS   Hey—did the moths eat up my plumes?

DICAEOPOLIS   Hey—shall I eat up the soup before dinner?

LAMACHUS   Listen, you. I'll thank you not to address any remarks to me.

DICAEOPOLIS   I'm not. It's just that this boy of mine and I have been having a long argument. (*To the servant*) Want to make a bet which tastes better, lice or thrushes? We'll leave it up to Lamachus.

LAMACHUS   God, what insults!

DICAEOPOLIS   (*to the servant*)   He says lice are lots better.

LAMACHUS   Boy! Take down my spear and bring it out here.

DICAEOPOLIS   Boy! Take off the spit with the sausage and bring it out here.

LAMACHUS   Boy! Hold the spear tight. I'm going to pull off the cover.

DICAEOPOLIS   And you, boy, hold this spit tight. (*As Lamachus pulls the cover off his spear, Dicaeopolis pulls the sausage off the spit.*)

LAMACHUS   Boy! Bring out the staff for my shield.

DICAEOPOLIS   Bring out the bread, the staff of my life.

LAMACHUS   Bring out my orbicular, be-Gorgoned shield.

DICAEOPOLIS   Bring out my orbicular be-cheesed soufflé.

LAMACHUS   This is an insult, and every man here knows it!

DICAEOPOLIS   This is a cheesecake, and every man here loves it.

LAMACHUS   Boy! Some oil on this shield. (*The servant puts some on, shines it up, and Lamachus looks into it.*) Ah! I see here in the bronze an old man who's going to stand trial for cowardice.

DICAEOPOLIS   Boy! A little honey on this cake. (*Holding it up and looking at it*) Ah! Here's an old man telling Lamachus, the Gorgon man, to go howl his head off.

LAMACHUS   Boy! Bring the armor for my breast.

DICAEOPOLIS   Boy! Bring the wine jug for *my* breast.

LAMACHUS   (*putting on the breastplate*)   With this I'm ready for my enemies.

DICAEOPOLIS   (*brandishing the jug*)   With this I'm ready for my friends.

LAMACHUS   Boy! Tie these blankets to the shield.

DICAEOPOLIS   Boy! Tie the rest of the food to the basket.

LAMACHUS   I'll take the knapsack and carry it myself.

DICAEOPOLIS   I'll take my coat—and I'm off.

LAMACHUS   Boy! Pick up my shield. Let's go! (*Holding out his hand, palm up*) It's snowing! Blast it! We'll have a cold time in the old fields tonight.

DICAEOPOLIS   Pick up the dinner. We'll have a hot time in the old town tonight.

(*They leave, Lamachus, with his servants and the orderly, stage left, for the front, and Dicaeopolis, with his servants and the messenger, stage right, for the feast.*)

CHORUS (*singing*)

> Goodbye! Good luck in your campaigns!
> What different paths the two men take!
> This one to don a wreath and drink,
> That one to freeze in a sentry post,
> This one to sleep with the sweetest girl
> And exercise his you know what!

(*To mark the interval in the action, the chorus continues with a song very much like a parabasis in character.*)

> May Zeus send to hell that spluttering writer
>   of prose and of verse,
> That cursed Antimachus.[1] He was the host at
>   the comedy feast,
> And *he* had the gall to refuse to invite me,
>   he left me to starve.
> Oh, may I live to see the day
> A sizzling roasted luscious squid
> Comes toward his plate, like a ship to port,
> And as he's set to eat it up,
> It's snatched and downed by a mangy pup!
>
> This is the first woe I wish on him. Next, when
>   he's on his way home,

---

[1] Antimachus, a dabbler in all forms of writing, was choregus for Aristophanes' first play and, when he gave the traditional banquet (cf. p. 47, n. 2), managed to find a pretext for not inviting the author.

Back from a ride, and it's night and he's sickish
    and shivering with ague,
I hope some Orestes[1] who's maddened from
    liquor will bash in his head.
And should he grope for stones in the dark,
May he lay his hand on a fresh-laid turd.
And should he clutch this missile and
Dash in, and fling, but miss his mark—
Then on Cratinus[2] may it park!

(A messenger races in, stage left, and knocks urgently on Lamachus' door.)

MESSENGER *(in tragic style, parodying the messenger speeches so common in Greek tragedy)*

O slaves who dwell in the house of Lamachus,
Quick, heat, oh, heat, some water in a vessel!
Prepare the lint and bandages and lotions,
Soft oil-soaked wool, and splints for injured ankles.
Your master's wounded, punctured by a stake's
Sharp point while leaping over a trench. And then,
By twisting back, he wrenched his ankle. Then
He fell and knocked his head upon a rock,
And broke the Gorgon off his shield. But when
His mighty tuft from a boastard's wing fell down
Upon the rocks, an awful cry he raised:
"O glorious eye of the sky, I look my last
On you. For now I leave the light of heaven.
I say to you that Lamachus is no more!"
And with these words he falls into a sewer—
Then springs erect, turns back his runaways,
And routs the raiders, prodding them with his spear.
But here he comes! Quick, open wide these doors!

(Enter, stage left, Lamachus wounded and supported by two grizzled campmates, and, stage right, Dicaeopolis drunk and supported by two

---

[1] Orestes, the famous figure of legend who slew his own mother, Clytemnestra, had been driven out of his mind by the Furies. "Orestes" became a slang term for "holdup man"; the chorus hopes that the one that meets Antimachus will be as insane as his eponymous ancestor—from drink.

[2] See p. 46, n. 1.

handsome blondes. *The lines from here to the close of the play are
sung.*)

LAMACHUS

Oh, oh!
These hateful, chilling woes! Oh, god,
I've been destroyed by enemy spear.
But it will be my chief lament
If Dicaeopolis sees me thus
And grins and jokes at my misfortunes.

DICAEOPOLIS

Oh, oh!
These lovely breasts, how firm and fruity!
Now kiss me sweetly, Goldilocks,
A lover's kiss with lips and tongue.
For I was first to drain my pitcher!

LAMACHUS

The troubles I have had! Oh, what a fate!
Ow, ow! Curses on these painful wounds!

DICAEOPOLIS

Well, well! Greetings to our Lamachus!

LAMACHUS

Oh, hateful trouble!

(*Dicaeopolis staggers up to him and plants a drunken kiss on him.
Lamachus fights him off, tooth and nail.*)

DICAEOPOLIS
(*aside*)   Now I'm in trouble.
LAMACHUS
Don't *you* kiss me!
DICAEOPOLIS
Don't *you* bite me!
LAMACHUS
To treat me thus! I'll pay you off!
DICAEOPOLIS
At the Pitcher Feast we go Dutch treat.

LAMACHUS

Apollo, god of healing, a cure, I pray!

DICAEOPOLIS

Today's the Pitcher Feast, not Healer's Day

LAMACHUS

Please hold me, hold my leg. Oh, oh,
Hold on to it, my friends!

DICAEOPOLIS

And you two grab my penis and
Hold on to it, my girls!

LAMACHUS

My head was struck by a flying stone.
I'm dizzy and my sight grows dark.

DICAEOPOLIS

I've got a hard on and I want
To screw in bed when night grows dark.

LAMACHUS

Oh, take me forth to Pittalus
And put me in his healing hands.

DICAEOPOLIS

And me to the judges and Chief of the
Feast,[1]
And put the wineskin in my hands.

LAMACHUS

Some enemy lance went through the bone
And left me with a dreadful wound.

(Lamachus is carried into his house groaning, followed by the messenger.)

DICAEOPOLIS *(holding out his pitcher upside down)*

You see this pitcher? Not a drop!
Hurray, hurray, I've won the day!

CHORUS

You want me to join in? Hurray,
Hurray for Dicaeopolis!

[1] Aristophanes' words here have pointed overtones. They are directed, on the surface, to the master of ceremonies of the Pitcher Feast and the judges of the drinking contest. But they are also directed to the master of ceremonies for the festival of the Lenaea, during which this play was being given, and to the judges who awarded the prize for the best play. The same is true of the remarks about victory in the following lines.

DICAEOPOLIS

What's more, I took it straight, yes, straight,
And drank it off without a stop.

CHORUS

Hurray for you, my noble friend!
Now take your wineskin, and goodbye.

DICAEOPOLIS

You follow me and sing with me:
"Hurray, hurray, I've won the day!"

CHORUS

To give you joy we'll follow you,
And sing for you, and your wineskin too,
"Hurray, hurray, you've won the day!"

(*They all leave the stage, singing and dancing wildly.*)

Greek New Comedy

/

Menander's The Grouch
The Woman of Samos
The Arbitration
She Who Was Shorn

The End of Old Comedy

In 404 B.C., after twenty-seven years of fighting, the war between Athens and Sparta finally ended in complete victory for Sparta. Athens was prostrate. Her empire had vanished, her armed forces had been destroyed, her treasury was empty.

Aristophanes' last two preserved plays, presented circa 392 and 388 B.C., show the results of the changed state of affairs. People were in no mood to listen to the merciless criticism that had been the very soul of his greatest plays; moreover, there was no longer any need to give it—it was too late. The chorus, as an important element of the play, has just about disappeared: it was too expensive for one, and had little to say for another. The invective and lashing satire is gone: in their unhappy circumstances, Athenians wanted to be amused, not lectured. Bowing to the public taste, Aristophanes turned to a type of play some of his earlier rivals had specialized in, one that concerned people in general and not specific individuals, one that poked fun at men's ways in general and not at their behavior as citizens at a given time and place. As Browning put it in his "Aristophanes' Apology":

> Aristophanes
> Surmounts his rivals now as heretofore,
> Though stinted to mere sober prosy verse—
> "Manners and Men," so squeamish gets the world!
> No more "Step forward, strip for anapaests!"
> No calling naughty people by their names.

Greek New Comedy

Although Athens soon revived politically and economically, the circumstances that had nourished Old Comedy never returned. From the beginning of the fourth century B.C. onward, people came to be increasingly interested in their lives as individuals rather than as members of the state. And, in 338 B.C., Athens fell under the domination of the kings of Macedonia, and freedom of speech became overnight a thing of the past. Throughout the Greek world people were no longer the masters of their own fate as they had been to a great extent in the fifth century B.C. What happened to them depended on the ambitions, or even whims, of a few kings; life was dictated from above and was terribly unsure. When people went to the theater they wanted to escape from what surrounded them twenty-four hours a day. The writers of comedy responded by moving even further in the direction Aristophanes had chosen in his last plays and, by the end of the fourth century B.C., they had created a new type of comedy, Greek New Comedy. Its purpose was entertainment, its subject was people, its chief source of humor gentle mockery of the manners of men. It swiftly became enormously popular, and eclipsed tragedy; all the available creative effort was being poured into the sock and no longer the buskin. As far as the history of literature is concerned, the new form is a greater achievement than Old Comedy: Old Comedy had come to an end even before the death of Aristophanes; New Comedy in a very real way is still alive on stage and screen.

Old Comedy is remarkable for the variety and ingenuity of its comic ideas. New Comedy is remarkable for its sameness. Euripides, Aristophanes' *bête noir,* became the darling of the practitioners of the new form: he had written many a play that was more romantic melodrama than tragedy, and they drew from these the inspiration for their plots. Their favorite formula has remained a favorite with writers and audiences ever since: a boy and girl in love who are kept apart by some obstacle, eventually surmount or remove it, and live happily ever after. Often the obstacle is the girl's low birth—she is a slave, perhaps, or a courtesan—and, with discouraging frequency, the solution is a last-act revelation that she really was a freeborn girl who had been exposed at birth, or captured by pirates as a child, or the like. Even when a playwright sought to explore interesting and vital ways of life and character he still made room in his plot for a pair of lovers; it was the frame on which he hung whatever he had to tell. The characters necessarily were as limited as the plots. In addition to the boy and girl, there are irate fathers, slaves (simple or clever as the situation required), old nurses, long-winded cooks, self-important soldiers. Mask-makers were able to keep on hand a stock series from which they could outfit readily all the casts of the comedies in a festival. There were no choruses as such; the chorus had dwindled to a group who came on to perform a brief song and dance to mark the breaks in the action, a substitute for a curtain. There were no lyric portions to be sung; all the dialogue was in a prosaic verse, most to be delivered in ordinary speech, some in recitative to flute accompaniment. And only minor, low-comedy characters wore the phallic symbol and the exaggerated padding about belly and buttocks.

Menander (ca. 342–291 B.C.)

There were at least three acknowledged masters in the field of New Comedy, Diphilus, Philemon, and Menander, but Menander was destined to outstrip the others. During his lifetime he was not overly successful: his rivals' more boisterous humor had greater popular appeal, so that, of the more than one hundred plays from his pen, only eight gained the prize. But after his death his reputation skyrocketed. He became known far and wide as one of Greece's greatest playwrights; critic after critic sang his praises. "O Menander and Life," exclaimed one, "which of you has copied the other?" Quintilian, a judicious critic of literature, has only the highest praise for him, particularly his trueness to life. Plutarch refers to him in terms that are nothing short of adulation. Yet, through some quirk of fate, not one play of this renowned and voluminous writer survived—that is, until 1905.

In the year 1905, Menander, dead for over a millennium and a half, was resurrected. Excavators, digging in Egypt, that storehouse of so many ancient treasures, came upon a tattered papyrus manuscript containing a selection of his works. Less than a third of the original was there, hardly a page was undamaged, yet it was a priceless find. The portion still readable preserved over one-half of one play and over one-third of two others. What is more, the most complete was a famous work, one frequently mentioned by ancient critics (*The Arbitration*), and another was a mature play from his best years (*She Who Was Shorn*); only one was a more youthful effort (*The Woman of Samos*). The discovery meant that Menander was no longer merely a highly touted shadow; we had at least enough to savor his quality if not to appreciate his full flavor.

And then, just a few years ago, the totally unexpected happened, a stroke of unbelievably good luck. Some Egyptian dealers in antiquities came up with eleven papyrus leaves, in an almost perfect state of preservation, which contained the whole of Menander's *Dyskolos* (*The Grouch*). No details of the find are to be had. We know that the place of origin was Egypt but nothing else; the dealers have been exasperatingly close-mouthed. As it happens, the first leaf of the eleven bears the page number "19"; the complete manuscript, then, contained a number of Menander's works. It is conceivable that the discoverers are holding back some of the find and that other plays will eventually appear on the market. The leaves were purchased by Martin Bodmer, a well known Swiss bibliophile, who turned them over to the eminent Swiss scholar Victor Martin for editing. In the spring of 1959 Martin published the Greek text—and the modern world got its first taste of what a complete play by Menander was like.

There is a question that troubles a good many critics of today when they consider Menander: How could he have achieved such a towering reputation when his plots and characters were so limited? More particularly, how could ancient critics have singled out trueness to life as his forte when his stock in trade was basically the same romantic stuff that made up so much of Greek New Comedy? *The Grouch* unfortunately does nothing to answer these questions—or enhance Menander's reputation; it is pretty bad. We can guess why from a notice prefixed to the play that gives some details about its production: it was put on, and won first prize, at the Lenaea in 317 B.C. In other words, Menander wrote it when he was but twenty-five years old; it must be one of his earliest efforts. (It's interesting to find that the Athenians thought it good enough for first prize; either their taste had degenerated since the days of Aristophanes, or the plays pitted against *The Grouch* were even worse, or both.) But what of mature plays like *The Arbitration* or *She Who Was Shorn*? In the battered remnants that have come down to us can we detect some trace of what had so captivated the ancient critics, some gleam of that trueness to life they praised so highly? Each reader will have to judge for himself.

The Grouch

/

DRAMATIS PERSONAE

Chaereas, a young man who makes his way by sponging on his rich friend Sostratus

Sostratus, a wealthy, young Athenian man about town, in love with Cnemon's daughter

Pyrrhias, servant (slave) of Sostratus

Cnemon, the grouch, a sour-tempered old farmer, father of the girl Sostratus loves

Cnemon's daughter

Davus, servant (slave) of Gorgias

Gorgias, a self-reliant, young Athenian farmer, stepson of Cnemon and half-brother of the girl Sostratus loves

Sicon, a chef

Geta, Sostratus' father's servant (slave) whose services Sostratus enlists in his own behalf

Simike, an elderly female servant of Cnemon's, his daughter's old nurse

Callippides, father of Sostratus

[*Myrrhina,* Cnemon's wife, mother of Gorgias by a former marriage]

SCENE   The scene is laid in Phyle, a country district outside Athens. In the center is the entrance to a grotto sacred to the god Pan and his nymphs. On either side are houses, stage right that of Cnemon, stage left that of Gorgias. The exit on stage left leads to Athens, that on stage right to the open country where Cnemon and Gorgias have their fields.

PROLOGUE

(*Out of a doorway made up to look like the entrance to a cave comes the god Pan. He is the mischievous fellow, goat from the waist down and man from the waist up except for goat's ears and horns, whose divine powers include, among others, that of inspiring lovers. The locale is a more or less unfrequented spot in Phyle, a country district about thirteen miles north of Athens, where a well-known sanctuary sacred to Pan was located.*)

PAN (*to the audience*) I want you to imagine that this (*with a sweeping gesture*) is Phyle, near Athens, and that this cave I've just come out of is the famous sanctuary of the nymphs that belongs to the people of Phyle and the others who manage to coax crops out of the stones around here. Now, the property on my right here belongs to Cnemon. He's a man whose one aim is to be anti-men. He's mean to everybody, dislikes being with people—being with people did I say? He's lived a good many years by now and so far he hasn't uttered a kind word in his life. The only conversations he ever starts are when he goes past my door—and that's only because I'm a neighbor and he can't avoid it. I'm convinced he regrets it the next minute.

Surprisingly enough, considering the sort he is, he took a wife. He married a widow right after she had lost her first husband and had been left with a son who was still just a child at the time. Cnemon led a miserable life with her, quarreling with her not only all day but most of the night too. They had a daughter. That made things even worse. (*Pauses and shakes his head sorrowfully over the fate of a child born into such a household.*)

When the situation got as bad as it could possibly be and her life was nothing but bitterness and hardship, his wife left him and went to live with the son she had had by her first husband. He has a scrap of land (*pointing*) adjoining here and he barely manages to squeeze enough from it to feed himself, his mother, and a single faithful old servant who once belonged to his father. He's a young fellow now, and wise beyond his years; the school of hard knocks has a way of accelerating a man's education. The old man lives alone with his daughter and an old hag of a servant and spends his days hauling wood, digging, slaving—and hating everyone in turn, beginning with his wife and neighbors here and going right on through to the outskirts of Athens. The girl has gotten this much benefit from the way she's been brought up: she simply doesn't know what it is to do wrong. And she's respected and worshiped me and my nymphs to the point where she's inclined us to make her our special charge. (*Leaning forward and speaking confidentially*) Now, a young fellow whose father owns farmland around here worth a fortune, and who lives in style in the city, went out hunting with his servant and happened to come to this place. And I've made him fall madly in love with the girl. (*Straightens up and pauses for a moment to let what he has just said sink in.*)

Those are the salient points. Please be good enough to stay, if you will, and watch the whole story unfold. (*Looking off toward the wings, stage left*) Well, I think I see our young lover and somebody with him coming this way. They're talking about how he fell in love.

ACT I

(*Sostratus and Chaereas enter, stage left. Sostratus is a fine-looking young man dressed in an elaborate hunting costume that obviously cost a good deal of money. He has an open, candid countenance, the sort that inspires immediate confidence, and an eager and enthusiastic temperament that is particularly appealing. It is clear from his manner at the moment that something significant has happened to him to which he has reacted strongly, as one of his nature would. His companion is totally different. He is also young but there is nothing open in his nature. He is, as a matter of fact, a professional scrounger, a quick-witted sort who makes his way by attaching himself to rich friends such as Sostratus and by rendering for them, in return for their hospitality, certain favors, often of a shady nature. Sostratus has just finished telling him something as they enter.*)

CHAEREAS What's this you tell me, Sostratus? You saw a respectable girl praying to the nymphs here (*gesturing toward the grotto*), you fell in love with her on the spot, and then turned around and left?

SOSTRATUS On the spot.

CHAEREAS (*smiling superciliously*) Pretty quick work. What did you do? Leave your house with the idea of falling in love with someone?

SOSTRATUS (*resentfully*) It may be a joke to you, Chaereas, but I'm in a bad way.

CHAEREAS (*quickly*) Oh, I believe you.

SOSTRATUS I consider you not only my friend but a man who gets things done. That's why I'm bringing you into this affair.

CHAEREAS (*with a professional air*) Well, Sostratus, here's how I handle affairs of this sort. If a friend of mine falls in love with some chorus girl and comes to me for help, I go right out and grab the girl to haul her off to him; I get drunk, I burn down her door, I don't listen to reason. The trick is to let him get her before you even find out her name. Because, if there's any delay, he'll get more and more infatuated, but if it's done quickly there's a chance he'll get over it quickly. On the other hand, if a friend brings up the subject of marriage with a respectable girl, then I'm totally different. I find out about her family, the way she lives, what her character's like. That way I'm in a position to leave my friend a reminder he'll never forget, to guide him.

SOSTRATUS That sounds fine. (*Aside*) But not for me.

CHAEREAS (*rubbing his hands energetically with the air of a man ready to get right to work*) Well, now, the first thing we have to do is get a full report on her.

SOSTRATUS I had Pyrrhias, the servant who went hunting with me, leave the house at the crack of dawn this morning.

CHAEREAS What for?

SOSTRATUS To speak to the girl's father or the head of the household, whoever he is.

CHAEREAS (*disgusted*) Oh, my god, what's this you're telling me?

SOSTRATUS (*unhappily*) I made a mistake. I guess you shouldn't use a servant for this sort of thing. But when a man's in love, it's hard for him to know what's the right thing to do. (*Looking around anxiously)* I've been wondering for some time now what's been keeping him. I told him to come right back to me as soon as he had found out the lie of the land.

(At this moment Pyrrhias bursts in, stage right, running at top speed and shouting.)

PYRRHIAS Gangway, everybody clear the road! Watch out, there's a lunatic after me, a raving lunatic!

SOSTRATUS *(grabbing him and forcibly holding him back)* What's the matter?

PYRRHIAS *(shouting)* Run for your lives!

SOSTRATUS What is it?

PYRRHIAS He's heaving things at me! Sticks and stones! He's going to kill me!

SOSTRATUS Heaving things? Where, you good-for-nothing?

PYRRHIAS *(looking around warily and not seeing anyone)* I guess he stopped chasing me.

SOSTRATUS You're darned right he did.

PYRRHIAS But I thought he was.

SOSTRATUS Now what's this all about?

PYRRHIAS *(still quaking)* Please! Let's get out of here.

SOSTRATUS Where?

PYRRHIAS *(pointing to Cnemon's house)* Away from that door. As far as we can get. That house you sent me to—the devil's own son lives there, a demon, a madman. What he did to me! I had to run for it and I kept stumbling and just about lost every one of my toes.

CHAEREAS Went after you, eh? He's mad. Or maybe he was drunk.

SOSTRATUS Oh, mad, no doubt about it.

CHAEREAS God, yes; out of his mind.

PYRRHIAS Sostratus, he'll kill us!

SOSTRATUS *(casting a wary eye at the house)* Watch the way you talk around here. *(He leads the two off to the side of the stage.)*

PYRRHIAS I can hardly talk, I'm so out of breath. Well, I knocked on the door and said I wanted the head of the house. Some old witch came out. From the very spot where I was talking to you just now, she pointed to where he was, on a hill dragging himself around to pick up wild pears—or maybe some wood to hang himself with.

CHAEREAS (*sarcastically*) Pretty violent carryings-on.

PYRRHIAS What did you expect? Well, I walked off the road into the field and headed toward him. I wanted to be real friendly and tactful, so I called out while I was still some distance away. "I beg your pardon," I said, "but I've come here to you because I'm very anxious about a matter that concerns you." He starts right in yelling at me, "You godforsaken good-for-nothing, what do you mean by trespassing on my property?" and then he picks up a clod and heaves it straight at my face.

CHAEREAS He can go to the devil!

PYRRHIAS I just about had time to blink and say "God damn you," when he picks up one of his vine stakes and starts clobbering me with it, hollering, "What business can you have with me, anyway? Can't you tell a public road from private property?"— all at the top of his lungs.

CHAEREAS (*nodding knowingly*) One of those crazy hicks.

PYRRHIAS It ended up with him chasing me about a mile and a half, all around the hill and down into the brush here, throwing clods and stones at me. Even his pears, when he didn't have anything better. He's a wild one, all right. Some godforsaken old crank! Please! Let's get out of here!

SOSTRATUS (*stubbornly*) What do you think I am, a coward?

PYRRHIAS (*frantically*) You don't understand. We're in danger. He'll eat us alive!

CHAEREAS He's probably sick and is having some sort of attack. That's why, if you ask me, Sostratus, I'd put off seeing him. Always remember that the best way to get anything done is to pick the psychological moment.

PYRRHIAS That makes sense.

CHAEREAS These half-starved hicks have mean tempers. Not just this one, but practically all of them. Tomorrow, first thing, I'll go see him by myself, now that I know where he lives. Right now you go home and take it easy. Everything will turn out all right. (*Takes his leave, stage left.*)

PYRRHIAS Let's do that.

SOSTRATUS (*to Pyrrhias angrily, gesturing toward the departing Chaereas*) He's delighted to get an excuse so quickly. I could see he wasn't any too anxious to come along with me, and took a dim view of my going after this marriage. But you! Damn you, anyway! How stupid can you be?

PYRRHIAS What'd I do that was wrong, Sostratus?

SOSTRATUS You trespassed on his property. No question about it.

PYRRHIAS But it couldn't be helped!

SOSTRATUS Would anyone have beaten you up if you hadn't done something wrong?

PYRRHIAS (*happening to look up in the direction of the wings, stage right*) Hey! Here he comes!

SOSTRATUS (*urgently*) Be a good fellow and go up to him.

PYRRHIAS No, you talk to him.

SOSTRATUS Oh, I couldn't. I'm no good at talking; nobody ever believes me.

PYRRHIAS (*looking toward the wings again, fearfully*) How would you describe someone like that, anyway?

SOSTRATUS He doesn't exactly look like the friendly type. My god, what a scowl! We'd better get a little further away from his door. Look—no one's with him and he's shouting away. If you ask me, he's a sick man. God in heaven, he scares me! It's the truth, let's face it.

(*Cnemon strides in, stage right, talking at the top of his lungs as he goes along. He's all that we have been led to expect: a sour-tempered old codger, gnarled and bent from a lifetime of work in the fields, and utterly indifferent to his appearance—he is dressed in worn work clothes that are a mass of tatters, and his hair is unkempt. His disposition has obviously not been improved by his recent contretemps with Pyrrhias.*)

CNEMON (*haranguing the world at large*) It's that fellow Perseus in the story who's the really lucky one. For two reasons. First, he had wings so he never had to meet anyone walking around on the ground. Second, he had some sort of gadget to turn anyone who bothered him into stone. I wish I had it right now—I'd fill the place with statues. God almighty, the way things are these days, life isn't worth living. Now people trespass on your property to come and jabber away at you. So help me, I used to live along this road, but I don't work this section of my property at all any longer. I've given it up. Too many people around. And now they even chase me up into the hills! (*Gritting his teeth and clenching his fists*) Oh, these crowds, these mobs! (*Noticing Sostratus in front of his house*) More trouble? Who's that in front of my door, anyway? (*Heads straight for Sostratus.*)

SOSTRATUS (*sotto voce, to Pyrrhias*) Is he going to hit me?

CNEMON (*as before*) A man couldn't find any privacy even if he
    wanted to hang himself!
SOSTRATUS (*sotto voce, to Pyrrhias*) He's got it in for me! (*Visibly
    braces himself. As Cnemon comes near, in his most courteous
    manner*) I beg your pardon. I'm waiting for someone here. I
    had an appointment with him.
CNEMON (*as before*) Didn't I tell you? (*To Sostratus*) What did you
    think this was, anyway, a public square? (*With ponderous
    sarcasm*) If you want to meet people in front of my door, why
    don't you be sensible about it? Rearrange everything, install a
    nice comfortable chair here. Better yet, build yourself a town
    hall. (*Charges into his house, slamming the door behind him.*)
SOSTRATUS (*dismayed at the prospect that lies ahead of him, to Pyrrhias*)
    This is awful! (*Shaking his head incredulously*) What a boor!
    It's downright sinful, if you ask me. And, if you ask me, ordinary
    measures aren't going to help. We've got to do something drastic.
    No question about it. (*Brightening*) Why don't I go see Geta,
    my father's servant? By god, that's what I'll do. He's a fellow
    with nerve and he knows his way around. He'll handle the old
    grouch, I know it. I have no intention of losing any time in this
    project; a lot can be accomplished in one day. (*There's a noise
    at Cnemon's door.*) Wait— someone's coming out.

(*The door swings open and Cnemon's daughter comes out. She is
dressed as simply as possible and is carrying a homely kitchen pot, but
somehow her radiant young beauty remains unimpaired. It has a special
quality that sets her off, raises her above everything about her. The
minute she closes the door and turns to the audience, it is apparent that
she is greatly upset.*)

GIRL (*to herself*) Oh, dear, this is simply terrible! What *am* I going to
    do? My old nurse went to draw some water and dropped the
    bucket in the well!
SOSTRATUS (*transfixed at the sight of the girl, to himself*) Ye gods! Ye
    gods in heaven! She's beautiful! She's irresistible!
GIRL (*to herself*) Papa had given orders when he left to heat up some
    water.
SOSTRATUS (*still in a daze, to himself*) Beautiful! Simply beautiful.
GIRL (*to herself*) And if he ever finds out about this, he'll beat her to
    within an inch of her life. Oh, dear, I don't have much time.

(*Turns and starts to walk toward the grotto.*) My darling nymphs, I'll take some of your water. (*Suddenly stops.*) Oh, there may be some people praying inside. I'd be mortified if I disturbed them.

SOSTRATUS (*recovering his wits, approaches her and addresses her in his most gallant manner*) May I? I'll fill it for you and bring it right back.

GIRL   Why, thank you!

SOSTRATUS (*as he walks toward the grotto*)   Just a lovely country girl. O Lord, I feel the pangs of love—there's no saving me now!

GIRL (*starting as she hears the creak of a door opening*) Oh, dear, someone's coming out. Maybe it's Papa! He'll beat me if he catches me outside here!

(*It is the door of Gorgias' house, not Cnemon's, that opens and Davus, Gorgias' servant comes out. The girl breathes a sigh of relief. Davus is an old, devoted family retainer who had once belonged to Gorgias' father. But, like many old men, he has a tendency to be cranky—and the long years of hard work he has put in helping the family eke out their bare existence hasn't helped matters.*)

DAVUS (*talking through the doorway to Myrrhina, Gorgias' mother, inside*)   I've spent enough time around here helping you. He's out there digging all by himself. I'd better go to him. (*Turns from the door and starts walking, muttering to himself.*) Oh, this poverty! Why do we have to have such a bad case of it? Why does it have to move into our house and live with us like a permanent guest?

(*Sostratus emerges from the grotto with the pot now full of water and walks toward the girl.*)

SOSTRATUS   Here you are.

GIRL   Please put it here.

DAVUS (*hearing the voices and noticing the two, to himself*)   What's that fellow after, anyway?

SOSTRATUS   Goodbye. Take care of your father. (*To himself, in despair*) Oh, my god, my god!

PYRRHIAS (*soothingly*)   Stop moaning, Sostratus. It's going to be all right.

SOSTRATUS   All right? How?

PYRRHIAS Don't worry. You just said you were going after Geta. Go
ahead. Tell him everything that's happened and bring him back
with you. (*The two leave, stage left.*)

DAVUS (*to himself*) What the devil's going on here? I don't like this
business of a youngster doing favors for a girl; it's bad stuff.
Cnemon, I hope you rot in hell! What do you mean by letting
an innocent girl go out by herself in a deserted place like this
without sending somebody along to look after her the way you
should? This youngster probably got wind of the situation and
sneaked in here figuring he had hit the jackpot. Well, I've got to
tell her brother about this as soon as I can so that we can arrange to keep an eye on her. Matter of fact, I think I'll go do
that right now. (*There's a sound of music and song; he looks
toward the wings, stage left.*) And I see that one of Pan's con-
gregations is coming here—and they're all a little high. If you
ask me, this is no time to get in their way. (*Leaves, stage right.*)

(*A chorus, dressed as worshipers of Pan, comes on and dances an
entr'acte.*)

ACT II

(*Davus enters, stage right, followed by a man dressed in work clothes
that, although worn, are clean and neat. It is Gorgias, Cnemon's stepson.
His mother had taken him from Cnemon's household when he was still
a child and it was the best thing she could have done: he has grown into
a sturdy, fine-looking young man; despite his dress, you can see at a
glance that he is no ordinary peasant. The hard life he is forced
to lead hasn't warped him; he has the intelligence and strength of
character to take a philosophical view of his situation.*

*Davus has just told him about the intruder and the two have come
to see if he's still around.*)

GORGIAS You mean to say you handled the situation that badly, that
carelessly?

DAVUS (*on the defensive*) What do you mean?

GORGIAS You should have realized then and there that, whoever he
was, he was making advances to the girl. You should have told
him that we don't want to catch him doing this ever again. What

you did was to turn your back on him as if it was none of your business. Davus, a man can't get out of family obligations, and that means I've got to keep an eye on my sister. Her father chooses to act like a stranger toward us, but we don't have to copy what that old grouch does. Because, if the girl gets involved in a scandal, the blame's going to fall on me too. Outsiders hear about only what's happened, not who's responsible for it. Let's go see the old fellow.

DAVUS   But, Gorgias, I'm afraid of him. The minute he catches sight of me heading for his door, he'll hang me on the spot.

GORGIAS (*nodding assent gloomily*)   Oh, he's a hard one to reason with, all right. I can see absolutely no way we can force him to behave better, or talk him into changing his ways. He's got the law to stop us from doing anything by force—and that temper of his from accomplishing anything by talk. (*Starts walking off.*)

DAVUS (*looking toward the wings, stage left*)   Wait a second. It wasn't a waste of time after all to come here. I told you he'd come back. There he is.

GORGIAS (*following Davus' glance*)   Is that the fellow you were telling me about? With the fancy jacket?

DAVUS   That's the one.

GORGIAS   One look and you can see he's up to no good.

(*Sostratus enters, stage left, so absorbed in his thoughts that he doesn't notice Davus and Gorgias.*)

SOSTRATUS (*to the audience*)   I couldn't get Geta. He wasn't in; my mother had sent him out to hire a chef. She's giving a party to celebrate some religious holiday. Don't ask me which—she goes in for this sort of thing every day of the week; goes around the whole town saying prayers. I said No, thank you, to the party and came back here. I've made up my mind to quit beating around the bush. I'm going to speak for myself. And I'm going to knock on the door right now so's not to give myself time for second thoughts.

GORGIAS (*coming forward*)   Mister, would you mind listening to me for a moment? I've got something important to tell you.

SOSTRATUS (*looking up in surprise, but responding with the courtesy that comes naturally to him*)   I'd be very glad to. What is it?

GORGIAS (*eyeing Sostratus closely and speaking earnestly and with con-*

viction) Some of us are well off and some not. But I'm convinced there isn't a man in this world whose situation is permanent; there's always a chance it can change. If a man's well off, things in life will keep going well for him only so long as he's able to handle his good luck and keep from doing wrong. When it comes to the point where he's led astray by the good things he has, then his life is going to take a turn for the worse. On the other hand, take people who aren't well off. If, in spite of all their handicaps, they can keep from doing wrong and can bear up under their fate like men of character, once they've proved themselves they can look forward to a change for the better eventually. What do I mean by all this? That you, no matter how well-to-do you are, shouldn't take this state of affairs for granted. Nor should you look down on us just because we're poor. You've got to make sure that, in people's eyes, you seem to deserve your good luck.

SOSTRATUS (*puzzled, not catching the drift of these remarks*) And just what do I seem to you to be doing now that isn't as it should be?

GORGIAS (*looking him straight in the eye*) I think you've been trying hard to do something mean and unworthy. You've got it in mind to talk a respectable girl into doing wrong. You're looking for a chance to do something you ought to pay for with your life.

SOSTRATUS (*stunned*) Oh, my god!

GORGIAS You have no right to spend your leisure time hurting people who don't know what leisure is. Remember, there's no one more bitter than a poor man who's been wronged. He's someone you should feel sorry for, to begin with; and, on top of that, remember to place the blame for what he puts up with where it belongs, on fate and not on any wrongdoing on his part.

SOSTRATUS (*finally realizing what lies behind all this, earnestly*) Mister, I'm ready to wish you all the luck, wealth and leisure in the world if you'll just listen to me for a moment.

DAVUS (*to Gorgias*) That's telling him, Gorgias! Good work!

SOSTRATUS (*to Davus, angrily*) And you listen too, blabbermouth! (*To Gorgias*) I saw a girl here. I fell in love with her. If this is wrong, then I guess I've done a wrong. What's there to complain about? I haven't come here to make advances to her. I want to see her father. Look, I'm a respectable Athenian citizen, I've got a good income, and I'm ready to take her without any dowry and give you my oath that I'll never stop loving her. (*With deep conviction*) Mister, may this god (*gesturing toward the grotto*) strike me dead on this spot if I came here to harm or try some underhand trick on you people. Believe me, I'm upset, terribly so, if I've given that sort of impression to you.

GORGIAS (*visibly impressed*) And if I've used stronger language with you than necessary, please don't let that trouble you. You've not only convinced me, but I'm ready to be your friend. And, my dear fellow, I want you to know that I'm no stranger to her. I'm her half-brother; she and I have the same mother. And, believe me, I can be a great help to you from now on.

SOSTRATUS (*eagerly*) A help? How?

GORGIAS I can see that you're a gentleman. I don't want to make up any excuses to get you away from here. I just want to make clear what the facts of the situation are. This girl's father is in a class by himself. There's no one like him alive today, and there never has been.

SOSTRATUS The old grouch? (*Grimly*) I know a little about him.

GORGIAS They don't come any worse. This property he's got is worth sixty thousand dollars. He always works it all by himself. Never gets anybody to help him, no slaves, no local hired hands, no neighbors. Does it all by himself. You see, his greatest pleasure in life is not to have to set eyes on another soul. He usually works with the girl at his side. She's the only one he'll talk to. As a matter of fact, he'd find it hard to exchange a word with anyone else. And he claims he won't let her marry until he can find a son-in-law exactly like himself.

SOSTRATUS You mean never!

GORGIAS (*urgently*) My dear fellow, don't go looking for trouble. You'll just be wasting your time. Leave it to us to put up with the situation. We're his relatives; it's our lot in life.

SOSTRATUS (*heatedly*) For god's sake, mister, haven't you ever been in love?

GORGIAS (*gloomily*) My dear fellow, that's out of the question.

SOSTRATUS Why? What's to stop you?

GORGIAS The sum total of all the troubles I'm up against. They don't give me a moment's respite.

SOSTRATUS I don't think you've had much experience with love. You're asking me to give up. (*Fervently*) That's no longer in my power, only in god's.

GORGIAS   It's not that you're doing us any harm, it's just that you're giving yourself a lot of trouble for nothing.

SOSTRATUS   Can't I get the girl somehow?

GORGIAS   No, you can't. Just come along with me and I'll prove it to you; it so happens he's working in the valley right near where I am.

SOSTRATUS   How?

GORGIAS   I'll make a remark about getting the girl married. The minute he hears something like that mentioned, he'll wade right in gleefully and attack everybody in creation, sneering at the lives they lead. And, if he gets a look at you, the picture of a gentleman of leisure, he won't be able to bear the sight of you.

SOSTRATUS   Is he out there now?

GORGIAS   Oh, no. But he'll go out a little later by the route he usually takes.

SOSTRATUS   (*eagerly*)   Now, please tell me this: will he have the girl with him?

GORGIAS   It depends. Maybe.

SOSTRATUS   (*resolutely*)   Then I'm ready to go to that place you mentioned. And, please, you've got to help me!

GORGIAS   How?

SOSTRATUS   What do you mean how? Take me to that place you mentioned!

GORGIAS   (*eyeing Sostratus' costume, and smiling*)   Why? You plan to stand around in that fancy jacket of yours while we work?

SOSTRATUS   (*ingenuously*)   Certainly. Why not?

DAVUS   He'll start right in heaving rocks at you and calling you a lazy good-for-nothing. No, you're going to have to dig right along with us. That way, if he happens to see you he'll think you're a poor man who has to work for a living and he may let you exchange a word with him.

SOSTRATUS   (*enthusiastically*)   Let's go! I'm ready to do whatever you say.

GORGIAS   (*forced by Sostratus' eagerness to acquiesce against his better judgment, hopelessly*)   What are you forcing all this trouble on yourself for? (*Shaking his head, goes to the front of his house and picks up a mattock and some extra work clothes.*)

DAVUS (*aside*) What I want is to put in such a day's work that we break this fellow's back. Then he'll stop coming around and bothering us.

SOSTRATUS Give me a mattock.

GORGIAS Here, take mine. I have some work to do on a fence I'm building; it's something I can't put off.

SOSTRATUS Let's have it. (*As he takes the mattock and work clothes, feelingly*) You've saved my life!

DAVUS (*unable to take any more of this*) I'll go along; you two follow me there. (*Goes out, stage right.*)

SOSTRATUS Here's the way I feel: if I get the girl, I'll live; if not, I'll kill myself on the spot.

GORGIAS If you really mean what you say, the best of luck to you! (*Follows Davus out.*)

SOSTRATUS (*to himself, looking at Gorgias' departing figure*) Ye gods! The very things you thought would stop me have made me twice as keen to go ahead. The girl's been brought up without any women around her. There's been no aunt or nurse to give her wrong ideas; she doesn't know a thing about the bad side of life. She's been left to herself, with a father who's a strait-laced old peasant. What a blessing to come upon a girl like that! (*Puts on the work clothes, shoulders the mattock, takes a few steps, then stops.*) This mattock weighs a ton! It'll kill me! Oh, well, I can't weaken; now that I've started I've got to sweat it out. (*Hurries out, stage right, to catch up with Davus and Gorgias.*)

(*A second later a man in a cook's outfit enters, stage left, pulling mightily on a rope, on the other end of which is a sheep that is pulling mightily in the opposite direction. The man is Sicon, the chef—or rather, chef and caterer—whom Sostratus' mother had sent Geta out to hire for her party. Sicon has no small opinion of himself and the importance of his profession. But if long on self-esteem, he's a bit short on brains.*)

SICON (*to himself*) This is some sheep! No ordinary animal, not this one. (*To the sheep*) Go to the devil! (*To himself*) If I pick it up and carry it, it gets a branch in its teeth, starts eating the leaves, holds on with all its might and pulls me back. If I put it down to walk, it won't go ahead, it just goes back in the opposite direction. Here I am, a chef, having to haul this thing all the way! I'm sick and tired of it! Thank god, here's the cave where we're going to sacrifice it. Pan, am I glad to see you! (*Looking back in the direction he had come from*) Geta! Look how far behind you are!

(*Geta, Sostratus' father's servant, enters. Geta is a young, agile, resourceful chap—but at this juncture he is in no position to display any of his talents, for he's bent double under a towering load of straw mats.*)

GETA   Those damn women piled enough on me to load four donkeys!

SICON   It looks as if a big crowd's expected. I can't even count all the mats you've got there.

GETA   What do I do with them?

SICON   (*pointing*)   Stack them here.

GETA   (*dumping his load*)   Here you are. (*Grumbling to himself as he straightens up painfully*) All she has to do is see Pan in a dream and I know just what happens: out we march to make a sacrifice to him.

SICON   (*overhearing and, being a highly superstitious sort, pricking up his ears*)   Who had a dream?

GETA   (*still put out because of the job that had been given him and in no mood for conversation, particularly Sicon's*)   Oh, don't bother me.

SICON   (*too obtuse to take offense*)   But tell me, Geta, who had a dream?

GETA   (*curtly*)   My lady.

SICON   (*on tenterhooks*)   What about? For god's sake, tell me!

GETA   (*disgusted*)   You'll be the death of me. She thought she saw Pan—

SICON   (*interrupting, pointing to the grotto*)   You mean the one from here?

GETA   (*patiently*)   The one from here.

SICON   Do what?

GETA   (*continuing*)   —take her son Sostratus—

SICON   (*interrupting again, with a knowing nod*)   A fine young fellow.

GETA   (*doggedly determined to end his sentence*)   —clap him in irons—

SICON   Oh, my god!

GETA   —give him some work clothes and a mattock, and order him to go digging in this field alongside here.

SICON   Amazing!

GETA   That's why we're making this sacrifice. It's an evil omen. We want to turn it into a good one.

SICON   (*awed*)   Now I understand. (*Galvanized into action by what he's just heard*)   All right, pick up the mats again and bring them inside. Let's get the seats set up in there and everything else all ready. Heaven help us, I don't want anything to hold up the sacrifice when they come. (*Noticing that Geta is standing there eying the stack of mats darkly, jovially*)   Wipe the frown off! You old good-for-nothing, I'll tie the feed bag on you today for real! All the food you want.

GETA   (*giving him a fishy stare*)   I've always had a good word to say for you and your cooking—but I don't trust you.

(*Geta picks up his load of mats and the two enter the cave. The stage is now empty, and the chorus re-appears to dance an entr'acte.*)

ACT III

(*The door of Cnemon's house opens and Cnemon comes out. He calls to Simike inside, the ancient female who is his only servant.*)

CNEMON   (*through the doorway*)   Simike! Lock the door and don't open up for anyone until I get back. And that probably won't be until after dark.

(*Cnemon turns from the door and is about to trudge out to his fields when he catches sight of Geta emerging from the cave. Geta walks forward and stands looking toward the wings, stage left, as if he were expecting someone. Suddenly a young servant girl enters, with a number of others behind her.*)

GETA   (*shouting to the girl*)   Plangon! Get a move on! We should have been done with the sacrifice by now!

CNEMON   (*aghast as he eyes the procession straggling in*)   What the devil does this mean? What's this crowd? Oh, damn them!

GETA   (*to one of the girls who is carrying a flute*)   Parthenis, some music for Pan! No silent processions for this god, that's what they say.

(By this time there is a whole group on stage, mostly girls plus a few men. They are Sostratus' mother's servants, and they are carrying all the paraphernalia needed for a sacrifice and a party: incense burner, holy cakes, holy water, kitchenware, tableware, and so on. Sostratus' mother herself is in the crowd. At this point Sicon comes out of the cave, takes one look at the group, and hurries forward to take over.)

SICON *(roaring at the servants)*   So you finally made it! Good god, this is disgusting! We've been sitting around here waiting all this time. We got everything we could all ready.

GETA *(joining in)*   Believe me, the sheep certainly is: it practically died waiting.

SICON *(as before)*   Of course. The poor thing's not going to hang around while all of you take it easy. Come on now, inside, all of you! *(As they start to file into the cave)* I want everything all set, the baskets, the holy water, the incense— *(To a final straggler)* Hey, you! Dumbbell! What are you gaping at? *(Hustles him inside. Cnemon is now alone on the stage.)*

CNEMON *(shaking his fist at the figures disappearing into the cave)*   God damn you! *(To himself)* They're going to keep me from my work. I can't leave the house now. *(Savagely)* These nymphs give me nothing but trouble! I guess I'll just have to tear my house down and move somewhere else. *(Gesturing toward the group in the cave)* They sacrifice like a bunch of thieves. They bring couches and jugs of wine—but not for the service. Oh, no, it's for themselves. The incense is for the service and so is the holy cake. They put that on the altar, all right, all of it. And then they add the animal's tail and its gall bladder because no one wants them. But the rest they gulp down therselves. *(Pounding on his door)* Simike! Hurry and open the door! *(To himself, worriedly)* I guess I'll have to stay around and keep an eye on things.

(The door is opened and Cnemon goes inside. A second later Geta comes out of the cave. His first words are addressed to one of the servants inside.)

GETA *(shouting through the entrance of the cave)*   You say you forgot to bring the pot? Why don't all of you go and sleep it off, you drunks! What are we going to do now? *(Leaves the entrance and makes his way toward Cnemon's door, grumbling to himself.)* It looks like I'll have to bother one of the god's neighbors. *(Knocks on the door and shouts)* Boy! *(Continues his chain of complaints, punctuating it with shouts to rouse someone within.)* God in heaven, if you ask me they don't grow them worse than that bunch of girls, anywhere.—Boy!—All they know how to do is get laid—Boy! Please!—and make nasty cracks about you if you catch them at it. Boy! What the devil is this? Boy! No one home? Ah—I think someone's coming.

(The door opens and Cnemon comes out.)

CNEMON *(raging)* Damn you, what are you hanging onto this door for? Speak up!

GETA *(taken by surprise)* Well, you don't have to bite my head off!

CNEMON By god, I'll eat you alive. *(Takes a threatening step toward him.)*

GETA *(beating a hasty retreat)* None of that, for god's sake!

CNEMON *(caustically)* Who are you, one of my creditors, you god-forsaken good-for-nothing!

GETA *(from a safe distance)* I'm no creditor. Look, I didn't come here to collect a debt. I don't have the sheriff with me. I just came to ask you for a pot.

CNEMON *(taken aback)* A pot?

GETA A pot.

CNEMON *(snarling)* Damn you, what do you think? That I'm the kind that can afford to sacrifice a whole ox and carry on the way you people do?

GETA *(aside)* If you want my opinion, you wouldn't sacrifice a snail. *(To Cnemon)* It's all right, my good man, I'll go. The servants told me to knock on the door and ask for a pot. That's what I did. I drew a blank. I'll go back and tell them so. *(To himself, as he walks away)* Ye gods! That old man's got fangs! *(Enters the cave.)*

CNEMON *(balefully watching Geta go off)* A bunch of wild animals! Come right up to your door and knock as if you were their best friend. *(Shaking his fist at the cave)* If I catch any of you coming up to this door, and if I don't make an example of him for everyone around here, you can take it for granted—*(pauses a second, then comes up with what to him is a terrible indict-*

ment) that I'm just another of the common herd! (*Turning to go inside*) I don't know why I let that one off so easy. He was lucky, whoever he was! (*Enters his house.*)

(*A second later Sicon comes out of the cave. His first words are addressed to Geta inside.*)

SICON (*through the entrance of the cave, disgustedly*)   You damn fool, he insulted you! Maybe you asked him like some dumb hay-seed would. (*Grumbling to himself as he walks toward Cnemon's door*) Some people just don't understand how to do things like this. I'm an expert at it. I've got thousands of customers back in the city and I pester their neighbors and borrow stuff from all of them. When you borrow from somebody you've got to use a little flattery. If some old gent answers the door, the first thing I do is call him "My dear sir"; if it's an old woman, I call her "Lady"; if it's a middle-aged woman, I call her "Madame"; if it's a servant, "My good man" or "My dear boy." (*Suddenly reminded of the servants' forgetfulness that caused him this trouble in the first place*) You ought to be hung, all of you! What stupidity! (*Knocking on the door*) Boys! Boys! Please! My dear sir, would you mind coming out? I'd like to speak to you.

CNEMON (*as he opens the door*)   You back again?

SICON   Yes, sir, for the same reason.

CNEMON (*eyeing him balefully*)   Are you deliberately trying to make me lose my temper? Didn't I tell you to keep away from this door? (*Turning and calling inside*) Simike! Bring me the whip!

SICON (*beating a hasty retreat*)   Oh, no, my dear sir, no, not that! For god's sake, not that! (*Starts to run away.*)

CNEMON (*armed with the whip and raging mad*)   Come back here, you!

SICON (*forgetting his principles*)   Well, god damn you—

CNEMON   Still jabbering, eh?

SICON (*getting control of himself again and stopping a safe distance away, resentfully*)   I only came here to ask you for a pot.

CNEMON   I don't have a pot and I don't have a cleaver, and I don't have salt or vinegar or anything else. I've told everybody in the neighborhood, once and for all, not to come near me.

SICON   You didn't tell me.

CNEMON   I'm telling you now.

SICON   Not very nicely, I must say. Please, couldn't you just tell me where I could borrow one?

CNEMON   (*to the world at large*) What did I tell you? (*To Sicon*) Are you going to keep on jabbering at me?

SICON   Well, thanks anyway.

CNEMON   I don't want any thanks from any of you.

SICON   All right then, no thanks.

CNEMON   (*as he turns to go inside, to himself*) What I have to put up with! And nothing I can do about it.

SICON   (*to himself*) He just about tore me to pieces! That's what I get for asking like a gentleman! God, it certainly makes a difference whose door you knock on. Now, if everybody around here is ready to take a poke at a man, things aren't going to be so easy for me. (*Thinking a moment*) I think the best thing would be to broil all the meat. At least I've got a broiling pan. (*Addressing, as it were, the whole district*) People of Phyle— GOODBYE! (*To himself again*) I'll just make do with what I have. (*Enters the cave.*)

(*Enter Sostratus, stage right. He looks all in: he is covered with dirt, sweat is streaming off him, his hair is disheveled, and he limps along holding his back.*)

SOSTRATUS   (*to himself*) If anyone's running short of trouble, the thing for him to do is go hunting in Phyle. Oh my aching back! And spine, and neck—why go into details? My whole body! (*Pauses and shakes his head mournfully.*) I acted just like a child. The minute I got out there I pitched right in, lifting the mattock way up, the way an old hand would, maybe even more so. I pegged away happily—but not for very long. Soon I began turning around to see whether the old man was coming with the girl. Next thing I knew I had to start pressing my hands on my back to straighten up. At first I did it without letting anyone see me, but then, when the work dragged on and on, I began to get curvature of the spine. Pretty soon I was stiff as a board. But everything was quiet: nobody came. And the sun began to roast me. There I was, barely able to straighten up each time and then going right down again fast with my whole body, like the boom on a crane, when Gorgias took a look at me and said, "Well, I don't think he's going to come today." "What should

we do then?" I shot right back at him. "Let's knock off for the
present. We'll look for him tomorrow," he said. Davus was there
and he relieved me at the mattock. Well, that's the way the first
round went. Then I came back here, god knows I can't tell why.
Things just automatically draw me to this place.

*(Geta appears at the mouth of the cave. His first words are to Sicon
inside.)*

GETA *(through the entrance of the cave, exasperated)* What's the
    trouble? Man dear, you think I've got sixty hands? I light the
    fire for you, follow you around, lug, wash, cut up the animal's
    innards, make the dough, carry everything around— *(Turns
    from the mouth of the cave rubbing at his eyes.)* Look at me—
    half blind from the smoke in there! If you ask me, I'm doing
    nothing but run this affair for them!
SOSTRATUS *(delighted to see him)* Hey, Geta!
GETA *(still rubbing his eyes, grumpily)* Who wants me?
SOSTRATUS I do.
GETA *(not recognizing Sostratus in his work clothes)* And who are
    you?
SOSTRATUS Don't you see me?
GETA *(finally recognizing him, and, knowing it probably means more
    work, not exactly overjoyed)* I see you. Sostratus.
SOSTRATUS Tell me, what are you doing here?
GETA What am I doing? We've just finished with the sacrifice and
    now we're getting dinner ready for you people.
SOSTRATUS Is my mother inside?
GETA Came a long time ago.
SOSTRATUS And my father?
GETA We're expecting him. But you go on in.
SOSTRATUS I've got some things to do around here first. *(To himself)*
    In some ways this sacrifice didn't come at a bad time at all.
    I'll go right now, just as I am, and invite Gorgias and Davus.
    Once they've joined in the festivities, they'll be of even more
    use as allies in getting me my bride.
GETA *(overhearing)* What! You're going to go out and invite more
    people to dinner! *(Changes his attitude abruptly and shrugs his
    shoulders.)* So far as I'm concerned there can be three thousand
    of you. I knew all along I wasn't going to get even a taste of

anything. Where am I going to get it from, anyway? Go on, invite the whole world. After all, you people just slaughtered a fine sheep, a beauty, really something to see. (*Gesturing toward the servants in the cave, sarcastically*) But those women —they're so charming—would they share anything with me? God, no! Not even a pinch of salt!

SOSTRATUS (*having had a moment, during Geta's grumblings, to think his plan over and more pleased than ever with it*) Geta, before this day is over everything's going to be all right. (*Turning toward the grotto, ebulliently*) Pan, this is one prophecy I'll take it on myself to make. (*Suddenly aware of his presumption, deferentially*) But I'll have a prayer for you every time I pass this way and I'll always treat you with every respect. (*Goes off, stage right, to get Gorgias and Davus.*)

(*The door of Cnemon's house flies open and Simike, Cnemon's aged servant, bursts out. She is in a state of alarm that borders on the pathological.*)

SIMIKE (*screaming*) I'm done for! It's all over! This is the end!

GETA (*stopped by the noise just as he was about to enter the cave*) Oh, damn, some woman's come out of the old man's house.

SIMIKE (*recovering somewhat, to herself*) What's going to happen to me? I wanted to see if I could get the bucket out of the well myself before Cnemon found out, so I tied his hoe to a rope. Well, it wasn't strong enough, and it was rotten anyway, and suddenly it broke.

GETA (*disgusted, aside*) Naturally!

SIMIKE (*to herself*) So now, heaven help me, I've lost the hoe down the well along with the bucket!

GETA (*aside*) Only thing left is to throw yourself in too.

SIMIKE (*to herself*) And it *would* happen just now, when he wants to shift some manure that's in the yard. He's been running around looking for the hoe, yelling bloody murder—(*hearing a noise at the door, starts*) and now he's coming out here!

GETA (*to Simike*) Run! Run for your life! Woman, he'll slaughter you! (*Sees Cnemon coming out.*) Too late. Better protect yourself!

CNEMON (*roaring*) Where's that thief?

SIMIKE (*terrified*) Please! I didn't mean to do it!

CNEMON (*savagely*)   Get inside!

SIMIKE (*as before*)   Please! Please! What are you going to do?

CNEMON   I'm going to tie you to a rope and lower you down the well myself.

SIMIKE (*shrieking*)   No! Oh, this is terrible!

CNEMON   What's more, by god, I'm going to use the same rope. And I only hope it's rotten through and through.

SIMIKE (*in despair, to herself*)   I'll call Davus. He's somewhere around.

CNEMON   Call Davus? How dare you talk like that, you old witch! Are you deaf? Get inside! Quick! (*Simike rushes inside. To himself, peevishly*) Right now this cutting myself off from everybody has me on the spot. Well, since no one else will, I'll go down the well myself. What else can I do?

GETA (*overhearing him, maliciously*)   We'll be glad to give you a rope.

CNEMON (*turning on him*)   Before you give me anything you can go fry in hell! (*Goes into his house, slamming the door behind him.*)

GETA (*to himself*)   Got so sore he had to run back inside. Poor devil, what a life he leads! Perfect example of the typical Athenian peasant: becomes an expert in hardship fighting it out with the rocks around here that grow nothing better than thyme and sage, and getting nothing good out of life. (*Stands silent for a moment pondering this. Then, hearing a noise, looks toward the wings, stage right.*) Here comes Sostratus. And he's got his guests with him. (*Looks again, not believing his eyes.*) They're some of the local farm hands! What a crazy idea! What's he bringing them here for? Where did he get to know them anyway?

(*Sostratus, Gorgias and Davus enter, stage right. Sostratus has issued his invitation and Gorgias has obviously been trying to beg off.*)

SOSTRATUS (*emphatically*)   I won't hear of your doing otherwise. We have plenty. God almighty, there isn't a man alive who can refuse to come to dinner when his friend's made a sacrifice and is holding a party. And remember, I've been a friend of yours a long time, even before I ever saw you. (*Handing Gorgias his work clothes*) Take these things, bring them inside, and then come right back.

GORGIAS   I can't leave my mother alone in the house.

SOSTRATUS Well, take care of whatever she needs. I'll meet you right away.

(Sostratus goes into the cave, and Gorgias, with Davus at his heels, into his house. The stage is now clear, and the chorus comes on and dances an entr'acte.)

ACT IV

(The door of Cnemon's house is flung open and Simike bursts out, wild-eyed and screaming at the top of her lungs.)

SIMIKE Help! Oh, my god, someone help!

(Sicon, attracted by the noise, emerges from the grotto.)

SICON *(grumbling)* In the name of all that's holy, can't you people let us carry on a service in peace! You insult us, you hit us, you scream—what a crazy household!

SIMIKE *(running up to him)* My master! He fell into the well!

SICON How?

SIMIKE How? He started to go down to get the hoe and the bucket, and he slipped and fell all the way to the bottom.

SICON *(a broad grin spreading over his face)* Well, by god, it couldn't have happened to a better man! Old lady, you've got a job now.

SIMIKE What?

SICON Pick up a boulder or a big rock or something like that and heave it in on top of him.

SIMIKE *(too distraught to resent Sicon's attitude)* Please! Go down after him!

SICON What? And become like that fellow in Aesop's fable and have to fight a dog in a well? Not on your life!

SIMIKE *(leaving him and running toward Gorgias' house)* Gorgias! Where in the world are you!

GORGIAS *(as he comes out of his house)* Here I am. *(Seeing the old woman)* Simike! What's the matter?

SIMIKE *(impatiently)* The matter? I'll tell it all over again: Cnemon fell into the well.

GORGIAS *(galvanized into action, rushes to the entrance of the grotto)*

Sostratus! Come on out here! (*As Sostratus dashes out of the cave, Gorgias turns to Simike.*) Show us the way! Come on, inside now! Quick! (*The three rush into Cnemon's house.*)

SICON (*watches them go in, then turns and addresses the audience with an air of great satisfaction*) I'll be damned! Now I believe in Providence. Cnemon, you cheapskate, so you wouldn't lend people a measly pot for a sacrifice, you had to begrudge it, eh? Now that you're down there, drink the well dry so you won't have to share the water with anyone. These nymphs here have taken a hand and given me my revenge—and it's just what you deserve. (*Puffing out his chest*) No one ever harmed a chef yet and got away with it. There's something sacred about our profession. A waiter's a different matter; you can do what you want to a waiter. (*Yielding to curiosity, walks over to Cnemon's door and puts his ear to it.*)

CNEMON'S DAUGHTER (*from inside*) Oh, my god! Oh, he's not dead, is he? Papa dear!

SICON (*to the audience*) Somebody's screaming and moaning. [Four lines are lost here in which Sicon very likely relayed to the audience whatever he could pick up about the way the rescue was going] . . . that way he'll be able to haul the poor devil out. (*Grinning*) Lord in heaven, can you imagine what a lovely sight it's going to be—the old man carried out here in front of the house, shivering away? Gentlemen, so help me, nothing would give me greater pleasure than to see him then. (*Walking to the cave and shouting into it*) You women in there! Let's hold a service for the rescue party. And say a prayer for the old man to be saved—provided he's left good and lame, a cripple. That way we'll have no trouble whatsoever from him even though he is the god's next-door neighbor and around here whenever anyone comes to sacrifice. This will mean a lot to me the next time someone hires me. (*Enters the cave.*)

(*The door of Cnemon's house flies open and Sostratus comes running out.*)

SOSTRATUS (*flushed and in a state of great excitement, to the audience*) Gentlemen! I swear to you, on my honor, by heaven, by all that's holy, I never in my whole life saw anyone pick a better moment to miss drowning by a hair. What a marvelous time I had! The minute we got inside there, Gorgias jumped into the well. The girl and I just waited around the rim. What else was there to do? Except that she kept tearing her hair and beating her breast and crying her eyes out and I, (*archly*) the fine fair-haired boy, stood by and played nursemaid. I kept begging and pleading with her not to carry on so, and all the time I just couldn't take my eyes off her. She's a work of art! And no ordinary one either. I forgot all about the old man groaning down there—except that it was a real nuisance to have to keep hauling away all the time. As a matter of fact, I nearly killed him: I was so busy looking at the girl that I let go of the rope a couple of times. But that Gorgias is an Atlas—and no ordinary one either; he managed to hang on and finally fished him out. As soon as the old man was safe, I had to come out here. I just couldn't hold myself in any longer. I practically went up to the girl and kissed her—that's how madly in love with her I am. I'm getting ready— wait; they're coming out. (*Cnemon's door opens, and Cnemon, supported by Gorgias and flanked by his daughter, comes hobbling out.*) My god! There's a sight for you! (*Moves off to the side, out of their range of vision.*)

(*Slowly Cnemon, Gorgias, and the girl make their way from the door to stage center. There they stand, the girl mute and terrified, and the old man kept from collapsing by his stepson's arm.*)

GORGIAS (*with great solicitude*)   Cnemon! Tell me, is there anything you want?

CNEMON (*weakly*)   What can I want? I'm a terribly sick man.

GORGIAS   Come on now, buck up!

CNEMON (*dully*)   It'll soon be all over, and then I won't bother you any more for the rest of time.

GORGIAS   See how bad it is to cut yourself off from everybody? You almost lost your life just now! At your age you've got to have someone keep an eye on you as long as you live.

CNEMON (*weakly*)   I'm seriously hurt and I know it. Gorgias, go call your mother. (*Shaking his head ruefully*) It certainly looks as if the only way we learn is by bitter experience. (*Turning to the girl*) My dear, will you take my arm and help hold me up?

SOSTRATUS (*aside*)   Lucky man!

CNEMON (*overhearing, turns, sees him—and revives at the prospect of being irascible again*)   And just what the devil are *you* standing around here for? [Eight lines are lost here. After concluding his remarks to Sostratus, Cnemon turned to his son and daughter and his wife, Myrrhina, who had come on stage in the meantime, and continued to unburden his heart, particularly his anguish at his crippled condition.] I would have preferred to die and not have been saved. And neither of you could have changed my mind about this. (*Holding up his hand as they attempt to protest*) Don't argue with me. (*Shaking his head ruefully*) I guess the big mistake I made was in thinking I was the one person who was completely self-sufficient, who'd never have need of anyone else. Well, now when I see how strange and sudden the end of a man's life can be, I realize how little I knew. A man has to have someone around who can look after him. (*Falls silent a moment, brooding. Then, passionately*) But, as god's my witness, what ruined me was seeing how everybody lived, the ways in which they went grubbing after money —I was convinced the person didn't exist who had a kind thought for anybody else. This was what blinded me. (*Dropping his voice and speaking with deep feeling*) Only now have I gotten the proof, from one man—Gorgias. He did something that only the finest sort of person would have done. I never let him come near my door, never helped him in the slightest, never said hello to him, never exchanged a word with him—and yet he willingly saved my life. Anyone else in his place would have said, and with good reason: "You never let me near your door, so I'm not going there now. You never went out of your way for me, so now I won't for you." Well, my boy, whether I die now—and the pain I'm in convinces me I will—or whether I live, I'm acknowledging you here and now as my son. Everything I happen to own you are to consider yours. (*Taking the girl's hand and putting it in Gorgias'*) I put her into your care. Get her a husband. (*Shaking his head sadly*) You see, even if I were a well man, *I* couldn't find one; after all, the man doesn't exist who could satisfy me. If I survive, just let me go on living the way I want. Everything else I leave to you to do—you've got good sense, thank god, and you're the natural choice as guardian of your sister. Divide my estate in two. Give her half as a dowry. You take the other half, run it yourself, and just give your mother and me enough to live on. (*Turning to the girl*) Help me, my dear; I want to go in and lie down. I think the sign of a man of good sense is that he doesn't say any more than he has to. (*Continuing right on, to Gorgias*) But there's one thing I want you to know, my boy. I want to say a few words to you about life and character. If there were only men of good will in this world, we wouldn't have any law courts, people wouldn't drag each other off to prison, there wouldn't be any wars, and we'd all be satisfied with a modest lot in life. But you probably like things the way they are, so you'd better live your life accordingly. (*Wryly*) Besides, you won't have a mean old grouch in your way any longer.

GORGIAS (*diplomatically*) Very well. I agree to everything you say. But I insist that you help me find a husband for my sister just as soon as we can. Someone who'll suit you.

CNEMON (*sharply*) Listen here, I meant every word I said. Now, in god's name, leave me alone!

GORGIAS You see, there's someone who wants to meet you—

CNEMON (*interrupting*) In god's name, no!

GORGIAS (*stoutly finishing his sentence*) —and ask your permission to marry her.

CNEMON (*starting to hobble toward his door*) It's none of my business from now on.

GORGIAS (*calling after him*) He helped save your life.

CNEMON (*stopping abruptly, interested*) Who is he?

GORGIAS (*pointing to Sostratus*) There he is. (*Beckoning to Sostratus*) Come here.

CNEMON (*scrutinizing him closely, to Gorgias*) He's all sunburned. Is he a farmer?

GORGIAS (*quickly*) Oh, yes! He's no rich playboy who sits around all day doing nothing.

[Five lines are lost at this point. Apparently Cnemon agrees to the match, leaves it to Gorgias to arrange the details, and, supported by his wife and daughter, goes inside to lie down.]

SOSTRATUS My father won't raise any objections.

GORGIAS Then, Sostratus, I hereby bequeath her to you, in front of these witnesses, and make over to you whatever portion of the estate it's fair for you to get as dowry. You entered into this affair with an honest heart and in all sincerity; and you didn't think it beneath you to do whatever you could to marry her. Here you are, a man raised in the lap of luxury, and yet you were willing to handle a mattock and dig away and not spare yourself. This is what shows whether a man understands the meaning of equality—if, even though he's rich, he can take orders from someone who's poor. That kind of man will be able to take the ups and downs of life in stride. You've given me enough proof of your character. I only hope you can stay just as you are.

SOSTRATUS (*swelling under Gorgias' paeans of praise*) I can even do better than that—but, well, this praising oneself isn't exactly the thing to do, you know. (*Turns away in embarrassment and happens to look toward the wings, stage left.*) There's my father! He couldn't have come at a better time.

GORGIAS (*looking, in surprise*) Is Callippides your father?

SOSTRATUS Of course.

GORGIAS Well, by god, he's one rich man who deserves every cent he has. When it comes to running a farm, nobody can beat him.

(*Callippides enters, stage left. He's a portly old fellow, dressed modestly but carefully and in the best of taste. He gives the impression of being affable and good-natured despite the fact that at the moment he's in a foul temper.*)

CALLIPPIDES (*as he comes on stage, to himself*) I've probably missed everything. They must have picked the bones of that sheep clean by now and all gone off into the fields.

GORGIAS (*to Sostratus, sotto voce*) My god! It sounds as if he's starving. Shall we tell him what's happened right now, or wait?

SOSTRATUS (*to Gorgias, sotto voce*) Let him eat first. He'll be easier to handle.

CALLIPPIDES (*seeing Sostratus*) Hey, Sostratus, have you people finished eating?

SOSTRATUS Yes, but there's some left for you. Go on in.

CALLIPPIDES That's just what I'm going to do. (*Hurries into the cave.*)

GORGIAS You go in too if you have anything you want to talk to him about in private.

SOSTRATUS You'll wait for me in your house, right?

GORGIAS I'll stay right there.
SOSTRATUS I'll call you in a little while.

(Sostratus goes into the cave and Gorgias into his house. The stage is now empty, and the chorus comes out and dances an entr'acte.)

ACT V

(Sostratus and Callippides emerge from the cave. Callippides' disposition has benefited enormously from the meal he has just put away, and the tête-à-tête with his son has, to all appearances, left him unperturbed. Not so Sostratus, who is clearly rather upset.)

SOSTRATUS *(unhappily)* Father, you haven't done everything I wanted —or expected of you.
CALLIPPIDES *(surprised)* What's the matter? Didn't I agree with you? I want you to have this girl you're in love with. I say you should marry her.
SOSTRATUS *(moodily)* Well, you don't seem very happy about it.
CALLIPPIDES Ye gods, I know this much: when a young fellow makes up his mind to take the plunge because he's in love, I say that's a marriage that's bound to last.
SOSTRATUS *(blurting out what's been troubling him)* Look here. In my opinion Gorgias is just as good as any of us. Since I'm marrying his sister, how can you refuse now to let him marry my sister in return?
CALLIPPIDES *(refusing to take the matter seriously)* Perish the thought! I don't want to acquire two impoverished in-laws. One in the family's enough.
SOSTRATUS *(refusing to take the matter lightly)* Ah, so it's money you're thinking about. Now *there's* something you just can't count on. If you're sure you can keep it to the end of your days, then go right ahead, don't share it with another soul. But you don't have the final say about it; everything you've got you owe to luck, not to yourself. So don't begrudge it to others, Father. Lady Luck can always take every penny away from you and give it all to someone who doesn't deserve it. That's why I insist, Father, that, so long as you have it in your hands, you be generous with it, help people, make life easier for as many

as you can. Such acts never die. If Fate ever deals you a blow, those you've helped will help you. You know, it's much better to have a friend you can see before your eyes than any treasure you've got buried out of sight.

CALLIPPIDES (*resentfully*)   Sostratus! You know the kind of man I am. I'm not going to take the money I've made to the grave with me. Anyway, how could I? It's all intended for you. (*Sighs good-naturedly.*) You want to win yourself a new friend? Go ahead, put him to the test, and good luck to you. But you don't need to preach sermons to me. Go on, hand the money out, give it away, share it. You've convinced me. Absolutely.

SOSTRATUS (*dubiously*)   You really mean that?

CALLIPPIDES (*heartily*)   Every word of it, believe me. Don't you worry your head about that.

SOSTRATUS (*finally convinced*)   Then I'll call Gorgias.

(*At this moment Gorgias emerges from the door of his house and walks toward them.*)

GORGIAS (*to the two of them, apologetically*)   I was on my way out, and, as I came to the door, I couldn't help overhearing every word you two said. (*To Sostratus*) What can I say? I consider you a true friend and I can't tell you how devoted I am to you. But I don't want a way of life that's beyond me. God knows I couldn't put up with it even if I wanted it!

SOSTRATUS   I don't know what you're talking about.

GORGIAS   I'm giving you my sister to marry. But to marry yours—well, thanks, but . . .

SOSTRATUS   What do you mean, "thanks but"?

GORGIAS (*blurting out something he has obviously been giving serious thought*)   I don't think I'd enjoy living a life of leisure on money that other people have worked for. I have to earn my own way.

SOSTRATUS   Gorgias! Stop talking nonsense! Don't you think you're good enough for her?

GORGIAS   Oh, I think I'm good enough for her, all right. But I feel it's wrong for a man with a modest portion to accept a large one.

CALLIPPIDES (*breaking in on the conversation before it gets too far off the ground*)   God in heaven, this is very noble and all that, but you're being silly.

GORGIAS How so?

CALLIPPIDES You have no money but you want to act like someone who does. (*Smiling*) All right, you've convinced me: I'll give you just a modest portion.

GORGIAS And now you've convinced *me*—doubly. If I don't accept your offer I'll not only be a poor man but a senseless one in the bargain. (*To Sostratus*) Your father has shown me the road to sanity.

SOSTRATUS (*rubbing his hands in delight*) Well, then, the only thing left to do is arrange the details.

CALLIPPIDES (*to Gorgias, solemnly*) My boy, I hereby betroth my daughter to you to be your lawfully wedded wife. And I'm giving you a dowry of ninety thousand dollars.

GORGIAS And I have thirty thousand that goes with my sister.

CALLIPPIDES You do? Now don't you give too much—

GORGIAS (*interrupting stoutly*) I have plenty.

CALLIPPIDES (*putting an arm around him, and smiling*) Keep all that you have, my boy. Now go and bring your mother and sister over here to meet the women in our family.

GORGIAS Yes, we must do that.

SOSTRATUS (*enthusiastically*) Let's all of us spend the night here and have a party. And tomorrow we'll hold a double wedding. Gorgias, bring Cnemon over. He probably stands a better chance of getting the attention he needs with us over here.

GORGIAS (*gloomily*) He won't come, Sostratus.

SOSTRATUS (*as before*) Talk him into it!

GORGIAS If I can. (*Turns and goes into Cnemon's house.*)

SOSTRATUS Father, you know what we ought to do now? Arrange a nice drinking session for us and a get-together for the women.

CALLIPPIDES (*dryly*) It'll be just the other way around, believe me: they'll have the nice drinking session, and we'll have the get-together. Well, I'll go ahead and get things ready for you fellows. (*Enters the cave.*)

SOSTRATUS (*to Callippides as he leaves*) Do that. (*To himself, musingly*) If a man's got sense he'll never give up, no matter how hopeless a situation is. There isn't anything you can't get—if you care enough and work hard enough for it. I'm the living proof. Not a man alive would have thought this marriage was possible—and yet I brought it off. And in just one day!

(The door of Cnemon's house opens and Gorgias comes out followed by his half-sister and his mother.)

GORGIAS *(to his mother and sister)*   Come, let's hurry.

SOSTRATUS *(calling to them)*   Right this way. *(Calling to his mother in the cave)* Mother, would you please make these people welcome? *(The two women enter the cave.)*

GORGIAS   Cnemon's not coming. He even begged me to take the old woman away so he could be completely by himself.

SOSTRATUS   What can you do with a man like that?

GORGIAS   That's the way he is.

SOSTRATUS   I hope he enjoys himself. Let's go in.

GORGIAS *(holding back)*   I'm terribly embarrassed when there are women around.

SOSTRATUS *(taking him by the arm and leading him in)*   Don't talk nonsense! Come on in, will you? You've got to remember that it's all in the family now. *(The two enter the cave.)*

(Cnemon's door opens and Simike comes out. She stops at the threshold to talk to Cnemon inside.)

SIMIKE *(through the doorway)*   All right, all right, I'll go too. Lie there all alone. Dear, dear, you're simply impossible! They were nice enough to invite you to the party, but you had to say no. Something dreadful is going to happen to you yet, I swear, worse than what you're reveling in now.

(Simike closes the door and starts walking toward the cave. At this moment Geta comes out of the cave and stands at the entrance, talking to the people inside.)

GETA *(grumbling at having to leave the party, particularly for such a purpose)*   All right, I'll go and see how he is. *(A mocking trill on the flute is heard from inside.)* Damn you, what are you tootling at me for? I still have things to do. Wait, will you? They're sending me to look in on the patient.

SIMIKE *(overhearing)*   Yes, one of you people should go inside and sit with him. My little girl is leaving me, and I want to go and see her and kiss her goodbye.

GETA *(his whole attitude changing as inspiration seizes him, heartily)*   You're absolutely right. You go ahead. I'll take care of him in the meantime. (*Watches Simike enter the cave. As soon as she disappears inside, to himself gleefully*) I've been just waiting for a chance like this. [Geta has two more lines which have been lost. After delivering them he calls through the mouth of the cave.] Sicon! Come on out here! Hurry! (*Waits impatiently during the few seconds it takes Sicon to appear.*) My god, you're slow!

SICON   Were you calling me?

GETA   I certainly was. Listen, do you want to get even for the insults you had to take a little while ago?

SICON (*in high dudgeon*) Me? Insulted? What the hell do you mean by that nonsense?

GETA (*excitedly*) The old grouch is fast asleep, all alone.

SICON (*forgetting his dudgeon and interested, but hesitant*) How's he doing anyway?

GETA   Not too bad.

SICON (*worriedly*) Do you think he could get up and start coming after us?

GETA   He's not going to do any getting up if you ask me.

SICON (*enthusiastically*) Those words are music to my ears. I'll go in there and ask to borrow things. That'll drive him out of his mind.

GETA   Wait. I've got a better idea. Let's first haul him outside and put him down here. Then let's bang on the door like this (*gesturing*) and ask to borrow things, and watch his temperature rise. Boy, will we have fun!

SICON (*worried again*) I'm scared of Gorgias. If he catches us, he'll tan our hides.

GETA (*gesturing toward the cave*) Listen to the racket in there. They're getting drunk. Nobody'll hear a thing. (*Grimly*) Listen—we've *got* to tame this grouch. Don't you see? We're his in-laws, he's one of the family now—and if he keeps on the way he is, what a cross to bear!

SICON (*nodding assent gloomily*) You're right.

GETA   The one thing to watch out for is that nobody sees you when you bring him out here. All right, you go a little ahead of me.

SICON (*heads toward Cnemon's door and then stops.*) Wait a second. Now don't you run away and leave me inside. (*Geta shakes his head vigorously to reassure him.*) And for god's sake, don't make any noise!

GETA   I'm not making a sound, I swear.

(*The two disappear into the house. A second later they emerge, Geta in the lead and Sicon after him, doubled under the weight of Cnemon, still asleep, slung on his back.*)

GETA (*whispering*)   Over here to the right.

SICON (*staggering over to the spot where Geta is standing, whispering*) Here you are.

GETA (*whispering*)   Put him down here. Now's the time!

(*The two walk stealthily up to the door of Cnemon's house and take their stand there.*)

SICON (*excitedly*)   I'll go first. Ready—you take the beat from me. (*Starts pounding on the door in a regular rhythm and shouting to the imaginary servants inside.*) Boy! Hey, boy! Hey there, boys! Boy! Boys!

CNEMON (*waking with a start and not yet fully aware of what is happening to him, groaning*)   Oh, my god, this is the end of me!

GETA (*joining Sicon in the measured pounding and shouting*)   Hey there, boys! Boy! Hey, boy! Boy! Boys!

CNEMON   My god, it's the end, the end. Who is it anyway? (*Painfully raising himself on his elbow and taking a look, disgustedly*) You're from over there, aren't you? What do you want?

SICON (*to the imaginary servants inside*)   I want to borrow some pots from you people. And a bowl.

CNEMON (*shouting*)   Lift me up, somebody!

SICON (*ignoring him*)   You have some, all right. I know it for sure.

GETA (*imitating Sicon*)   And seven pot stands and twelve tables. (*To imaginary servants outside*) Hey, boys! Tell them inside there what we need. We're in a hurry.

CNEMON (*snarling*)   I don't have a thing.

GETA   You don't, eh?

CNEMON   No, I don't. I told you so a thousand times.

SICON (*taunting him*)   Should I go away then?

CNEMON (*to himself*)   Oh, my god, my god, how did I get out here? Who put me down here? (*To Sicon*) Yes! Get out of here!

SICON   All right, I'll get out. (*Deliberately turns his back on Cnemon, faces the door, and starts the rhythmic pounding all over again*) Boy! Hey, boy! Women! Men! Boy! Answer the door!

CNEMON (*raging*) Are you crazy? You'll break down the door!

SICON (*to the imaginary servants inside*) Bring us nine rugs.

CNEMON Where are they going to get them?

SICON (*as before*) And a tablecloth, a good one, an imported one. And it's got to be a hundred feet long.

CNEMON (*in despair*) Why doesn't someone come out? The old woman—where's the old woman?

SICON I'll try some other house.

CNEMON Go right ahead, both of you. (*Shouting frantically*) Simike! Simike! (*To Sicon, who is still planted at the door*) God damn you to hell, now what do you want?

SICON I want a bowl. A big metal bowl.

CNEMON (*shouting desperately*) Lift me up, somebody!

SICON You've got one, all right. And I know you've got the tablecloth too.

CNEMON There's no boy here and I don't have a bowl. (*Gnashing his teeth*) I'll kill that Simike!

(*Geta, who had been standing by passively the past moment, signals Sicon to keep quiet, steps forward, and stands over the helpless Cnemon.*)

GETA (*disgustedly*) Stop complaining and go back to sleep! (*Speaking slowly and with great emphasis*) You keep away from people. You hate women. You can't bear the idea of going to a friendly party. Well, you're going to put up with every one of these things. There's no one around to help you. Go ahead, start foaming at the mouth.

SICON Now, you're going to hear every single thing . . . [Two and a half lines are lost here in which Sicon launched into a description of what was going on in the cave.] For the first time in their lives your wife and your daughter have had a change in their luck: they've been having a good time. (*Clearing his throat and making other obvious preparations for an extended harangue*) To begin at the beginning, I undertook the arrangements for a party for these gentlemen. (*Indicates by a gesture the people in the cave. Cnemon falls back and closes his eyes wearily.*) You hear me? Wake up!

CNEMON (*muttering ruefully*) I am awake, damn it.

SICON You want to go back in your house, eh? You're going to hear me out first. (*Resuming his narrative manner*) There wasn't any time to waste so I laid out the places and set the tables myself. It was my responsibility and I did it. You hear me? (*Striking his chest*) I'm a chef, that's what I am, and don't you forget it!

GETA   The man's got no guts.

(*A burst of music and song and laughter is heard from the cave. Cnemon raises his head wonderingly and Sicon seizes the chance to rub it in.*)

SICON   By now someone in there has taken a fine old wine, poured it into the punch bowl, mixed it with spring water from the cave, and has been going the rounds inviting the men to have a drink. And someone else has been doing the same for the women. But it's like trying to irrigate a desert! You understand that, don't you? And one of the serving girls who got soused put a veil over her pretty little face, jumped out on the dance floor, and has been singing and swaying to the beat. And another joined hands and has been dancing with her.

CNEMON   God! What an ordeal I have to put up with!

SICON   Get in there and start dancing!

CNEMON   Damn you! What do you want from me, anyway?

SICON   Get in there, you old hick!

CNEMON   God damn it, no!

SICON   Do you want us to carry you in there?

CNEMON   (*in despair, to himself*)   What can I do?

SICON   Dance!

CNEMON   All right, carry me in. I'm probably better off putting up with it, no matter how bad it's going to be.

GETA   Now you're talking sense. (*To Sicon and a slave, one of a group that has clustered in the meantime about the entrance to the cave*) We've won! Donax, and you, Sicon, my fellow victors, pick him up and carry him inside. (*To Cnemon*) And you watch yourself; if we catch you making any trouble again, you're not going to get off so easily, believe me. (*Shouting*) Bring us garlands and a torch, someone!

SICON   (*taking a garland from a slave and handing it to Geta*)   Here, take this one. (*As Geta claps it on Cnemon's head, Sicon comes forward and addresses the audience.*) If you enjoyed the way we won the fight with this old troublemaker, let's have a hearty round of applause from all of you, every boy, youth, and man here!

And may that maid who loves to laugh, the noble goddess of victory, be on our side forever!

The Woman of Samos

/

DRAMATIS PERSONAE

Demeas, a well-to-do, elderly citizen of Athens

Chrysis, the woman of Samos; a youngish, good-looking woman whom
Demeas had taken in and made his common-law wife

Moschion, a young man about town, adopted son of Demeas

Niceratus, Demeas' neighbor, a poor, elderly citizen of Athens

Parmeno, Demeas' valet (slave)

A cook

[*Plangon,* daughter of Niceratus]

SCENE A street in Athens. Two houses, Demeas' and Niceratus',
front on it.

[All that is preserved are two long segments from the last half, less
than a third of the original play. The opening lines plunge us right into
a rapid-fire series of misunderstandings. The problem is to reconstruct
the events that had led up to these.

The central figure is Demeas, an elderly, well-to-do Athenian. Demeas
is the kindly and genial type; the members of his household owe their
very presence there not to any ties of blood or law but to his benevolence.
His grown son, Moschion, was a foundling whom he had taken in as
a baby and raised as his own, and the lady of his house, the youngish,
handsome Chrysis, was a woman from the island of Samos whom he

had come upon alone and penniless and had sheltered and made his common-law wife. Under normal circumstances Demeas was affable and expansive, given to indulging a pixieish sense of humor; on the day this play portrays, however, circumstances were far from normal.

The house next door belongs to his good friend Niceratus. Demeas was rich, lived comfortably, and was by nature easygoing; Niceratus was poor, worked long and hard, made every penny count, and had a prickly sensitiveness. His family consisted of his wife and grown daughter, Plangon.

The two friends, as it happened, left Athens for an extended trip. Just before they went off, Chrysis confided to Demeas the news that she was in an interesting condition. It didn't interest Demeas: he left her with explicit orders to expose the infant. It wasn't that he suspected cuckoldry—his relation with Chrysis was one of real love that was amply reciprocated—but rather that, under the law, the issue of a union such as theirs would be illegitimate. She dutifully obeyed. But at the very same time another complication involving an unwanted infant was in the making: the adult children of the two households, Moschion and Plangon, had been having an affair and, as always happens under such circumstances in Greek New Comedy, Plangon became pregnant.

Like Chrysis, she had her baby shortly before its grandfathers were scheduled to return home. Something had to be done, and quickly. Moschion very likely could have trusted in his father's good nature, made a clean breast of everything to him, and offered to marry the girl—he genuinely loved her—, but he was afraid that Demeas, for all his easygoing ways and cordial relations with Niceratus, would take a dim view of an alliance with a girl who had no dowry. Moreover, resolution and courage were not exactly the boy's strong points. He took his problem to the women of the two households, Chrysis and Plangon's mother, and the consensus was a bold and brilliant scheme: to pass the baby off as the one Chrysis had just disposed of. Accordingly, it was smuggled into Demeas' house and Chrysis took it over. A situation of this sort could hardly be kept secret from the servants, particularly from Parmeno, Demeas' valet, so they were let in on it and sworn to silence.

The scheme worked, although not without complications. Demeas wasn't exactly overjoyed on his return to find Chrysis fondling an infant contrary to his orders; he grumbled about it, but she eventually managed to talk him into letting her keep the child. What he did next raised the hopes of all concerned for a much happier solution of the problem: he called in Moschion and announced that arrangements were about to be made for him to marry Plangon at once; perhaps Niceratus had done Demeas some great favor during their trip together or perhaps Demeas, having heard vague rumors that his son was playing around, was employing the parental therapy standard in Greek New Comedy of marrying him off as quickly as possible to a respectable bride, and Plangon filled the bill even though she was penniless. Moschion, of course, agreed with alacrity.

So Demeas went inside his house and broke the unexpected news to the staff that there was going to be a wedding that very day. With so much to be done on so short notice there was, naturally, a good deal of confusion, and he stayed around to make sure that things were progressing properly. And so it happened that he stumbled upon what looked like incontrovertible evidence that something was rotten in the state of his household. He came out to reveal it to the audience, and the preserved part of the manuscript—probably the beginning of Act III—opens with his speech.]

ACT III

(Demeas comes out of his house, extremely upset. He walks forward and faces the audience.)

DEMEAS *(to the audience)* As soon as I went inside, since I was very anxious to get started on the wedding, I simply announced to the servants what was going to happen and ordered them to make all the necessary preparations—clean up, do the baking, get everything set for the ceremony. Things were getting done, all right, but, as you'd expect, there was some confusion because of the rush. The baby had been sort of left on a couch out of the way and was screaming its head off. And everybody was hollering at the same time: *(imitating the voices)* "Bring some flour. Bring some water. Bring some oil. Bring some charcoal." I pitched in myself, and helped hand out things. That's how I happened to go into the pantry and, since I was busy there picking out extra supplies and looking things over, I didn't come right out. Well, while I was in there, one of the women came down from the second floor into the room in front of the pantry.

We do our weaving there, and you have to go through it either
to get to the staircase or the pantry. It was Moschion's old nurse;
she used to be one of my slaves until I freed her. She saw the
baby screaming there with nobody near it and, having no idea
that I was inside and that she ought to watch what she was saying, she went up to it and started to talk to it the way they do
(*imitating her*): "Sweet little baby," and "My precious, where's
your mommy?" And she kissed it and rocked it, and, when it
stopped crying, she says to herself, "Dear me! It seems just yesterday that I was taking care of Moschion when he was no
bigger than this and now he's got a baby of his own." [Two or
three lines are lost here.]

While she was prattling on, one of the serving girls came
running in, and the old one shouts at her: "Here you! Take
care of this baby! What is this? His own father's getting married
and you're not giving his little one the least bit of attention!"
Right away the other one whispers to her (*dropping his voice
and imitating her*), "What are you talking so loud for, you fool?
He's in there." "No! Where?" "In the pantry!" And then, speaking in her natural voice, she says (*raising his voice*), "Nurse,
Chrysis is calling for you," and then (*lowering it again*), "Hurry!
We're lucky, he hasn't heard anything." So the old one went off
somewhere mumbling to herself (*mimicking her*), "Dear me,
this big mouth of mine!"

Then I came out, very calmly, just as you saw me come out a
little while ago, acting as if I hadn't heard or didn't know a
thing. But when I was walking out, I noticed that Chrysis had
the baby and was nursing it herself. So one thing we know for
certain: it's her baby. But who the father is, I or—no, gentlemen,
I'm not going to say it to you, I'm not even going to suspect it.
I'm reporting the facts, what I heard with my own ears. I'm not
angry with anybody—not yet. (*As the calm he has been struggling to maintain starts to desert him, emphatically*) Good god,
I know that boy of mine; he's always been thoroughly decent,
always been as considerate toward me as a son should. (*Shakes
his head worriedly.*) Yet, when I consider that it was his own
nurse who said it and that it was something I wasn't supposed to
hear, and when I look back at the way that woman of mine
fondled the child and forced me to let her keep it against my

will—I can go out of my mind! (*Looks toward the wings, stage left, and sees someone approaching.*) Good—here comes Parmeno back from downtown just in time. But first I've got to let him take the help he's hired into the house.

(*Demeas steps back to let Parmeno, who is carrying a shopping bag and is followed by a cook and some other servants he has hired in town for the wedding party, pass into the house. They come on stage without noticing Demeas. The cook—whose job included butchering the animals as well as cooking them—is, as always in Greek New Comedy, long-winded and self-important. He has clearly been wagging his jaw all during the walk from downtown.*)

PARMENO (*maliciously*) For god's sake, cook, I don't know why you bother carrying a knife around. You can kill anything you want with that tongue of yours.

COOK (*suspiciously*) Are you trying to make fun of me, you moron?

PARMENO (*with practiced innocence*) Who, me?

COOK (*grumbling*) Well, god knows it looks that way to me. If I ask a simple question like how many tables you plan to set, how many ladies there'll be, when you want to serve, whether we need a caterer, whether you have enough dishes, whether the kitchen is out-of-doors, whether everything else—

PARMENO There you are, my friend. See? You're killing me. One stroke. Real professional job.

COOK Go to the devil!

PARMENO (*with elaborate politeness*) You first, by all means. (*To the whole group at his heels*) Inside everybody!

DEMEAS (*to Parmeno just as he is on the point of following his task force indoors*) Parmeno!

PARMENO (*knowing very well it's Demeas calling but anxious to delay the inevitable moment when he would be quizzed on what was going on, without turning around*) Somebody calling me?

DEMEAS Yes, you.

PARMENO (*turning around reluctantly*) Oh, hello.

DEMEAS Take that bag inside and come right back here.

PARMENO Right. (*Goes into the house.*)

DEMEAS (*gesturing toward the departing figure of Parmeno, to the audience*) If you ask me, nothing gets by that fellow. He knows

everything that's going on around here. Knows everybody else's
business, if anyone does. He's coming out now.

PARMENO (*turning at the door to talk to Chrysis inside*)   Chrysis, give
the cook whatever he asks for. And, for god's sake, keep that
old hag of a nurse away from the wine. (*To Demeas, but still
standing a safe distance away near the door; with affected cheeri-
ness*) Now, what would you like?

DEMEAS   What would I like? For you to get away from that door!
(*Parmeno takes a minuscule step nearer.*) Further!

PARMENO (*finally giving up and coming near him*)   Here I am.

DEMEAS (*sternly*)   Now listen, Parmeno. So help me, there are lots
of reasons why I don't want to give you a beating—

PARMENO (*with his practiced air of innocence*)   Me? What'd I do?

DEMEAS (*emphatically*)   You're hiding something from me. (*As
Parmeno opens his mouth to protest*) I've noticed it, all right.

PARMENO (*excitedly*)   I swear to god! I swear by all that's holy! I swear
on a stack—

DEMEAS (*interrupting, curtly*)   Cut it out. Don't do any swearing.

PARMENO (*aggrieved*)   But, see here, you've got the wrong idea. I
never—

DEMEAS (*interrupting*)   Look at me!

PARMENO (*deflated, knowing the jig is up*)   I am.

DEMEAS (*grimly*)   Out with it: Whose baby is that?

PARMENO (*in a desperate attempt to switch the conversation*)   Hey,
look!

DEMEAS (*not falling into the trap*)   I'm asking you: Whose baby
is that?

PARMENO   Chrysis'.

DEMEAS (*intently*)   And the father?

PARMENO   You.

DEMEAS (*exploding*)   Parmeno, that's the end of you—you're lying
to me!

PARMENO   Who, me?

DEMEAS (*with ominous calm*)   You see, Parmeno, I know the whole
story. I know it's Moschion's; I know that you know it too; and
I know that he's the reason she's taking care of it now.

PARMENO (*blustering*)   Who says so?

DEMEAS   Don't worry, I know it. Just tell me this—I'm right, yes?
(*Steps toward him menacingly.*)

PARMENO (*cringing*) Yes—but we kept it secret—

DEMEAS (*roaring*) Secret! (*Shouting to the servants in the house*) Inside there! Someone bring me a whip for this godforsaken slave of mine.

PARMENO Oh, no! Oh, god, no!

DEMEAS (*between his teeth*) So help me, I'm going to skin you alive.

PARMENO Skin me alive?

DEMEAS (*as a slave comes out and hands him a whip*) Right now.

PARMENO (*to himself, agonized*) I'm a goner! (*Whirls around and takes off, stage left.*)

DEMEAS (*shouting after him*) Hey, you! Where are you going, you good-for-nothing! (*To the slave*) Go get him! (*Losing all control, starts wildly quoting phrases from Euripides*) Oh, how sharper than a serpent's tooth, oh, that this too too solid flesh would thaw, oh— (*suddenly getting hold of himself*) Hey, Demeas, what are you raving for? Gone mad? What are you raving for, anyway? Get hold of yourself. Buck up. Moschion hasn't done anything wrong to you. (*To the audience*) Gentlemen, this may sound like a risky thing to say, but it's the truth. Let's suppose Moschion did what he did with malice aforethought, either because he hated me or because he was so much in love with her. He'd feel the same way now as he did then; it would be war between us for the woman. But he's cleared himself of all guilt on that count: when I told him about the marriage he was honestly glad to hear about it. I thought he was so eager because he was in love with the girl—but he was just anxious to escape from the clutches of that Helen of mine in there (*gesturing toward the house*). She's to blame for what happened. She must have gotten her hands on him sometime when he was drunk and not in his right mind. Mix youth with wine and that's the sort of thing that happens—even in the case of a youngster who never wished the slightest harm to those near and dear to him. I simply cannot bring myself to believe that a boy who's so decent and well behaved toward everyone else would have deliberately acted this way toward me. And the fact that he's an adopted child doesn't make a particle of difference; what I look at is not his birth but his character. (*His thoughts shift from Moschion to Chrysis and his self-control begins to disintegrate.*) Oh, but that whore, that ruination— (*recovering again*) What's this

for, Demeas? It's not going to get you anywhere. You've got to
be a man now. Forget about your love for her and, for your son's
sake, just do all you can to hush up this awful thing that's
happened. She's a bad woman; throw her out on her ear and
let her go to the devil. You've got a good excuse—because she
insisted on keeping the infant. Don't mention a single thing
else. Stiff upper lip and don't weaken. Show what you're made
of.

*(As Demeas stands there absorbed in thought, the cook comes out of
the door. He's looking for Parmeno.)*

COOK *(to himself)*   Maybe he's out here in front of the house. Hey!
   Parmeno! *(Aggrieved)* He's run out on me. And he didn't even
   lend me a hand for a minute.
DEMEAS *(suddenly makes up his mind, wheels around, charges toward
   the door and, en route, roars at the cook)*   Out of my way!
COOK *(as he's jostled aside)*   Hey! What's the matter with you? *(Turns
   back to the street)* Parmeno! *(What had happened a second
   earlier suddenly sinks in.)* Some old man just ran in like a
   lunatic; wonder what the trouble is? *(Shrugging his shoulders)*
   What's it to me? *(Turning back to the street)* Parmeno!
   (Stopping again to think over what had just happened) God
   almighty, you ask me, it was a lunatic, all right. Sure howled like
   one. Now, won't it be just fine if he gets into the dishes I've
   laid out and smashes them all to pieces. *(Demeas' door starts to
   open)* Someone's coming out. Parmeno, I'd like to wring your
   neck for bringing me here! I'll get out of the way over here.
   (Moves off to the side where he can stay unobserved.)

*(The door opens and Demeas, Chrysis, and the nurse holding the
baby come out.)*

DEMEAS *(angrily)*   You heard me. Get out of here!
CHRYSIS *(in tears)*   Where in the world can I go?
DEMEAS   Go to the devil!
CHRYSIS *(sobbing)*   Oh, my god, my god!
DEMEAS *(mimicking her)*   "Oh, my god, my god." *(Sarcastically)* By
   all means, let's have tears; always good for some sympathy.
   (Mumbling to himself) I've got an idea I'll keep you from—
CHRYSIS *(looking up at this first hint of what is causing her banishment)*
   Doing what?

DEMEAS (*remembering, just in time, his decision to stick strictly to the keeping of the infant*) Nothing. (*Brutally*) You've got the baby; you've got the nurse. Now beat it!

CHRYSIS Just because I wanted to keep the child, for that reason and—

DEMEAS What do you mean "and"? For that reason, period. That's about the size of it.

CHRYSIS (*pathetically*) I don't understand!

DEMEAS (*abandoning his resolution and casting about, guiltily, for some stronger justification*) Well, you didn't know how to fit in with people of my class.

CHRYSIS (*startled*) I didn't know what? What's that you say?

DEMEAS Look here, Chrysis, you haven't forgotten that when you came here you had only the clothes on your back.

CHRYSIS What about it?

DEMEAS Back in those days, when you were down on your luck, I was everything to you.

CHRYSIS (*humbly*) Have I changed?

DEMEAS (*aware that he is getting into just what he wanted to avoid, and shamed by her attitude*) Enough of this talk. You've got everything that's yours. Look, I've even given you a servant. Now leave the house.

COOK (*nodding sagely, to himself*) One of these cases of a man losing his temper. (*Self-importantly*) I'd better go up to him. (*Coming forward and addressing Demeas*) I beg your pardon, but you ought to watch out that—

DEMEAS (*turning on him with a snarl*) What are you butting in for?

COOK (*taken aback*) You don't have to bite my head off!

DEMEAS (*disregarding him and turning back to Chrysis*) Some other girl will be very glad to take your place, Chrysis, and thank her lucky stars too.

COOK (*to himself*) What's it all about?

DEMEAS But you've got yourself a son. Now you've got everything.

COOK (*to himself*) Hasn't bitten me yet. (*Going up to Demeas again*) I beg your—

DEMEAS (*roaring*) If you butt in again, I'll break your skull!

COOK (*muttering*) If I butt in again, I deserve it. See? I'm going right inside. (*Scuttles through the door of Demeas' house.*)

DEMEAS (*watching the cook go off, scornfully*) Big shot. (*Turning back to Chrysis*) Wait until you start living on the town—you'll see yourself as you really are. Girls in your situation, Chrysis, to make a few dollars to keep alive, become call girls and drink themselves to death. If they prefer not to kill themselves off quickly that way, the alternative is slow starvation. Nobody will learn this lesson better than you, I know it. And you'll learn what kind of woman you are and what a mistake you made. (*As she goes near him to plead*) Stay where you are! (*He stalks into the house and slams the door.*)

CHRYSIS (*sobbing, to herself*)   Oh, my god, what's happening to me!

(*Niceratus enters, stage right. The day was one of those rare occasions when this sour skinflint was genuinely happy: his penniless daughter was in a few hours to be married off to one of the better catches in Athens. And Demeas was footing the bill for the wedding. The least Niceratus could do was to take care of the formal sacrifice, so, accompanying him on stage, is a marvelously scrawny and decrepit sheep, one that, as his own description reveals, has everything except flesh.*)

NICERATUS (*to himself, not noticing at first the forlorn figures of Chrysis and the nurse*)   This sheep will take care very nicely of all that's required for the gods. The goddesses, too. It's got blood, plenty of bile, good bones, big spleen—it'll satisfy the celestial requirements. I'll make hash out of the skin to send as a present to my friends; (*dolefully*) that's all there'll be left of it for me. (*Catching sight of Chrysis*) My god, what's this? That can't be Chrysis crying there in front of the door. It is, at that. (*Going up to her*) What's the matter?

CHRYSIS (*bitterly*)   What do you think? That fine friend of yours has thrown me out.

NICERATUS   My god! Who? Demeas?

CHRYSIS   Yes.

NICERATUS   What for?

CHRYSIS   For keeping the child.

NICERATUS (*unsympathetically*)   Yes, I heard from my womenfolk that you had found a baby and were raising it. Crazy idea! He's a push-over, that man.

CHRYSIS   He didn't get angry at first. It was only after a while, just now. First he tells me to get things ready inside for the wedding and then, right in the middle of everything, he rushes in at me like a lunatic and throws me out!

NICERATUS   Demeas must have gone mad—

[There is a gap of about 140 lines at this point, but it isn't too difficult to reconstruct what happened. Niceratus took Chrysis and the nurse and baby into his house. This gave Chrysis an opportunity to review strategy with her accomplices, Niceratus' wife and daughter. Everything hinged on the wedding: it had to go on at all costs since it provided the only possible way out of the whole mess. And, at all costs, neither of the old men was to learn that Plangon was an unmarried mother—Demeas because he might use the information to call everything off, and Niceratus because he'd fly into a rage if he heard of anything that might jeopardize the marriage. And so the women renewed their determination to stick to the original strategy. Act III very likely ended at this point.

Act IV probably opened with Moschion on stage. When Demeas had first announced to him the plans for marrying him to Plangon, he had gone off to celebrate what looked like the end of all his troubles. He came back to find that the scheme had backfired so badly that the trouble he was now in was far worse than what he had originally tried to get out of. Without wasting any time he got hold of Demeas and made a clean breast of the whole matter. The old man, euphoric at the news, immediately became his old self. He couldn't wait to reinstate Chrysis and get going on the wedding once again. He rushed out to share the news with Niceratus and got as far as telling him that the baby in his house wasn't Chrysis' at all, but Plangon's. The result was exactly what the women were afraid would happen: Niceratus, jumping to the conclusion that Demeas was telling him this by way of leading up to an announcement that the wedding was off, flew into a rage. When the text picks up again, the misunderstandings on both sides are flourishing: Demeas—discreetly omitting any mention of Moschion's part in the proceedings—is trying to convince his neighbor that his daughter's misstep is really nothing to take seriously. Under the circumstances these are his genuine sentiments, but Niceratus, naturally misinterpreting them, is about to stalk off in bitter disappointment.]

ACT IV

(Niceratus and Demeas are on stage and Demeas has just finished his defense of Plangon, explaining that what she had done was really "nothing at all.")

DEMEAS (*as Niceratus starts to stalk off*)   Hey! Come back!

NICERATUS (*misunderstanding Demeas' readiness to excuse Plangon*)
"Nothing at all" eh? Goodbye! (*To himself as he rushes into his house*) That upsets everything. It's all over now.

DEMEAS (*to himself*)   My god, will he be mad when he hears what really happened! He'll howl! He's tough and he's rough, the kind that wants everything his own way. (*Shaking his head in remorse*) How could I ever have sunk so low as to suspect what I did! God, I deserve to be killed. (*There's a roar from inside Niceratus' house*) God almighty, listen to him howl! (*Goes to the door and puts his ear to it. Listens, then incredulously*) That's what he's saying—he's yelling for fire. (*Listening again*) He says he's going to roast the baby. What am I going to have to do? Stand looking at my grandson cooking? There's the door again. (*Scuttles away as the door is flung open.*) It's no man coming through, it's a hurricane!

(*Niceratus rushes out breathing fire; obviously the women have stuck to their original story that the baby is Chrysis'.*)

NICERATUS (*excitedly*)   Demeas! Chrysis is starting a revolution against me. She's making terrible trouble.

DEMEAS   What's that you say?

NICERATUS   She's talked my wife into denying everything. My daughter too. She's keeping the baby from me; says she won't give it up. (*Between his teeth*) So don't be surprised if I murder her with my own hands.

DEMEAS (*genuinely alarmed*)   Murder her?

NICERATUS   Sure. She knows the whole story.

DEMEAS   Niceratus! Don't do it!

NICERATUS (*over his shoulder as he rushes back into the house*)   I just wanted to warn you.

DEMEAS (*to himself*)   He's out of his mind—there he goes galloping off again. (*Worriedly*) What do you do in a case like this? So help me, I know I've never gotten into a mess like this before. (*Shaking his head ruefully*) When you come right down to it, it's best to stick to the facts, no question about it. My god, there goes the door again!

(*Niceratus' door flies open, and Chrysis bursts out. In her rush she doesn't notice Demeas.*)

CHRYSIS (*screaming*)   In the name of heaven, what am I to do! Where
    can I run? He'll take the child from me!

DEMEAS (*shouting at her*)   Chrysis! This way!

CHRYSIS   Who's there?

DEMEAS   Inside with you!

(*She ducks behind him, and Demeas plants himself in front of her.
A second later Niceratus comes running out of his house.*)

NICERATUS (*shouting, to Chrysis*)   Hey you! Where are you running
    to?

DEMEAS (*aside*)   So help me, it looks as if I'm going to be a sparring
    partner today. (*To Niceratus*) What's the hurry? Who are you
    after?

NICERATUS (*between his teeth*)   Demeas, out of my way. I'm going to
    get that baby and get the story out of those women, and don't
    try to stop me.

DEMEAS (*aside*)   Mad! (*As Niceratus squares off*) You want to fight,
    eh?

NICERATUS (*as before*)   I sure do.

DEMEAS (*to Chrysis*)   Damn it, inside quick! (*To Niceratus, trucu-
    lently*) That's just what I want too. (*As the two start flailing
    away*) Chrysis! Hurry! He's stronger than I am!

(*Chrysis scoots into the house and, a second later, the two oldsters,
out of breath, stand apart glaring at each other. Demeas has succeeded
in keeping his back to his door.*)

NICERATUS (*accusingly*)   You hit me first. I'm a witness.

DEMEAS   And you were chasing after a respectable woman and were
    going to take a stick to her.

NICERATUS   Dirty swindler!

DEMEAS   Dirty swindler yourself!

(*Another moment of silence as they puff and glare.*)

NICERATUS   She wouldn't give me the baby.

DEMEAS (*exploding*)   This is ridiculous! It's mine!

NICERATUS   It is not! (*Starts pushing Demeas from his door.*)

DEMEAS (*roaring*)   This is an outrage! Help!

NICERATUS   Holler your head off. I'm going inside and kill that woman.
    There's no other way.

DEMEAS (*aside, resignedly*) Here we go again. (*To Niceratus*) I'm not going to put up with this. (*As Niceratus again tries to shove his way to the door*) Where do you think you're going? Stand back!

NICERATUS Don't you dare raise your hand to me!

DEMEAS Then get hold of yourself.

NICERATUS Demeas, you're out to do me wrong, I can see it. What's more, you know the whole story.

DEMEAS (*testily*) Then ask me about it and stop being a nuisance to that woman.

NICERATUS (*giving voice to a suspicion that has gradually been growing in his mind, that Moschion is going to use the baby as an excuse to back out of the marriage*) Has that son of yours pulled a fast one on me?

DEMEAS Stop talking nonsense. He's going to marry the girl. That's not what's the matter. (*Soothingly*) Let's you and I take a little walk over here.

NICERATUS (*taken aback*) Take a walk?

DEMEAS And you can pull yourself together.

(*Demeas takes the bemused Niceratus by the arm and starts walking him up and down the stage. Demeas, completely his old self, has a mischievous glint in his eye as he chats with his slower-witted neighbor.*)

DEMEAS Tell me, Niceratus, you've seen that play, haven't you, the one that tells how Zeus once turned himself into a golden shower, trickled down through the roof of a house, and seduced a girl shut up inside?[1]

NICERATUS (*puzzled*) What about it?

DEMEAS Maybe we have to be ready to expect anything. Think now: Do you have any leaks in your roof?

NICERATUS Lots. But what's that got to do with it?

DEMEAS Once Zeus turned himself into gold. Another time into water. See? He's responsible for what happened. Lucky thing we discovered it so quickly.

NICERATUS (*still puzzled by Demeas' straight face, but growing suspicious*) Lucky thing I've discovered you're kidding me.

DEMEAS (*pretending to be in dead earnest*) So help me, I'm not. You're in exactly the same situation Acrisius was. If his daughter had the honor of a visit from Zeus, your daughter—

[1] He is referring to the mythological story of Danae, the daughter of Acrisius.

NICERATUS (*convinced that all this double talk is just Demeas' way of gently breaking the news that Moschion won't go through with the marriage after all*) God almighty! Moschion's pulled a fast one on me!

DEMEAS (*quickly*) He'll marry her! Stop worrying! (*Resuming his former soothing tone*) I'm absolutely convinced this was a celestial visitation. You think it's something amazing, but I can name thousands of these celestially sired children. You see them on the street all the time. First of all, take Chaerophon. He scrounges a life of luxury without paying a cent. You have to have divine blood in you to do that, right?

NICERATUS (*resignedly*) Right. (*Shrugging*) Why should I bother? I'm not going to argue with you over nothing at all.

DEMEAS (*nodding approvingly*) Very sensible remark, Niceratus. Take Androcles. Look how old he is. Yet he still goes out on the town, runs around, does plenty of scrounging, and keeps his white hair nice and black. You couldn't kill him off even if you slit his throat. Another case of divine blood, right? (*Guiding him toward his door*) Now, run along and pray that everything will be all right. Start the ceremony. My son's coming to get your girl right away. It's all Fate's doing.

NICERATUS So many things are.

DEMEAS Very sensible remark. Just because my boy lost his head then, don't you go and lose yours now. Go inside and make sure everything is all set.

NICERATUS I will.

DEMEAS Everything's ready at my end.

NICERATUS (*shaking his head admiringly*) You're a pretty smart fellow, Demeas. (*Enters his house.*)

DEMEAS (*to himself*) Thank the good lord none of my suspicions turned out to be true!

(*Demeas enters his house. The stage is now clear, and a chorus enters and dances an entr'acte.*)

ACT V

(*The door of Demeas' house opens and Moschion comes out. He has something on his mind—and makes his way downstage to unburden himself to the audience.*)

MOSCHION   I had a hard time clearing myself a little while ago, and
when I did I felt pretty good about it. I figured I got a lucky
break and I was satisfied with it. But now that I've had time
to collect my wits and know what the score is, I'm really burned
up. It drives me crazy—my father was willing to believe I could
stoop so low! I don't want to change anything now that involves
the girl, and there are a lot of other things that keep me tied
down—I gave her my word, we've known each other so long
and so intimately, and I love her—but if it weren't for all this,
I wouldn't give him a second chance to make such accusations.
I'd clear out of Athens; I'd be off to Asia and join the foreign
legion there. That's what a real man would do, but I'm not
going to do it, and all for your sake, Plangon, my sweetheart.
I can't—because I can't tear myself away; all I can think about
is how much I love you. (*Falls silent for a moment, building
up again his righteous indignation.*) But I can't sit back like
some spineless clod and just let this pass by. (*Brightening as he
gets an idea*) I'm going to tell my father that I'm clearing out.
I want to give him a scare by bluffing, if nothing else. When he
sees I'm dead serious about what he did this time, he'll think
twice before he's unfair with me hereafter. (*Notices Parmeno
entering, stage left*) Well, look who's here, just in time. Just
the man I want.

PARMENO   (*not noticing Moschion, to himself*)   God almighty, that
was a miserably stupid stunt I pulled. Absolutely innocent, and
yet I got scared and ran away from Demeas. And what'd I do
to be scared about? Let's examine the record, item by item.
Moschion seduces a respectable girl—nothing you can charge
Parmeno with there. She gets pregnant—Parmeno not guilty.
The baby goes into our house—*he* brought it in, not I, and someone else in the household blabbed about it. What's Parmeno
done wrong in all this? Nothing. So why did you get so panicky
and run away like that, stupid? Don't be ridiculous! He said
he'd skin you alive to make you talk! Doesn't make a particle of
difference whether you deserve it or not, skinning's no fun, no
fun at all.

MOSCHION   Hey!

PARMENO   (*turning*)   Oh, hello.

MOSCHION   Cut out the jabbering and go inside. Quick!

PARMENO To do what?

MOSCHION Bring me my overcoat and a sword.

PARMENO A sword? For you?

MOSCHION And make it snappy.

PARMENO What for?

MOSCHION Shut up. Go and do as you're told.

PARMENO What's up?

MOSCHION (*taking a threatening step toward him*) Do you want a beating?

PARMENO (*with alacrity*) No, sir! I'm going! (*Doesn't move.*)

MOSCHION (*angrily*) What are you waiting for? (*Parmeno hustles into the house. Moschion continues, to himself.*) My father's sure to come out now and plead with me to stay. I'll let him plead away for a while; that much I've got to do. Then, when it looks like the right moment, I'll give in. The important thing is to sound as if I meant it. (*His courage ebbing*) Oh, my god, that's the one thing I can't do! (*Listening at the door*) I thought so—he's coming out now.

(*The door opens but it is Parmeno, not Demeas, who comes out, and he is empty-handed.*)

PARMENO (*earnestly*) I think you're way behind the times; you don't know what's going on inside. You haven't heard the right story and you're getting all upset for no good reason. Forget these ideas of yours and go on inside.

MOSCHION (*grimly*) Where are my things?

PARMENO (*disregarding the question and continuing as before*) Your wedding's going on. (*Carried away by the spirit of the occasion*) They're killing the fatted calf—

MOSCHION (*ominously*) Listen, you—where are my things?

PARMENO (*again disregarding the question*) They're waiting for you. Been waiting a long time. Aren't you going to go in and join your bride? You're a lucky fellow! Everything's going fine. Buck up! What more do you want?

MOSCHION (*advancing on him*) Are you telling me what to do, you little stinker?

PARMENO (*the high spirits suddenly drained out of him*) Moschion! What are you doing!

MOSCHION (*slapping him hard*) Now are you going to hurry in there
and bring me the things I told you to?

PARMENO You cut my lip!

MOSCHION Are you still blabbering?

PARMENO (*quickly*) I'm going. (*Reproachfully*) God almighty, the
trouble I run into!

MOSCHION (*menacingly*) Still hanging around?

PARMENO (*making a last, desperate attempt*) I tell you, they're really
holding the wedding.

MOSCHION (*chasing him inside*) Inside, and hurry! And report back
to me. (*To the audience*) My father'll come out now. (*Struck
by a new thought*) But, gentlemen, what if he doesn't plead
with me to stay? What if he gets angry and lets me go? I didn't
think of that before. What am I going to do? (*Reassuring himself*) He wouldn't do a thing like that. But supposing he does?
After all, anything can happen. God almighty, if I do an about-
face now, I'll look like a fool!

[The text breaks off at this point, but we must be fairly near the end
of the play. Almost certainly Demeas came out, rescued his unheroic
son from his heroics, and then, finally, went ahead with the wedding.]

The Arbitration

1

DRAMATIS PERSONAE

Smicrines, an elderly, well-to-do Athenian, father of Pamphila and
father-in-law of Charisius

Chaerestratus, a friend and neighbor of Charisius

Syriscus, a charcoal burner, slave of Chaerestratus

Davus, a goatherd (slave)

Onesimus, Charisius' valet (slave)

Habrotonon, a young professional entertainer (slave), hired by
Charisius

Pamphila, daughter of Smicrines and wife of Charisius

Charisius, a young, well-to-do Athenian, recently married to Pamphila

Sophrona, Pamphila's old nurse

SCENE A street on the outskirts of Athens. Two houses front on it,
Chaerestratus' and Charisius'. The exit on stage left leads downtown,
that on stage right to the open country.

ACT I

[Less than a quarter of this act is preserved. The loss is not so serious
as it might appear since a large part of the act was given over to introducing the characters and conveying to the audience the information

it had to have in order to follow the action, and most of this can be deduced from the surviving portions. Probably the exposition was made through an initial scene in dialogue between several of the minor characters, followed by a formal statement by an actor playing the role of Prologue.

What the audience learned was this: Charisius had married Pamphila five months ago. Four months before the wedding, at the Tauropolia, an all-woman festival that was held at night, a drunken youth had crashed the affair and attacked her; in the struggle she had somehow managed to grab his ring but, in the darkness, had had no chance to see his face. As will happen in the world of the theater, whether that of the Greek comic stage or of Hollywood, she became pregnant. Luckily, soon after the wedding, her husband left on an extended trip and she was able to keep her condition a secret; and he was still away when her baby was born. Since she loved Charisius deeply and didn't want to run any risk of spoiling her newly launched marriage, she took advantage of his absence to get rid of the child. She swaddled him up, tied to him a packet containing the ring and a few other distinctive bits of jewelry—"birth tokens" as the Greeks called them—and, helped by her old nurse, smuggled the pathetic bundle out of the house and left it in some brush on a nearby hillside. It was her misfortune, however, that in some way Charisius' valet, Onesimus, got wind of what was going on and, when Charisius returned, informed him that the wife he was convinced was so innocent and chaste had just gotten rid of an illegitimate child. Charisius, who was a thoroughgoing prig, a holier-than-thou sort, decided then and there to end the marriage. But he was unwilling to initiate proceedings and submit her to public scandal and himself to public ridicule; instead he did what is done so often today: he set about giving her open-and-shut grounds for divorcing him. He moved into his friend Chaerestratus' house next door. He began to throw money around right and left on a series of around-the-clock wild parties. He even hired a professional entertainer, Habrotonon, as his mistress. The pose, of course, was not easy for him to maintain since conduct of this kind was uncharacteristic.

Pamphila, though alone in Charisius' house and utterly miserable, was determined to stick it out in the vague hope that all would somehow work out. But not her father, Smicrines. This crusty old businessman, the kind who goes through life getting full value for every cent spent, was horrified by the stories he was hearing of his new son-in-

law's extravagance. Concerned about the dowry he had provided, as
well as about his daughter (he, of course, knew nothing about her
child), he came to visit her. The first scene we have preserved starts
at this point.]

(*Chaerestratus, Charisius' friend and neighbor, comes on stage from
his house. As he does, Smicrines enters, stage left, grumbling to himself.*)

SMICRINES That man and his drinking! I'm downright shocked. I
don't mean about his getting drunk. No, what's inconceivable
to me is that anyone would drive himself to drink when it costs
a dollar a glass!

CHAERESTRATUS (*aside*) I was expecting this. Once he breaks in on
us, that's the end of our fun with the girls.

SMICRINES (*to himself*) Why should I care? He's the one who'll be
sorry. But there's the dowry—he takes a hundred and twenty
thousand dollars from me, and then doesn't even consider himself a part of his wife's household! Sleeps away from home.
Even hires a mistress from a pimp. (*Throwing up his hands,
horrified*) At sixty dollars a day!

CHAERESTRATUS (*aside*) Sixty dollars? He knows everything, down to
the details.

SMICRINES (*to himself*) Enough to feed a man for a month. (*Making
a mental calculation*) And six days besides.

CHAERESTRATUS (*aside*) He's got it all figured out—a dollar and a
half a day, just enough to get you a bowl of soup if you get
hungry.

(*One of the girls comes out of Chaerestratus' house and addresses
him.*)

GIRL Chaerestratus, Charisius is waiting for you. (*Pointing to
Smicrines*) Who is *that*?

CHAERESTRATUS Pamphila's father.

GIRL What's the matter with him? He looks as sour as a professor.

CHAERESTRATUS The poor devil heard about the entertainer and . . .

[Some thirteen lines are lost here. Apparently the girl innocently
suggested they tell Smicrines that his son-in-law was now staying with
Chaerestratus.]

CHAERESTRATUS   If you know what's good for you, you won't tell him.
GIRL (*pouting*)   But I want to.
CHAERESTRATUS (*losing his temper*)   Oh, go to the devil! Just try it.
   You'll be sorry.
SMICRINES (*to himself*)   I'm going inside now to find out exactly how
   things stand with my daughter. Then I'll figure out how to get
   at him. (*Enters Charisius' house.*)
GIRL   Shall we tell Charisius he's here?
CHAERESTRATUS   We'd better. That old fox can ruin a household.
GIRL (*still smarting under Chaerestratus' angry words*)   There's quite
   a few I wish he would.
CHAERESTRATUS   Quite a few?
GIRL   That one, for example, next door. (*Points to Chaerestratus'
   house.*)
CHAERESTRATUS   Mine?
GIRL   Yes, yours! Let's go in and see Charisius.
CHAERESTRATUS   Let's. (*Looking toward the wings*)   As a matter of
   fact, a bunch of youngsters are coming this way and they're a
   little tight—this is no time to run into any trouble with them.
   (*Hurries her off into the house.*)

(*The stage is now empty, and a chorus comes on—the "bunch of
youngsters"—and dances an entr'acte.*)

ACT II

(*Smicrines comes out of Charisius' house. He hasn't accomplished
very much: Charisius, of course, was not in the house, and his daughter,
hugging the hope that time is somehow on her side, refuses to go along
with his plans. As he walks slowly, buried in thought, away from the
entrance, two slaves, Davus and Syriscus, enter stage right, arguing.
Behind them is Syriscus' wife, holding an infant. Davus, a goatherd,
is shrewd, has a keen eye for what's best for himself, and doesn't waste
words. Syriscus, a charcoal burner, is almost the exact opposite: open,
absolutely honest, somewhat scatterbrained, and richly endowed with
the gift of gab.*

   *Their argument is about the infant the woman is carrying and it
has reached an impasse.*)

SYRISCUS (*heatedly*) You're evading justice.

DAVUS (*angrily*) No, damn you, you're out to skin me. I don't have to give you what's not yours.

SYRISCUS Then we'll have to have somebody arbitrate the matter.

DAVUS All right, let's arbitrate it.

SYRISCUS But who?

DAVUS Anyone will do for me. (*Disgustedly*) I'm getting what I deserve. Why did I ever let you in on the deal?

SYRISCUS (*pointing to Smicrines*) Are you willing to take him as judge?

DAVUS I'll risk it.

SYRISCUS (*going up to Smicrines*) I beg your pardon, could you spare us a minute of your time?

SMICRINES (*jolted out of his thoughts*) You? What about?

SYRISCUS (*pointing to Davus*) He and I have a little disagreement.

SMICRINES (*impatiently*) What's that got to do with me?

SYRISCUS We're looking for somebody to arbitrate it, somebody impartial. If you have the time, would you please settle it for us?

SMICRINES (*testily*) Go to the devil! What is this—workmen in overalls going around arguing lawsuits?

SYRISCUS (*unabashed*) What if we do. It's a simple matter and won't take long to explain. Please do us the favor. And please don't think it's beneath you. (*Oratorically*) Justice should triumph all the time, everywhere, and whoever comes along should be concerned to do his part. It's a duty we all share in life.

DAVUS (*aside, sarcastically but a little worried*) I've got a real lawyer on my hands here! (*Shaking his head disgustedly*) Why did I ever let him in on the deal?

SMICRINES (*curtly*) Tell me, will you stand by whatever I decide?

SYRISCUS Absolutely.

SMICRINES I'll hear the case. Why not? (*Turning to Davus*) You there, you who aren't saying anything, you speak first.

DAVUS (*flatly, without wasting any words*) I'll tell you what went before too and not just what passed between me and him, so you'll have the whole matter clear in your mind. I was pasturing my flock in the brush near here about a month ago, and, all by myself, I found an infant that someone had abandoned. There was a necklace with it and some pieces of jewelry like this. (*He shows some trinkets.*)

SYRISCUS (*breaking in*)   These are what we're arguing about.

DAVUS (*to Smicrines, angrily*)   He's not letting me talk!

SMICRINES (*turning to Syriscus*)   Don't interrupt or I'll let you have it with this stick!

DAVUS   And serve him right.

SMICRINES   Keep talking.

DAVUS   I will. I picked up the baby and its things and went home. I was going to raise it. At least, that was the idea I had at the time. But, that night, just as happens to everybody, I had second thoughts on the matter. I thrashed it all out in my mind. What do I want the trouble of raising a child for? Where would I get the money? What do I want with such worries? That's how I felt. Next morning I went out with my flock again. (*Gesturing toward Syriscus*) This fellow came to the same place to cut out some stumps—he's a charcoal burner. I had known him before, and we got to talking. He saw I was down in the mouth, and says, "What's on your mind, Davus?" "What's on my mind?" I say. "That I don't mind my own business!" And I told him what happened, how I found a baby and took it home. So, then, before I could tell him the whole story, he begins begging, keeps interrupting me with, "Davus, give me the baby and heaven will reward you. You'll be lucky. You'll get your freedom. I've got a wife," he tells me, "she lost a baby in childbirth." (*Pointing to the woman*) There she is over there; she's got the baby with her now.

SMICRINES (*turning to Syriscus*)   Did you beg him?

DAVUS (*to Syriscus, sharply*)   How about it, Syriscus?

SYRISCUS (*unabashed*)   I did.

DAVUS   He certainly did, the whole day long. He kept pestering me and jabbering away at me, so finally I gave in. I gave it to him. It was nothing but "bless you, bless you," when he left. He even grabbed my hands and kept kissing them.

SMICRINES (*to Syriscus*)   Did you?

SYRISCUS (*as before*)   I did.

DAVUS   He went away. Now he and his wife meet me and all of a sudden claim they should get the things that were with the baby—little things, some trash, nothing at all, believe me. He says he's getting a raw deal because I claim I should keep them, and won't give them up. What I say is that he ought to be grateful for the share he begged out of me. Just because I didn't give him everything is no reason why I have to submit to an investigation. Suppose *he* had found the baby while he was walking along with me, and it was a case of finders-sharers? He still would have gotten only what was his share and I what was mine. (*Turns to Syriscus, and his voice rises with indignation*) But I found it all by myself! You weren't even there at the time! (*Shaking his head incredulously*) And you think you should keep everything and I should have nothing! (*Falls silent for a moment, still shaking his head, then resumes, more calmly, again addressing Syriscus.*) Let's cut it short. I gave you, of my own free will, something that belongs to me. If you're satisfied, keep it. If you're not, if you've changed your mind, just give it right back. Then there's no question of your doing anybody any wrong or anybody doing you any. But you just can't have everything. You can't take what I gave you of my own free will and then squeeze the rest out of me. (*Turning back to Smicrines*) I've had my say.

SYRISCUS (*to Smicrines, a little timidly, since he's afraid of the stick if he talks out of turn*) Is he done?

SMICRINES Are you deaf? Certainly he's done.

SYRISCUS Good. That means it's my turn. (*With candor*) He found the baby all by himself, and everything he says is the absolute truth. It all happened that way. I don't deny it. I got the baby by begging him for it, on my knees. It's the truth. (*Pauses to let this sink in, then proceeds melodramatically*) I happened to learn from some shepherd he'd been chatting with, fellow who works for the same master, that he had also found some jewelry with the child. (*Adopting the pose and manner of a trial lawyer*) Your Honor, my client has made a personal appearance to claim this jewelry. (*To his wife*) Hand me the baby. (*Turning to Davus*) Davus, my client is here for his necklace and birth tokens. He claims that they were intended for his neck, not your pocket. And I'm representing him, since he's my ward. You made him so yourself, when you gave him to me. (*Hands the baby back to his wife and again addresses Smicrines*) Your Honor, as I see it, what you have to decide is whether this jewelry, gold or whatever it is, should be kept in escrow for the child until he grows up, in accordance with the will of the

mother, whoever she was, or whether this crook is to cheat him
out of it, just because he was the first to find something that
didn't belong to him. (*Turning to Davus*) You want to know
why I didn't ask you for the jewelry when I got the baby?
Because at that time I was in no position to; I didn't know the
facts. And I'm not coming now to ask for one single thing for
myself. Finders-sharers? Don't talk of "finding" something when a
party's been wronged. That isn't finding, it's stealing! (*Turning
back to Smicrines*) And there's this to think about (*looking off
into the distance, dreamily*): for all we know this child is above
our station. Even though he's been brought up among working
people, the time may come when he'll show the stuff he's made
of and go in for the sort of things gentlemen do—lion hunting,
or an army career, or sports. (*Facing Smicrines again*) I'm sure
you've been to the theater and remember lots of situations like
this. There's the one where an old goatherd, fellow who wore
clothes the same as mine, found those heroes Neleus and
Pelias. When he realized they were above his station, he
told them the whole story, how he found them and brought them
up, and he gave them a little bag full of their birth tokens, and
this was the way they found out everything about themselves.
They started out as goatherds and ended up as kings. But if a
Davus had taken these tokens and sold them off to make himself
fifty dollars, they would have gone through the rest of their
days without ever knowing how high their station in life really
was. What good is it for me to go ahead and raise the child if
Davus is going to destroy the one hope of ever saving him?
(*Carried away by his own eloquence, again gazing off into
space, dreamily*) Why, once birth tokens saved a man from
marrying his sister. Another time they helped a man find his
mother and rescue her. Once they saved a brother. Life is full of
pitfalls for every one of us. We've got to have foresight, we've
got to be on the alert, we've got to look far ahead, as best we
can. (*Pauses to recover from this verbal flight, and returns to
the matter at hand.*) "Give it right back if you're not satisfied,"
he tells me, and he thinks he's got a strong point there. What's
the justice in that? (*Turning to Davus*) You find you have to
give up what belongs to the baby, so you're out to get your
hands on the baby too. (*Sarcastically*) I suppose Fate preserved

that jewelry just to make life easier for a crook like you from now on. (*To Smicrines*) I'm done now. Decide whatever you think is right.

SMICRINES (*promptly*) It's simple. The baby keeps whatever was left with it. That's my decision.

DAVUS Fine. But what about the baby?

SMICRINES (*indignantly*) Good god, do you think I'd give it to you, the man who was out to cheat it? No! It goes to the man who came to the rescue and went after you when you tried to cheat it.

SYRISCUS (*fervently*) God bless you!

DAVUS (*outraged*) God almighty, what a hell of a decision! I found everything and I have to cough it all up; he found nothing and he gets everything. You mean I have to hand it all over?

SMICRINES (*curtly*) That's what I mean.

DAVUS (*as before*) What a hell of a decision! I'll be god damned!

SYRISCUS Come on, let's have the stuff.

DAVUS My god, what I have to put up with!

SYRISCUS Open up that pouch and show us what's in it. I know you've got the stuff there. (*To Smicrines, who is starting to move off*) Please, wait just a second and make him hand the things over.

DAVUS (*grumbling to himself*) Why did I ever let him (*gesturing toward Smicrines*) handle the case?

SYRISCUS Hand it over, you stinker!

DAVUS (*handing the jewelry over*) The dirty, lowdown treatment I have to put up with!

SMICRINES (*to Syriscus*) Have you got everything?

SYRISCUS I think so; unless he swallowed something when I was arguing my case and he knew he was going to lose.

DAVUS (*still dumbstruck, to himself*) I wouldn't have believed it!

SYRISCUS (*to Smicrines as he walks off, stage left*) Goodbye, and thanks! (*Admiringly*) All our judges ought to be like that.

DAVUS (*to himself*) A dirty deal, so help me. Never heard a worse decision in my life.

SYRISCUS You were a crook.

DAVUS Listen, you crook you, you better keep this stuff safe until that baby grows up, because, believe me, I'm going to keep an eye on you as long as I live.

SYRISCUS On your way, on your way! (*Davus leaves, stage right, and*

Syriscus addresses his wife.) Take all this and bring it inside to
our master, Chaerestratus. We'll spend the night here, pay
what we owe, and go back to work in the morning. But first
let's check these things over, every one of them. Got a box?
(*She shakes her head.*) Then spread out your skirt and put
them there.

(*At this point Onesimus, Charisius' valet, comes out of Chaerestratus'
house. He's nattily dressed, as one would expect of the personal attendant
of a rich master. He rather prides himself on knowing his way around,
on being a man of the world. He also likes to know everything that's
going on, and has a flair for successful snooping—witness his learning of
Pamphila's baby.*)

ONESIMUS (*muttering to himself as he comes out of the door*) Never
saw such a slow cook. By this time yesterday people were having
their after-dinner drinks.

SYRISCUS (*to his wife as they examine the child's jewelry*) This looks
like a rooster. (*With a grin*) Wouldn't try to eat it, though. Here,
take it. Here's something with stones. And here's a little ax.

ONESIMUS (*his curiosity piqued, looks over the pair's shoulders; then,
to himself*) What's going on here?

SYRISCUS (*as before*) Here's a gold-plated ring; it's iron underneath.
It's got a seal: a bull or a goat, I can't make it out. "Made by
Cleostratus" it says.

ONESIMUS (*breaking in*) Let me see it.

SYRISCUS (*absentmindedly*) Here. (*Suddenly realizing what he has
done*) Hey, who are you?

ONESIMUS (*goggling at the ring*) Just can't be!

SYRISCUS Who can't be?

ONESIMUS The ring.

SYRISCUS (*testily*) What do you mean, ring? What are you talking
about?

ONESIMUS It's my master's ring! It's Charisius'!

SYRISCUS You're out of your mind.

ONESIMUS One that he lost.

SYRISCUS (*reaching for the ring*) Damn you, give me that ring back!

ONESIMUS (*holding it out of reach*) Give you our ring? Where did
you get it, anyway?

SYRISCUS (*indignantly, to himself*) God damn it, what the hell's going

on here? What a job it is to keep a poor orphan's property safe!
The minute someone comes along he's out to get his hands on it.
(*To Onesimus*) You heard me! Give me that ring!

ONESIMUS Are you kidding? God damn it, it belongs to my master!

SYRISCUS (*with the jewelry still in his hands, decides to finish taking
inventory before tackling Onesimus in earnest. Growling to himself*) He'll get any of this stuff over my dead body! I'll haul
'em into court, one after the other—my mind's made up. This
stuff's the baby's, not mine. (*To his wife as he resumes the inventory*) Here, take this, it's some kind of necklace. And a piece
of red cloth. Now go inside. (*Straightening up and turning to
Onesimus*) Now what's this you were telling me?

ONESIMUS (*startled out of his fascinated study of the ring*) Who me?
Oh, it belongs to Charisius. He got drunk once and lost it; at
least that's what he said.

SYRISCUS (*relieved to hear that the alleged owner is his master's best
friend*) All right. I'm in Chaerestratus' household. Take good
care of it, or give it back to me and I'll keep it safe for you.

ONESIMUS (*hastily*) I don't mind taking care of it.

SYRISCUS Makes no difference to me. Looks to me as if we're both
headed for the same place (*pointing to Chaerestratus' house*).

ONESIMUS Look, there's a party going on now and maybe it isn't a good
time to tell him about all this. How about tomorrow?

SYRISCUS (*grimly*) I'll be around. Tomorrow I'm ready to let anyone
you want arbitrate the case. (*To himself, as he watches Onesimus
go off into Chaerestratus' house*) I didn't come off so badly the
last time. Looks like I'll have to stop everything else and start
practicing law. Only way a man can keep anything nowadays.
(*Follows Onesimus into the house.*)

(*The stage is now empty, and the chorus re-appears to perform an
entr'acte.*)

ACT III

(*Onesimus emerges from Chaerestratus' house. It is clear that something is very much on his mind.*)

ONESIMUS (*to himself*) Five times I started to go up to Charisius to
show him this ring. I was right at his side, we were face to face—

and I just couldn't go through with it. Now I'm sorry about what
I told him before. He goes around saying: "You! You had to go
and tell me these things! I hope to god you break your neck!"
I only hope he doesn't make up with his wife; then he'll get rid
of me—I'm the one who told him all about her; I know too much.
It's a good thing I held off just now from adding anything more
to the mess. It could land me in a lot of trouble.

*(Habrotonon, the entertainer that Charisius had hired, now appears
at the doorway of Chaerestratus' house. Habrotonon is a slave, owned
by a slave dealer who hires her out. She does not consciously rebel at
her lot, but, like any slave, she dreams unremittingly of that remote yet
possible moment when she may gain her freedom, and is ready to grasp
at whatever promises to bring it even a mite closer. A girl in her walk
of life must learn to use her wits to get along; Habrotonon has become
adept at the art. She is no doubt hard—she could hardly be otherwise
and get by—but still young and attractive enough to keep this from
showing. Aware of her undeniable charms and with the professional's
pride in her skill at her trade, she is understandably resentful when her
services are contracted for and go unused—as is the case at the moment
with her present employer.*

*She is leaving the house to get away from the unwelcome advances of
some drunk. Her first words are addressed through the door to him.)*

HABROTONON   Stop bothering me and let me go. Please! (*She manages
    to wrench herself loose, and leaves the doorway, muttering to
    herself.*) I guess I've been making a fool of myself without
    realizing it. I thought he wanted me to make love to, but the
    way that man hates me—it's something out of this world! My
    god, he won't even let me sit next to him at the table; I've got to
    be somewhere else.

ONESIMUS (*to himself, staring gloomily at the ring in his hand*)   Maybe
    I should give it back to the fellow I got it from. (*Thinking for a
    moment*) No, that'll get me nowhere.

HABROTONON (*to herself*)   He's in a bad way. What's he throwing away
    all this money on me for? My god, I could enroll as a vestal
    virgin right now for all that's gone on between him and me. I've
    been sitting around for three days now, chaste as a bride in
    white, as the saying goes.

ONESIMUS (*to himself*)   How in heaven, how could—

(His soliloquy is interrupted by Syriscus, who suddenly rushes out from Chaerestratus' house.)

SYRISCUS *(excitedly, to himself)* Where is he? I've been looking for him all over the house. *(Suddenly seeing Onesimus)* Hey, mister, give me back that ring or else show it to the fellow you were going to. Let's get this settled. I've got to get going.

ONESIMUS *(confidentially)* Look, old man, here's the situation. This is my master's ring. It's Charisius', all right; I'm sure of it. But I simply can't bring myself to show it to him. You know, if I hand him this ring, I just about make him the father of the child it was left with.

SYRISCUS Don't be silly. How?

ONESIMUS He lost it at the Tauropolia, the women's festival, the one that goes on all night. What I figure is, he crashed the party and attacked some girl, and then she had this baby and abandoned it. That's what must have happened. Now, if we could only find *her* and produce this ring, we'd be getting somewhere. But as things stand now, we'd only be getting people suspicious and upset.

SYRISCUS *(not able to follow Onesimus' reasoning and suspicious)* That's your problem. But if you're trying to shake me down, if you've got the notion that I'm going to pay you off to get the ring back, you're out of your mind. I'm not the kind that makes deals.

ONESIMUS *(quickly)* I'm not asking you to.

SYRISCUS All right. I'm going to town now. When I'm finished running some errands there, I'm coming right back to look into what's to be done about all this. *(Exits stage left.)*

HABROTONON *(who has been listening in on the conversation with growing curiosity)* Onesimus, the baby the woman is nursing inside now, is that the one this charcoal burner found?

ONESIMUS So he says.

HABROTONON Poor little baby. It's so cute.

ONESIMUS And this ring was with it. *(Looking around furtively and dropping his voice to a whisper)* It's Charisius'!

HABROTONON *(passionately, her sudden indignation born of her resentment at her own sorry fate)* Oh, how *could* you! When there's a chance this child may actually be your master's son, are you going to stand by and see him brought up in slavery? I could murder you! And I'd have every right.

ONESIMUS (*taken aback by Habrotonon's vehemence and on the defensive*) But, as I was saying before, nobody knows who the mother is.

HABROTONON (*thoughtfully*) Did you say he lost it at the Tauropolia?

ONESIMUS Yes, he was drunk. I heard about it from the boy who was attending him.

HABROTONON (*as before*) He must have gotten in by himself and gone after one of the women who were spending the night there. The same sort of thing happened once when I was there.

ONESIMUS (*surprised that one of Habrotonon's profession had had an opportunity to get to a woman's festival*) When *you* were there?

HABROTONON Yes, last year's festival. I'd been hired to play for a party of girls and I went along with them. I wasn't then . . . (*Catching Onesimus' knowing and mocking look, she breaks off and adds sharply*) I didn't even know what a man was!

ONESIMUS (*leering*) Oh, sure.

HABROTONON (*angrily*) I didn't, I tell you!

ONESIMUS (*hurriedly changing the subject*) But this girl it happened to—do you know who she was?

HABROTONON (*thoughtful again*) I could find out. She was a friend of the girls I was with.

ONESIMUS Did you happen to hear who her father was?

HABROTONON I don't know a thing about her except that, if I saw her, I'd recognize her. She was simply beautiful. And I heard she was rich.

ONESIMUS (*hopefully*) Maybe it's the same one.

HABROTONON I wouldn't know. Anyway, she was there with us, and then she wandered off somewhere. Then, all of a sudden, we see her running toward us all by herself, crying and tearing her hair. And her dress! It was one of those south Italian gowns, simply beautiful, and very sheer fabric, and it was ruined. The whole thing was just a *rag*.

ONESIMUS (*patiently enduring the female's eternal interest in clothes and anxious to get back to the main point*) And she had this ring?

HABROTONON (*firmly*) Maybe she did, but I didn't see it, and I'm not going to make anything up.

ONESIMUS (*more up in the air now than even before*) What should I do now?

HABROTONON That's your worry. But if you've got any sense, you'll take my advice and make a clean breast of it to Charisius. If the baby belongs to a girl from a good family, why must we keep what's happened a secret?

ONESIMUS First let's find out who she is. (*Pleadingly*) Habrotonon, I need your help for this.

HABROTONON (*quickly*) Oh, I couldn't. Not until I know who attacked her. I'd be afraid of starting something with those girls I told you about, for no reason. You never can tell; maybe someone else, one of the men with him, got the ring as security and then lost it. When they were gambling Charisius might have thrown it into the pot, or maybe he lost a bet and ran short and handed the ring over. When men get to drinking, any of a thousand things like that are bound to happen. I don't want to go looking for the girl or breathe a word about it until I find out who attacked her.

ONESIMUS (*nodding assent gloomily*) You've got a point there. (*In despair*) What in the world is a man to do?

HABROTONON (*thoughtfully*) Onesimus, listen. I've got an idea. See if you like it. (*Pausing to make sure he is listening and eying him closely to note the effect*) Suppose I pretend that the whole thing happened to me. Suppose I take this ring and go in to see him.

ONESIMUS (*eagerly*) Go on, I'm following you.

HABROTONON (*warming to the subject*) The minute he sees me with it, he'll ask me where I got it. I'll say (*melodramatically*), "At the Tauropolia—when I was still a virgin." Then I'll make believe that everything that happened to her happened to me. Most of it I know, anyway.

ONESIMUS Terrific!

HABROTONON And if it hits home—

ONESIMUS (*interrupting in his excitement*) Good, good!

HABROTONON —he'll fall right into the trap. He's been drinking, you know, so he'll spill the whole story first. I don't want to slip up anywhere, so I'll let him do the talking. I'll just say Yes to whatever he says.

ONESIMUS Very good. God, yes. *Very* good!

HABROTONON   When I have to say something, I'll make up the sort of
thing you can't go wrong on. Like (*melodramatically*), "Oh,
what a *brute* you were! The way you went after me!"

ONESIMUS   Good, good!

HABROTONON   (*as before*)   "And when you threw me down you were
so *rough!* My poor dress was absolutely ruined!" (*Dropping the
histrionics and abruptly becoming matter-of-fact again*) Before
I do anything, I want to go inside and get the baby. I want to
cry over it, pet it—and find out from that woman just where she
got it.

ONESIMUS   (*aghast at the breakneck pace at which things are suddenly
moving*)   My god!

HABROTONON   And my last line will be (*melodramatically*), "Charisius!
You are the father of a child!" And then I'll produce the baby.

ONESIMUS   (*maliciously*)   Habrotonon, you could make a fortune as a
crook.

HABROTONON   (*deliberately ignoring him*)   If it works, and he does
turn out to be the baby's father, then we'll have lots of time
to look for the mother later.

ONESIMUS   (*a train of thought suddenly started in his mind by
Habrotonon's last remark*)   You forgot to mention that you'll get
your freedom. He'll buy it the minute he's convinced you're the
mother. No doubt about it.

HABROTONON   (*deprecatorily*)   Oh, I don't know. I hope so.

ONESIMUS   (*mimicking her*)   Oh, you don't know, eh? (*Coming closer
to her*) How about me, Habrotonon? Do I get any thanks for
what you'll get out of all this?

HABROTONON   (*sweetly*)   Of course! You know I'll always feel that
whatever I get I owe to you.

ONESIMUS   (*bluntly*)   Suppose you just don't go looking for the girl?
Suppose you just double-cross me and drop the whole business?
What then?

HABROTONON   (*quickly*)   My god! What makes you think I want anything to do with children? (*Fervently*) Just let me get my freedom. God knows that's all I want out of all this.

ONESIMUS   (*somewhat reassured*)   I hope you get it.

HABROTONON   Well? Do you like my idea?

ONESIMUS   I like it—with this condition. (*Grimly*) The minute you try any funny stuff, I'm going to let you have it. And I can do it, too. (*Relaxing his tone*) Right now, let's see how things go.

HABROTONON   So it's a deal?

ONESIMUS   Right.

HABROTONON (*anxious to clinch things before Onesimus has any second thoughts*) Quick, give me the ring!

ONESIMUS   Here, take it.

HABROTONON (*fervently, as she goes into Chaerestratus' house*) Holy Lady of Persuasion, stand by me now! Please put the right words in my mouth!

ONESIMUS (*to himself, shaking his head in awed admiration*) The female of the species knows her way around. When she sees she can't get her freedom through making love, that that's a dead end, she takes another route. A poor slob like me, with the brains knocked out of my head, I could never figure out what to do about such things. Result—I'll be a slave all my life. (*Brightening*) Maybe, if she pulls it off, I'll get something from her. I certainly deserve it. (*Clapping a hand to his brow*) What's the matter with me? Lost my mind? Expect gratitude from a woman? I'll be satisfied if she doesn't add to my troubles. Right now, Pamphila's situation is pretty shaky. The minute Charisius finds out it's a girl from a good family who's the mother of his child, he's going to marry her and get rid of his wife. Anyway, if you ask me, I've done a neat job of keeping myself in the clear; I've kept my fingers out of this mess. And, from now on, no more meddling: if anyone catches me sticking my nose into other people's business, or talking out of turn, I hereby give him permission to cut my tongue out. (*Noticing someone approaching, stage left*) But who's this coming? (*Looking closely*) It's Smicrines, back from town, and he's burning up; maybe he's learned the truth from someone. I'm going to make myself scarce. (*Hurries into Chaerestratus' house.*)

[The second half of the act (130-odd lines) is fragmentary. Just enough is preserved to enable us to follow the plot.

When Smicrines comes on stage he delivers in soliloquy a tirade that makes it clear his trip to town has only multiplied his misgivings. This, however, is only the beginning. A cook now comes out of Chaerestratus' house, and his lines reveal that Habrotonon's ruse has been brilliantly successful: Charisius has ended the party, sent everybody home (this is how the cook got into the act; he was told to pack up and go), acknowledged the baby, and installed Habrotonon in the house. By the time the cook leaves, the old man is seething.

And so, when Chaerestratus comes out of his house and tries to defend Charisius, he doesn't get very far. Smicrines vows that he's not only going to rescue his daughter from all this, but, what's more, is going to summon Chaerestratus as a witness and compel him to testify to the treatment she's been subjected to. The act closes as he enters Charisius' house to get Pamphila.]

ACT IV

(Pamphila and Smicrines emerge from Charisius' house. They have obviously been arguing. Now that Charisius has established Habrotonon in his house and plans to raise the child, Smicrines wants his daughter to have nothing more to do with him. Pamphila, loyal to her husband and desperately hopeful that some way out will be found, refuses to leave. The argument continues on stage.)

PAMPHILA *(stubbornly)* You've got to convince me I need to be rescued. Otherwise you'll be treating me like a slave, not a daughter.

SMICRINES *(exasperated)* Convince you! What for? Isn't it clear as day? Pamphila, the situation cries out to high heaven. *(As she starts to move away from him)* All right, all right. If I have to talk you into it, I'm ready. There are three things I'm going to point out to you. First, there's not a chance of salvaging this marriage, neither on your side, nor his. [About 23 lines are lost here, in which Smicrines evaluated the feasibility of Charisius' keeping the two women in separate households.] Think of the expense. Double each year for the women's festival in June. Double each year for the women's festival in October. He'll run through his money, you've got to realize that. And that means he's ruined, right? Now let's look at it from your side. He'll tell you he has a business appointment. He'll go out and stay out. And you'll be miserable, believe me. You'll wait around, you'll hold up dinner. And he'll be drinking with that entertainer, no question about it; he only went out to be with her. Come, get out of this house. [Another, larger, segment is lost here in which Smicrines evaluated the feasibility of the two women living under the same roof.] A respectable girl is no match for a whore, Pamphila. She's been around, she knows all the tricks; she won't stop at anything, she knows how to get around a man.

(The rest of Smicrines' speech is lost. Apparently all his talk has no effect and, finally, he leaves. At this moment, Habrotonon comes out of Chaerestratus' house holding the baby. Her first words are addressed to someone inside.)

HABROTONON *(through the doorway)* I'm going to take the baby out. The poor thing's been crying its heart out all this time. There's something the matter with it.

PAMPHILA *(seeing Habrotonon, the source of her present torment, to herself)* Oh, god! Have mercy on me!

HABROTONON *(hearing Pamphila's voice, looks up, recognizes her, and whispers to the baby, excitedly)* Baby darling, you're going to see your mommy! She came out here just at the right time!

PAMPHILA *(to herself)* I'll get out of here.

HABROTONON *(stationing herself near the door to Charisius' house, so Pamphila can't avoid her)* May I see you a moment, please?

PAMPHILA *(frigidly)* Are you speaking to me?

HABROTONON Yes. *(Pleadingly)* Please! Look at me! Do you know me? *(Aside)* She *is* the one I saw that time. *(To Pamphila, warmly)* I am *so* glad to see you!

PAMPHILA *(confused)* But—who are you?

HABROTONON Here, let me take your hand. Tell me, dear, weren't you at the Tauropolia last year? In one of those beautiful south Italian gowns?

PAMPHILA *(suddenly noticing the necklace the baby is wearing and, disregarding the question, urgently)* Tell me, please, where did you get this child?

HABROTONON *(quickly)* Oh, my dear, do you recognize something it's wearing? Please tell me. Don't be afraid of me!

PAMPHILA *(still confused but sensing the glimmer of a possibility)* Aren't you the mother?

HABROTONON *(speaking rapidly and with all the persuasion at her com-*

mand) I pretended I was—not to cheat the real mother, but
to gain time to find her. And I have—just now. For you are the
girl I saw that night!

PAMPHILA *(turns away, lowers her head in shame, and remains silent.
Then, with eyes averted and speaking in almost a whisper)* Do
you know who the father is?

HABROTONON *(almost shouting)* Charisius!

PAMPHILA *(straightens up, startled. Stares at Habrotonon, incredulous)*
My dearest girl, are you sure of this?

HABROTONON   Absolutely. *(Pointing to Charisius' house)* You *are* the
mistress of this house, aren't you?

PAMPHILA   Yes, yes.

HABROTONON   Then thank your lucky stars. God *has* had mercy on
you. *(The door of Chaerestratus' house starts to open.)* Wait!
Someone's coming out next door. Take me inside your house. I'll
tell you the rest of the story there.

*(The two women hurry into Charisius' house. A second later
Onesimus emerges from Chaerestratus' house. It is obvious that he is
considerably perturbed.)*

ONESIMUS *(to the audience)*   He's going out of his mind. By god, he *is*
out of his mind. He's really gone out of his mind; clean out of
his mind, I swear. Charisius, I mean. Had an attack of manic
depression or something. How else can you explain something
like this? Just now, for the longest while he was squatting outside the back door with his ear glued to it. I guess his father-in-
law must have been inside discussing the situation with
Pamphila. Well, the way that man's color changed—I just can't
talk about it. Then he bursts out with *(imitating Charisius)*,
"Sweetheart! What wonderful things to say!" and gives himself
a blow on the head, real hard. Then, a little while later
(imitating him again), "What a wonderful wife I had. . . . I'm
miserable, miserable." Finally, when he heard all they had to
say, he went inside and there he started to rant and tear his
hair and even have fits. He kept saying over and over: "I'm the
guilty one. I committed a wanton attack; I became the father of
an illegitimate child. She was merely the tragic victim of someone like me. And yet I didn't have a shred of commiseration for
her, not the slightest thought of forgiveness for her. I'm just a

brute, a pitiless brute." He keeps shouting these awful things about himself, he's all worked up, his eyes are bloodshot—I'm scared. I'm scared stiff. In his condition, if he sees me, the fellow who told on her, he's liable to kill me. That's why I sneaked out of the house. But where am I going to go? What am I going to do? I'm a goner, I'm sunk! (*The door of Chaerestratus' house opens.*) He's coming out now. God in heaven help me—if you can!

(*Having nowhere else to go, Onesimus ducks into Charisius' house. A moment later, Charisius comes out of Chaerestratus' house.*)

CHARISIUS (*to the audience, bitterly*)   There I was acting like some saint, always with an eye on my reputation, reading the books on what's right and what's wrong, pure, above reproach—well, the good lord has treated me just as I deserve. He showed me up: "You, with all your wind and big talk, you poor fool, you're only human. Your wife runs into trouble through no fault of her own, and you can't take it. Well, I'm going to show the world that you've fallen as low as she. And, when she hears about it, she'll treat you with sympathy and understanding, even though at this moment you're denying her everything that's her due. Everybody's going to know you for what you are—a miserable, stupid cad. Just compare the thoughts you've been having about her with what you heard her tell her father—not exactly the same, are they? She told him she had become a partner in your life and that it was her duty not to desert when trouble came along. And you, holier-than-thou Charisius, you treated her like a brute. [Three lines are lost here.] Nor will her father treat her very nicely." (*Having completed this imaginary divine rebuke, he paces up and down for a moment in silence. Then, defiantly*) What do I care about her father? I'll lay it on the line to him: "Smicrines, I don't want any trouble from you. My wife's not going to leave me. What are you upsetting her for? What are you pressuring her for?"

(*At this moment Onesimus, with Habrotonon behind him, bursts out of Charisius' house. He sees Charisius and makes an abrupt about-face but it is too late; Charisius has already seen him.*)

CHARISIUS (*eyeing him balefully*) What! You again?

ONESIMUS (*quaking, aside*) I'm in trouble, real trouble. (*To Habrotonon*) Please! Don't desert me now!

CHARISIUS You little sneak, were you standing here listening to what I was saying?

ONESIMUS (*terrified*) No! I swear, I just came out.

[Four lines are lost here. The altercation apparently continued until Habrotonon stepped forward to take a hand in the proceedings.]

HABROTONON (*to Charisius*) You don't know anything about what's happened!

CHARISIUS What?

HABROTONON The baby's not mine!

CHARISIUS Not yours?

[Another four lines are lost in which Habrotonon presumably explains that Onesimus had given her the ring and that she had pretended the baby was hers. But this only succeeds in inciting Charisius in his overwrought state to go after Onesimus again.]

CHARISIUS (*advancing on Onesimus menacingly*) Well, Onesimus, what have you got to say? You were testing me, eh?

ONESIMUS (*pointing to Habrotonon*) She talked me into it, I swear to god!

CHARISIUS (*coming even closer*) So you were going to put one over on me, you little sneak? Why—

HABROTONON (*rushing in between the two of them, frantically*) Please, please! Don't hit him! The baby's your own wedded wife's, no one else's!

CHARISIUS (*dully*) If only it were . . .

HABROTONON (*in her excitement almost shrieking*) It is, I swear it!

CHARISIUS (*his attention finally caught by the intensity of the girl's manner*) What are you saying?

HABROTONON I? The truth!

CHARISIUS You mean it's Pamphila's baby?

HABROTONON And yours, of course.

CHARISIUS (*dazedly*) Pamphila's? Habrotonon, please now, don't get me all excited . . .

[About twenty lines, the last of the act, are lost here, in which Habrotonon presumably convinces him that the child is really his wife's and the three go into Charisius' house.]

ACT V

[The first ninety lines are for the most part lost. Enough is left to show that Chaerestratus and a friend—or, more likely, a servant—named Simias, are involved and that the topic of their discussion is Habrotonon; very likely the audience learned that she had gotten the freedom she yearned for so passionately. They leave and the stage is empty. A second later Smicrines enters, stage left, dragging after him Sophrona, Pamphila's old nurse, the one who had helped her dispose of the child at the outset. Smicrines, in complete ignorance of all that has happened, is bent on rescuing his daughter—and what's left of the dowry.]

SMICRINES Sophrona, so help me, I'll bash in that skull of yours. Are you laying down the law to me too? So, "It's very rash of me to carry off my daughter," is it, you lying old hag? I suppose I should sit back and waste my breath talking about the dowry I turned over, while that fine husband of hers swallows it up? You're telling me to do that too, eh? Don't you know it's better to strike while the iron is hot? (*As she opens her mouth to answer*) Another word out of you and you'll be sorry! (*To himself*) What am I—a defendant before Sophrona? (*To her again*) You go and reason with her—if ever you get to see her. Because, Sophrona, so help me, when we go home from here—remember that pond we passed?—I'm going to drown you there if I have to hold you under water all night. I'm going to make you see things my way and put an end to this taking sides against me. (*Reaches the door of Charisius' house and tries to open it.*) This door is locked; I've got to bang on it. (*Shouting*) Inside there, somebody open this door! Open up, I say! (*Moves off to the side, pulling Sophrona after him, to see if any servants are around.*)

(*Onesimus comes to the door. Now that everything has ended so happily, he has been restored to favor, and has resumed his former role of the worldly wise sophisticate.*)

ONESIMUS (*to himself as he opens the door*) Who's knocking at this
door, anyway? Oh, it's that grouch Smicrines, coming for his
dowry and his daughter.

SMICRINES (*snarling*) Yes! It's Smicrines, damn you, and with good
reason! A sensible businessman doesn't waste time. The way
you people are robbing me—it's unbelievable! In the name of
god—

ONESIMUS (*interrupting with a calculatedly irritating patience, like a
kindly priest dealing with a not overly bright member of his
congregation*) Now, Smicrines, do you think god has so much
time on his hands that he can go around parceling out a daily
dose of good and bad to each one of us?

SMICRINES (*testily*) What are you talking about?

ONESIMUS (*as before*) I'll explain it to you. At a rough guess there
are a thousand cities in the world. Say, thirty thousand people in
each. Now, can god go around damning or saving every single
one of them? How? Some working day you'd have him put in!
What then? Will you conclude that he doesn't care about us
mortals? Not at all—he's given each of us our character to be
the captain of our soul. This is the guardian that's always with us;
it damns us when we treat it badly and saves us when we don't.
This is our god, and this is what's responsible for whether we live
happily or unhappily, every one of us. Just win its favor by not
doing anything stupid or out of place, and you'll live happily.

SMICRINES (*snarling*) And I suppose, you little sneak, my character
is doing something stupid right now?

ONESIMUS (*solemnly*) It's ruining you.

SMICRINES (*outraged*) Of all the insolence!

ONESIMUS (*with an air of great patience and righteousness*) Smicrines,
do you think it's the right thing to do, to take your daughter away
from her husband?

SMICRINES Who's talking about the right thing? It's simply something
that's got to be done.

ONESIMUS (*to Sophrona, shaking his head*) You see? According to this
fellow's way of thinking, a man must do the wrong thing.
(*Shaking his head commiseratingly*) Some other god, not his
character, is ruining this man. (*To Smicrines*) Well, this time
just as you were rushing to do something wicked, sheer luck
has saved you. You've arrived just in time to find everybody

reconciled and all your troubles solved. (*Sternly*) But, Smicrines, I warn you—don't let me catch you doing anything rash again. (*Grandly*) Right now I consider you absolved of any such charges. You may go in and say hello to your grandson.

SMICRINES (*fuming*) Grandson? I'll have you horsewhipped!

ONESIMUS (*scornfully*) You thought you were so smart. You were as thick as the others! Is that the way you kept an eye on a grown-up daughter? Look at the result—now we have a prodigy to raise, a baby that needed only five months of pregnancy!

SMICRINES (*utterly confused*) I don't know what you're talking about.

ONESIMUS I'll bet the old woman here does. (*Turning to Sophrona*) Sophrona, my master was the one who grabbed her and dragged her off from the dancing at the Tauropolia—understand me?

SOPHRONA (*nodding vigorously*) Oh, yes.

ONESIMUS And now they've recognized each other and everything is fine.

SMICRINES (*to Sophrona*) What does he mean, you lying old hag?

SOPHRONA (*quoting from Euripides' play, the* Auge, *in which Heracles identified a child of his by a ring*)

For Nature wished it so. She spurns all laws—
And fashioned womankind for just this cause.

SMICRINES (*more confused than ever*) Have you gone out of your mind?

SOPHRONA (*sharply*) I'll recite a whole speech from the *Auge* if you don't start using your brains, Smicrines.

SMICRINES (*testily*) You and your histrionics are going to make me lose my temper. You really understand what he's talking about?

SOPHRONA (*firmly*) Every word.

ONESIMUS Believe me, she knew about it a long time ago.

SMICRINES This is terrible!

SOPHRONA It's the best thing that's ever happened! (*To Onesimus*) If what you say is true and the baby . . .

[The rest of the act is lost, but the plot is virtually complete at this point: Charisius and Pamphila had been reconciled by the end of Act IV, and now Smicrines joins them. If Habrotonon and Onesimus had not received their freedom earlier, they very likely were given it before the final curtain.]

She Who Was Shorn

I

DRAMATIS PERSONAE

Polemon, a wealthy, young professional army officer
Sosias, his orderly (slave)
Glycera, a free-born, but poor, girl living with Polemon
Doris, her maid (slave)
Moschion, a young man about town, adopted son of Myrrhina
Davus, servant (slave) of Moschion's family
Pataecus, an elderly friend of Polemon
[*Myrrhina,* foster-mother of Moschion]

SCENE A street in Corinth. Three house entrances front on it: the one in the middle is that of Myrrhina and Moschion, her adopted son; on one side is that of Polemon, on the other that of Pataecus. The exit on stage left leads downtown, that on stage right to the open country.

ACT I

[About 120 lines are lost before the preserved portion begins, but we can deduce with a fair degree of certainty what they told.

The first scene introduced the protagonists of the play, Polemon and Glycera. Polemon was a young but experienced professional army officer who had spent all his adult years in the field and always among men; though basically of a good, even fine, character, he could at times act violently and impulsively, a failing that had hardly been helped by his way of life. He had been successful in his chosen career and had made enough money to buy a house and settle down. He had even been lucky enough to come upon a very desirable girl to live with. Glycera was young, attractive, and charming, but, since she was poor—in other words, had no dowry—life as Polemon's common-law wife offered her, despite its obvious disadvantages, as comfortable a mode of existence as she could ever have hoped for. Moreover, she at the very least admired and respected him, and perhaps even loved him, while he was un-questionably very much in love with her.

After presenting the two, the scene must then have revealed the event that gives the play its name. Polemon, who had been away on campaign, returned unexpectedly one evening; the first sight that met his eyes was Glycera embracing Moschion, his neighbor's son, a pampered young playboy who rather fancied himself a ladies' man. Polemon, reacting instinctively, inflicted on Glycera an injury more visible and humiliating and lasting than the most merciless beating would have been. He treated her as the French did the girls who had taken German lovers during World War II: he cut off her hair. A moment later, as so often happens after an unthinking act, he was ap-palled by what he had done; unable to bear the sight, he fled into the house of his neighbor and friend, Pataecus.

The stage is now empty and a formal Prologue enters, Lady Ignorance, to tell the audience some facts it needs to know in order to follow the plot; she is a fitting enough choice for Prologue since ignorance is, in a sense, the mainspring for the play's action. Her words make clear both why Glycera was so poor and why she had been in the embrace of the boy next door.

The story she tells is this. Eighteen years ago, an old woman found in the fields an infant set of twins, a boy and a girl, and took them home. From this point on, we have the Prologue's own words.]

LADY IGNORANCE   She kept the girl but gave the boy to a rich woman
   —(*gesturing toward the house alongside Polemon's*) she lives here
   —who had no children of her own. That's the way it happened.
      Well, the years passed and, what with the war and things
   at Corinth going from bad to worse, the old woman was at the

end of her rope. The girl was now grown up—she's the one
you saw in the first scene—and, when that young hothead you've
just seen came along, since he was no stranger but a local
Corinthian boy and had fallen in love with the girl, the old
woman gave her to him, letting him think it was her own
daughter. But because she was by this time quite old and weary,
and had a feeling that her end was at hand, she decided not to
keep anything secret from the girl. The old woman told her she
was a foundling, gave her the baby clothes she had been found
in, and disclosed to her the unexpected news that she had a
blood brother. The old woman did this because she was minded of
the troubles that always happen in life, occasions when the girl
would need some help, and, so far as she could see, the boy
was her only relative. Besides, she wanted to guard against the
possibility that through ignorance, through my doing, the two
might involuntarily get involved with each other; for the old
woman was well aware that the boy was rich and drank too
much and the girl attractive and young, and that there was
nothing secure about the union she had entered into.

Now, the old woman died and, not long ago, the officer bought
this house (*gesturing toward Polemon's house*). Although the
girl has been living just next door, she's kept quiet about having
a brother. She doesn't want to disturb things when his prospects
look so bright. She wants him to enjoy everything his good
fortune has brought him. Well, as luck would have it, last night
he saw her when she happened to send her maid out on an
errand; as I mentioned, he's the type that will make advances
and when he went walking he always saw to it that he stayed
near her house. He saw her at the door, ran right up, took her
in his arms, and kissed her. She knew it was her brother, of
course, and didn't try to break away—and at that moment along
comes the officer and sees everything. You've heard what happened next from his own lips: how he took himself off telling
her that he wanted to see her later and how she stood there
crying, brokenhearted, over the way circumstances wouldn't per-
mit her to do what she wanted.

Now, all of this has erupted because of what's to come: to get
him (*with a gesture toward Polemon's house*) to whip himself
into a lather—it's all my doing, of course; it's not his way to be

like that—, to get the disclosures that are in store under way, and
to have the twins find out who they are. If any of you are re-
volted by what's happened and consider it disgraceful, you'll
change your mind. God can turn even evil into good. Goodbye,
dear audience, be kind to us, and enjoy what you are going to
see.

(*It is the morning after Polemon's violent act. The door of Pataecus'
house, where Polemon is now staying, opens and Sosias, his orderly,
comes out. Sosias is a tough old-line army man, and he takes a very
dim view of such unmilitary conduct as getting upset over a woman.*)

SOSIAS (*to himself, scornfully*)   Well, our man who's so set against
women having hair, who was stomping around a while ago
spoiling for a fight, is now flat on his back crying his eyes out.
Just now, when I left, breakfast was being served and all his
friends had rallied round to buck him up. (*Gesturing toward
Polemon's house, where Glycera was still staying*) Since he's
got no way of knowing what's going on here, he's purposely
sent me out to get him a coat. (*Grumbling*) He doesn't really
need it; just wants me to have the exercise.

(*At this moment, the door of Polemon's house opens and Doris,
Glycera's maid, comes out. She turns and speaks to Glycera inside.*)

DORIS (*through the doorway*)   I'll go and see, ma'am.
SOSIAS (*to himself*)   It's Doris. (*Admiring the change that has taken
place since he and Polemon had left to take the field*) Look at
her—not bad! Nothing wrong with the way these girls are living,
if you ask me. But I'd better get going. (*As Doris leaves the
threshold of Polemon's house, Sosias enters it.*)
DORIS (*to herself, as she crosses over to the door of Myrrhina's house*)
There's nobody around outside; I'll have to knock. (*Indignantly*)
I pity the poor girl who has an army man for a husband. They're
all a bunch of lawbreakers; you can't trust any of them. What
my poor mistress has to put up with! (*Shouting*) Hey, someone,
open the door! (*To herself*) That brute will be delighted that
she's crying now, if he hears about it; that's just what he's after.
(*A servant finally opens the door.*) Please tell . . .

[About seventy lines are missing here, but what happened can be
reconstructed. Sosias came out of Polemon's house with the coat—his

grumbling to the contrary, his master could well use it; the only clothes
he had was the uniform on his back—and went into Pataecus' house
to deliver it. Doris and Myrrhina then came on stage. Doris explained
the situation to Myrrhina and asked her to take Glycera in. She agreed,
Glycera hurried over, and Myrrhina sent the family servant, Davus,
with a group of slaves to transfer Glycera's possessions. Davus responded
with alacrity—he was under the impression that Myrrhina was aiding
and abetting a love affair for that pampered son of hers. When the
text resumes, he and his men have left Polemon's house and are approaching Myrrhina's door.]

DAVUS (*hustling his squad, loaded down with Glycera's belongings, into
    Myrrhina's house*) Boys, there's a mob of youngsters heading
    this way, and they're drunk. (*To himself*) My congratulations
    to our mistress—she's moving the girl into our house. That's
    what I call a mother! I've got to find Moschion. If you ask me,
    this is just the time for him to get here—and fast!

(*Davus goes off, stage left. The stage is now empty, and a chorus—
the "mob of youngsters" Davus had mentioned—enters and dances
an entr'acte.*)

ACT II

(*Davus and Moschion enter, stage left. Moschion is a dashing, handsome young fellow, fastidiously groomed, and wearing clothes that, although obviously expensive, are a trifle too flashy to be in the best of
taste. More than his dress, however, his whole bearing reveals at a
glance the spoiled, only son of an indulgent mother.*)

MOSCHION (*menacingly*) Davus, you're a godforsaken faker. You've
    told me lots of things before that turned out to be lies. If you're
    lying to me now—
DAVUS If I'm lying to you now, you can hang me.
MOSCHION That's letting you off too easy.
DAVUS (*unabashed*) Go right ahead. Treat me like an enemy. But
    supposing it's true? Suppose you really find the girl in your
    house? Since I arranged the whole deal for you—I had to talk
    for hours to get the girl to move in, and to get your mother to

take her in and do everything you'd want—what do I get out
of it?

MOSCHION *(blandly)* Well, Davus, what would you like best to do
for a living?

DAVUS *(warily)* Let me think it over.

MOSCHION *(who, obviously having taken a lot from Davus in the past,
is glad to get the chance to turn the tables for once)* Don't you
think making little ones out of big ones would suit you perfectly?

DAVUS *(in alarm, not sure whether Moschion is joking)* The rock
pile? Me?

MOSCHION *(to the audience, pointing to Davus)* If you ask me, he's
heading right in that direction.

DAVUS *(with a shudder)* Don't mention the word!

MOSCHION *(assuming an air of serious deliberation)* I'd like to see you
become military governor of Greece and paymaster general of
the armies.

DAVUS What? And have a gang of soldiers slit my throat when they
catch my fingers in the till?

MOSCHION Why don't you become commissioner of public works?
Then you could really steal. You could pocket eighty-five per
cent of every contract and nobody'd notice it.

DAVUS *(very seriously)* Moschion, I'd like to run a little stall downtown, sell groceries or cheese. I swear, I don't want to become
a millionaire. No, that's what I'd really like.

MOSCHION *(putting on an air of being incensed at him for not having
a more ambitious spirit)* What? Like some old hag of a
peddler?

DAVUS I just want my three squares a day. And I say I've earned it.
I told you what I did for you.

MOSCHION All right. Go peddle cheeses, and god be with you.

DAVUS Amen. *(As they reach the door of Myrrhina's house)* Well,
the girl you're dying for is here. So, in you go.

MOSCHION Good idea; that's what I'll do. And now it's up to me to
hand her a line and get the laugh on a certain damned gold-
braided colonel.

DAVUS Right.

MOSCHION But, first, Davus, you go in and scout the whole situation.
Find out what she's doing, where my mother is, how they feel

about my coming in. I don't need to go into details with you in this sort of thing; you're a smart boy.

DAVUS I'm off.

MOSCHION (*calling out as Davus goes into the house*) I'll walk around in front of the door here and wait for you. (*To himself, as he struts up and down*) She let me know how the land lay when I went up to her yesterday evening. When I ran toward her, she didn't run away; just put her arms around me and kissed me. (*Smugly*) You ask me, I'm not so bad to look at, and not so bad to be with; by god, I'm the type girls go for. It's my luck, knock on wood.

(*Davus comes running out.*)

DAVUS (*excitedly*) Moschion, she's got herself all dressed up, and she's sitting down inside!

MOSCHION (*to himself, rapturously*) Sweetheart!

DAVUS Your mother's walking around arranging god knows what. But breakfast is on the table and I think, from what's going on, they're waiting for you.

MOSCHION (*smugly, to the audience*) Didn't I tell you? I'm not bad, not bad at all. (*To Davus*) Did you tell them I was here?

DAVUS No, I didn't.

MOSCHION You go right inside and tell them!

DAVUS Right. Back I go. (*Hurries back into the house.*)

MOSCHION (*to himself*) She's going to be embarrassed when I come in, of course, and she'll hide her face. They all do it. The first step is to kiss my mother and win her over completely; get the flattery going and spend every minute just doing things for her. You'd think this was all her affair, the way she's handled it! Ah, someone's coming out. (*Davus comes out and walks slowly toward Moschion, shaking his head; obviously he is puzzled about something.*) Well, what's the story? Davus! What are you hanging back like that for?

DAVUS God in heaven! The whole thing's crazy. I went in and I told your mother you were here and she says: "None of that! How did he hear about it? Did you go and tell him this poor girl was so frightened she had to come running to us?" "Sure," says I. "Oh, I hope you drop dead!" says she, "And you can just clear out of here right now. I'm busy." What more can I tell you?

We've lost everything. She certainly wasn't overjoyed to hear you were around.

MOSCHION (*eyeing him balefully*)   I'm going to give it to you—you've been pulling a fast one on me!

DAVUS   Don't be ridiculous. Your mother—

MOSCHION (*suddenly aware of the implications of the conversation just reported to him*)   What did you just say? Something about her not coming here of her own free will? She didn't come because of me? (*Accusingly*) Then just how did you talk her into coming here for my sake?

DAVUS (*with an air of utter incredulity*)   I said I talked her into coming? As god's my witness I did nothing of the sort! (*With injured innocence*) You couldn't have said anything more untrue.

MOSCHION (*taking a threatening step toward him*)   You didn't tell me just now that you talked my mother into taking her in for my sake?

DAVUS   Well, you see—(*as Moschion raises an arm*) yes, I did say that. Yes, it comes back to me now.

MOSCHION   And that you thought she was doing it just for me?

DAVUS   I don't want to say that—(*as Moschion's arm goes up again*) but I admit I urged her.

MOSCHION (*with an air of finality*)   That does it. Come here!

DAVUS (*still acting the innocent*)   Where?

MOSCHION (*grimly*)   Not very far.

DAVUS (*sparring desperately for time*)   Moschion, there's something or other you ought to know—er—I—er—at that time—er—(*as Moschion takes a threatening step closer*) wait, just a second!

MOSCHION (*his patience exhausted*)   Are you still trying to fool around with me?

DAVUS   No, I swear to god! (*Suddenly getting an idea to get himself out of his fix*) Listen to me, please. Maybe she doesn't want to give in, you understand, right off the bat, just like that. Maybe she feels she ought to get to know you and hear what you've got to say. Sure, that's it. Remember, this is no chorus girl or cheap whore who's come to you.

MOSCHION   Now you're making sense again.

DAVUS   Give it a try. You know how it is. She's left her house—I wasn't kidding you there. So if you'll just be willing to hold off

for three or four days, she'll come around. I've got it on good
authority. (*Desperately*) You have to listen to me now!

MOSCHION (*with ominous calm*) You've figured out a fine full four-
day furlough for me. All right, Davus, I'll just tie you up in the
meantime. Where do you want to be left? (*Dropping his assumed calm, angrily*) A minute ago you were making sense and
now you're back to nonsense.

DAVUS Give me a chance to think in peace, will you? Why don't you
reform and be a nice fellow—and go inside.

MOSCHION (*suspiciously*) And let you run away?

DAVUS (*scornfully*) Oh, sure. How far do you think I'd get, anyway,
on the money I've got? No, I've got an idea that if you go inside
you could straighten things out a bit.

MOSCHION All right. I agree. You win. (*He goes into the house.*)

DAVUS (*mopping his brow, to himself*) Lord, that was close! I'm still
shivering. This isn't going to be as easy as I thought.

(*Davus is just about to follow Moschion into Myrrhina's house when
he notices Sosias come out of Pataecus' house. Sosias had earlier brought
Polemon a coat to wear; now he is bringing back part of Polemon's
uniform. He is getting fed up with these comings and goings and is
grumbling as he comes on stage.*)

SOSIAS (*to himself*) He's sent me back with this tunic and sword to
get a look at what she's doing and report back to him. I'm just
about ready to tell him I caught her lover in the house—*that*'d
bring him here on the double. No, I won't; I pity him too much.
Never saw such a poor devil, not even in a nightmare. What a
homecoming he's had! (*Enters Polemon's house.*)

DAVUS (*to himself, unobserved by Sosias*) So, the army's back, eh?
That's not so good; no, sir, not good at all. (*Suddenly aware of
what would happen if Myrrhina's husband were to barge in and
discover what was going on*) But I haven't yet entered the chief
debit in the books: if my master happens to get back from the
country in a hurry and makes an appearance—what a riot *he'll*
raise!

(*The door of Polemon's house opens and Sosias appears. He has
found out that Glycera is gone. As he comes out, he shouts at the
servants inside.*)

SOSIAS (*through the doorway*)   You let her get away, you godforsaken
dumbbells; you let her get out of the house!
DAVUS (*to himself*)   Here he comes back—and he's sore! I'd better get
out of the way. (*Moves off to a spot on the side from where, unobserved, he can overhear and keep an eye on Sosias.*)

(*Sosias starts toward Pataecus' house to make his report, and then
suddenly stops short as a thought strikes him.*)

SOSIAS (*to himself*)   That's it! She's told us to go to the devil, and
she's gone off to her lover next door.
DAVUS (*to himself*)   That's no orderly, that's a mind reader our colonel
has there. He's hit the nail on the head.
SOSIAS (*turning around and going up to Myrrhina's house*)   I'll knock
on the door. (*He knocks.*)

(*Davus, deciding the time is ripe to take a hand, comes out of his
hiding place.*)

DAVUS   Hey, you! What the devil are you after? Where do you think
you're going?
SOSIAS (*gesturing toward Myrrhina's house*)   You belong here?
DAVUS   Maybe. But what are you poking your nose around here for?

(*At this point, in answer to Sosias' knock, Doris comes to the door.
Sensing what is happening, she moves off to the side to listen.*)

SOSIAS (*angrily*)   God in heaven, are you people out of your mind?
Some nerve you have to keep a free-born woman locked up in
violation of the rights of her legal guardian!
DORIS (*aside*)   Just like a sniveling good-for-nothing like you to think
up something like that!
SOSIAS (*with a sweeping gesture toward Polemon's house*)   Maybe you
think we don't have guts? We're not men, eh?
DAVUS (*sneering*)   Men? Tin soldiers!
SOSIAS (*backing down a bit since all he could muster was a parcel of
slaves and since his own courage had a way of getting unstuck
easily*)   Yeah? But when an iron man leads them, we won't
have any trouble taking you people on.
DAVUS   This is a damned outrage!
SOSIAS   Come on, admit you've got her. (*Turning to Polemon's house
and calling to one of the servants there*)   Hey, you! Hilarion!

Come here! (*No movement from the house. He turns back to Davus.*) He's gone somewhere. He happened to see it all, and he says you've got her.

DAVUS   We don't have her.

SOSIAS   You people are going to feel sorry for this. Who do you think you're fooling around with, anyway? What sort of nonsense is this? Why, we'll launch a full-scale attack, storm that miserable shack of yours, and take it in a minute. Better tell lover-boy to strip for action.

DAVUS (*shaking his head in mock sorrow*)   You poor guy—pretty tough waiting around all this time because you thought we had her in our house.

SOSIAS   Our commando troops will sweep the field before you can bat an eye—tin soldiers, eh?

DAVUS (*scornfully*)   I was joking: you're just a hick.

SOSIAS (*blustering*)   Well, you city types—

DAVUS (*who knows that Sosias is just so much wind, and has listened to enough of it, interrupting*)   Listen—we haven't got her.

SOSIAS (*screaming with rage*)   Yahhh! Wait till I get my spear—

DAVUS (*turning away, disgustedly*)   Oh, go to hell. I'm going in now—and I'm staying there until you come to your senses.

(*Davus goes into Myrrhina's house. As Sosias stands there, baffled, Doris calls to him from the spot where she has been standing unobserved.*)

DORIS   Sosias!

SOSIAS (*swiveling around and starting to bluster the minute he sees her*)   Doris, just come over here, and I'll give it to you. You're to blame for all this.

DORIS (*urgently*)   Oh, Sosias, please! Please tell him that she got terribly frightened and ran away to some woman.

SOSIAS (*puzzled*)   To some woman? Got terribly frightened?

DORIS   That's right. She's gone to Myrrhina, her neighbor here. So help me, it's the truth!

SOSIAS (*disgusted and infuriated*)   Don't you realize where she's gone? That's just where her lover is! (*He takes a step toward her.*)

DORIS (*retreating*)   Now, don't be hasty, Sosias!

SOSIAS (*as before*)   Go on, get out of here! To go lie—

[About sixty lines are lost at this point. Presumably Sosias reported what he had found out to Polemon and suggested they follow out the threat he had made to Davus and break into Myrrhina's house. To Sosias this procedure had two advantages: it would enable him to get even with Davus, and Polemon to carry Glycera off by force. Since Polemon was by training prejudiced in favor of such pseudo-military actions in the first place, and since he had had too much to drink in the second, he agreed. They sallied forth at the head of a motley group of household slaves; even Habrotonon, a courtesan who had been hired to help cheer Polemon up, joined the "army." Fortunately Pataecus, the only clear head around, got them to agree to hold off until he had a chance to talk with Myrrhina and find out whatever he could that would throw light on Glycera's reasons for choosing to flee there.]

ACT III

(*As the act opens, Polemon and Sosias and their ragtail army are milling about in front of Myrrhina's house. The door opens and Pataecus, his parley with Myrrhina finished, comes out.*

Pataecus is old enough to be Glycera's father. You can see at a glance why Polemon had gone to him for help: his face is that of a man who has endured a good deal of suffering and from it learned compassion and calmness and resignation; clearly he is someone you can come to for sympathy and understanding, and can trust implicitly.

Sosias, with Polemon at his side and a few men at his back and more than a few drinks inside, is in no mood to give up the present promising opportunity to square accounts with Davus. The moment he catches sight of Pataecus he calls out to Polemon.)

SOSIAS (*excitedly*) Here he comes—and they've bribed him. Believe me, he's out to betray you and our army.

PATAECUS (*to Sosias, firmly but not unkindly*) Now, stop playing soldier boy and be a good fellow and go on home and sleep it off. You're not in good shape. (*Turning to Polemon*) I'll talk to you: you're not so drunk.

POLEMON (*pained*) Not so drunk? All I've had is just about one drink, damn it! I could see all this coming, so I kept an eye on myself.

PATAECUS Good. (*Firmly*) Now, I want you to do what I tell you.

POLEMON (*quietly*) What do you want me to do?

PATAECUS (*relieved at this reaction*) Now you're talking the way you should. All right, I'll tell you what it is.

SOSIAS (*realizing that Pataecus is on the point of winning out, shouts to Habrotonon, who has brought her flute with her and is acting as bugler for this "army"*) Habrotonon! Sound the charge!

PATAECUS (*to Polemon, mildly exasperated*) First, will you please send him away with that army of his?

SOSIAS (*to Pataecus, shouting*) What a way to fight a war! Demobilize the army? What we need is a full-scale attack! (*To Polemon*) This here Pataecus is ruining everything I've done. What's he know about being an officer?

POLEMON (*losing his temper, to Sosias*) For god's sake, get out of here!

SOSIAS (*grumbling*) All right, all right, I'm going. (*As he lurches away, he passes near the tempting figure of Habrotonon.*) Habrotonon, I really thought there was a job for you here. If a fellow wants to make an attack (*leering at her*) you're handy to have around; you know how to take a position. (*She eludes him as he makes a pass at her.*) What are you running away for, you whore? Embarrassed—you? This bothers you? (*Sosias, followed by his "army" moves off to the side of the stage, leaving Polemon and Pataecus alone in the center.*)

PATAECUS Now, Polemon, if something like what you've told me about had happened and the woman were your wife—

POLEMON (*interrupting impatiently*) What a thing to say, Pataecus! She *is*.

PATAECUS Ah, there's a difference.

POLEMON (*raising his voice in his vehemence*) I've always thought of her as my wife.

PATAECUS You don't have to shout. (*Gently*) All right, who betrothed her to you?

POLEMON (*taken aback by the question*) Who betrothed her to me? (*Weakly*) She did.

PATAECUS Very good. Maybe at one time she did like you. But she doesn't any longer. And, since you've treated her in a way you shouldn't have, she's left you.

POLEMON (*aggrieved*) What are you saying? In a way I shouldn't have? Now that's the most unkind cut of all!

PATAECUS I'm sure you'll admit that what you're doing now is madness. (*Vehemently*) What are you after? Who's this person you're out to abduct anyway? That girl is her own mistress. (*Firmly*) When a lover's not doing well, he has only one course left—persuasion.

POLEMON (*indignantly*) What about the fellow who ruined her while I was away? Hasn't he done me a wrong?

PATAECUS (*sympathetically but firmly*) He certainly has—and if you ever have it out with him, you can take him to court. But if you try any rough stuff, he'll have the law on you and he'll win. What he did gives you a legal cause of action, not carte blanche to go and take your own revenge.

POLEMON (*in desperation*) Not even now? (*that is, after, as he supposes, Glycera has been seduced into leaving*)

PATAECUS Not even now.

POLEMON (*wildly*) God in heaven, I don't know what to say—except that I'll burst a blood vessel! Glycera's left me. Pataecus, you hear? She's left me! Glycera! (*Getting control of himself with a visible effort*) Well, you're a good friend of hers and you've often talked things over with her in the past, so, please go and have a talk with her. I beg you, be my intermediary.

PATAECUS You can see I do think it's what's called for.

POLEMON (*anxiously*) You're a pretty good talker, aren't you, Pataecus?

PATAECUS (*dryly*) Pretty good.

POLEMON (*his control slipping away, and starting to talk wildly again*) You've got to be good, Pataecus. My life depends on it. If I've ever done her the least wrong—if I haven't every minute tried to—if you'd only take a look at the clothes I've bought her— (*Starts to pull him into the house.*)

PATAECUS (*anxious to get going on his difficult mission, and holding back*) It's all right—

POLEMON (*brushing aside Pataecus' reluctance and pulling him toward the door*) In the name of god, Pataecus, come look at them! Then you'll really feel sorry for me.

PATAECUS (*to himself, exasperated at the delay*) Oh, for god's sake!

POLEMON Come on. What dresses! And you ought to see how she looks when she puts one of them on. You've probably never seen her.

PATAECUS (*in a forlorn effort to get out of going inside*) Yes I have.

POLEMON (*absorbed in his own thoughts and not hearing him*) With that tall figure of hers—she was really something to see. (*Getting hold of himself again*) But what am I doing babbling about tall figures and things that don't concern us now? I must be out of my mind.

PATAECUS (*soothingly*) No, no; not at all.

POLEMON You mean that? Oh, but you've got to take a look at those clothes. Come on in. (*Literally hauling the reluctant Pataecus into the house*) After you.

PATAECUS (*resignedly*) I'm coming.

(*The two enter the house, followed by the "army" and, in the rear, Sosias. He is just lurching through the door when Moschion comes out of Myrrhina's house.*)

MOSCHION (*to the retreating army*) All right. Inside with the whole damn bunch of you. On the double. (*To himself, quoting a line of poetry*) "With lance in hand at me they sprang." They couldn't storm a bird's nest, not that gang. (*Imitating Davus' way of speaking*) "They've got a real regiment," he tells me. It's a great regiment, all right. Look at it. (*Pointing to Sosias reeling through the doorway*) One man. (*He paces up and down, deeply troubled; to the audience*) There are a lot of fellows in a bad way these days—with one thing and another, there's a bumper crop of them right now all over Greece—but I don't think there's a man among them all as badly off as I am. As soon as I went in, I didn't do any of the things I usually do— didn't go in to see my mother, didn't ring for any of the servants —I just went into a back room out of everybody's way and I lay down. I was all set. I sent Davus to my mother to tell her that I was home—just that, nothing else. But he finds their break- fast still on the table, forgets all about me, and stays to stow away a meal. In the meantime, I was lying there thinking to my- self, "Any minute my mother will be here with a message from my sweetheart telling me under what arrangement she says she'll come to me." I was working up a little speech myself—

[About 157 lines are lost at this point. Somehow or other, during this portion of the play, Moschion learned some highly disquieting news: that Davus had duped him and Glycera had come to his house not to join him but to escape from Polemon; and that he is a foundling. He

was even shown some of the objects—"birth tokens"—(see page 128)
that had been found with him.

Toward the end of this missing section, Pataecus and Glycera came
on stage. Pataecus presumably pleaded Polemon's cause as he had
promised and offered her generous terms if she would come back. When
the text resumes, Glycera is presenting her side of the matter, indignantly making clear to him the reason for her move next door. We are
by now somewhere in Act IV.]

ACT IV

*(Glycera and Pataecus are standing in front of Myrrhina's house. She
is refuting Pataecus' suspicion—which he had got from Polemon—that
she had fled to Myrrhina's to join Moschion as a mistress.)*

GLYCERA (*vehemently*)   My dear man, if that were the case, how could
I possibly have run to his mother? Obviously I didn't come here
to be his wife; (*bitterly and with irony that is, of course, lost on
Pataecus*) our different family backgrounds, you know. Well, if
not that, then did I come to be his mistress? In that case, for
god's sake wouldn't I have done everything I could to keep it
a secret from his parents—and wouldn't he have too? But he
went right ahead and introduced me to his father [*she is referring to Myrrhina's husband*]. Would I have deliberately acted
so senselessly? Deliberately made an enemy of Myrrhina, and
left all of you with an impression of me that you could never
get rid of? (*Her bitterness now mingled with anguish*) Have I
no sense of shame, Pataecus? Did you come here because you
were convinced, like the others, by what you had heard? Did
you take me for that sort of girl?

PATAECUS (*with conviction*)   God forbid! And may heaven help you
convince everybody else that what you tell me is true. As for
myself, I'm convinced.

GLYCERA   But I still want you to go away. (*Bitterly*) Let him insult
some other girl from now on.

PATAECUS (*soothingly*)   It was a terrible thing to do, but he didn't
really mean it.

GLYCERA (*as before*)   It was an ungodly thing to do. My god, you
wouldn't even treat a slave girl that way!

[Sixteen lines are lost here in which Glycera presumably revealed to Pataecus that she was a girl of good family and asserted that she had birth tokens to prove it. When the text resumes, she is talking about them. As it happens, the chest they were in was still in Polemon's house; she had left it there in her distraught state and, since it had been hidden away, Davus and his squad had overlooked it when they transferred her belongings.]

GLYCERA   I want you to do me a favor. I got these birth tokens from my mother and father and I've made a practice of always having them at my side where I can keep an eye on them.

PATAECUS   Well, what do you want to do about them?

GLYCERA   I want them brought here (*pointing to Myrrhina's house*).

PATAECUS   Then you're going to give Polemon up once and for all? (*She nods resolutely. He sighs resignedly.*) All right, my dear; now, what do you want from me?

GLYCERA   I want your permission to take them.

PATAECUS   All right—although I think it's ridiculous. (*Returning to the attack*) You ought to look at all sides—

GLYCERA   (*cutting him short*) I know what's best for me.

PATAECUS   Well, if that's the way you feel . . . Do any of the servants know where these things of yours are?

GLYCERA   Doris does.

PATAECUS   Have someone call her out here. (*Pataecus is hard to discourage. As a servant goes off to fetch Doris, he makes one last try*) Glycera, for god's sake, while there's still a chance, on the terms I've been telling you about—

(*At this point Doris, answering the summons, comes out of Myrrhina's house. Doris is in tears—her emotions are easily engaged and the whole affair has been getting her down.*)

DORIS   Ma'am!

GLYCERA   What's the matter?

DORIS   All this trouble!

GLYCERA   Doris, bring out that chest, you know, the one with those embroidered things in it that I gave you to take care of. Come on! What are you crying about? (*Doris goes off into Polemon's house.*)

PATAECUS   God in heaven, I've put up with—

[About 8 lines are lost here. When the text resumes, Doris has brought out the chest and Glycera and Pataecus are discussing a piece of fabric with embroidered figures on it that they found there.]

PATAECUS   Yes, I saw it then. (*Not looking at the piece and struggling to rouse a dim memory*) And the next one, wasn't it a goat or a bull or some such animal?

GLYCERA   It's a stag, my dear, not a goat.

PATAECUS   Something with horns, I remember that. And the third one is a winged horse. (*Aside, and not overheard by Glycera, who is preoccupied with the things in the chest, in anguish*) These things are my wife's! My poor wife's!

(*Absorbed in what they are doing, they are unaware that Moschion has come out of Myrrhina's house. He walks from the door aimlessly and moodily, jolted by the new knowledge that he is a foundling. After a moment he notices the two and, unobserved, draws near. The piece of embroidery catches his eye—and he steps back in astonishment on seeing that it is identical with a piece that had, but a short while ago, been shown to him as one of his birth tokens.*)

MOSCHION   (*aside, agitated*)   When I see this (*gesturing toward the embroidery that Glycera is holding*) I can only believe that my real mother had a daughter, too, whom she abandoned the same time she did me. And if this is what happened, then she's my sister and, heaven help me, I'm ruined! (*Carefully concealing himself, he eavesdrops intently.*)

PATAECUS   (*in a daze at the melodramatic turn events have taken, aside*)   Oh, God! What do they mean, these relics from my past?

GLYCERA   (*with no inkling of what her tokens convey to Pataecus, and only concerned to prove that they are really hers*)   Go ahead and ask me anything you want about them.

PATAECUS   (*intensely*)   Tell me, where did you get these?

GLYCERA   They were found with me when I was an infant.

MOSCHION   (*suddenly aware he had, in his excitement, been edging closer and closer to them, to himself*)   Back a little! Moschion, you're on the crest of a wave headed right for the crisis of your life!

PATAECUS   (*as before*)   Was it only you who was abandoned? (*Urgently*) Tell me!

GLYCERA   No. A brother was abandoned with me.

MOSCHION (*aside*)   Ah—that's one of the things I wanted to know.

PATAECUS   How did you become separated?

GLYCERA   I could tell you the whole story if I wanted; I've heard it all. But, please, ask me only about myself because I can talk about that. I swore to her that I wouldn't talk about the rest.

MOSCHION (*aside*)   Another clue for me. Plain as day: it's Myrrhina she swore to. (*Visibly shaken, he speaks unsteadily.*) I've got to find my bearings. . . . (*He slumps down to a seat and stares ahead vacantly, deaf for the moment to what is going on about him.*)

PATAECUS   Who was it who took you and brought you up?

GLYCERA   A woman found me lying there. She brought me up.

PATAECUS   Did she ever mention where she found you?

GLYCERA   She mentioned a spring in a shady spot.

PATAECUS (*dazedly, to himself*)   The very place he told me about after he exposed them.

GLYCERA (*caught up by Pataecus' words*)   Who was that? If it's no secret, let me know too.

PATAECUS (*slowly, uttering the words with visible effort*)   The one who exposed you was a slave. But the one who refused to raise his own children . . . was . . . I.

(*He stands with head bowed and eyes averted. Glycera stares at him. Her joy at discovering her father is for the moment overbalanced by her sense of injury at the life she has been forced into by his one and only act as a father.*)

GLYCERA   *You* exposed me? My own father! (*Agonizedly*) Why, why?

PATAECUS (*speaking in a low voice and, eschewing ordinary language, selecting his words with extreme care*)   My child, Fate does many incredible things. Your mother, soon after giving birth to you, left this life. And just the day before she died—

GLYCERA   What happened? Oh, I'm almost afraid to hear!

PATAECUS   I became a pauper—I who had always lived in comfort.

GLYGERA   In one day? Oh, god, how terrible! But how?

PATAECUS   I received the news that the ship which represented my whole livelihood had gone down in a storm in the Aegean.

GLYCERA   A terrible stroke of luck—for me!

PATAECUS   I thought that to try to raise two children, now that I was a beggar, was completely senseless, like trying to sail with a pair of anchors dragging. (*Both are silent for a moment.*) Do you have the rest of the things, my child?

GLYCERA   Which ones?

PATAECUS   Whatever was left with you.

GLYCERA   Let me list them. There were a necklace and a little jeweled adornment to identify us.

PATAECUS   Let's take a look at that.

GLYCERA   We can't.

PATAECUS   Why?

GLYCERA   My brother got all the rest, you know.

(*Moschion has come out of his trance and is now aware of what is passing between Pataecus and Glycera.*)

MOSCHION (*aside*)   My god! This man is my father!

PATAECUS   Could you give me some details?

GLYCERA (*thinking*)   There was a purple belt.

PATAECUS (*nodding*)   Yes, there was.

GLYCERA   With dancing girls embroidered on it.

MOSCHION (*recognizing from the description one of his birth tokens, aside*)   So you know about that!

GLYCERA   And a woman's wrap of sheer fabric and a gold headband. There, I've listed them all.

PATAECUS (*going toward her, his arms open wide*)   My dear girl, I can't restrain myself—

(*As Pataecus goes to embrace Glycera, Moschion rushes forward and reveals himself.*)

MOSCHION (*wildly*)   If I go away, you won't need to have anything to do with me! (*Seeing them staring at him*) I've been here all the time—I've overheard everything you said!

PATAECUS   God in heaven, who is this?

MOSCHION   Who am I? Your son!

[At this dramatic climax there is a break of at least a hundred lines. Undoubtedly there was a highly charged rapprochement between father and son, and protestations and explanations between sister and brother. And Glycera's belongings must have made a second trip, this time from Myrrhina's house to Pataecus'. Installing Glycera there involved, naturally, dispossessing Polemon, and the soldier, in the course of being told why, learned of Glycera's great good luck. The news plunged him into even deeper depths of despair: in the light of her new rank, his brutal act seemed worse than ever and his chances of getting her back even more remote. When the text resumes, he is bewailing his sorry state to Doris. We are now somewhere in Act V.]

ACT V

(Doris and Polemon are standing in front of his house. Polemon is in bad shape: he is drawn and haggard, his hair is unkempt, and his clothes are in utter disarray.)

POLEMON (*wildly*)   And so, I decided to hang myself!

DORIS (*taking him seriously and horrified*)   No! You mustn't!

POLEMON (*as before*)   But what am I going to do, Doris? Without Glycera what good is this miserable life of mine?

DORIS (*reassuringly*)   She'll come back to you.

POLEMON (*shaking his head in a vigorous negative*)   Oh, god! You don't know what you're saying.

DORIS   She will—if you're ready and willing to behave yourself from now on.

POLEMON (*babbling with excitement*)   I will, I will. I'll watch every step I make. My dear girl, you're right, you're absolutely right. You go to her. Doris, I'll set you free first thing tomorrow. Listen, here's what you've got to say— (*As Doris turns and runs into Pataecus' house, to himself*) She's gone in. Oh, Glycera, you've got me completely in your power! (*Paces up and down for a moment in silence. Then, with bitter self-recrimination*) It was no lover you kissed that time; it was your brother. And I was so jealous and hipped on getting even, I thought you were deceiving me and I went berserk on the spot. So, I was going to hang myself—and a good thing too. (*To Doris as she comes out of Pataecus' house, eagerly*) Doris, my girl! What's the news?

DORIS (*excitedly*)   It's good. She's coming out to see you.

POLEMON (*incredulously*)   She was joking.

DORIS   Lord, no! She's all dressed up. Her father can't take his eyes off her. You know what you ought to do? Arrange a party right now to celebrate her good luck and the happy ending of all these troubles!

POLEMON (*enthusiastically*) By god, that's a great idea! My cook's inside; just came back from shopping. I'll have him prepare a pork roast.

DORIS What about all the trimmings?

POLEMON Let him worry about those later. I want him to get going on the pig. And I want to grab a garland from some altar and put it on.

DORIS (*smiling as she observes his far from partylike general appearance*) Oh, yes, that'll make you look lots more convincing for the occasion.

POLEMON You can bring her out now.

DORIS She'll be out any minute. Her father too.

POLEMON (*nervous as a schoolboy*) He too? (*As the door of Pataecus' house starts to open*) Oh, my god! (*Loses his nerve completely and bolts into his house.*)

DORIS (*calling after him*) Hey! What are you doing? (*To herself*) He's gone. What's so terrible about a door opening? Well, I'll go in too; maybe there's something I can lend a hand with.

(*Doris follows Polemon into his house. A moment later Glycera, elegantly dressed, and Pataecus enter.*)

PATAECUS I was simply delighted when you said you were willing to be reconciled. When you are riding high, to be willing to accept what is fair—that's the mark of the Greek character. (*To his slaves in the house*) Someone go call Polemon.

POLEMON (*bursting out from behind his door where he had obviously been eavesdropping*) I'm coming! (*He hurries over to them, then stands embarrassed and ill at ease.*) I heard that Glycera had found the ones she was looking for, so I was inside arranging a party to celebrate the good news.

PATAECUS (*nodding vigorously*) You're absolutely right. Now listen to me; I have something to tell you. (*Solemnly*) Do you, Polemon, take this woman for your lawfully wedded wife?

POLEMON (*promptly*) I do.

PATAECUS Her dowry is ninety thousand dollars.

POLEMON Fine!

PATAECUS (*warningly*) From now on, forget that you're a soldier. Absolutely no more of this going wild and flying off the handle.

POLEMON (*fervently*) A man who missed ruin by a hair to fly off the handle again? God, no! What's more, I'll never even find any fault in my Glycera. (*Turning to her*) Sweetheart! Are we reconciled?

GLYCERA As it turned out, your going berserk was the beginning of our happiness.

POLEMON How true!

GLYCERA And for that reason I forgive you.

POLEMON (*turning to Pataecus*) Pataecus, you'll come to the party?

PATAECUS There's another marriage I've got to look after. I'm getting Philinus' daughter for my son.

POLEMON Well!—

[The manuscript breaks off here, but we are almost certainly within a few lines of the end of the play.]

Roman Comedy

/

Plautus' The Haunted House
The Rope
Terence's Phormio
The Brothers

The Spread of Greek New Comedy

When Aristophanes sat down to write a comedy, he had in mind its presentation at a particular place and time: the Theater of Dionysus in Athens during either of the two great Dionysiac festivals. A century later Athenian drama had become as ubiquitous in the Greek-speaking world as the movies in America: it was played in theaters from Italy to deep in Asia Minor, some of which were even grander and more capacious than that at Athens. The goal of every aspiring playwright and actor was still Athens—it was to take another century before she had to share this distinction with other cities—and Athenian audiences had, as before, the privilege of being the first to see the new productions. But they were no longer the last. Athens was now Broadway and Hollywood combined, not only the spiritual home of the drama but the source of theatrical fare for the rest of the Greek world as well. Professional troupes presented the latest hits of Menander or Diphilus before audiences in the Aegean Isles, Asia Minor, North Africa, and—most important of all for the history of the theater—southern Italy.

As early as 700 B.C., two centuries and a half before Aristophanes was born, the lower part of Italy, from Naples through Sicily, had been largely taken over by Greeks, and their populous and well-to-do cities dotted the region. By the fourth century B.C., each had its own theater where the local folk could see everything from native farces and skits to the latest imports of New Comedy from Athens or revivals of the *chef d'œuvres* of Euripides.

The Beginnings of Roman Comedy

To the north of this area lay Rome. In Aristophanes' day it was an obscure little nation. By Menander's time it had become an important state, already of some size and showing a penchant for expansion. Between 300 and 200 B.C., the Romans, in the opening stages of the great push that was ultimately to carry them the length and breadth of the Mediterranean, extended their frontier southward to the coasts of Sicily and swallowed up, along with everything else, the Greek towns they found there. In the process they developed a hearty appetite for Greek culture, including a considerable taste for that delectable dish, Greek drama. In 240 B.C., a Greek named Livius Andronicus adapted a Greek comedy and tragedy for presentation before a Roman audience, and Roman drama was launched.

The Greeks did not actually open Roman eyes to the theater, for Rome had a drama of its own. Village fiestas featured several types of short, boisterous farce, including one in which song and dance played an important part. But it was all rather primitive fare. The Latin versions of Greek plays that Livius introduced quickly took their place alongside the native product and, in larger communities, easily outstripped it in popularity. Livius was followed by Gnaeus Naevius (ca. 270–201 B.C.), Rome's first native playwright, who, in addition to adapting Greek works, inaugurated true Roman drama by writing completely original Latin comedies and historical plays. His efforts seem to have had a good deal of merit, but unfortunately almost nothing from his pen has been preserved. The distinction of having produced the earliest Latin plays to survive—and of being, at the same time, an outstanding figure in the history of the Western theater—belongs to a younger contemporary of Naevius, the comic playwright Plautus.

Plautus (ca. 254–184 B.C.)

Titus Maccius Plautus was, first and foremost, a man of the theater. Tradition has it that he made his living for a while as an actor in native farces. It may well be true: his plays give every indication that the author was intimately aware of what went on behind and in front of the stage as well as on it.

The conditions under which a playwright worked in the Rome of Plautus' day were far different from those that faced the poets of Greek New Comedy. The latter wrote for the sophisticated Athenian audience, and their end was recognition, to win a prize at a festival of Dionysus. Plautus wrote to amuse a motley, far from sophisticated crowd of Romans, and his end was to make money.

In Plautus' time there were at least four annual festivals whose programs included drama, and special events such as the funerals of great men or victory celebrations provided still further opportunities for a playwright. On none of these occasions were plays featured, as in Greece. They were offered as just one more item on a bill of fare of popular entertainment: the Roman officials who ran the festivals simply hired a theatrical troupe along with the required number of gladiators, boxers, wrestlers, funambulists, and so on. The troupes, small groups of five or six actors, generally of Greek extraction, were managed by a *dominus gregis,* or "leader of the troupe," who entered into a contract with the appropriate officials to supply a given number of plays. They paid him a lump sum and provided the facilities: a temporary wooden structure consisting of a long, low, narrow stage with a backdrop that presented two or three house fronts, and temporary wooden bleachers for the audience. It was the job of the *dominus* to find scripts for his troupe to put on. He either bought them himself or recommended their purchase by the officials.

Plautus was, therefore, in much the same position as a dramatist of today. He had to peddle his plays to the Roman equivalent of a Broadway producer; they had to pass the hard-eyed scrutiny of a man who knew that, if what he bought failed to please, he was not likely to be offered a contract when the next festival came around. And, when presented, they had to compete, not with other plays, but with gladiatorial combats and boxing and wrestling events.

Plautus pleased. During his lifetime he became a famous and successful writer. He sold upward of fifty comedies, of which twenty have been preserved more or less in their entirety. And these show why he pleased: to Plautus the play was not the thing; the audience was. The customers were rude Romans who had come to laugh from the belly, and he did his level best to accommodate them. He had no hesitation in interrupting the flow of the action at any point for a scene of pure slapstick or for a series of jokes, much the same way a screen writer today will interrupt the action of a scenario for the intrusive rendition of a popular song; he labeled the characters by making up broadly comic names for them; he explained every turn of the plot painstakingly to make sure the slowest wits could follow it; he even explained the jokes to make sure everyone got them. He added songs to vary the fare and appeal to the traditional Italian taste for music. At all costs he kept the pot of the action boiling, the stream of gags and puns and comic alliterations flowing swiftly and steadily. It is pointless to criticize

Plautus for not providing real endings for his plots, for introducing characters and then abruptly dropping them, for making, in a word, the most elementary mistakes in playwriting; his defense would very likely have been the same one offered us today by the writers who grind out television scripts or carpenter successful Broadway farces: he was giving the audience what it wanted.

In fashioning a play Plautus, following in the footsteps of Livius, began with a Greek original, a work by one of the writers of Greek New Comedy. But he quickly parts company with Livius who more or less faithfully rendered his originals into Latin. Since a strict translation of a play by Menander or even the more boisterous Diphilus would have had as little appeal for a Roman audience as one of Bernard Shaw's for the crowd at a baseball game, Plautus generally took from the Greek only the outline of the plot, the characters, and selected segments of the dialogue, and then stepped out on his own. In a sense he worked the way playwrights of today do when they convert a "legitimate" comedy into a musical. Along with his revamping of the dialogue, he replaced the relatively simple metrical pattern of the original with one more complex and, perhaps as a carry-over from his youthful days as an actor in native farce, introduced frequent scenes in song and dance (since the music for these portions has been lost, Plautus poses for the modern reader the same problem Aristophanes does [cf. page 5], although to a lesser degree). None of the Greek plays he adapted has survived, and we consequently can't be certain of the exact extent of his changes, but it is clear that they were far-reaching. *The Rope,* for example, very likely has much less in common with the play by Diphilus from which it was taken than, say, *My Fair Lady* has with Shaw's *Pygmalion.*

Plautus has been as popular after death as he was during his lifetime. Probably no one writer has had so profound an influence on the history of comedy. If he owes a debt to his Greek predecessors, later playwrights of the highest stature have evened the score by being indebted to him, from Shakespeare in the sixteenth century (*The Comedy of Errors* is based on *The Twin Menaechmi*) to Giraudoux in the twentieth (*Amphitryon 38* is an adaptation of the *Amphitruo*). It was Plautus who—along with Terence—kept the spirit of Greek New Comedy alive for the modern world and enabled it to make its great contribution to later literature, the novel as well as the theater. Dickens' Sam Weller, Wodehouse's Jeeves, the girls in the movies who come from the wrong side of the tracks and then turn out to be the long-lost daughters of eminently eligible parents—these and countless others are lineal descendants of Tranio, Trachalio, Palaestra, and others of Plautus' dramatis personae.

That as many as twenty of Plautus' plays have been preserved forces the compiler of an anthology to make some hard decisions. Even after he has eliminated those that are clearly of second rank, he is left with half a dozen or so that qualify for inclusion. The two presented here illustrate the variety of the playwright's output. *The Haunted House* is an example of Plautus at his best, when he was writing pure farce. The most popular of his works in this vein is *The Twin Menaechmi*, and it may be argued that I should have chosen it instead; I felt, however, that there was much to be said for selecting a play that is less widely known and, in my judgment, just as successful. The other, *The Rope*, is an example of his more romantic style. The plot, one typical of Greek New Comedy, is as important to the play as the purely comic scenes, and these, in line with the general tenor of the work, are of a somewhat higher order of humor than the unabashed tomfoolery of *The Haunted House*.

Both Plautus and Terence wrote their plays to be acted without breaks. Subsequently editors introduced act divisions. Since these have by now become traditional, and are useful as well, I have retained them.

The Haunted House

/

DRAMATIS PERSONAE

Grumio, a farm hand (slave)

Tranio, servant of Theopropides (slave)

Philolaches, a young man about town, son of Theopropides

Philematium, his mistress

Scapha, her maid (slave)

Callidamates, a young man about town, Philolaches' best friend

Delphium, his mistress (slave)

Theopropides, a well-to-do, elderly citizen of Athens, father of Philolaches

A moneylender

Simo, a well-to-do, elderly citizen of Athens, neighbor of Theopropides

Phaniscus }
Pinacium } servants of Callidamates (slaves)

SCENE A street in Athens. Two houses front on it: Theopropides' and Simo's. In the center of the stage is a small altar. The exit on stage left leads downtown, that on stage right to the country.

ACT I

(Grumio, "the purse," an ancient, gnarled servant in worn farm clothes, comes out of the door of Theopropides' house. He turns and shouts to someone inside.)

GRUMIO *(through the doorway)* Damn you, come on out of that kitchen! I've had enough of your smart talk among the pots and pans. Out of the house, you ruination of the household! By god, if I live long enough to see you out on the farm, I'll get even with you once and for all. You heard me: come on out of that kitchen, you stinker! What are you hiding for?

(There emerges from the doorway a young fellow who, although dressed in servant's clothes, is a model of sartorial elegance and carries himself in as debonair a manner as the most sophisticated man about town. It is Tranio, Theopropides' valet. It takes brains and unremitting activity to maintain a position in the household and keep from being demoted to farm hand or some status even lower; Tranio's wits are razor sharp and his energy is unflagging.)

TRANIO What the devil do you mean by shouting like that in front of the house? Where do you think you are, anyway? On the farm? Now get the hell away from here and back to your barn. Beat it! Get away from this door! *(As Grumio stands there sullenly, Tranio hauls off and boxes his ear.)* There—was that what you were waiting for?

GRUMIO *(nursing his ear)* Damn! What did you have to hit me for?

TRANIO *(blandly)* For being alive.

GRUMIO *(grimly)* I'll stand for it—now. But just let the old man get back, just let him get back safe and sound. Here he is away on a trip, and you're eating him out of house and home.

TRANIO Clear case of mis-statement. Dumbbell, how can I eat him *out* of house and home when he's not *in* the house?

GRUMIO *(baffled)* So our city slicker, our toast of the town, objects to me because I come from the farm, eh? I think I know why, too: because you're going to wind up there yourself pretty soon— pushing a millwheel. It won't be long before you increase the rural population—by adding one more member to the chain gang. So long as you enjoy it so much and can get away with it, go right ahead—have your parties, run through the money, ruin the old man and that fine young son of his. Drink twenty-four hours a day, live like a bunch of Greeks, buy yourselves mistresses and set them free, feed the scroungers, live off the fat of the land. I suppose these were the orders the old man left when he went abroad? Is this how he's going to find his property was taken care of? Is this your idea of what a good servant should do? Ruin not only his master's property but his son as well? Because, in my opinion, that boy is ruined, now that he spends all his time doing the things he does. And yet, before this, there wasn't a boy in all Athens more careful about his money or his morals. Now he's running a record for exactly the reverse—thanks to you and the education you're giving him.

TRANIO   Why the devil do you worry about me and what I do? Listen, haven't you got any cows on the farm to worry about? I *like* drinking and making love and having girl friends. Anyway, it's my hide that's at stake, not yours.

GRUMIO (*truculently putting his face close to Tranio's*)   Listen to him talk! Pretty tough, eh?

TRANIO (*wincing*)   Get away, damn you! Whew, do you smell of garlic! You're the real barnyard type—goat, pig, dirt and dung all mixed together.

GRUMIO   What do you expect? Everybody can't smell like a rose just because you do—or sit at the head of the table, or eat the fine food you do. You can have your guinea hen and your fancy fish and fowl. I'm content to live out my life on cheap garlic. You're a lucky fellow and I'm a poor devil. That's all right with me— just so long as I get my reward and you get what's coming to you.

TRANIO (*loftily*)   Why, Grumio, I think you're jealous because I have it so good and you so bad. That's just how it should be: I was cut out for running around with women and living like a king, and you for running around with the cows and living like a dog.

GRUMIO (*shaking his finger at him*)   You know what I think? That the executioners are going to make a sieve out of you. Because, once the old man gets back, that's how many holes they're going

to punch in you when they nail you to a cross—after they've
whipped you through the streets.

TRANIO (*as before*) How do you know it won't happen to you first?

GRUMIO Because I've done nothing to deserve it. But you have—and
are still at it.

TRANIO (*moving toward him menacingly*) Save your breath—unless
you're interested in seeing the daylights beaten out of you.

GRUMIO (*giving up morality and reverting to the real purpose of his
trip to town*) If you people are going to give me the feed I
need for the cows, let's have it; if not, just go right on the way
you've been: live like a bunch of Greeks, get drunk, eat, stuff
yourselves, clean out the kitchen.

TRANIO Oh, shut up and go back to the farm. I want to go down to
the docks to see about some fish for dinner. I'll have someone
bring your feed to the farmhouse tomorrow. (*As Grumio stands
there*) Well, what are you staring at me now for, jailbird?

GRUMIO If you ask me that's just what you're going to be. And soon.

TRANIO (*smugly*) If things stay the way they are in the meantime, I'm
not going to worry about that "soon" of yours.

GRUMIO Is that so? There's one thing you'd better remember: it's a
lot easier to end up in hot water than in clover.

TRANIO I've had enough out of you. Back to the farm! On your way!
Damn it, you're not going to waste another minute of my time.
(*Exits stage left.*)

GRUMIO (*to himself*) Gone off, has he? And without giving a second
thought to anything I said. Oh, god, please, please send the old
man back as fast as you can before everything's ruined, house
and home and farm. He's been away three years now and he'd
better get back—we won't scrape through more than a few
months on the scraps we're down to. (*The door of Theopropides'
house opens and a figure appears in the doorway.*) Here's the
master's son, a fine young boy gone wrong. (*Shaking his head
sorrowfully*) I'd better get back to the farm.

(*Grumio exits, stage right. Since he had been introduced solely to
help purvey to the audience the necessary background, he does not
reappear.*
*Philolaches, "the gambler," enters. He is a well-dressed, good-looking
young fellow who, although endowed with a good deal of intelligence,*

is short on will and courage; his face at the moment shows signs of
some wild living. He is deep in thought, and walks slowly downstage to
unburden himself to the audience.)

SONG

PHILOLACHES *(thoughtfully)*

> I've wracked my brains, thought long and hard,
> Gone over the evidence in my mind—
> Whatever mind I have, that is—
> And argued it both pro and con,
> To figure out what I'd compare
> Or liken a man to, when he's born.
> And here's what I've found:
> A man when he's born is exactly like
> A house that's just been built.
> I'll explain my line of reasoning,
> And prove I'm right in what I say.
> And you, when you hear my words, will feel
> I'm sure, the same way.
> Now listen while I state my case;
> I want you to know it as well as I.

> The moment that a house is done,
> All made to plan, the paint still fresh,
> We think it's fine, applaud the builder,
>   And use it as model for one of our own;
> We spare no effort, no expense,
>   To get us a house that is just the same kind.

(Pauses, then proceeds with more feeling)

> But if a lax, good-for-nothing moves in,
> Someone lazy and careless, with a wife
> Who's no better, it's bad for the house—
> Then a good house gets badly kept up.
> All too often what happens is this.
> Comes a windstorm. It smashes the drains
> And the rooftiles. The owner, of course,
> Won't replace them. The rain trickles through,
> Then gets into the walls. They spring leaks,
> And the beams start to rot. The whole house
> Is run down—and the builder's work lost.

Now, we can't blame the builder for the way
    people act:
Even trifling repairs they put off and won't make
Till the walls tumble down; then the whole thing's
    rebuilt.
That's enough about buildings. Now let me
    show why
You're to think that a man's like a house newly
    built.

(Resumes his original thoughtful manner)

The parents are builders of a child;
They lay the child's foundation, raise
Him, work with care to give him strength.
There's nothing they begrudge, no expense
They think too great, to make of him
A worth-while man and citizen.
An education tops it all,
The study of law and literature.
With all their energy and cash
They strive to make a paragon
  That others will copy with sons of their own.
The army calls; a cousin guides
  Him through—he can still feel his builders'
             strong hands.
So only after he's served his hitch
  Are there signs how this building is bound
            to turn out.

(Pauses, then again proceeds with more feeling)

Now take *my* case. Just as long as my builders
Kept an eye cocked on me, I was good.
The first moment I struck out on my own,
I destroyed all the work of my builders.
For a windstorm of indolence came.
First it smashed in all feelings of shame,
Then it broke through the roof of my will.
I was lax about making repairs.
Soon there poured on my body a rainstorm of love.
It got into my breast and leaked through to my heart.
I have lost my good name, all my sense of respect.
My integrity, property, trustworthiness.

I'm a house that's run down: there's such rot in the beams,
No repairing can keep it from total collapse;
Its foundation is gone, it's beyond any hope.

How it hurts to compare what I'm now
With the man I once was! No one else
Trained as hard: I spent days working out
With the discus and javelin and spear,
On the mat, in the ring, round the track,
On a horse, and with arms in the field—
A fine model of hard and clean living for all.
Every worth-while young fellow took lessons from me.
Now I'm nothing—and *I'm* all to blame, I can see.

(*Philolaches steps back to an unobtrusive corner of the stage as the door of his house opens. Two women come out. The first is Philematium, "cute kiss," a radiantly beautiful young girl, exquisitely dressed. Philematium had been a courtesan, that is, the property of a slave dealer who, having provided her with an exacting training in all the arts of pleasing men, made his living by hiring her out. But, just the day before, Philolaches had bought her—at a stiff price; courtesans, particularly young and handsome and accomplished ones, came high—and set her free. The second woman is her servant Scapha, "the cup." Scapha is everything Philematium is not, a bent, sour-visaged, cynical old crone who, to judge by her name, has a weakness for the bottle. She carries a mirror, make-up box, jewel box, and other paraphernalia for a woman's toilet.*)

PHILEMATIUM (*stretching luxuriously*)   Scapha, I haven't enjoyed a
   bath so much in ages. And I don't know when I've felt cleaner.
SCAPHA (*indulgently*)   Wait until you see how things turn out, I always say. For example, this year the harvest turned out fine.
PHILEMATIUM (*puzzled*)   And just what does the harvest have to do
   with my bath?
SCAPHA (*pointedly*)   No more or less than your bath has to do with
   your harvest.
PHILOLACHES (*watching the two unobserved, aside*)   O my lovely,
   lovely beloved! (*To the audience*) There's the windstorm that
   raised the roof with my will power. And then love and passion
   poured into my breast, and I'll never be able to make any repairs.
   The walls of my heart are drenched. My whole house is a ruin.

PHILEMATIUM (*worriedly*)   Scapha dear, do you think this dress is
   becoming? I want to be sure Philolaches likes the way I look.
   (*Rapturously*) He's my darling; I owe everything to him.

SCAPHA   You're such a nice girl, why not make do with your nice sweet
   ways to set you off? Lovers aren't in love with a woman's clothes
   but with what's in them.

PHILOLACHES (*aside*)   So help me, that was very nicely said, Scapha.
   The old witch knows a thing or two. She has a nice idea of the
   way lovers feel.

PHILEMATIUM   Well, what about it?

SCAPHA   What about what?

PHILEMATIUM   What about looking at me and telling me if this becomes me?

SCAPHA   You're so pretty that whatever you wear becomes you.

PHILOLACHES (*aside*)   Scapha, for saying that you get a gift from me
   today. I can't let you give compliments to the girl I love and
   not get something for it.

PHILEMATIUM (*impatiently*)   Now, don't just yes me.

SCAPHA (*indulgently*)   You're such a silly girl. What do you prefer?
   That I tell lies and run you down or tell the truth and compliment you? Lord knows I'd much rather have people lie to pay me
   a compliment than tell the truth and find fault or poke fun at
   my looks.

PHILEMATIUM (*passionately*)   I love the truth. I *want* people to tell
   me the truth. I hate lies.

SCAPHA   All right. (*With mock solemnity*) I swear, by your love for me
   and Philolaches' for you, you're a lovely girl.

PHILOLACHES (*aside*)   What's that, you old witch? How did you swear?
   By my love for her? What's the matter with adding by her love
   for me? That settles you. That gift I promised you is all off.
   You've just lost it.

SCAPHA (*shaking her head disapprovingly*)   It amazes me that such
   a smart, sensible, and well-trained girl like you can do such silly
   things.

PHILEMATIUM   Please, you must warn me if I'm making any mistakes.

SCAPHA (*vehemently*)   You're certainly making a mistake in having
   eyes for just one man, and giving yourself all to him and forgetting about the others. (*Scornfully*) Devoting yourself to one
   lover! That's being a married woman, not a mistress.

PHILOLACHES (*stunned, aside*)   God in heaven! What sort of plague is this upon my house? I'll be damned if I don't kill that old hag. I'll starve her; I'll let her freeze to death!

PHILEMATIUM (*sharply*)   Scapha, I don't want any wrong ideas from you.

SCAPHA (*scornfully*)   You *are* a silly girl. What do you expect? That he'll be your loving friend forever? I'm warning you: you'll get older, he'll get colder—and then he'll leave you.

PHILEMATIUM (*worriedly*)   I hope not.

SCAPHA (*bitterly*)   What you don't hope for happens more often than what you do. All right. If my saying so won't make you believe the truth, maybe some facts will. Compare what I am now with what I used to be. Men once fell in love with me just as much as they do with you. I went ahead and gave myself to one man. And, god help me, as soon as these hairs turned gray, he left me in the lurch. If you ask me, the same thing will happen to you.

PHILOLACHES (*beside himself, aside*)   I can't hold myself back—I'll scratch that bitch's eyes out.

PHILEMATIUM (*firmly*)   He paid the price from his own pocket to free me—me and only me—to be his alone. So I feel I owe it to him to devote myself to him, to be his alone.

PHILOLACHES (*rapturously, aside*)   So help me, there's a fine girl, one with real character. By god, I did the right thing: I'm glad I spent every cent I had for her sake.

SCAPHA (*witheringly*)   God, what a fool you are!

PHILEMATIUM   Why?

SCAPHA   Because you care about his being in love with you.

PHILEMATIUM (*with asperity*)   And why shouldn't I care?

SCAPHA   You've already got your freedom. At this very moment you have what you were after. But he—if he doesn't keep on loving you, he's thrown away every penny he paid for you.

PHILOLACHES (*raging, aside*)   God damn it, I'll murder that hag! That filthy tongue of hers is corrupting the girl. That old woman's a bawd, that's what she is.

PHILEMATIUM (*with conviction*)   I'll never be able to give him the thanks he deserves from me, never! (*Sharply*) Scapha! Stop trying to make me think any less of him.

SCAPHA   Just remember one thing: if you're going to devote yourself to him alone, now when you're lovely and young, you'll be sorry when you're old.

PHILOLACHES (*as before*)   God, I wish I could turn myself into a case of lockjaw. I'd close that foul mouth. I'd kill that blasted bitch.

PHILEMATIUM (*resolutely*)   Now that I have what I wanted, I ought to act toward him just as I did before he gave in—when I was doing all I could to be sweet to him.

PHILOLACHES (*aside*)   So help me, for those words I'm ready to pay what I did all over again—and murder Scapha in cold blood.

SCAPHA (*ironically*)   Well, if you've got it in writing that he'll provide for you forever, that he's going to be your own true love till the end of your days, then I suppose you should devote yourself entirely to him—and start dressing like a wife.

PHILEMATIUM (*loftily*)   A good name is money. If I keep mine, I'll be rich enough.

PHILOLACHES (*rapturously, aside*)   So help me, even if I have to sell my own father, I'll do it before I'll ever let that girl be in need as long as I'm alive.

SCAPHA   What's going to happen to all the others who were in love with you?

PHILEMATIUM   They'll be even more in love with me when they see the gratitude I show to someone who's earned it.

PHILOLACHES (*as before*)   I wish I'd be given the news right now that my father's dead—I'd disinherit myself and turn the whole estate over to her.

SCAPHA   He'll go through every cent he has before long. Drinks and parties all day and all night, nobody trying to save a penny, nothing but eat, eat, eat . . .

PHILOLACHES (*between his teeth, aside*)   All right, damn you, I'll find out how economically I can live—and I'll start with you: you're not going to eat or drink a thing in my house for ten days in a row.

PHILEMATIUM (*sharply*)   If you have anything nice to say about him, you can say it. But if you're simply going to run him down, believe me, I'll give you a beating.

PHILOLACHES (*exultantly, aside*)   I couldn't have spent the money I paid for her any better if I had put it on the altar for god almighty himself. You see how she loves me? From the bottom of her heart. Pretty smart of me: I paid to set her free—and got a defense attorney for my money.

SCAPHA (*grumbling*) All right, all right. I can see that, for you, no other man in the world can compare with Philolaches. So I'll just say Yes; I don't want any beatings on his account.

PHILEMATIUM Scapha, quick, the mirror and my jewel box. I want to be all ready when my sweetheart comes.

SCAPHA (*handing her the mirror and box*) It's the woman who has to worry about her looks and her age that needs a mirror. But what do you need one for? You're a mirror of beauty yourself.

PHILOLACHES (*aside*) Scapha, I must reward a compliment as pretty as that. So today I'll give a special present—to Philematium.

PHILEMATIUM Is everything in place? How's my hair-do? Is it attractive?

SCAPHA On an attractive girl like you, how could it help but be attractive?

PHILOLACHES (*aside*) Did you ever hear of anything worse than that old woman? All she could say before was No; now it's nothing but Yes.

PHILEMATIUM My powder, please.

SCAPHA What in the world do you want with powder?

PHILEMATIUM For my cheeks.

SCAPHA You might just as well try to make ivory shine by putting soot on it.

PHILOLACHES (*aside*) Make ivory shine with soot? That's not bad. Good for you, Scapha.

PHILEMATIUM Then give me my lipstick.

SCAPHA No, I won't. You *are* a silly girl. What do you want to do? Mess up a beautiful work of art with some splashes of fresh paint? At your age you don't need any make-up—no rouge, no powder, none of that junk.

PHILEMATIUM All right, then, take the mirror. (*Before handing it over she takes a last look and, pleased with what she sees, kisses it.*)

PHILOLACHES (*writhing, aside*) Oh, god, oh, god! She's kissed the mirror! If I only had a stone to smash that thing into bits!

SCAPHA (*handing her a towel*) Now take this towel and wipe your hands.

PHILEMATIUM What for?

SCAPHA You held the mirror. I'm afraid your hands'll smell of the silver. We don't want Philolaches to suspect that silver's ever crossed your palm.

PHILOLACHES (*shaking his head in reluctant admiration, aside*)   I don't know where I've ever seen a wiser old bawd than that filthy-minded hag. That's a pretty good idea she had about the mirror.

PHILEMATIUM   Don't you think I need some perfume?

SCAPHA   Absolutely not.

PHILEMATIUM   Why?

SCAPHA   Because the right smell for a woman is no smell at all. You know those patched-up, toothless old crones who drench themselves with perfume and cover up their ugly spots with make-up? Well, once sweat starts mixing in with all that, they begin to smell like some sauce a cook's concocted: you don't know what the smell is from, but you do know it's pretty bad.

PHILOLACHES (*again shaking his head admiringly, aside*)   Clever old crone—you'll never see one smarter. (*To the audience*) It's the truth and most of you know it, you fellows with old hags at home who bought you with their dowries.

PHILEMATIUM   Look at my jewelry and my dress. Are they becoming?

SCAPHA   *I* don't have to bother about them.

PHILEMATIUM   Then who should?

SCAPHA   I'll tell you: Philolaches—so he'll buy you only what he thinks you'll like. You see, a lover just uses jewelry and clothes to buy himself a mistress; he's not interested in those things himself. So why go to the trouble of parading them before him? Anyway, jewelry's for an ugly woman and gowns are for an old one to hide her age. A good-looking girl is better looking in the nude than in a gorgeous gown. Good looks are ornament enough.

PHILOLACHES (*aside*)   And I've held back long enough. (*Stepping out of his hiding place, to Philematium*) Well, what are you doing?

PHILEMATIUM   Trying to look my best to please you.

PHILOLACHES   You look fine as is. (*To Scapha, gesturing toward the toilet articles*) Get inside and take all this stuff with you. (*To Philematium*) Philematium, sweetheart, let's have a drink together.

PHILEMATIUM (*tenderly*)   Yes, lets. Anything you want I want too, sweetheart.

PHILOLACHES (*exulting*)   It's cheap at ten thousand dollars to hear you talk that way.

PHILEMATIUM (*caressing him*)   Oh, make it five; I want to give you a bargain, when I hear *you* talk that way.

PHILOLACHES (*banteringly*) Even at my price you still owe me five.
Figure it out if you like: I paid fifteen thousand for you.

PHILEMATIUM (*reproachfully*) Why do you have to throw that in my
face?

PHILOLACHES (*vehemently*) Throw it in your face? I only wish they'd
throw it in mine! What an investment! Best place I've found in
years to put my money.

PHILEMATIUM And I certainly could find no better place for my love
than you.

PHILOLACHES That means our account with each other balances perfectly: you love me, I love you, and we both think this is just as
it should be.

PHILEMATIUM Then come, sit down. (*Calling*) Boy! Water for washing, please. And bring a table here. And see if you can find the
dice. (*Servants hurry out and set a table and two couches near
the door. Philolaches and Philematium sit down on one.*) Do
you want scent with the water?

PHILOLACHES What do I need it for? I'm sitting alongside attar of roses
itself. (*Hearing a noise, looks off, stage right.*) Hey, isn't that my
old friend there with his girl? (*Peering harder*) That's who
it is, Callidamates and his girl friend. This is wonderful, honey!
See? Here comes the rest of our gang, heading this way for their
half of the handout.

(*Three people enter, stage right. In the lead is Callidamates, "lady-
killer," a good-looking, flashily dressed, young man about town. With
him is his mistress Delphium and a servant. Callidamates has already
been to one drinking party—and shows unmistakable signs of the fact.*)

SONG

CALLIDAMATES (*to the servant*)

Now I want you to come to Philolaches' house.
You're to meet me there later—and you'd better be prompt!
Do you hear? Now get going; you know what to do.

(*The servant scurries off, stage right. He turns to Delphium.*)

I just *had* to get out of that place where I was:
Oh, my god, was I bored with the drinks and the talk!
Now I'll go for some fun to Philolaches' house.
There's a man with some life. He can show us a good time.

(He tries to walk on; the wine he has taken aboard hits him and he starts weaving unsteadily.)

Shay there, what d'ya think? Had me too much to drink?

DELPHIUM *(resignedly)*

Oh, you're always like this. Let's get on.

(She swivels him around as he starts to stagger off in the wrong direction.)

No, no, here!

CALLIDAMATES *(boozily)*

How 'bout holding me up in those sweet li'l' arms?

DELPHIUM *(patiently)*

If you want me to, sure. *(Puts her arms around him.)*

CALLIDAMATES

You're a good li'l' girl.
Come on, you lead the way.

(They get under way, clinging to each other.)

DELPHIUM *(as he starts to crumple)*

Don't you fall—stand up straight!

CALLIDAMATES *(boozily happy)*

Like a sweet li'l' mom with her big baby boy.

DELPHIUM

Just watch out that you don't sit down here in the street.
(Seductively)
There's a couch at his house; it's all ready for us.

CALLIDAMATES *(stopping and weaving about sleepily)*

'Ats all right. Go ahead. Lemme fall.

DELPHIUM *(disgustedly)*

Well, I will!

CALLIDAMATES (*holding her tightly*)

If you do, what I've got in my arms goes down too.

DELPHIUM (*resignedly*)

If you fall, I fall too; it's the street for us both.

CALLIDAMATES (*with drunken finality*)

So we'll lie on the ground till some guy picks us up.

(*Delphium gives up, lowers her arms, and stands looking at him as he sways and struggles to keep his balance.*)

DELPHIUM (*disgustedly*)

Oh, you're crocked.

CALLIDAMATES (*argumentatively*)

Thaz what *you* shay. Me crocked? Nosirree!

DELPHIUM

Sure, sure. Give me your hand. I don't want you in splints.

CALLIDAMATES (*reaching out his hand*)

Here it is.

DELPHIUM (*taking it and trying to tug him along*)

Now come on!

CALLIDAMATES (*blankly*)

Come on where?

DELPHIUM

Don't you know?

CALLIDAMATES (*thinking hard; then, with drunken gravity*)

Oh, yes, now it comes back to me. Sure. We go home.
To a party. (*Turns about and starts heading offstage.*)

DELPHIUM (*swiveling him around toward Philolaches and Philematium*)

No, here!

CALLIDAMATES

I remember. You're right.

*(As they head slowly toward Philematium and Philolaches, the latter
gets up from his seat. Philematium starts to pull him down.)*

PHILOLACHES

Do you mind if I get up to meet them, my sweet?
Out of all of my friends, he's the one I like best.
I'll be back in a second.

PHILEMATIUM *(sighing)*

To me that's a year.

(Philolaches walks over to Callidamates and Delphium.)

CALLIDAMATES *(hollering in the general direction of Philolaches' house)*

Anyone here?

PHILOLACHES *(coming up to him)*

Yes, there is.

CALLIDAMATES *(throwing his arms around him)*

Hey, Philolaches! Good!

Hearty greetings, the best friend I have in the world!

PHILOLACHES *(steering him to the couch)*

Same to you. Have a seat. Now then, where have you been?

CALLIDAMATES *(collapsing onto the couch)*

Where a man can get drunk as a lord.

PHILEMATIUM *(to Delphium)*

Now, my dear,

Won't you please have a seat?

PHILOLACHES *(beckoning to a servant and gesturing toward Callidamates)*

Get him something to drink.

CALLIDAMATES

Right now, I'm for a nap. *(Slumps over and falls fast asleep.)*

PHILOLACHES (*smiling indulgently*)

> Same old Callidamates.

DELPHIUM (*to Philematium, helplessly*)

> I don't know what to do with him next.

PHILEMATIUM (*patting her hand reassuringly*)

> > You just let
> Him alone.

PHILOLACHES (*to the servant in charge of the drinks, gesturing toward Delphium*)

> Fill her glass. Now a drink for us, too.

ACT II

(Philolaches, Philematium, and Delphium are seated, and Callidamates snoring away, as at the end of Act I. The three settle back, drinks in hand, for a gay, relaxed session—and Tranio bursts in, stage left, running at top speed. Without noticing the group near the door, he comes to a halt, catches his breath, and turns to the audience.)

TRANIO (*with great excitement*) God almighty is out with all his might to finish off Philolaches and me. No sense even trying to be brave; that's out the window. Any hopes we had are dead. Our guardian angel himself couldn't guard us now, even if he wanted to. Down at the dock I just got a look at a ten-ton load of terrible trouble. (*Frantically*) The old man's boat got in—and, Tranio, you're sunk!

(*Paces up and down for a moment shaking his head gloomily, then brightens.*) Any of you want to make a little money by taking on a crucifixion in my place? Where are some of those the-hell-with-the-whips-and-handcuffs types? Or how about those fellows who join the army, run right up to the enemy's batteries and get themselves punctured by a dozen spears for a couple of cents a day? (*Calling*) Thirty thousand dollars for the first soldier to storm and take my cross—(*lowering his voice*) on this condition: first he gets nailed up with two nails in each hand and foot and then, when this is nicely taken care of, let him ask me for the cash. Hey, what am I hanging around here for? I've got to get going and get home. (*Spins about and starts running toward the group at the door.*)

PHILOLACHES (*to his companions*)   Ah, dinner at last. Here's Tranio back from the docks.

TRANIO (*shouting*)   Philolaches!

PHILOLACHES   What's the matter?

TRANIO   You and I—

PHILOLACHES (*interrupting in alarm*)   You and I what?

TRANIO   —are sunk!

PHILOLACHES (*jumping up*)   Why?

TRANIO   Your father's back!

PHILOLACHES (*roaring*)   What! What's that you say!

TRANIO   We're washed up—your father's back.

PHILOLACHES   Where in heaven's name is he?

TRANIO   At the dock.

PHILOLACHES   Who says so? Who saw him?

TRANIO   I did. With my own eyes.

PHILOLACHES   Oh, my god! (*Dazedly*) What's happening to me?

TRANIO (*impatiently*)   Why the devil ask me what's happening to you? You're being served drinks.

PHILOLACHES (*desperately*)   Did you see him yourself?

TRANIO   Myself. With my own eyes.

PHILOLACHES   Are you sure?

TRANIO   Sure, I'm sure.

PHILOLACHES   Tranio, I'm a dead man if you're telling the truth.

TRANIO   What good would it do me to lie to you?

PHILOLACHES   What do I do now?

TRANIO (*taking command of the situation, gestures toward the table and the things on it*)   Get all this stuff out of here. (*Pointing to Callidamates, who is snoring away undisturbed*) Who's that asleep there?

PHILOLACHES   Callidamates. Delphium! Wake him up.

DELPHIUM (*poking him*)   Callidamates! Wake up!

CALLIDAMATES (*jumping up with a start*)   I'm awake. Gimme drink. (*Collapses back on the couch immediately, and starts snoring away again.*)

DELPHIUM (*disgustedly*) Oh, wake up. (*Shaking him and shouting*) Philolaches' father's come back!

CALLIDAMATES (*murmuring sleepily*) Tell him go take nice long trip.

PHILOLACHES (*gloomily*) He just had one. I'm going to have one too —to hell.

CALLIDAMATES (*too drunk and sleepy to hear straight*) Toot in hell? (*Shaking his head with drunken gravity*) Can't be done.

PHILOLACHES (*impatiently*) For god's sake, will you wake up? (*Shouting in his ear*) My father's back!

CALLIDAMATES (*staring at him boozily*) Father's back? You jus' tell 'm go 'way again. Whaz he have to come back for, anyway?

PHILOLACHES (*to Tranio*) What am I going to do? My father'll come back and find a party going on, me drunk, and the house full of women. It's a pretty miserable business for a man to have to dig a well when he's dying of thirst—as bad as my having to figure out what to do when my father's already here.

TRANIO (*pointing to Callidamates, disgustedly*) Look at him! Head on his chest and off to sleep again. Wake him up.

PHILOLACHES (*shaking him*) Wake up, will you? I tell you my father'll be here any minute!

CALLIDAMATES (*blinking blearily*) Whazzat? Father? (*Gets up and starts staggering about.*) Gimme shoes. Gotta go get sword. By god, gonna kill 'at father right now. (*Collapses again on the couch.*)

PHILOLACHES (*hopelessly*) You'll be the ruin of me!

DELPHIUM (*to Callidamates*) Please! Can't you keep quiet?

TRANIO (*to the servants*) Pick him up and get him inside—right now.

(*Two servants pick Callidamates up and start hauling him into the house.*)

CALLIDAMATES (*roaring as he's carried off*) Bring me a chamber pot or, damn you, I'll let go on the both of you!

(*They all watch him being taken off. There is a moment of silence as they stare at each other blankly.*)

PHILOLACHES (*hopelessly*) I'm sunk.

TRANIO (*clapping him on the shoulder*) Cheer up! Old Dr. Tranio will fix you up just fine.

PHILOLACHES (*as before*) I'm a goner.

TRANIO Don't talk that way. I'll think up something to settle the whole business. Will you be satisfied if I not only keep your father out of the house when he gets here, but even chase him away? (*Philolaches stares at him unbelievingly. Tranio turns to the servants.*) Go inside now and (*gesturing toward the table and couches*) take all this stuff in with you. Quick!

PHILOLACHES (*worriedly*) Where do you want me to be?

TRANIO (*gesturing toward the girls*) Just where you want to be—with these two.

DELPHIUM I think we girls had better leave.

TRANIO (*confidently*) Delphium, you don't need to budge an inch. This isn't going to change things—you people can do all the drinking you want, inside.

PHILOLACHES I'm in a cold sweat already worrying where all this smooth talk of yours is going to lead us.

TRANIO Listen, can't you take it easy and do what I tell you?

PHILOLACHES (*without conviction*) All right, I will.

TRANIO First of all, Philematium, you go inside. You too, Delphium.

DELPHIUM We'll do anything you say, Tranio.

TRANIO (*leering*) God, I wish it were true! (*The two girls go in. He turns to Philolaches.*) Now, listen carefully. Here's what I want you to do. First of all, shut the whole house up. Right now. Then make sure no one inside makes a sound.

PHILOLACHES I'll take care of it.

TRANIO Just as if there wasn't a soul living here.

PHILOLACHES Right.

TRANIO And I don't want anyone to answer the door when the old man starts knocking.

PHILOLACHES Anything else?

TRANIO Yes. Have one of the boys bring out the key. I want to lock up from the outside.

PHILOLACHES (*desperately*) Tranio, I'm trusting everything to you. My life, my future—it's all in your hands.

TRANIO (*calling after him as he goes into the house*) It doesn't make a particle of difference whether master or servant's the better man. (*Waits until Philolaches is inside, out of earshot, then addresses the audience.*) Anyone, the highest or the lowest, even if he's got no guts at all, can create a mess at a moment's notice. What you've got to watch out for—and it's the mark of genius—

is how to handle the mess, once you've made it, so that there are
no repercussions, no one gets into trouble, and you don't wind
up with a black mark against you that'll last a lifetime. Now,
that's just what I'm going to do with what we've stirred up here.
Everything's going to end nice and tidy, and none of us are going
to suffer the least bit. (*A servant pops his head out of the door.*)
What do you want, Sphaerio?

SPHAERIO (*handing him a key*)   Here's the key.

TRANIO (*nodding approvingly*)   You're a boy who obeys orders.

SPHAERIO   Philolaches told me to beg you to please, please scare his
father off somehow and keep him out of the house.

TRANIO   Well, you just tell him I'll make the old man so scared he
won't even look at the place; he'll cover his eyes and scoot. Give
me the key. You go in and close the door. I'll lock it from outside.
(*Sphaerio goes in. Tranio locks the door and turns to the
audience.*) Let him come now. Will I put on a show for him!
While he's right here, in the flesh. (*Smirking*) I'd better—
there's no money left for one at his funeral. (*Moving off far to
one side*) I'll get away from the door. I can man a lookout post
from here, and start handing him a line the minute he comes
along.

(*As Tranio takes up his post at the side of the stage, Theopropides,
"the seer," enters, stage left, dressed in traveling clothes; two servants,
loaded with baggage, are at his heels. Theopropides is a wizened old
fellow whose prime interest in life is business and the making—and
saving—of money. It's difficult to see how he could be successful, since
his dominant characteristic, mockingly pointed up by his name, is an
almost unbelievable gullibility.*)

THEOPROPIDES (*looking up to heaven*)   Father Neptune! Many thanks
for letting me off and sending me home still alive. But, believe
me, if you ever hear of my getting within a foot of the water
hereafter, you can go right ahead and finish what you started to
do this last trip. Just keep away from me, far away, from now
on. I've trusted in you all I'm ever going to.

TRANIO (*from his hiding place, aside*)   Oh, lord, Father Neptune, what
a mistake you made! What a wonderful chance you just passed
up!

THEOPROPIDES (*to the audience*)   Here I am, back after three years in
　　　Egypt. Well, I expect the whole family will be glad to see me.
TRANIO (*aside*)   Not nearly so glad as we'd be to see the fellow who
　　　brings your death notice.

(*Theopropides goes up to the door of his house and tries it.*)

THEOPROPIDES (*to himself*)   Hey, what's this? The middle of the day
　　　and the door locked? I'll knock. (*Pounding on the door*) Hey!
　　　Anyone inside? Open up!
TRANIO (*aloud but as if to himself*)   Who's that over there in front of
　　　our house?
THEOPROPIDES (*turning and seeing him, to himself*)   There's my
　　　servant Tranio.
TRANIO (*with effusive heartiness—but without moving*)   Well,
　　　Theopropides! It's a pleasure to see you back safe and sound.
　　　How've you been?
THEOPROPIDES   Pretty good all along. (*Straightening himself up
　　　proudly*) You can see for yourself.
TRANIO   Fine, that's just fine.
THEOPROPIDES   What's the matter with all of you? Are you out of your
　　　minds?
TRANIO   What do you mean?
THEOPROPIDES   Here you are walking around outside, and not a soul
　　　inside, no one to answer the door. I almost broke it down bang-
　　　ing on it.
TRANIO (*with a convincing air of incredulity*)   You mean you touched
　　　that house?
THEOPROPIDES (*irritably*)   And why shouldn't I? You heard me—I al-
　　　most broke down the door banging on it.
TRANIO (*switching from incredulity to horror*)   You touched the door!
THEOPROPIDES (*as before*)   Yes, I touched the door. What's more, I
　　　banged on it.
TRANIO   Oh, my god!
THEOPROPIDES   What's the matter?
TRANIO   That's bad, that's very bad.
THEOPROPIDES   Now what's this all about?
TRANIO (*shaking his head gloomily*)   I can't tell you what a terrible
　　　thing you just did.
THEOPROPIDES (*a bit worried*)   What do you mean?

TRANIO (*shouting frantically*) Run for your life! Get away from that house! Run! This way, over here where I am. (*Leaving the servants by the door, Theopropides scuttles over to where Tranio is standing. Tranio eyes him as if he were on his deathbed.*) So you touched the door!

THEOPROPIDES (*bewildered*) Now how could I knock without touching it?

TRANIO (*like a prophet of doom*) You've just murdered—

THEOPROPIDES (*interrupting, alarmed*) Murdered whom?

TRANIO —your whole family.

THEOPROPIDES (*relieved at the answer, angrily*) You can go straight to hell! You and your superstitions!

TRANIO (*darkly*) I'm afraid there's no way you can take the curse off yourself or the rest of the family.

THEOPROPIDES Why? Now just what is this sudden new state of affairs, anyway?

TRANIO (*pointing to the two servants still standing near the door*) Hey, tell the both of them to get away from there.

THEOPROPIDES (*shouting*) Get away from there!

TRANIO (*calling to the servants*) Don't touch that house! (*As they approach him*) Now knock on wood! (*They hurry off, stage left.*)

THEOPROPIDES For god's sake, will you tell me what this is all about?

TRANIO (*with an air of great sorrow*) It's been seven months since we moved out of that house. And no one has set foot in it since.

THEOPROPIDES But why? Tell me why!

TRANIO (*whispering*) Take a look around. Anybody who can overhear us?

THEOPROPIDES (*craning his neck in all directions*) All clear.

TRANIO (*as before*) Take another look to make sure.

THEOPROPIDES (*going through the same business*) Not a soul. You can talk now.

TRANIO (*hoarsely*) There's been a crime committed!

THEOPROPIDES (*blankly*) I don't understand.

TRANIO (*as before*) You heard me. A horrible crime was committed. A long, long time ago.

THEOPROPIDES (*as before*) A long, long time ago?

TRANIO Yes. We just found out about it.

THEOPROPIDES What kind of crime? Who did it? Tell me!

TRANIO (*tragically*) A host murdered a guest in cold blood! (*Furtively*) If you ask me, it was the fellow who sold you this house.

THEOPROPIDES (*goggle-eyed*)   Murder!

TRANIO (*nodding vigorously*)   And then he robbed the body—a guest
in his own home, mind you—and buried it here in the house.

THEOPROPIDES   What makes you think any such thing happened?

TRANIO (*confidentially*)   I'll tell you the whole story. Listen. One
night your son ate out. When he got back home from dinner,
we all went to bed. We fell fast asleep. It so happened I
had forgotten to put out one of the lights. I got up—and all of
a sudden he lets out a yell at the top of his lungs.

THEOPROPIDES   Who? My son?

TRANIO   Sh! Let me talk. Listen. He said the corpse of the murdered
man came to him in a dream—

THEOPROPIDES (*interrupting, with relief*)   Then it was just a dream?

TRANIO   That's right. But listen. He said that this corpse told him that
this is the way—

THEOPROPIDES (*interrupting, incredulously*)   In a dream?

TRANIO (*impatiently*)   What was it supposed to do? Come around and
chat in broad daylight? It was a corpse, dead for sixty years!
(*Disgustedly*) Sometimes you're pretty stupid, Theopropides.

THEOPROPIDES (*meekly*)   All right, I'll keep quiet.

TRANIO   Now here's what the corpse said to him in his dream: (*striking
a pose, and with a sepulchral delivery*) "I am a stranger from
across the sea. My name is Overwaterman. I live here. This
house was given to me as my abode. For the world of the dead
refused to receive me because I departed this life before my time.
I trusted a man—and he betrayed me. My own host murdered
me here and, without giving me proper burial, secretly threw
me into a pit in this house. He did it to get my money, the
fiend! Move away from here this instant. This house is evil.
There's a curse on it!" (*Switching to a frightened whisper*) You
have no idea what queer things go on here—it'd take me a year
to tell you. (*A noise is heard from inside—Philolaches and his
guests, forgetting their orders, are whooping it up. Tranio, thinking fast, ostensibly addresses Theopropides but in tones that will
carry to those inside.*) Sh! Quiet!

THEOPROPIDES (*quaking*)   Oh, my god! What's happening?

TRANIO (*whispering hoarsely*)   There was a noise at the door! (*As-
sumes an attitude of abject terror and, pointing to Theopropides,
pretends to address the ghost.*) He was the one who knocked!

THEOPROPIDES (*his teeth chattering*) I don't have a drop of blood left
in my veins! Dead men are coming to put me in my grave, and
here I am still alive!

TRANIO (*aside*) I'm sunk! That bunch in there will queer my act. Now
I'm really scared—the old man may catch me red-handed!

THEOPROPIDES What are you muttering about?

TRANIO (*frantically*) You've got to get far away from that door! For
god's sake, please, run for your life!

THEOPROPIDES (*starting off, then suddenly stopping*) Where should I
go? (*Seeing Tranio still standing there*) Hey! You run too!

TRANIO (*reassuringly*) I've got nothing to be afraid of. The ghosts
aren't after me.

(*The party inside gets wilder—unmistakable noises are heard and
someone starts shouting.*)

VOICE FROM WITHIN Hey, Tranio!

TRANIO (*again trying to warn those inside by pretending to talk to the
ghost*) If you've got any sense you won't call for *me*. I shouldn't
have to pay for it, I didn't knock on the door.

VOICE FROM WITHIN Say there—

TRANIO (*sotto voce, to the voice*) Shut up!

THEOPROPIDES (*overhearing*) Who are you telling to shut up?

TRANIO (*as if to the ghost*) Go away! Go away from here!

THEOPROPIDES Tranio, is there something the matter with you? Who
were you talking to just now?

TRANIO (*as if tremendously relieved*) Ah, so it was you who called
me, was it? So help me, I thought it was the ghost kicking up
a fuss because you knocked on the door. But what are you
standing there for? Why don't you do as I say?

THEOPROPIDES What should I do?

TRANIO Run for your life! Cover your head and don't look back!

THEOPROPIDES Why don't you run too?

TRANIO The ghosts aren't after me.

THEOPROPIDES (*with some asperity*) I heard you the first time. If that's
the case, what were you so scared about a minute ago?

TRANIO Don't worry about me, I tell you. I can take care of myself.
You just get going again, as fast as those legs of yours can carry
you. And start saying your prayers.

THEOPROPIDES (*as he scurries off, stage right*) Please, god, I need your
help!

TRANIO (*watching him go off*) Me too—to put one over on this old man. God help me, what a beautiful mess I started today!

ACT III

(*Enter a moneylender, stage left. He does not notice Tranio, who is still standing, as at the end of the last act, off to the side.*)

MONEYLENDER I haven't seen a fouler year for lending money than this since I've been in the business. I drag around the business district all day long, from dawn to dark, and I can't lend a sou to a soul.

TRANIO (*to himself*) Oh, god, now my number's up for real! There's the moneylender who made us the loan we needed to buy the girl and pay our bills. The jig's up unless I can think of something in time to keep the old man from finding out about the whole business. I'd better have a talk with him. (*Suddenly noticing Theopropides hurrying in, stage right*) What in the world brings him back so soon? Oh, oh, maybe he's heard something. I'd better have a talk with *him*. Damn it all, I'm scared. There's nothing worse than a guilty conscience—and that's precisely my problem now. Well, no matter how things stand, I've got to keep the pot boiling—there's no other way. (*To Theopropides as the latter comes up to him, sourly*) Where are you coming from?

THEOPROPIDES (*excitedly*) I just met the man I bought the house from.

TRANIO You didn't tell him what I told you, did you?

THEOPROPIDES Of course I did. Everything.

TRANIO (*aside*) Oh, my god, there go all my plans down the drain.

THEOPROPIDES Now what are you muttering about?

TRANIO (*quickly*) Nothing. Tell me—you told him, eh?

THEOPROPIDES Of course. The whole story from beginning to end.

TRANIO Well, did he admit the murder?

THEOPROPIDES He did not. He denied everything.

TRANIO (*as if he can't believe his ears*) Denied it? Of all the dirty—

THEOPROPIDES That's what I said. Kept insisting there wasn't a word of truth in it.

TRANIO (*sparring for time*) Think now—you're sure he didn't confess?

THEOPROPIDES I'd have told you if he had. What do you think we ought to do now?

TRANIO (*switching from incredulity to righteous indignation*) What do I think? Damn it all, haul him up before a judge and have it out with him! (*Aside*) But make sure you get one who'll believe my side of the story. (*To Theopropides*) You'll win the case easier than taking candy from a baby.

MONEYLENDER (*his attention caught by the voices, to himself*) There's Tranio, Philolaches' servant. They're the pair that haven't paid me my interest—to say nothing of the principal.

(*Tranio abruptly leaves Theopropides and starts walking toward the moneylender.*)

THEOPROPIDES (*calling*) Where are you going?

TRANIO (*over his shoulder*) Nowhere in particular. (*To himself as he walks*) Tranio, you're just a poor unlucky devil born under the wrong star. (*Gesturing toward the moneylender*) He has to turn up just when the old man is here. What a spot to be in! Now I'm getting it from both sides. Well, I'll tackle this fellow first.

MONEYLENDER (*to himself*) He's coming to see me. The country's saved—there's some hope for my money.

TRANIO (*to himself*) He looks happy—has he got the wrong idea! (*As he comes up to him*) Well, Mr. Hatecashman, glad to see you.

MONEYLENDER Glad to see you too. How about my money?

TRANIO (*banteringly*) Oh, come on, you vulture. The minute I come within range you start firing at me.

MONEYLENDER (*to himself*) Just as I thought—the man doesn't have a penny.

TRANIO (*to himself*) Just as I thought—the man's a mind reader.

MONEYLENDER What are you playing around with me for?

TRANIO What are you after me for?

MONEYLENDER Where's Philolaches?

TRANIO (*putting an arm around him affectionately*) You know, you couldn't have picked a better time to drop around than this very minute.

MONEYLENDER (*suspiciously*) Why?

TRANIO (*trying to lead him off to the side of the stage further away from Theopropides*)   Come on over here.

MONEYLENDER (*without budging, and raising his voice excitedly*)   How about paying me my interest?

TRANIO (*with an anguished glance in Theopropides' direction to see whether he has heard*)   I know you've got a good pair of lungs. You don't have to yell.

MONEYLENDER (*as before*)   Damn it, I'll yell if I want.

TRANIO   Why don't you be a nice fellow and listen to me?

MONEYLENDER (*suspiciously*)   And just what do you want me to be a nice fellow and listen to you for?

TRANIO (*urgently*)   Do me a favor. Go on home.

MONEYLENDER (*taken aback*)   What! Go home?

TRANIO (*as before*)   Come back around noon.

MONEYLENDER (*suspiciously*)   Will you pay me the interest then?

TRANIO   Sure we'll pay it. Just go.

MONEYLENDER   Why should I go to all that trouble? Why should I wear myself out by going away and coming back? Suppose I just stay here until noon?

TRANIO (*quickly*)   Oh, no! Go on home. I swear, it's no trick. Just get going. (*Starts trying to pull him away.*)

MONEYLENDER (*without budging*)   I don't want to. Not until that interest—

TRANIO (*interrupting quickly, and tugging*)   Please! Go on home!

MONEYLENDER (*brushing him off his arm*)   No. Pay me my interest. What are you people fooling around with me for?

TRANIO (*loudly*)   Fine, fine. (*Dropping his voice*) Listen to me: just go home.

MONEYLENDER   Damn it, I'm going to call Philolaches.

TRANIO (*needled into dropping his friendly approach for a moment*)   Go ahead. Holler your head off. You're so happy when you yell.

MONEYLENDER   I'm only asking for what's mine. You've been putting me off like this for days. If I'm a nuisance, just pay me my money. I'll go away. That's all you have to do and there'll be no more arguments.

TRANIO (*ready to try anything in his desperation*)   All right, we'll give you your money back.

MONEYLENDER (*shouting*)   Not on your life! First I want my interest!

TRANIO (*switching to the offensive*)   What's that? If you aren't the limit! What did you do, come here to test your lungs? Go on, do your damnedest. He's not going to pay you. He doesn't owe you a dime.

MONEYLENDER (*incredulously*) Doesn't owe me a dime?

TRANIO You're not going to get a penny out of him. (*Scornfully*) And don't worry—he's not going to skip town just to get out of paying you your interest. Not when he's offered to pay back the principal right this minute.

MONEYLENDER I'm not after the principal. First he's got to pay me the interest.

TRANIO Stop making a nuisance of yourself. You can do what you like; no one's going to pay you. I suppose you think you're the only one around here who lends money?

MONEYLENDER (*screaming*) I want my interest! Come on, let's have that interest. Are you people going to pay me my interest right now or not? I want my interest!

TRANIO (*holding his hands over his ears*) Interest, interest, interest! That's the only word this fellow knows. Get out of here! I've never seen a worse vulture than you in my life.

MONEYLENDER God damn it, you can't scare me with that talk.

THEOPROPIDES (*his attention finally attracted by the voices, to himself*) Things are getting warm with those two; I'm getting burned all the way over here. (*Walking toward them and calling as he does*) Tranio, what's this interest this fellow wants?

TRANIO (*to the moneylender*) Look, here comes his father. He just got back from abroad. He'll pay you your interest and your principal, so don't come around bothering *us* any more. Worry about whether *he'll* keep you waiting for your money.

MONEYLENDER (*grimly*) Wherever it comes from, I'll take it.

THEOPROPIDES (*now alongside Tranio*) Well, what about it?

TRANIO (*disingenuously*) What about what?

THEOPROPIDES This fellow. Who is he? What's he after? Why does he keep mentioning my son's name? Why is he saying such things to you, right to your face? What's this debt of his, anyway?

TRANIO (*cavalierly, with an air of washing his hands of the whole dirty business*) For god's sake, Theopropides, will you please have the money paid and stop this foul vulture's mouth?

THEOPROPIDES (*thunderstruck*) I have it paid?

TRANIO (*scornfully*)   Yes. Stuff it in this creature's mouth.

MONEYLENDER   Gagged with money? I don't mind in the least.

TRANIO (*as before, to Theopropides*)   Listen to him! Isn't he the perfect moneylender type? (*Shaking his head in disgust*) Worst breed of men alive.

THEOPROPIDES (*grimly*)   I don't care what he is or who he is or where he comes from. What I want to know—and what you're going to tell me—is, what does all this talk about money mean?

TRANIO (*elaborately casual*)   Oh, Philolaches owes him a few pennies.

THEOPROPIDES (*as before*)   How many?

TRANIO (*glibly*)   About twenty thousand dollars. You wouldn't call that very much, would you?

THEOPROPIDES (*gulping*)   So that's a few pennies, eh? And there's interest due on it too, I hear.

TRANIO   Twenty-two thousand all told, principal plus interest.

MONEYLENDER   Correct. And that's all I'm after, no more.

TRANIO (*shifting to high dudgeon*)   Damn it, I'd like to see you ask for a penny more! (*To Theopropides, airily*) Tell him you'll pay it so he'll go away.

THEOPROPIDES (*incredulously*)   *I* tell him I'll pay it?

TRANIO (*blandly*)   That's right. Tell him.

THEOPROPIDES   Me?

TRANIO   Sure, you. Go on, tell him. (*Pulling Theopropides off to the side, out of earshot*) Listen to me. Go ahead and promise it to him. It's all right, *I'm* telling you to do it.

THEOPROPIDES   You listen to *me*. What happened to the money?

TRANIO   It's in a safe place.

THEOPROPIDES (*promptly*)   Then *you* pay him off, if it's so safe.

TRANIO (*inspiration coming to him*)   Your son bought a house.

THEOPROPIDES (*taken aback*)   A house?

TRANIO   A house.

THEOPROPIDES (*exultantly*)   *Very* good. That Philolaches is a chip off the old block. The boy's a businessman already.

TRANIO (*glibly*)   Sure. After your house turned out to be the way I told you about, he went right out and bought another one.

THEOPROPIDES (*relishing the news*)   So he bought a house, you say?

TRANIO   That's what I said. (*Enthusiastically*) But can you guess what kind?

THEOPROPIDES (*smiling happily*)   How could I?

TRANIO (*as if unable to express what he has to say in words*)   Mm-mm!

THEOPROPIDES   What do you mean?

TRANIO (*as before*)   Don't ask me.

THEOPROPIDES   Why not?

TRANIO (*disregarding the question, ecstatically*)   Absolutely beautiful. Bright as a mirror.

THEOPROPIDES (*enthusiastically*)   Fine, fine. (*Curbing his enthusiasm somewhat*) But how much did he have to pay for it?

TRANIO (*deprecatorily*)   Only sixty thousand dollars. This twenty thousand was what he gave as down payment. He raised the money from him (*gesturing toward the moneylender*) and we turned it over to the seller. You follow me?

THEOPROPIDES (*nodding*)   Fine, fine.

MONEYLENDER (*calling to Tranio*)   Hey, it's almost noon.

TRANIO (*to Theopropides, airily*)   Please pay this fellow off so he doesn't asphyxiate us with his verbal belching.

THEOPROPIDES (*to the moneylender*)   All right, mister, you can take this matter up with me.

MONEYLENDER   It's understood I'm to get the money from you?

THEOPROPIDES   Come for it tomorrow.

MONEYLENDER   In that case I'll go. If I get it tomorrow, it's all right with me.

TRANIO (*aside*)   I hope to god he goes straight to hell tomorrow! He's ruining every single solitary plan I made. Damn these money-lenders! Foulest breed of men alive—and the most unreasonable.

THEOPROPIDES   Where is this house my son bought?

TRANIO (*aside*)   Oh oh, sunk again.

THEOPROPIDES   Why don't you answer my question?

TRANIO (*reassuringly*)   I'll tell you where it is, all right. It's just that I'm trying to remember the name of the owner.

THEOPROPIDES (*helpfully*)   Try and think.

TRANIO (*desperately, aside*)   I don't know what to do—(*getting a second inspiration*) unless I throw our neighbor next door into the pot and say that Philolaches bought his house. The best lie is the biggest one; that's what I've always heard. All right, that settles it. I've got to say it, so I will.

THEOPROPIDES (*patiently*)   How about it? Did you think of it?

TRANIO (*as if struggling to remember*)   Damn that name! (*Aside*) I mean damn this old man. (*To Theopropides*) It's your next-door neighbor. It's his house Philolaches bought.

THEOPROPIDES (*savoring the news*)   So he closed a deal with him, eh?

TRANIO   He closed it if you'll pay the price. If you don't, it's wide open. Good location, eh?

THEOPROPIDES   Good? The very best. (*Enthusiastically*) I'm dying to look over the house. Tranio, knock on the door and call one of the servants out.

TRANIO (*to himself*)   Sunk again! What do I say now? Here I am, stranded on the same old rock again. Now what do I do? God, I can't think of a way out of this one. Caught in the act!

THEOPROPIDES (*impatiently*)   Go on, call one of the servants. Hurry now. Ask him to show us around.

TRANIO   Listen, there are women in the house. First we have to see whether they're willing to have us or not.

THEOPROPIDES   You're right. You go and ask permission. I'll wait here until you come out.

TRANIO (*muttering to himself as he walks toward Simo's door*)   God damn you to hell, Theopropides! You've stymied every one of my plans. (*As he approaches the door, it opens and a figure appears.*) What luck! The owner's coming out. Just in time. (*Moving off to the side*) I'll move off here until I can call my cerebral senate into session. Then, when I hit on a plan, I'll tackle him.

(*Simo leaves the door of his house and, without noticing Tranio nearby or Theopropides off to the side, walks downstage. Simo is about the same age as Theopropides and, like him, considers money of prime importance in life. But in one key respect he is vastly different: Theopropides, because it means spending, disapproves of fast and free living; Simo is fascinated by it. The reason for this is the nature of Simo's home life: he chose to marry a considerably older woman for her money —and there is no doubt whatsoever which of the two is boss.*)

SONG

SIMO (*to the audience*)

> Not in over a year has my wife been this nice—
> Or have I had a dinner that pleased me as much.
> She just served me a meal that was fit for a king.
> Ah, but then she suggested I go take a nap.
> Not a chance. When I saw I was getting a meal
> That was special, I knew it was no accident.
> What she wants is to get me in bed—the old bitch.

And to nap right on top of a meal? Nosirree.
So I left her inside and I sneaked out the door—
And I bet that by now she's as sore as a boil.

TRANIO (*aside*)

This old man's in for trouble by the time evening
comes.
She'll start scolding at supper—and continue in bed.

SIMO (*thoughtfully*)

The more thought that I give it, the more I'm con-
vinced
That the men who have married old maids for their
money
Have to do without sleep; that's how much they hate
bed.
For example, take me. I just made up my mind
That I'd rather go out for a walk into town
Than stay home to go climb into bed with my wife.

(*Shaking his head worriedly*)

I don't know whether *your* wives have tempers or
not,
But I certainly know about mine. And I know
She'll be worse after this than she's been in the past.

TRANIO (*aside*)

Now if your way of life turns out badly for you,
Don't start trying to blame it on heaven, old boy.
Blame it all on the man who deserves it—yourself.
But it's time now for me to speak up.   ·
                (*Gesturing toward Simo*)   He's my man:
It just came to me now—how to catch this poor fish
And get *me* off the hook. I'll go up to him now.

(*Walks from his place near Simo's door downstage to where Simo is
standing.*)

TRANIO (*heartily*)

Glad to see you.

SIMO

               Why, Tranio, good afternoon.

(*They shake hands.*)

TRANIO (*solicitously*)

> How's your health been these days?

SIMO

> > > > Not too bad. What's with you?

TRANIO (*gravely*)

> I am shaking the hand of the finest of men.

SIMO

> Mighty nice of you, son, to say that.

TRANIO (*emphatically*)

> > > > > It's the truth.

SIMO

> Well, it's mutual: I'm shaking hands with the worst.
> (*Confidentially*)
> I say, tell me how long—

TRANIO (*interrupting*)

> > > > How long what?

SIMO (*smirking, with a gesture toward Theopropides' house*)

> > > > > You in there
> Can keep up all these carryings-on.

TRANIO (*summoning up his blankest expression*)

> > > > > I don't know
> What you mean.

SIMO (*winking archly*)

> > > You know perfectly well what I mean.
> (*Clapping him on the shoulder*)
> I'm on *your* side, my boy. You must live while you
> can.
> We must always remember that life's pretty short.

TRANIO

> Now just what—oh, of course. I was slow to catch
>   on:
> It's the way we've been living you're talking about.

SIMO (*enviously*)

> You've been hitting it up, and it's right that you
>   should.
> What with choice meat and fish and the very best
>   wines,
> You've been living the life!

TRANIO (*assuming an air of deep despond*)

> It's all part of the past.
> Not a one of those goodies is left to us now.

SIMO

> What's the reason?

TRANIO

> We're done for, we're sunk.

SIMO

> You don't say!
> Just when things were all going so smoothly for you.

TRANIO

> That's the truth. We just lived as we liked. It was
>   great.
> But the wind has been taken right out of our sails.

SIMO

> How is that? In what way?

TRANIO

> In the worst way of all!

SIMO

> Why, I thought you were safely in port.

TRANIO

Oh, god, no!

SIMO

What's the matter?

TRANIO

I'm sunk, I'm a wreck!

SIMO

How is that?

TRANIO

Well, a ship crossed our path and rammed into our boat.

SIMO

Very sorry to hear it. But tell me what happened.

TRANIO

In a word: the old man just came back from abroad.

SIMO (*shaking his head gloomily*)

Oh, that's bad, very bad. It's the whip for you, boy! Then a session in irons, then up on the cross.

TRANIO (*in his best help-a-dying-man manner*)

I implore you—please, Simo, don't tell him a word!

SIMO

Don't you worry. He won't get a thing out of me.

TRANIO (*fervently*)

You're a true friend in need, a defender in court!

SIMO (*distastefully*)

Any clients of mine will be hardly your sort.

TRANIO (*with a let's-get-back-to-business air*) Now, here's what Theopropides sent me to you for. He—

SIMO (*interrupting*) First answer this question. Does the old man know anything about your carryings-on?

TRANIO Not a thing.

SIMO He hasn't pitched into his son yet?

TRANIO He's as mild as a summer breeze. He sent me to ask a favor of you: will you please let him t. ke a look around your house.

SIMO (*puzzled*) But it's not for sale.

TRANIO (*quickly*) I know that. But the old man's thinking of adding to our house: a set of rooms for the women, a bath, a porch, a colonnade . . .

SIMO What made him dream all that up?

TRANIO It's like this. He's out to marry his son off as fast as he can. That's why he wants the wing for the women. Then he heard some architect or other say that your house was a marvelous job. So he wants to use it as a model if you have no objections. He's particularly interested in copying yours because he heard it's so well shaded all day long, even in summer.

SIMO God, no! When it's shady everywhere else, there's sun there from morning till night. There's no shade anywhere, except whatever's down in the well.

TRANIO Can't get the right shade, eh? How about something in pastel?

SIMO (*curtly*) Don't be funny. It's just the way I've described it.

TRANIO He wants to take a look around anyway.

SIMO (*shrugging*) Let him, if he wants. And if there's anything about it he likes, he can go right ahead and copy it.

TRANIO Shall I tell him to come, then?

SIMO Sure, tell him.

TRANIO (*to the audience as he walks over to where he had left Theopropides standing*) They say that two men, Alexander the Great and Agathocles, performed the greatest deeds. How about me for Number Three? I'm doing some marvelous deeds, and all by myself. (*Gesturing first toward Theopropides and then toward Simo*) I'm taking both these old fellows for a ride. Not a bad business, this one I've just opened up. Stables have saddle horses for hire—and I have saddle men. And can they take it! Any load you give them!

(*Tranio comes up to Theopropides. The old man has been left alone so long he has started to doze. Tranio looks him over distastefully.*)

SONG

TRANIO (*to himself*)

> Is now the time to tackle him?
> It is. Wake up, Theopropides!

THEOPROPIDES (*startled out of his doze*)

> I say, who's calling?

TRANIO

> > > Tranio,
> A superfaithful servant to
> His master.

THEOPROPIDES (*still half asleep*)

> > > Where're you coming from?

TRANIO

> From where you sent me. It's all set.

THEOPROPIDES (*finally fully awake*)

> But tell me, what kept you there so long?

TRANIO

> Simo was busy. I had to wait.

THEOPROPIDES (*testily*)

> You're always late. It's a habit of yours.

TRANIO (*as if hurt*)

> Just keep in mind the proverb, please:
> "To drink and whistle, both at once,
> Is not an easy thing to do."
> Just how could I have possibly been
> Both here with you and there with him?

THEOPROPIDES

> Well, what's he say?

TRANIO

> Look all you like.

THEOPROPIDES

> Let's go. You first.

TRANIO

> I'm off.

THEOPROPIDES

> I'm behind.

(They start walking over to where Simo is standing. When they come near, Tranio stops.)

TRANIO

> He's waiting there before the door.
> You see how down in the dumps he looks?
> It broke his heart to sell this house.

THEOPROPIDES

> It did?

TRANIO

> He *begged* me to persuade
> Philolaches to sell it back.

THEOPROPIDES *(vehemently)*

> No dice. It's every man for himself.
> Suppose the house turned out a bad buy;
> Fat chance we'd have of handing it back!
> Whatever profit's in a deal
> You pocket and take home with you.
> A businessman feel pity? No!

TRANIO

> You're holding things up. Come on, let's go.

(He starts walking again toward Simo.)

THEOPROPIDES (*sotto voce*) Anything you say, Tranio. (*He tags along after him.*)

TRANIO (*sotto voce*) There he is. (*To Simo*) Here's your man, Simo.

SIMO Glad to see you back safe and sound, Theopropides.

THEOPROPIDES Thanks very much.

SIMO Tranio's been telling me you want to look over the house.

THEOPROPIDES Yes, but if we're going to put you to any trouble . . .

SIMO No trouble at all. Go on in and take a look around.

THEOPROPIDES But the women—

SIMO (*interrupting testily*) Don't bother yourself one bit about the women. (*Graciously*) Feel free to look the whole place over just as if it was your own home.

THEOPROPIDES (*sotto voce, to Tranio*) "As if?"

TRANIO (*sotto voce, quickly*) Sh! Don't needle him in his present state about selling you the house. Look at him. Can't you see how down in the mouth he is?

THEOPROPIDES (*sotto voce, nodding vigorously*) I certainly can.

TRANIO (*sotto voce*) So don't let him see you gloating and crowing. And don't mention a word about your having bought it.

THEOPROPIDES (*sotto voce, nodding sagely*) Got you. Very good idea. I'm beginning to think you're a very sensitive person, Tranio. (*To Simo*) It's all right, then?

SIMO Go right in and look around all you want. Take your time.

THEOPROPIDES This is very nice of you, Simo.

SIMO Glad to do it.

(*They go up to the door.*)

TRANIO (*assuming the air of a professional*) You see the vestibule and foyer he has here in front of the house?

THEOPROPIDES (*nodding approvingly*) Very nice. Very nice indeed.

TRANIO Look at these gateposts he has here. (*Winking at the audience and gesturing covertly toward Theopropides and Simo*) See how solid and thick they both are?

THEOPROPIDES I don't think I've ever seen a finer pair.

SIMO Believe me, I once paid a pretty price for them.

TRANIO (*quickly taking advantage of Simo's casual use of tenses, sotto voce to Theopropides*) Did you hear that? He "once paid." He looks as if he's ready to break down and cry.

THEOPROPIDES (*to Simo*) How much did you pay for these posts?

SIMO   Fifteen hundred dollars for the pair. Not including the freight.

(*Theopropides starts at the figure, and begins examining the posts closely.*)

THEOPROPIDES (*frowning*)   Damn it, they're in much worse shape than I thought at first.

TRANIO   Why?

THEOPROPIDES   Good god, termites have gotten at both of them. Down at the bottom.

TRANIO (*winking at the audience*)   Green. Yes, sir, if you ask me, they were both made out of green wood. That's what's wrong with them. Well, they'll still give good service if you work pitch into them. No cheap, wine-guzzling foreign carpenter did this job. You see the way these double doors fit?

THEOPROPIDES (*approvingly*)   I certainly do.

TRANIO (*winking at the audience and gesturing toward the old men*)   See how fast asleep they are?

THEOPROPIDES   Fast asleep?

TRANIO (*smirking*)   I mean to say, look at them side by side. Well, are you satisfied?

THEOPROPIDES (*enthusiastically*)   The more I look at it, the more I like it.

TRANIO   See that mural? The one that shows a crow putting it over on two vultures?

THEOPROPIDES (*looking all around*)   No, I don't.

TRANIO (*looking straight at him*)   But I do. A crow standing right between two vultures. And he's taking turns skinning each one of them alive. Here, look toward me. Then you can see the crow. (*As Theopropides does so*) You see it now?

THEOPROPIDES (*bewildered*)   I don't see any crow there.

TRANIO   Then look where you and Simo are. If you can't see the crow, maybe you can make out the vultures.

THEOPROPIDES (*peevishly*)   Enough of this. I don't see any birds painted anywhere.

TRANIO   Never mind. It's all right. It's your age: you can't see so well.

THEOPROPIDES   Well, whatever I do see, I like very much.

SIMO   You've got to see more; it's really worth your while.

THEOPROPIDES   Good idea.

SIMO (*calling to a servant*)   Boy! Take him around the house. Show

him the rooms. (*To Theopropides, apologetically*) I'd run you
around myself but I've got some business in town.

THEOPROPIDES (*indignantly*) Run me around? Cut that out—none of
that stuff. I don't care what happens, I'd sooner go wrong than
let anyone give me the run-around.

SIMO I meant run you around the house.

THEOPROPIDES In that case I'll go in. But no run-around, mind you!

SIMO Sure, sure.

THEOPROPIDES All right, then I'll go in. (*Heads for the door.*)

TRANIO (*holding him back*) Wait a minute. I want to see whether
there's a dog—

THEOPROPIDES (*with alacrity*) Right. Take a look.

TRANIO (*through the doorway*) Sst! Beat it, dog! Out of the way! Get
the hell out of here! Still hanging around, are you? Sst! Beat it!

SIMO He's not dangerous. He's as gentle as a puppy. You can go right
in. Well, I'm off to town. (*Leaves, stage left.*)

THEOPROPIDES (*calling after him*) Thanks very much. Have a nice
walk. (*To Tranio*) Have someone get that there dog away from
the door. I don't care if he isn't dangerous.

TRANIO (*reassuringly*) Just look at him. See how quietly he's lying
there? You don't want people to think you're that fussy and
afraid, do you?

THEOPROPIDES Well, have it your own way. All right, follow me in.

TRANIO I'm right at your heels.

ACT IV

(*Callidamates' servant Phaniscus, "the lamp"—he lights his master's
way home at night—, enters, stage right. He has come back, in accordance with the orders issued him, to pick up his master at Philolaches'
house. Before going to the door he walks downstage and faces the audience.*)

SONG

PHANISCUS (*to the audience*)
>   Your servant who's afraid of the whip,
>   Though his conduct has been perfect,

Is just the kind a master finds
    He can use to best advantage.
For what good are the other kind
    Who are tough and scared of nothing?
When once they've earned some punishment
    They'll do things that are idiotic:
You'd think they're out to win at track
    When you see them start in running!

(Emphatically)

But if ever they're caught and brought back, it's the end:
The whole sum they could bank from a lifetime of tips
Won't come near what they'll book for their backs from the whips!

(Pauses, then resumes confidentially)

The plan that *I've* worked out is this:
I see to it my nose is clean—
That keeps me from an aching back.
And that's the way it's always been.
My platform is: a skin that's whole,
No truck with whips and the whipping pole.
By doing all my master says
I keep a roof above my head:
When blows rain down on everyone else,
There's not a single drop on me.
Just how a master will behave
Depends on what his servants do.
If they are good, then he'll be good;
When they are bad, then he is too.

(Pauses again, then resumes with considerable warmth)

Now, I know what I'm talking about. Why, the bunch
At our house is the worst set of servants alive.
"Oh, the hell with the tips, let 'em bring on the whips,"
Is their attitude. So, when you ask one of them
To go call for the master, he answers you back:
"Oh, stop bothering me. I won't go. Why don't you?
So you're busy and late? I know why—for a date.
You just want some time off to go out and make hay."

So for all my good work what reward do I get?
A long walk out-of-doors. No one else of that whole
Pack of servants is willing to call for the master.
But tomorrow A.M. he will hear what has happened,
And he'll dress them all down with the finest cowhide.
To sum up: it is *my* back that counts and not theirs;
    I'd rather see them in the tanning trade
    Than me doing business in hangings!

(Phaniscus turns and starts toward Theopropides' door. As he does, Pinacium, "the notebook"—he keeps track of appointments—, his fellow servant, comes hurrying in, stage right.)

PINACIUM *(calling)*

    Hey, Phaniscus, wait for me!
    Hold it. Hey there, turn around!

(Rushes up to Phaniscus and grabs him.)

PHANISCUS *(pulling himself free and walking on)*

    Stop that! Don't annoy me now!

PINACIUM *(jeering)*

    What's the matter? Too good for me?
    Stop, you stinking parasite!

PHANISCUS *(stopping and eyeing him distastefully)*

    Just how am I a parasite?

PINACIUM *(sneering)*

    I'll tell you how. To feed your face
    You let them lead you by the nose.

PHANISCUS *(truculently)*

    Well, that's the way I like it, see?
    It's my affair. What's it to *you?*

PINACIUM *(as before)*

    Oh, yeah? You only act so tough
    Because you're master's fair-haired boy.

PHANISCUS

    Oh, boy, do my eyes hurt!

PINACIUM

How come?

PHANISCUS

All this hot air you're handing me.

PINACIUM

Aw, cut those phony jokes of yours.
If you went in for carpentry
You'd turn out wooden nickels, boy.

PHANISCUS (*loftily*)

You can't get *me* to swap insults.
The master knows the sort I am.

PINACIUM (*promptly*)

God, yes! A doormat, all his own.

PHANISCUS (*as before*)

If you weren't drunk, you'd have more respect.

PINACIUM

You don't take any orders from me,
So I won't take a one from you.

PHANISCUS (*grabbing him and propelling him toward the door*)

This time, damn you, you're coming along.
And hold your tongue. Enough of that talk.

PINACIUM

All right, all right, I'll knock on the door.

(*Starts pounding vigorously and calling at the same time.*)

Whoever's in there, you'd better come out
And save this door from a horrible end.
Hey, someone come and open this door!

(*To himself*)

So, no one's coming, eh? Of course—
The lazy good-for-nothings are drunk.

(*Suddenly starts backing away from the door.*)

> That means I'd better be on the alert.
> If they do come out, I'm bound to get hurt!

(*The door of Simo's house opens, and Tranio and Theopropides come out.*)

TRANIO   Well, what kind of buy does it look like to you?

THEOPROPIDES (*beaming*) I couldn't be more pleased.

TRANIO (*putting on an air of being unsure*) You don't think we paid too much now, do you?

THEOPROPIDES (*with conviction*) If ever I've seen a house simply given away, it's this one.

TRANIO   So you like it?

THEOPROPIDES   Like it? Lord, I love it!

TRANIO   The women's rooms are all right? And how about the colonnade?

THEOPROPIDES   Marvelous. I think it's bigger than the ones on the main square downtown.

TRANIO   As a matter of fact, Philolaches and I measured all the colonnades in town.

THEOPROPIDES   What did you find?

TRANIO   They're all shorter.

THEPROPIDES   Ye gods, it's a terrific buy. Damn it all, if he offered me two hundred thousand for it, cash on the barrel head, I wouldn't take it.

TRANIO   Damn it all, even if you wanted to, I wouldn't let you.

THEOPROPIDES (*rubbing his hands delightedly*) We've made one fine investment in this buy.

TRANIO (*with affected modesty*) I think it's fair to say that I was the one behind it all. It was I who talked Philolaches into going to that moneylender and borrowing the cash for the down payment.

THEOPROPIDES   Right. You saved the day. So I owe Simo forty thousand, eh?

TRANIO   Not a penny more.

THEOPROPIDES   He'll have it today.

TRANIO   Good idea. That way he can't back out. (*Casually*) Tell you what: give me the money and I'll pay him off.

THEOPROPIDES (*losing some of his expansiveness*) No, you might try to pull something on me, if I gave it to you.

TRANIO (*reproachfully*) I deceive you? Not even as a joke! What makes you think I'd do such a thing.

THEOPROPIDES (*eyeing him narrowly*) What makes you think I'd let down my guard and trust you with anything?

TRANIO (*switching from reproachfulness to injured innocence*) Because I've never once deceived you since I've been in your household.

THEOPROPIDES (*smugly*) Naturally. I never gave you the chance.

TRANIO (*loftily*) You ought to be grateful for having a servant with my character.

THEOPROPIDES I think it's pretty smart of me to spot you as the one man to keep an eye on.

TRANIO (*aside*) I agree with you.

THEOPROPIDES Now, go to the farm and tell Philolaches I'm home.

TRANIO Whatever you say.

THEOPROPIDES Tell him to hurry into town with you.

TRANIO Right. (*Aside, as he walks away*) Now I'll go through this gate here (*pointing*) to the rest of the gang and explain how everything's under control at my end and how I got rid of the old man.

(*Tranio leaves to sneak around to the back of Theopropides' house and get in by the rear door. Theopropides remains, buried in happy thought, near Simo's door. At this moment Phaniscus and Pinacium resume their conversation.*)

PHANISCUS (*listening intently at the door*) There's no sound of any party going on the way there usually is. There's no singing, and I can't even hear any talking.

THEOPROPIDES (*his attention caught by the voice, to himself*) What's going on here? What are those two after at my house? What do they want, anyway? What are they peeking inside for?

PINACIUM Well, I'll begin banging on the door again. (*Pounding and shouting*) Hey, open up! Tranio! Are you going to open this door or not?

THEOPROPIDES (*to himself*) Now this is very curious.

PINACIUM (*as before*) How about it? Going to open up for us? We're here to get Callidamates.

THEOPROPIDES (*calling to them, sharply*) Hey, boys! What are you doing there? What are you trying to break down the house for?

PHANISCUS   Look, old man, what are you sticking your nose into what's none of your business for?

THEOPROPIDES *(taken aback)*   None of my business?

PHANISCUS   That's right. What are you anyway, a newly appointed investigator, guardian, overseer and judge of other people's property?

THEOPROPIDES   That house you're in front of is *my* property.

PHANISCUS   What are you talking about? *(To Pinacium)* Has Philolaches sold it? Or is this old man trying to put one over on us?

THEOPROPIDES *(sharply)*   I don't tell lies. Just what are you doing here anyway?

PHANISCUS   If you must know, our master's at a party here.

THEOPROPIDES   Your master's at a party here?

PHANISCUS   That's what I said.

THEOPROPIDES   Now don't try to be funny, boy.

PHANISCUS   We came to get him.

THEOPROPIDES   Who?

PHANISCUS *(impatiently)*   Our master. How many times must you be told?

THEOPROPIDES *(indulgently)*   My dear boy, nobody lives here. I don't mind telling you this because you look like a nice, decent boy to me.

PHANISCUS   You mean a young fellow by the name of Philolaches doesn't live here?

THEOPROPIDES *(as before)*   He used to, but he moved out a long time ago.

PINACIUM *(to Phaniscus)*   This old fellow must be off his rocker.

PHANISCUS *(to Theopropides)*   Mister, you can't be right. I know for sure he lives here—unless he moved out today or yesterday.

THEOPROPIDES   You're wrong. No one's been living in this house for the last six months.

PINACIUM   Wake up, will you?

THEOPROPIDES   Who? Me?

PINACIUM   Yeah, you.

THEOPROPIDES *(sharply)*   Now, don't annoy me! I'm talking to this boy here. *(To Phaniscus)* Nobody lives here.

PHANISCUS   He lives here, all right. Yesterday, and two days ago, and three days ago, and four days ago, and five—well, ever since his father went abroad, he's been throwing a nonstop party here. They haven't quit drinking for three days in a row.

THEOPROPIDES (*taken aback*) What's that you say?

PHANISCUS I simply said they haven't stopped drinking for three days in a row—or having women in the house or acting like a bunch of Greeks or having musicians and entertainers around.

THEOPROPIDES (*bewildered*) Who's been doing these things?

PHANISCUS Philolaches.

THEOPROPIDES Which Philolaches?

PHANISCUS I think his father's name is Theopropides.

THEOPROPIDES (*aside*) Oh, my god! I'm done for if what this fellow says is true. Better get to the bottom of all this. (*To Phaniscus*) So you say that this Philolaches, whoever he is, was in the habit of throwing wild parties along with your master, eh?

PHANISCUS That's what I said. Right in this house.

THEOPROPIDES (*gently*) My boy, you don't look that stupid. I suspect you stopped off for a snack on the way and had a bit more to drink than was good for you.

PHANISCUS What do you mean?

THEOPROPIDES (*as before*) I only say this because I'm afraid you've made a mistake and come to the wrong house.

PHANISCUS Listen, I know the way here and where I am now. Philolaches lives here, Theopropides' son. Same fellow who bought a chorus girl and set her free after his father went abroad on business.

THEOPROPIDES (*thoughtfully*) Philolaches did that, eh?

PHANISCUS (*nodding*) Right. Her name is Philematium.

THEOPROPIDES How much did he pay?

PHANISCUS Fif—

THEOPROPIDES (*roaring*) Fifty thousand!

PHANISCUS Good god, no. Fifteen.

THEOPROPIDES And he set her free, eh?

PHANISCUS He sure did. After laying out fifteen thousand.

THEOPROPIDES Let's get this straight. You say Philolaches bought a chorus girl for fifteen thousand.

PHANISCUS Right.

THEOPROPIDES And then set her free?

PHANISCUS Right.

THEOPROPIDES And that once his father had left for overseas he kept throwing wild parties along with your master?

PHANISCUS Right.

THEOPROPIDES What about this: did he buy this house next door?

PHANISCUS Wrong.

THEOPROPIDES Another thing: did he give the owner twenty thousand as a down payment?

PHANISCUS Wrong again.

THEOPROPIDES Good god, you're ruining everything!

PHANISCUS Oh, no. He is. Especially his father.

THEOPROPIDES That's no joke.

PHANISCUS I wish it was. You look as if you might be a friend of the old man's.

THEOPROPIDES Lord in heaven, from what you say that poor father's in a bad way.

PHANISCUS Oh, the fifteen thousand is nothing compared with what he's spent on fancy living.

THEOPROPIDES (*bitterly*) He's ruined his own father.

PHANISCUS The worst of all, though, is a servant by the name of Tranio. He could go through a millionaire's bankroll. So help me, I feel sorry for that poor old father. When he finds out what's happened, the poor fellow'll eat his heart out.

THEOPROPIDES (*clinging to a last straw*) If you're telling the truth.

PHANISCUS What have I got to gain by lying?

PINACIUM (*pounding and hollering again*) Hey in there! Isn't anyone going to open this door?

PHANISCUS What are you banging away for? There's no one in there. If you ask me, they've moved the party somewhere else. Let's go right now—

THEOPROPIDES (*interrupting worriedly*) I say, boy—

PHANISCUS (*disregarding the interruption*) —and keep looking for them. Follow me.

PINACIUM I'm right behind you.

THEOPROPIDES You leaving now?

PHANISCUS You're a free man. Your back doesn't have to worry about welts. To make mine immune I have to maintain a healthy respect for the master and keep an eye on him. (*Exits, followed by Pinacium, stage right.*)

THEOPROPIDES (*to himself*) Oh, my god, this is the end of me! What's the use of talking about it? Have I been taken for a ride! Egypt was just the halfway mark—I've been hauled to the end of the world. I'm lost! I don't know where I'm at! (*Recovering somewhat as he sees Simo enter, stage left*) Now I'll get the truth.

Here comes the fellow my son bought the house from. (*To Simo as he approaches*) Well, how are things going?

SIMO Going? I'm coming. Just got back from downtown.

THEOPROPIDES Anything new there?

SIMO Yes.

THEOPROPIDES What?

SIMO I saw a funeral.

THEOPROPIDES (*impatiently*) What's so new about that?

SIMO I saw the fellow's body. They told me that up to the time he died—he was still alive.

THEOPROPIDES (*disgustedly*) You and your jokes!

SIMO What are you doing hanging around asking people for news?

THEOPROPIDES I just got back from abroad today.

SIMO (*quickly*) Look, if you're thinking of being invited to dinner, I'm sorry. I'm eating out tonight.

THEOPROPIDES The thought never crossed my mind.

SIMO But tomorrow, unless someone invites me first, we can have dinner together if you like. At your house.

THEOPROPIDES That thought never crossed my mind either. (*Worriedly*) Are you very busy right now? Can you spare me a minute?

SIMO By all means.

THEOPROPIDES As I understand it, Philolaches turned over to you twenty thousand dollars, right?

SIMO As *I* understand it, he hasn't given me a cent.

THEOPROPIDES Then maybe my servant Tranio gave it to you?

SIMO (*snorting*) That one? Not a chance!

THEOPROPIDES You didn't receive this money as a down payment?

SIMO Are you dreaming?

THEOPROPIDES (*angrily*) I? You must be, if you're thinking you can call the whole deal off by putting on this act.

SIMO What deal?

THEOPROPIDES The deal my son made with you while I was away.

SIMO He made a deal with me while you were away? What kind of deal? When?

THEOPROPIDES I owe you forty thousand dollars.

SIMO (*responding automatically*) Not to me you don't. (*Reversing his field as the import sinks in*) Wait—if you owe it to me, you'd better pay it. (*Warming up to the subject*) **A** man shouldn't go back on his word. So don't try to back out.

THEOPROPIDES   Believe me, I won't. I owe it to you and I'll pay it. Just don't you try to deny that you've already received twenty thousand.

SIMO (*exasperated*)   For god's sake, stand still and look at me and answer this question: How come your son owed me that twenty thousand you're talking about?

THEOPROPIDES   I'll tell you, all right. Tranio says the boy bought your house from you for sixty thousand dollars.

SIMO   Bought my house from me? Is that what he told you? Why, he told me you wanted to marry your son off and consequently wanted to do some adding to your house.

THEOPROPIDES   I wanted to add to my house?

SIMO   That's what he told me.

THEOPROPIDES   Oh, my god, this is the end! (*Choking with rage*) I'm even losing my voice! Simo, I'm ruined, I'm done for!

SIMO   You mean Tranio put one over on you?

THEOPROPIDES (*roaring*)   One? Everyone in the book. It's a crying shame the way he took me in today.

SIMO   What's that you say?

THEOPROPIDES   Just what I'm telling you: Tranio pulled the fast one of the century on me today. Please, will you do me a favor and help me out?

SIMO   What do you want?

THEOPROPIDES   I'd like you to come with me.

SIMO   All right.

THEOPROPIDES   And lend me some servants and some whips.

SIMO   Help yourself.

THEOPROPIDES   And while we're getting them, I'll tell you just how he made a monkey out of me. (*The two enter Simo's house.*)

ACT V

(*Tranio emerges from the side gate he had sneaked through a little earlier. Things are not going well for him: his less brazen accomplices have intimated that they're ready to make a clean breast of the whole business.*)

TRANIO (*to the audience*) The man who gets scared when things look bad isn't worth a tinker's damn. Come to think of it, what is a tinker's damn anyway? Well, when Theopropides sent me off to the farm to get Philolaches, I just sneaked through this alley (*pointing*) to our back yard. Then I opened the gate between the yard and the alley and led out my whole battalion, males and females. After I had liberated my forces from the siege and led them to safety, I decided to call a special senate meeting of the gang. And then, after I call it to order, what do they do but refuse to give me the floor. So, since I see they're going to sell me out—and in my own market at that—I'm going to go right ahead and do what most people do when things are touch and go: stir up such a mess there's no possible way of straightening it out. After all, I can't hide things any longer from the old man, no matter what I do. [Four lines are lost here.] I'll steal a march on them: I'll make contact with the old man before they do and hit him up for a treaty. But I'm wasting time. (*Turns to go, then stops.*) Wait—someone's coming out of Simo's door. (*The door opens wide.*) There's Theopropides. I want to get a line on what he's going to say. (*Moves off to the side of the stage.*)

THEOPROPIDES (*through the doorway to some servants inside*) Now, you stand right there where you are, behind the door, so that you can jump out on the double the minute I call you. Then get those handcuffs on him fast. (*Turning away, to himself*) I'll wait for that joker of mine in front of the house and, as sure as I'm alive, what I'll do to his hide today will be no joke!

TRANIO (*aside*) Oh, oh, it's all out in the open now. Tranio, old boy, you'd better start to figure out what you're going to do next.

THEOPROPIDES (*to himself*) I've got to play this fish with finesse when he comes along. I'm not going to let him see the hook right off. I'll feed him the line gradually. I'll make believe I don't know a thing about what's been going on.

TRANIO (*aside, derisively*) Smart boy, there. Subtlest brain in all Athens. About as hard to put one over on him as it is on a rock. Well, here goes. (*Walks toward Theopropides.*)

THEOPROPIDES (*not noticing him, to himself*) Now if he'd only come along this minute.

TRANIO (*calling to him cheerily*) If it's me you're looking for, here I am in the flesh, right before your eyes.

THEOPROPIDES (*with patently false heartiness*) Well, Tranio! How are you making out?

TRANIO The countryside-lovers are coming back from the country. Philolaches will be along very soon.

THEOPROPIDES (*as before*) I must say you came along just at the right time. (*Dropping his voice*) I've got an idea that our neighbor here (*gesturing toward Simo's house*) is a crook who'll stop at nothing.

TRANIO Why?

THEOPROPIDES He says he doesn't even know you people.

TRANIO (*as if thunderstruck*) Doesn't know us?

THEOPROPIDES And that you never gave him a cent.

TRANIO Aw, come on. You're kidding me. I can't believe he'd say such a thing.

THEOPROPIDES Well, you're wrong. He says you absolutely did not. And he says he never sold his house to Philolaches.

TRANIO You mean to tell me he says we never paid him any money?

THEOPROPIDES Do you know he even agreed, in case I wanted it, to swear out an affidavit that he never sold his house or received any money? [One line is missing here.] I told him the very same thing myself.

TRANIO What did he say?

THEOPROPIDES (*pointedly*) He offered to let me question every one of his servants—under torture.

TRANIO (*nervously*) That's ridiculous. He'd never let you do *that*.

THEOPROPIDES He most certainly is going to let me.

TRANIO (*with an air of having come to a difficult but final decision*) The thing to do is to hale him into court. I'll go get him. (*Turns as if to head for Simo's door.*)

THEOPROPIDES (*holding him back*) Hold it. I think I'll take him up on his offer. (*Pausing, as if seriously deliberating it*) Yes, that's what I'll do.

TRANIO No, leave him to me. I'd like to see him claim he still owns the house, in front of *me*.

THEOPROPIDES But first I want to grill those servants of his.

TRANIO Absolutely right. I agree. You should.

THEOPROPIDES Suppose I have them brought out here?

(Realizing that he is close to disaster—a session on the rack for Simo's servants undoubtedly would be followed by one for him—Tranio saunters casually to the altar in the center of the stage; since it stood in a consecrated spot no one who sought refuge there could be touched. He seats himself comfortably on it.)

TRANIO *(blandly)* You should have done that earlier. In the meantime I'll just take over this altar.

THEOPROPIDES *(biting his lip)* What do you want to do that for?

TRANIO Don't you know anything? To keep those servants from running here for protection when you start your inquisition. I'll guard it for you. That way there's no chance of that grilling of yours coming to nothing.

THEOPROPIDES Tranio, you get off there.

TRANIO No sir!

THEOPROPIDES Tranio, I don't want you on that altar.

TRANIO *(innocently)* Why?

THEOPROPIDES *(thinking hard)* I'll tell you. Don't you see? That's just what I want them to do. Let them run to this altar. Then I'll have a reason to hale *him* into court, and it'll be lots easier to collect damages.

TRANIO *(as if giving the matter serious thought)* No, you go ahead with what you started to do. Why do you want to make more trouble for yourself? You have no idea what a ticklish business it is to go before a judge.

THEOPROPIDES In that case, come on over here. There's something I want your advice on.

TRANIO *(blandly)* Oh, I can give it to you from here, just as I am. I think better sitting down. *(Smirking)* Besides, advice from a divine spot is bound to have more weight.

THEOPROPIDES Now, Tranio, I want you to stop fooling around and get off of there. *(As Tranio swivels about and jauntily faces the audience)* Look at me!

TRANIO *(grinning)* I already have. *(Turns back and looks him over distastefully.)*

THEOPROPIDES *(summoning up a ghastly smile in an attempt to look genial)* See?

TRANIO *(cheerily)* Oh, I see, all right. You know, if somebody came between us now, he'd starve to death.

THEOPROPIDES   Why?

TRANIO   Because he couldn't make a cent out of either of us. We're both so infernally clever.

THEOPROPIDES   (*in utter bafflement*)   Oh, god!

TRANIO   (*solicitously*)   What's the matter?

THEOPROPIDES   You've been lying to me!

TRANIO   (*all innocence*)   I? How?

THEOPROPIDES   You've been doing a fine job of pulling my leg.

TRANIO   (*solicitously*)   But please make sure I've done it enough. How are the muscles? All nice and relaxed?

THEOPROPIDES   (*roaring*)   You've pulled all the brains out of my head! I've found out about everything you did. I got to the bottom of it, I did. By god, I even got beneath the bottom.

TRANIO   Look, I'm never getting off this spot. Not unless I want to.

THEOPROPIDES   (*raging*)   You'll get off, all right. Damn you, I'll have 'em bring wood out here and light a fire around you.

TRANIO   (*unruffled*)   Roast me? Oh, don't do that: I taste much better boiled.

THEOPROPIDES   (*shaking his fist*)   I'll make an example of you, that's what I'll do.

TRANIO   You want to make an example of me because you're so pleased with me, is that it?

THEOPROPIDES   (*giving up, wearily*)   What was my son like when I went away? Just tell me that.

TRANIO   Well, he had hands, feet, fingers, ears, eyes, lips—

THEOPROPIDES   (*disgustedly*)   I asked you about something different.

TRANIO   Well, I'm telling you about something different. (*His attention caught, looks off, stage right.*) I see your son's best friend is coming this way. If you want to keep at me you'll have to do it with him around.

(*Enter Callidamates, a little bleary-eyed and disheveled but otherwise in fair shape.*)

CALLIDAMATES   (*to the audience*)   I got rid of the effects of that binge; managed to sleep it off. And then, as soon as I wake up, Philolaches tells me his father's back from abroad and explains how that servant of his made such a fool of the old man when he arrived at the house. Philolaches says he's scared to look his father in the face—so here I am, appointed sole spokesman for the company, to arrange a peace pact with pater. (*Turns and notices the two at the altar.*) I'm in luck; there he is now. (*In his best greetings-to-a-long-lost-friend manner*) Well, Theopropides! Back safe and sound. It's a pleasure to see you. You eat at my house tonight, that's what you do.

THEOPROPIDES (*unenthusiastically*) Oh, hello, Callidamates. Thanks for the invitation, but I can't.

CALLIDAMATES Why not?

TRANIO (*to Theopropides*) Oh, say yes. I'll go instead of you, if you're not interested.

THEOPROPIDES (*angrily*) Damn you! More funny stuff out of you?

TRANIO (*with injured innocence*) Just because I said I'd go to a dinner party instead of you?

THEOPROPIDES (*grimly*) You won't be going. I'm arranging the sort of invitation you deserve—to a hanging.

CALLIDAMATES (*to Theopropides*) Come now, forget all this and promise me you'll come to dinner. (*As Theopropides remains sullenly silent*) What do you say? (*Waits a minute without getting an answer, then turns to Tranio.*) And you there, what did you run to this altar for?

TRANIO (*gesturing covertly toward Theopropides*) Some nitwit came along and scared me. (*To Theopropides*) Go ahead, tell him what I did. Now we have an umpire to hear both sides. Go ahead, state your case.

THEOPROPIDES (*eyeing him balefully*) I say that you corrupted my son.

TRANIO Now, just listen to me. I admit that he carried on, that he bought a mistress and set her free, and that he went out and borrowed money—and I don't mind telling you it's all used up. But has he done anything different from what all the young fellows in the best families do?

THEOPROPIDES (*sarcastically*) I see I have to watch my step. Pretty slick talker, aren't you?

CALLIDAMATES (*to Theopropides*) Now just let me decide this matter. (*To Tranio*) Get off. I'm going to sit there.

THEOPROPIDES (*to Callidamates*) By all means. The case is all yours.

TRANIO (*without budging*) There's something tricky going on. (*To Callidamates*) First you see to it that I have nothing to be afraid of and that you be the one to worry instead of me.

THEOPROPIDES (*to Callidamates*)   The one thing I care about is the way he made a fool of me. Everything else is secondary.

TRANIO   I did a good job and I'm proud of it. Look, you've got gray hair. At your age you ought to have more sense.

THEOPROPIDES (*to Callidamates, helplessly*)   What can I do with him?

TRANIO (*promptly*)   If you were a friend of Diphilus[1] or Philemon you could tell them how your servant made a fool of you. You could supply them with some wonderful Old-Man-Gets-Duped plots for their plays.

CALLIDAMATES (*to Tranio*)   Keep quiet a minute, will you? Let me have a chance to talk. (*To Theopropides*) Please listen to me.

THEOPROPIDES (*stony-faced*)   I'm listening.

CALLIDAMATES (*very seriously*)   You know that I'm your son's best friend. He came to me for help. It's understandable: he's ashamed to look you in the face because he knows that you know what he did. He's young and he behaved stupidly. I beg you, please forgive him. After all, he's your own son. And you know that boys his age usually play around that way. What's more, whatever he did, we did with him; we're all to blame. About that money for the loan and the interest and the price of the girl— we'll get together and dig it up. We'll pay it. It won't cost you a cent.

THEOPROPIDES (*mollified—particularly by Callidamates' offer*)   You know, there isn't anyone else who could have pleaded his case before me so effectively as you. I'm not angry with him any longer—and I won't hold any grudge against him. As a matter of fact, even now, with me back, he can go right ahead and run around with women or drink or do whatever he likes. If he's ashamed of himself—of having spent all that money—then I consider that punishment enough.

CALLIDAMATES   He's terribly ashamed.

TRANIO   Now that you've pardoned *him*, how about *me*?

THEOPROPIDES (*exploding*)   You? Damn you, I'm going to have you strung up and whipped to within an inch of your life!

TRANIO (*mockingly*)   Even if I'm terribly ashamed?

THEOPROPIDES (*between his teeth*)   So help me, as sure as I'm alive, I'm going to see that you die.

[1] See p. 67.

CALLIDAMATES (*to Theopropides*) Please forgive us all. I beg you, for my sake let Tranio off.

THEOPROPIDES Ask me for any other favor and I'll do it. But don't ask me to let this pest go without paying the price for what he did to me.

CALLIDAMATES Please. Let him off.

THEOPROPIDES (*as Tranio lounges against the altar, grinning insolently*) Let him off? Look at the way the stinker is standing there!

CALLIDAMATES (*as Tranio opens his mouth*) Tranio! If you've got any sense, you'll keep your mouth shut!

THEOPROPIDES (*to Callidamates, angrily*) And you can keep yours shut if you're still out to try this "let-him-off" business. And I'll keep his shut too—with the whip.

TRANIO No need for that, believe me.

CALLIDAMATES Come on. Please. I'm asking you as a special favor.

THEOPROPIDES Don't ask me for any favors.

CALLIDAMATES Please!

THEOPROPIDES You heard me—don't ask me for any favors.

CALLIDAMATES I heard you, but it doesn't make any difference. Please, for my sake pardon this one slip of his.

TRANIO (*to Theopropides*) What are you worried about? I'll turn around and make another slip tomorrow and then you can do a bang-up job of punishing me for both at once.

CALLIDAMATES (*to Theopropides*) Please! Will you let him go?

THEOPROPIDES (*to Tranio*) All right, I'll let you go. (*Gesturing toward Callidamates*) But don't you forget to thank this fellow here for it. (*Walks downstage and addresses the audience.*) Ladies and gentlemen, the play is over. May we please have your applause?

The Rope

/

DRAMATIS PERSONAE

Sceparnio, Daemones' servant (slave)

Plesidippus, a wealthy young Athenian residing in Cyrene

Daemones, an elderly Athenian living in straitened circumstances near Cyrene

Palaestra, a beautiful young courtesan, the property of Labrax

Ampelisca, an attractive young courtesan, also the property of Labrax

Ptolemocratia, priestess of the shrine of Venus

Fishermen

Trachalio, Plesidippus' valet (slave)

Labrax, a slave dealer

Charmides, an elderly vagabond who has recently struck up an acquaintance with Labrax

Roughneck ⎫
⎬ slaves of Daemones
Cutthroat ⎭

Gripus, a fisherman, slave of Daemones

[*Daedalis,* wife of Daemones]

SCENE   A barren shore near Cyrene. In the background are, stage right, Daemones' simple cottage, and, stage left, a shrine of Venus consisting chiefly of a modest temple with an altar in front. The exit near the temple (stage left) leads to Cyrene. That near the cottage (stage right) leads to the beach; sand and rocks and a patch of reeds are visible near it.

PROLOGUE

(The Prologue, dressed in a spangled costume and wearing a glittering star on his forehead, steps forward. He represents Arcturus, the constellation that, rising in September and setting in November, marks the period of the equinoctial storms.)

ARCTURUS   I am from the city of the celestials, fellow citizen of him who holds sway over all peoples, all seas, and all lands. My appearance is as you see: a bright star that glitters and gleams, that rises and sets in heaven and on earth, forever and ever, in its season. My name is Arcturus.

At night I shine among the gods in the sky; by day I walk among men on earth. Other stars, too, come down here from heaven: great Jove, lord of gods and men, assigns us stations, one here and another there, all over the world. We find out for him what men are doing, how they are behaving, particularly which are reverent and honest so that he can show them his favor. If we find people trying to win cases by bearing false witness, or forswearing themselves to deny a debt, we note their names and report them to Jove. From day to day he knows precisely who here on earth is out to do wrong. When rascals go into a trial ready to perjure themselves and trick a judge into awarding them the verdict, *he* reopens the case, reviews it, and passes a sentence so stiff it far outweighs whatever they may have won.

In another set of records he keeps a list of the good. And if the wicked have the idea that they can get on it by winning him over with gifts and offerings, they're wasting their time and money. Why? Because he has no mercy for men who are two-faced. The appeal of the honest man finds favor far more easily than that of the wicked despite all their gifts. And so I advise those of you who are good, who live your lives in reverence and honesty, to go on in this way so that you may reap your reward in time to come.

But now I want to tell you about the play; after all, that's what I'm here for.

(*Gesturing toward the scene behind him*) To begin with, this city is Cyrene; that's the way Diphilus[1] wanted it. This cottage on the seashore and the farm alongside it belong to Daemones. He's an old man who came here as an exile from Athens. He's not a bad man; he didn't leave his homeland because of any wrong he had done. It's simply that, in helping others, he got himself involved and, through his generosity, dissipated a hard-earned fortune. He once had a daughter, and he lost her, too, when she was a little child: she was kidnaped. The kidnaper sold her to a dealer in courtesans, one of the worst men alive.

Now the pimp who bought her brought the girl here to Cyrene. A certain young fellow, an Athenian—which makes him the girl's fellow citizen—happened to see her one day as she was coming home from her music lesson. He fell in love with her, went straight to the pimp, and arranged to buy her for fifteen thousand dollars. He paid a deposit and had a contract drawn up. But the pimp, true to type, didn't care the least bit either about keeping his word or about the contract he had signed. He happened to have staying with him an old fellow from Agrigentum in Sicily, someone just like himself, a scoundrel who'd sell his own mother. This fellow began to rave about how beautiful the girl was, as well as all the others the pimp owned. And he began to talk the pimp into going to Sicily with him: he kept telling him there were lots of fast livers in Sicily, that courtesans made big money there, and that he could become a rich man there. He convinced him. And so the pimp secretly chartered a vessel and, one night, moved everything out of his house and put it on board. He told the boy who had bought the girl that he was going to the shrine of Venus to make a sacrifice and pay off an obligation—(*pointing*) this is the shrine right here—and even invited the young fellow to share the remains of the animal and have lunch with him there. Then he went straight to the ship and sailed off with his girls. Word reached the boy of what had happened, that the pimp had left town, but by the time the young fellow made it down to the waterfront the ship was already far out at sea.

[1] See p. 67.

When I saw that the pimp was carrying the girl off, I stepped
in to help her and hurt him. I raised a storm and stirred up the
waves. You all know that I, Arcturus, am the fiercest constellation of all; things get stormy when I rise and worse when I set.
Right now both the pimp and his cohort are castaways, sitting
on a rock; their ship's been shattered. The girl and one other
from the troupe got frightened and jumped out of the vessel into
the ship's boat; at this moment the waves are carrying them to
shore near where old Daemones lives in exile. As a matter of fact,
the storm ripped off his roof with all its tiles. (*As the door of the
cottage opens and a figure comes out*) That's his servant there,
coming out. In a minute you'll see the young fellow who arranged
to buy the girl from the pimp. Goodbye and good luck!

ACT I

(*Daemones' servant, Sceparnio, "the wood chopper," comes out of the
cottage carrying a spade. Sceparnio, a young fellow in his twenties, is
the sort whose face feels more comfortable wearing a scowl than a smile,
and his disposition has not been improved by years of work for a penniless master. His expression is even more sour than usual as he looks over
the damage done to the cottage during the night.*)

SCEPARNIO (*to the audience*)   God in heaven, what a storm we had
here last night! The wind took the roof right off the cottage.
Wind? That was no wind; that was a hurricane right out of a
play by Euripides! Look how it ripped all the tiles off the roof!
It's made the cottage a lot brighter—put in some new skylights
for us.

(*Unnoticed by Sceparnio, Plesidippus enters, stage left, followed by
three friends; all are wearing coats and carrying swords. Plesidippus is
a good-looking young fellow, well and expensively dressed. His face at
the moment shows signs of worry and strain. He and his friends are deep
in conversation as they come on stage.*)

PLESIDIPPUS (*apologetically*)   And so I rushed you away from your
own affairs and all for nothing; I wasn't able to get my hands
on that pimp down at the dock. But I didn't want to let up for
one minute, I didn't want to give up hope; that's why I've kept

you with me all this time. I've come out here to take a look around this shrine of Venus; he told me he was going to make a sacrifice here.

SCEPARNIO (*to himself, eying the spade distastefully*) If I've got any brains, I'd better start getting some of this blasted clay ready.

PLESIDIPPUS (*overhearing, to his friends*) Wait—I hear someone talking.

(*The door of the cottage opens and Daemones comes out. Daemones is middle-aged. Though he is dressed in worn work clothes, there is something about his manner and carriage that indicates he was not born a peasant.*)

DAEMONES (*calling*) Hey, Sceparnio!

SCEPARNIO (*as he turns around*) Who wants me?

DAEMONES The man who paid good money for you.

SCEPARNIO (*sourly*) Why don't you come right out with it and call me your slave?

DAEMONES We're going to need lots of clay, so there's lots of digging for you to do. It looks as if we'll have to re-roof the whole cottage. Daylight's coming through everywhere; there are more holes up there than in a sieve.

PLESIDIPPUS (*to Daemones*) Good morning, Dad. (*Noticing Sceparnio*) Good morning to you both.

DAEMONES Good morning.

SCEPARNIO What do you mean by calling him "Dad"? You his— (*Eying his rather dandified dress distastefully*) What are you anyway, male or female?

PLESIDIPPUS (*astonished*) I? I'm a man.

SCEPARNIO Well, my man, go find your father further on.

DAEMONES (*sorrowfully*) I once did have a little daughter, but I lost her. She was the only child I had; I never had a son.

PLESIDIPPUS (*politely*) God will give you one.

SCEPARNIO (*snarling*) And he'll give you, whoever you are, what you won't want. Bothering busy people with your blabbering!

PLESIDIPPUS (*pointedly ignoring him, to Daemones; gesturing toward the cottage*) Do you live here?

SCEPARNIO What do you want to know for? What are you doing, casing the place? Looking for someone to rob?

PLESIDIPPUS (*turning on him*)   You must be one important and trusted slave to be able to answer for your master when he's present—and insult a gentleman.

SCEPARNIO   And you must be one nervy boor to be able to come up to the house of a total stranger who doesn't owe you the time of day and make a nuisance of yourself.

DAEMONES   Keep quiet, Sceparnio. (*To Plesidippus*) What would you like, my boy?

PLESIDIPPUS (*testily*)   I'd like to see that slave of yours get what's coming to him for taking it on himself to do the talking when his master's around. (*Politely*) If you don't mind, there are a few questions I'd like to ask you.

DAEMONES   Well, I'm busy right now, but I'll be glad to help even so.

SCEPARNIO (*quickly*)   Why don't you go down to the swamp and cut some canes for the roof while the weather's still clear?

DAEMONES (*curtly*)   Quiet! (*To Plesidippus*) Now, what can I do for you?

PLESIDIPPUS (*eagerly*)   Tell me, have you seen a fellow around here with curly gray hair? A sneaking, wheedling, lying—

DAEMONES (*interrupting, grimly*)   Lots of them. It's because of men like that that I live the way I do.

PLESIDIPPUS   I mean right here, at the shrine. Fellow with two girls with him, coming to make a sacrifice? Yesterday or maybe this morning?

DAEMONES (*shaking his head*)   No, my boy, I haven't seen anyone come here to make a sacrifice for a good many days now. And when they do, I see them all right—they always drop in to get water or fire or borrow dishes or a knife or a spit or a cooking pot or something. You'd think I kept a kitchen and a well for Venus and not myself. But they've left me alone for quite a while now.

PLESIDIPPUS (*in anguish*)   You know what you've just done? Pronounced my death sentence!

DAEMONES   Believe me, if I had my way, you'd be alive and healthy.

SCEPARNIO (*to Plesidippus*)   Listen you, if you're hanging around this shrine to beg some scraps to fill your belly, you'll do a lot better having lunch at home.

DAEMONES (*to Plesidippus*)   What happened? Someone invite you to lunch and not show up?

PLESIDIPPUS   Exactly.

SCEPARNIO   It's all right; *we* don't mind if you go home from here with your belly empty. Why don't you try Ceres' shrine instead? She handles the commissary; Venus only deals with love.

PLESIDIPPUS (*half to himself, bitterly*)   The way that man put one over on me is a crying shame!

DAEMONES (*happening to look off, stage right*)   Good god! Sceparnio, what are those men doing there in the surf?

SCEPARNIO   If you ask me, they're going to a fancy breakfast.

DAEMONES   Why?

SCEPARNIO   Because they took a bath last night.

DAEMONES (*gazing intently*)   They've been wrecked at sea!

SCEPARNIO   Sure. Take a look at the roof of our cottage—we've been wrecked on land.

DAEMONES   Poor fellows! Tossed overboard and having to swim for it.

PLESIDIPPUS (*trying to follow the direction of his gaze*)   Where do you see these men, anyway?

DAEMONES (*pointing*)   There, toward the right. See? Near the beach.

PLESIDIPPUS   I see them now. (*To his friends*) Follow me. I only hope one of them is that blasted crook I'm after. (*To Daemones and Sceparnio*) Well, take care of yourselves. (*They rush off, stage right.*)

SCEPARNIO (*calling after him*)   We've got it in mind; we don't need any reminders from you. (*Watches them go off, then suddenly gives a start*) Oh, my god in heaven, what's that I see?

DAEMONES   What is it?

SCEPARNIO (*excitedly*)   Two girls in a boat, all by themselves. Look at the way the poor things are being tossed about! (*Gazes intently in silence for a moment.*) Good, good! The waves just carried the boat away from the rocks and toward the shore; there isn't a helmsman alive who could have done better. I don't think I've ever seen the surf this bad in my life! If they can only get clear of those breakers they'll be all right. Now's the moment they have to watch out for—oh, a wave just hit them and one fell overboard—wait, it's shallow there—she can swim out easily. Good work! She's on her feet—she's coming this way—she's safe! (*Turning his head as if looking in a slightly different direction*) The other's just jumped out of the boat to get on shore—oh, she lost her nerve, she's fallen in the water, she's on her knees—no, she's safe! She's wading out—now she's on the beach—oh, oh, she turned to the right, she's going off in that direction. Damn! That poor girl's going to do a lot of hiking today!

DAEMONES   What do you care?

SCEPARNIO (*still gazing intently*)   If she falls off that cliff she's heading toward, she'll finish her hike in a hurry.

DAEMONES (*with some asperity*)   If you were going to eat at their expense tonight, Sceparnio, I think you should worry about them. But if you're going to eat at mine, you'd better pay attention to me.

SCEPARNIO   True. You're absolutely right.

DAEMONES   Follow me.

SCEPARNIO   I'm right behind.

(*The two enter the cottage. A moment later Palaestra, "the struggler," enters, stage right. Her face is haggard, her hair dripping, her clothing drenched, and she barely has the energy to drag herself along. Despite all this, we can see that she is a remarkably fine-looking young girl. She makes her way downstage and addresses the audience.*)

SONG

PALAESTRA

The tales they tell of men's mishaps are mild,
Compared to actual experience.
It seems that Heaven's pleased to leave me thus—
A frightened castaway in lands unknown.
Oh, god, what can I say? That I was born
For this? Have I received this as reward
For all my honest and devoted prayer?
For me to undergo such hardships would
Be understandable if I had sinned
Against my parents or, perhaps, my god.
But when I've striven so to lead a life
That's free of all such blame, this treatment is,
O god, unfair, unjust, and undeserved.
What mark hereafter will you place on guilt
If such is the reward for innocence?
If I were conscious that I'd done you wrong,
Or that my parents had, then I would be
More reconciled to all this misery.

(Pauses a moment, then resumes with bitterness and passion.)

But the crimes of my owner are the cause of my grief.
It is *his* sins I suffer for—his, and not mine!
All he owned has gone down with his ship in the sea;
I am all that is left of his worldly possessions.
And that girl who escaped in the boat at my side,
Even she has been lost; I'm alone, all alone.
If she'd only been saved! Then at least, with her help,
This sad blow would have been a bit lighter to bear.
For what hope have I now or whose help can I seek?
I'm deserted, alone in a desolate spot
Where there's nothing but rocks and the sound of the sea,
Where there isn't a chance of my meeting a soul.
All I own in this world are the clothes on my back,
And I've no idea where to find shelter or food.
Oh, it's hopeless! Why try to go on with my life?
I don't know where I am; it's a place strange to me.
How I wish that some person would come and point out
Where a road or a path is! I'm so at a loss
I can't make up my mind to go right or go left;
It's all wild—not a sign of a field can I see.
All the horrors of cold and distraction and fear
Have me now in their grasp. Poor dear parents of mine,
You can have no idea of your daughter's despair!
I was born a free girl, but my birth was in vain—
At this moment how more of a slave could I be
Had I been one from birth? Oh, what good have I been
All these years to the parents who cherished me so!

(She staggers back to the rocks on stage right, sinks down on them, and buries her face in her arms. The next moment there enters, stage right, the companion she thought had been lost. Ampelisca, "tender grape," is a pretty girl with an attractive, gay, vivacious manner. Right now she is as bedraggled and forlorn as Palaestra. She makes her way downstage and addresses the audience.)

AMPELISCA

Oh, what act could be better or more suitable now
    Than to sever my soul from my body?
For my life is a torment and my breast is beset
    By an army of cares that destroy me!

In the face of all this I've no stomach for life,
   All the hope that once buoyed me is ended:
For I've roamed everywhere, used my voice, eyes, and ears,
   Crept through thorns, to track down my companion;
She's been lost without trace, and I have no idea
   Where to turn, in what place to go searching.
And I haven't been able to meet anyone
   I could speak to and ask for directions.
Why, this region's a desert—in all of the world
   There's just no place so lonely and barren.
Yet as long as I live—granted she's alive too—
   I'll persist in the search till I find her.

PALAESTRA (*to herself, raising her head in alarm*)

    Whose voice is that I hear?
    Was that a sound nearby?
    Oh, god, I'm so afraid!

AMPELISCA (*to herself*)

    Did I hear someone speak?

PALAESTRA (*in desperation*)

    O god of hope! Please help!

AMPELISCA (*to herself, hopefully*)

    Does this mean my release
    From misery and fear?

PALAESTRA (*to herself, listening intently*)

    I'm absolutely sure
    I heard a woman's voice.

AMPELISCA (*to herself, listening intently*)

    A woman's somewhere here—
    I heard a woman's voice.

PALAESTRA (*dubiously*)

    It can't be Ampelisca!

AMPELISCA (*calling uncertainly*)

    Palaestra! Is that you?

PALAESTRA (*jumping to her feet, excitedly*)

Oh, I *must* make her hear me—I'll call out her name!
Ampelisca!

AMPELISCA (*calling*)

Who's there?

PALAESTRA

It's Palaestra! It's me!

AMPELISCA (*looking about without seeing her*)

I can't see where you are.

PALAESTRA

I'm in all sorts of trouble.

AMPELISCA

I've a share in it too—one as big as your own.
But I'm dying to see you.

PALAESTRA

And I to see you.

AMPELISCA

Let's both talk and we'll follow the sounds. Where are you?

PALAESTRA

Over here. Come this way. Now walk up to me. Come!

AMPELISCA (*walking slowly and hesitantly toward her*)

This is the best I can do.

PALAESTRA (*as she comes near*)

All right, give me your hand.

AMPELISCA (*doing so*)

Here it is.

PALAESTRA (*grabbing it, pulling her near, and embracing her*)

Ampelisca! You're safe! You're alive!

AMPELISCA (*tearfully*)

Yes—and now that I'm able to touch you, Palaestra,
You've restored the desire to go on with my life.
But I scarcely believe that you're here in my arms!
Oh, my dear! Hold me tight! How you make me forget
All my troubles!

PALAESTRA

You've taken the words from my mouth!
But we ought to get out of this place.

AMPELISCA

And go where?

PALAESTRA

Shall we follow the beach?

AMPELISCA

Go wherever you like;
I'll be right at your heels. But we're both sopping wet—
Are we going to tramp up and down in these clothes?

PALAESTRA

Yes, we must. We just have to take things as they come.

(*Starts trudging off with Ampelisca close behind and then suddenly stops and points.*)

What is that, do you think?

AMPELISCA

What is what?

PALAESTRA

Don't you see?
There's a shrine over there.

AMPELISCA

Over where?

PALAESTRA

On the right.

AMPELISCA (*following the direction of her hand*)

> I can make out a spot that would serve for a shrine.

PALAESTRA

> It's so pleasant a place that I'm sure we shall find
> There are people about. Now let's pray that the god
> Dwelling here will have pity on us in our plight,
> And will come to the rescue and bring to a close
> All these torments and terrors, these worries and woes!

(*As the two girls slowly make their way toward the little temple that marks the shrine, the door opens and Ptolemocratia, the priestess, comes out. She is an elderly woman dressed in flowing white robes that, although spotlessly clean, have obviously seen better days. Her face is kindly and serene.*)

PTOLEMOCRATIA (*to herself*)

> The sound of prayer just roused me now
> To step outside. But who has come
> To ask my mistress for a favor?
> The goddess they implore is quick
> To yield, and loath to hide, her grace,
> A patroness both kind and good.

PALAESTRA (*timidly*)

> Good morning, Mother.

PTOLEMOCRATIA (*responding perfunctorily*)

> > Morning, girls.

(*Suddenly aware of their appearance*)

> Tell me, where have you come from, my dears?
> You're in rags! And you're both sopping wet!

PALAESTRA

> Well, right now from a place that's nearby.
> But our homeland is far, far away.

PTOLEMOCRATIA (*in mock-tragic style*)

> Then you came o'er the blue of the sea
> On a charger of canvas and wood?

PALAESTRA

Yes, we did.

PTOLEMOCRATIA (*reproachfully*)

> But you should have come here
> Dressed in white and prepared to give gifts.
> This is simply unheard of, my dears—
> Coming into this shrine in this way.

PALAESTRA (*taken aback*)

> From two castaways fresh from the sea?
> Tell me, where would you have us find gifts?

(*The two girls drop to the ground and embrace Ptolemocratia's knees.*)

> Here we are on our knees at your feet.
> We need help! We don't know where we are,
> We don't know what's in store for us next.
> Oh, I beg you, please pity our plight.
> Give us shelter and save us, please do!
> We are homeless and hopeless, and all
> That we own you can see on our backs!

PTOLEMOCRATIA (*gently*)

> Now I want you to give me your hands
> And get up from your knees, both of you.
> There's no woman alive with a heart
> That's as tender as mine, I am sure.
> But this shrine's very humble, my girls.
> I can barely keep living myself.
> And the offerings for Venus come from me.

AMPELISCA

> Then is this one of Venus' shrines?

PTOLEMOCRATIA

> Yes, it is, dear. And I am in charge.
> We'll make do. You will both be put up
> Just as well as my means will permit.
> Come with me.

PALAESTRA

> We're most grateful to you
> For a welcome so friendly and kind.

PTOLEMOCRATIA

It's a duty I've always in mind.

(*Ptolemocratia and the girls enter the temple.*)

ACT II

(*A group of fishermen, dressed in rags and carrying tackle, enters, stage left.*)

FISHERMEN (*to the audience*)

> The poor man leads a sorry life
>   In every mode and manner,
> Especially if he has no trade
>   Or never became a craftsman;
> For then he needs must make his way
>   With just his own resources.
> This tackle here makes pretty clear
>   The kind of money *we* make;
> These hooks and rods, which mark our trade,
>   Provide us with our living.
> Each day we hike from town to beach
>   To forage for our rations.
> We get our exercise this way—
>   The poor man's calisthenics.
> We grub for limpets, oysters, clams,
>   Sea urchins, mussels, scallops.
> Then next we turn to rock and rod
>   To try our luck at fishing.
> We fill our bellies from the seas;
>   And when the seas don't fill them,
> We take a swim—if not the fish,
>   We clean and salt the fishers!—
> Then sneak back home and climb in bed
>   Without a thing for supper.
> With seas as rough as they are right now,
>   There's not much hope for fishing;
> Unless we find a clam or two,
>   We've had today's collation.
> To get some help, let's proffer to
>   Kind Venus veneration.

(Trachalio, "bull-necked," Plesidippus' servant, enters, stage left. He's a burly young fellow, honest and good-natured at heart, and gay in temperament. He rather fancies himself as a man of importance, and with—or without—provocation often begins orating instead of talking.)

TRACHALIO *(to himself, worriedly)* And I watched so carefully all the way so's not to miss that master of mine on the road! When he left the house he said he was going to go to the waterfront, and gave me orders to meet him here at this shrine of Venus. *(Catching sight of the fishermen)* Now, that's convenient: there are some fellows over there I can ask. *(Calling)* Hail, heroes of the hook and half shell, despoilers of the deeps, members of the Honorable Order of the Empty Belly, how're you doing? How're you dying?

FISHERMAN The way fishermen always do—of optimism followed by starvation.

TRACHALIO Did you happen to see a young fellow come along while you've been standing here? Husky, red-faced fellow looking as if he meant business? He had three others with him; they were all wearing cloaks and daggers.

FISHERMAN Nobody answering to that description's come along, so far as we know.

TRACHALIO How about an old guy, pretty big, with a bald forehead like an old satyr, a fat belly, bushy eyebrows, and a dirty look? A low-down, filthy, lying, thieving, swindling crook? Had two good-looking girls with him?

FISHERMAN Anyone with those sterling virtues ought to be headed for a town jail, not a temple of Venus.

TRACHALIO But did you see him?

FISHERMAN No. He hasn't been here. So long. *(They leave, stage right.)*

TRACHALIO *(calling after them)* So long. *(To himself)* I thought so; I had a suspicion this would happen. They've put one over on that master of mine: that damned pimp skipped town. Took passage on a ship and took the girls away. I'm a prophet, that's what I am. The lousy liar! He even invited Plesidippus for lunch out here. Well, the best thing I can do is wait around here until Plesidippus shows up. And while I'm at it, if I see the priestess,

I'll quiz her and find out if she knows anything more about all this. She'll tell me.

(The door of the temple opens and Ampelisca comes out, carrying a pitcher. Her first words are addressed to the priestess inside.)

AMPELISCA *(through the doorway)*   Yes, I understand. I'm to go to the cottage right next door to the shrine, knock, and ask for water.

TRACHALIO *(pricking up his ears, to himself)*   Now whose voice is that the wind has wafted to mine ears?

AMPELISCA *(turning at the sound)*   Who's that talking out there, please? *(Seeing him)* Look who's here!

TRACHALIO *(turning, to himself)*   Isn't that Ampelisca coming out of the temple?

AMPELISCA *(to herself)*   Isn't that Trachalio, Plesidippus' valet, I see?

TRACHALIO *(to himself)*   That's who it is, all right.

AMPELISCA *(to herself)*   That's who it is, all right. *(Calling)* Trachalio! Hello there!

TRACHALIO *(going up to her)*   Hello, Ampelisca. What have you been doing with yourself?

AMPELISCA *(bitterly)*   Spending the best years of my life in the worst possible way.

TRACHALIO   Don't say things like that!

AMPELISCA *(as before)*   Sensible people should tell the truth—and listen to it. But where's Plesidippus?

TRACHALIO *(looking at her blankly)*   What a question! He's inside with you people, isn't he?

AMPELISCA *(emphatically)*   He is not. He hasn't been here today.

TRACHALIO   Hasn't been here?

AMPELISCA   You never said a truer word.

TRACHALIO *(grinning)*   Rather unusual for me. Well, when will lunch be ready?

AMPELISCA *(taking her turn at looking blank)*   What lunch are you talking about?

TRACHALIO   You people are making a sacrifice here, aren't you?

AMPELISCA   My dear boy, will you please wake up?

TRACHALIO   But I know for certain our masters were getting together for lunch here. Labrax invited Plesidippus.

AMPELISCA *(bitterly)*   I'm not at all surprised. Exactly what you'd expect of a pimp—as ready to cheat a goddess as a man.

TRACHALIO   You mean you people and Plesidippus *aren't* making a
    sacrifice here?

AMPELISCA *(scornfully)*   You're a prophet.

TRACHALIO   What are you doing around here, then?

AMPELISCA *(breathlessly)*   We were in terrible trouble, scared to death,
    in danger of losing our lives, with not a thing to our name and
    not a soul to help us. And the priestess here took us in. The
    two of us—me and Palaestra.

TRACHALIO *(excitedly)*   You mean Palaestra's here? His sweetheart's
    here?

AMPELISCA   Of course.

TRACHALIO *(as before)*   Ampelisca, that's the best possible news you
    could have brought me. But what was this danger you were in?
    I'm dying to hear about it.

AMPELISCA   Trachalio, last night our ship was wrecked!

TRACHALIO   What ship? What are you talking about?

AMPELISCA   Didn't you hear what happened? The pimp wanted to
    move all of us to Sicily without anybody knowing about it. So
    he loaded all his belongings on board a ship. And now he's lost
    everything!

TRACHALIO *(exulting)*   Good work, Father Neptune! Congratulations!
    Nobody can play the game better than you: you hit the jackpot;
    you gave that liar his lumps. But where is our pimping friend
    Labrax now?

AMPELISCA   Probably died of drink. Neptune was serving in the big
    glasses last night.

TRACHALIO *(chuckling)*   And he probably insisted on bottoms up,
    every round. Ampelisca, I love you! You're so sweet! What
    honeyed words you have for me! *(Suddenly becoming serious)*
    But how were you and Palaestra rescued?

AMPELISCA   I'll tell you just how it happened. We saw that the ship
    was being carried toward the rocks, and we both got so scared
    we jumped into the ship's boat. Then, while everybody on board
    was busy having the shakes, I hurried and cast off the rope.
    The storm carried us away from them, to the right. And then
    we were tossed about by the wind and waves in the worst way
    imaginable, all night long. Finally, just this morning, the wind
    drove us up on the beach. We were half dead!

TRACHALIO I know. That's what Neptune always does. (*Grinning*) Most meticulous purser in the business: any bad merchandise around, and he heaves it right overboard.

AMPELISCA Oh, go to the devil!

TRACHALIO You almost did, Ampelisca, my girl. (*Becoming serious*) I knew that pimp would do something like that; I said so all along. You know what I really ought to do? Grow a beard and be a prophet.

AMPELISCA (*tartly*) Considering that you knew all about it, you and that master of yours certainly took good care not to let him get away.

TRACHALIO (*defensively*) What should he have done?

AMPELISCA (*angrily*) If he really loved her, you wouldn't have to ask such a question! He should have kept his eyes open night and day, been on his guard every minute. My god! That Plesidippus of yours certainly took fine care of her! Shows how much she mattered to him!

TRACHALIO (*reproachfully*) Why do you say that?

AMPELISCA (*severely*) It's plain as day, isn't it?

TRACHALIO Can't you understand? Why, you take a fellow who goes to a public bath: he watches his clothes like a hawk and still he gets robbed. There are so many people around, he doesn't know which one to keep an eye on. It's easy enough for the crook to spot the man *he* wants to keep his eye on, but it's tough for the fellow who's on guard to spot the crook. (*Quickly changing the subject*) But how about taking me to Palaestra?

AMPELISCA Just go inside the temple here. You'll find her sitting there crying her eyes out.

TRACHALIO Crying? That I'm sorry to hear. What's she crying about?

AMPELISCA I'll tell you what she's crying about: she's all broken up because the pimp took away a little jewel box she had in which she kept some things that were her only means of identifying her parents. She's afraid it's lost.

TRACHALIO Where was this box?

AMPELISCA On board with us. He kept it locked up in a satchel. He wanted to make sure she'd never be able to find her parents.

TRACHALIO What a criminal thing to do! A girl who ought to be free and he wants to keep her a slave!

AMPELISCA   It must have gone down to the bottom with the ship. The pimp had all his money in the same satchel.

TRACHALIO   (*comfortingly*)   Oh, someone's probably dived down and rescued it.

AMPELISCA   The poor girl is simply miserable at the thought of having lost those things.

TRACHALIO   All the more reason for me to go in and cheer her up. I don't want her to go on tormenting herself that way. I know for a fact there are lots of people whose affairs turned out much better than they ever expected.

AMPELISCA   And I know for a fact there are lots who expected their affairs to turn out well and they never did.

TRACHALIO   When you come down to it, the best medicine for trouble is a level head. Well, if there's nothing more I can do for you, I'll run along inside. (*Enters the temple.*)

AMPELISCA   Go ahead. (*To herself*) And I'll do that errand for the priestess and ask them next door for some water. She told me they'd give it to me right away if I said it was for her. (*Walking toward the cottage*) I don't think I've ever met anyone nicer than that old lady. I think she deserves every kindness god or man can do for her. There we were, castaways, frightened to death, drenched to the skin, helpless, half alive, and she took us in and was so sweet and generous and open and unbegrudging—just as if we were her own daughters! She even tucked up her robe and heated the water herself so that we could take a bath. Well, I don't want her to be held up on my account, so I'll go where she told me right now and get some more water. (*Knocking on the door of the cottage*) Hello there! Anyone inside? Anyone there to open this door? Will someone please come out?

SCEPARNIO   (*throwing the door open and looking past her as he does*) Who's the wild animal trying to break this door down?

AMPELISCA   Here I am.

SCEPARNIO   (*breaking into a pleased smile as he sees her, to himself*) Hey, here's a piece of luck. Damn it all, that's one good-looking girl there!

AMPELISCA   Good morning, mister.

SCEPARNIO   Good morning to *you*, miss.

AMPELISCA   I've come here to—

SCEPARNIO (*interrupting with a leer*) It's a little too early in the morning for me to entertain you, my girl. Come back later this evening and I'll really take care of you. (*Putting his arm around her*) Well, how about it, baby?

AMPELISCA (*deftly fending him off*) Hey, don't you get so familiar with those hands!

SCEPARNIO (*aside*) Lord in heaven, this is Lady Venus herself! Look at those eyes—this girl's the lively type. And those cheeks! Like silt—silk, I mean. And those breasts! And that mouth calls for a kiss. (*Makes another pass at her.*)

AMPELISCA (*as before*) Can't you keep your hands off me? I'm for your betters, boy!

SCEPARNIO Come on, little one, just one little hug, nice and gentle, like this. (*Tries to get an arm around her again.*)

AMPELISCA Later on, when I'm not busy, you and I'll have time to play around, but right now I have a favor to ask and please just tell me yes or no.

SCEPARNIO All right, what do you want?

AMPELISCA (*holding up the pitcher*) If you had any brains, this would show you what I want.

SCEPARNIO (*making an obscene gesture*) And if you had any, this would show you what *I* want.

AMPELISCA (*remembering her instructions, importantly*) The priestess of the shrine of Venus sent me to ask you for some water for her.

SCEPARNIO (*tapping his chest*) *I'm* lord and master around here. Unless you ask me for it, you don't get a drop. We risked our own necks to dig this well, and we did it with our own tools. (*Leering*) And no one gets a drop without asking me nicely.

AMPELISCA What's the matter? You won't give me some water? What any stranger would give to another?

SCEPARNIO What's the matter? You won't give me what any friend would give to another?

AMPELISCA (*enticingly*) I? Of course I will. I'll do anything you want, honey.

SCEPARNIO (*aside*) Congratulations, old boy, you're in; she just called you "honey." (*To Ampelisca*) Sure I'll give you the water. I don't want you to fall in love with me and get nothing for it. Give me the pitcher.

AMPELISCA Here it is. And please hurry.

SCEPARNIO (*taking the pitcher*) You wait here. I'll be right back—honey. (*Enters the cottage.*)

AMPELISCA (*worriedly*) What should I tell the priestess took me so long? (*Gazes about abstractedly, and her eye falls on the sea.*) Ugh! When I look at that water, I get frightened even now. (*Starting*) Oh, my god, what's that I see on the beach? It's the pimp and his friend from Sicily! And I, like a poor fool, thought the two of them had drowned! That means more trouble in store for us than we had thought. But what am I waiting for? I've got to hurry into the temple and tell Palaestra so that we can throw ourselves on the altar before that filthy pimp comes here and catches us. I'd better run—every minute counts!

(*She hurries into the temple. A second later Sceparnio comes out carrying the pitcher.*)

SCEPARNIO (*smiling fatuously, to himself*) Lord, oh, lord, I never thought water had so much happiness to offer. It was a sheer pleasure to draw it—the well never seemed that shallow before. Practically no work at all to haul it up. Sceparnio, knock on wood, you're quite a guy. Got yourself a love affair going today, eh, boy? (*Calling*) Where's my pretty girl? Here's your water. (*Putting the bucket on his head and mincing about*) See? This is the way I want you to carry it, like a lady. Want me to like you? Then do it just like this. (*Calling*) Sweetie-pie, where are you? Come on and get your water. Where are you? (*Grinning even more fatuously*) Well, what do you know—the little devil's playing hide-and-go-seek. Boy, did she fall for me! (*Calling*) Where are you? (*After waiting a moment in silence*) Hey, are you going to come and get this pitcher? Where are you? Come on, no more games, I'm serious. How about taking this here pitcher? (*Removes the pitcher from his head and starts searching in earnest.*) Where the devil are you? Good god, I don't see her anywhere. Is she playing a trick on me? (*Slamming the pitcher down, angrily*) I'll just leave the blasted pitcher right in the road. (*Starts walking away, then stops abruptly.*) Wait a second—what if someone walks off with it? That's no ordinary pitcher; it belongs to the shrine. I'll get into trouble. (*Excitedly*) I think that girl framed me—wanted me to get caught with a holy pitcher on me. If anyone sees me with this thing, the judge'll have every right to throw the book at me. Look—it's even got its name on it—it practically shouts to high heaven whose it is. Holy god, I'm going to call the priestess out here right now to get her pitcher. I'm heading right for her door! (*Rushes up to the door and starts shouting frantically.*) Hey! Ptolemocratia! Come on out and get your pitcher! Some blamed girl brought it to me. (*Waits a moment; then, getting no reply, disgustedly*) I'll have to carry it in. Fine business if, on top of everything else, I've got to deliver the water right to the house!

(*Sceparnio goes into the temple. A second later Labrax, "the shark," enters, stage right. He is wet, bedraggled, and shivering.*)

LABRAX (*to himself*) If anyone wants to become a beggar, just let him trust himself, body and soul, to Father Neptune. Believe me, whenever you do business with him, this (*indicating his appearance*) is the way he sends you home. I remember a story about a girl who always refused to set foot on a ship with Hercules—she was a smart one, all right. But where's that guest of mine who's been my ruination? Oh, there he is. Look at him taking his time!

(*Charmides enters, stage right, in the same condition as Labrax.*)

CHARMIDES (*sourly*) What the devil's the hurry, Labrax? I can't keep up when you go that fast.

LABRAX (*bitterly*) I wish to god you had gone to the gallows in Sicily before I ever set eyes on you. You're to blame for getting me into this!

CHARMIDES And I wish to god I had spent the night in the town jail rather than let you take me home with you that day. There's only one favor I want from heaven—that from now on till the end of your days, your guests be the same breed as yourself, every one of them.

LABRAX The day I took you in I let Bad Luck walk right in the front door. Why did I ever listen to a good-for-nothing like you? Why did I ever leave here? Why did I get aboard that ship? (*Thinking of the money he took from Plesidippus*) I've lost even more than I owned!

CHARMIDES I'm not surprised that ship went down—not when it was carrying a crook like you and all that crooked stuff you had.

LABRAX   You ruined me, you and that slick talk of yours.

CHARMIDES   How about that filthy meal you served me? Believe me, Thyestes and Tereus[1] didn't get worse.

LABRAX   (*holding his stomach*)   Oh, god, I feel sick. Hold my head, will you?

CHARMIDES   Damn you, I hope you puke up your lungs while you're at it.

LABRAX   Poor Palaestra and Ampelisca. I wonder where they are now.

CHARMIDES   Probably feeding the fish down in the drink.

LABRAX   It's all your doing that I'm a beggar now. I had to listen to that big talk of yours!

CHARMIDES   (*grinning maliciously*)   You ought to be grateful to me. You never knew how to get along before. I taught you how to get along swimmingly.

LABRAX   Why don't you go straight to hell and leave me alone?

CHARMIDES   That's just what I was going to invite you to do.

LABRAX   God, there isn't a man alive worse off than I am.

CHARMIDES   Oh, yes there is. One lots worse off—me.

LABRAX   How so?

CHARMIDES   Because you deserved what you got. I didn't.

LABRAX   Look at those bulrushes. I envy them. Always nice and dry.

CHARMIDES   I'm practicing to be a Spanish dancer. I'm shivering so much, every time I speak I clack like a castanet.

LABRAX   That Neptune sure runs a cold bathing establishment. I leave the place, have all my clothes on, and I'm still freezing. And he doesn't even have a hot-drink counter. Only drinks he serves are cold and salty.

CHARMIDES   The fellows I envy are the blacksmiths. Around a fire all day. Always nice and warm.

LABRAX   What I'd like to be right now is a duck. Come straight out of the water and still be dry.

CHARMIDES   I think I'll get me a job playing a ghost with a stock company.

LABRAX   Why?

CHARMIDES   Listen to the terrific clatter I can make with my teeth. (*Shaking his head ruefully*)   If you ask me, being cleaned out of everything I owned was just what was coming to me.

LABRAX   Why?

[1] Mythological characters who had been served their own sons.

CHARMIDES How could I have had the nerve to get aboard a ship with someone like you? I'll bet you made all those waves yourself, just to spite me.

LABRAX I listened to you, that's what I did. You kept telling me girls made big money where you came from. You promised I'd rake in the cash there.

CHARMIDES And you expected to swallow up the whole island of Sicily in one gulp, like a damned vulture.

LABRAX Talk about swallowing, I wonder what whale got my satchel. I had all my money in it.

CHARMIDES Probably the same one that got my wallet. The inside pocket was full of cash.

LABRAX Do you know that all I've got left to my name is this shirt and this rag of a coat? I'm done for!

CHARMIDES You and I could set up a perfect partnership. We'd hold identical shares.

LABRAX If only my girls were still alive, there'd be some hope. If that young fellow Plesidippus sees me now, the one I took a down payment from for Palaestra, he's going to make real trouble for me—and soon.

CHARMIDES What are you crying about, stupid? So long as that tongue of yours is alive, you've got what it takes to get you out of any debts you owe.

(The door of the temple opens, and Sceparnio comes out, looking puzzled.)

SCEPARNIO *(to himself)* What's going on here, anyway? Two girls inside the temple, holding on to the altar and crying their eyes out. The poor things are scared to death of someone but I don't know who. They said they'd been shipwrecked last night and tossed up on the beach this morning.

LABRAX *(to Sceparnio, eagerly)* Say there, mister, where are these girls you're talking about?

SCEPARNIO Here, in the temple.

LABRAX How many of them are there?

SCEPARNIO Two.

LABRAX *(half to himself)* I'll swear they're mine.

SCEPARNIO And I'll swear I don't know about that.

LABRAX What do they look like?

SCEPARNIO   Not bad. I could go for either one of them—if I was good and drunk.

LABRAX   They're pretty young, aren't they?

SCEPARNIO   You're pretty much of a nuisance, aren't you? Go on in and take a look if you want.

LABRAX   (*to Charmides, excitedly*)   Charmides! Those girls in there must be mine!

CHARMIDES   Whether they are or they aren't, you can go to hell for all I care.

LABRAX   I'm going into that temple this minute. (*Rushes into the temple.*)

CHARMIDES   (*calling after him*)   I wish you were going straight to hell this minute. (*To Sceparnio*) Say, how about playing host and giving me a place where I can stretch out and get some sleep?

SCEPARNIO   Stretch out wherever you want. No one's stopping you. It's a free country.

CHARMIDES   But look at me—these clothes I'm wearing are wringing wet. How about putting me up in your house and giving me some dry clothes until these get dry? I'll make it up to you sometime.

SCEPARNIO   (*pointing to a homely coverall of rushes hanging up alongside the cottage*)   See that mat there? That's all I've got. It's dry, and if you want it you're welcome to it. It's my coat, and it doubles as umbrella when there's rain. Here, give me your things and I'll dry them out.

CHARMIDES   (*backing away suspiciously*)   Oh, no. Isn't the cleaning out I got at sea enough for you? Do you have to put me through it all again on land?

SCEPARNIO   I don't give a damn whether you get cleaned out or rubbed out. I'm not trusting you with anything of mine without security. Go ahead—freeze to death or sweat to death, get sick or get well. Who cares? I don't want any foreigners around the house, anyway. And that's that. (*Stomps into the cottage.*)

CHARMIDES   (*calling after him*)   Hey, where are you going? (*To himself*) Whoever he is, the man must be a slave dealer—doesn't know what it is to feel pity. But what am I standing around here in these wet clothes for? Why don't I go into this temple here and sleep off last night's party? Drank too much; lots more than I wanted. You'd think we were cheap wine, the way Neptune watered us. Maybe he was figuring on giving us a salt-water laxative. When you come right down to it, if he had kept on serving drinks much longer we'd have gone to sleep then and there; this way he let us go home—half alive, but alive. Well, I'll see what my fellow drunk is doing inside here now. (*Enters the temple.*)

ACT III

(*Daemones comes out of the cottage shaking his head wonderingly.*)

DAEMONES (*to the audience*) It's amazing the way heaven plays tricks on us mortals. The amazing dreams heaven sends you when you're asleep! A person's not left in peace and quiet even in bed. Last night, for example, I had an incredible dream, something unheard of. I dreamed that an ape was trying to climb up to a swallow's nest and get his hands on the swallows, but couldn't quite make it. After a while it came to me to ask for the loan of a ladder. I refused, pointing out that swallows were descended from Philomela[1] and Procne, and I pleaded with it not to do any harm to what were, in effect, my fellow countrymen. That just made it more belligerent than ever, and it threatened to beat me. It hauled me into court. There I lost my temper and, somehow or other, managed to grab the filthy creature around the middle and chain it up. (*Scratching his head perplexedly*) Now, what does it all mean? I've thought all morning but I just can't figure it out. (*A clamor is heard in the temple.*) What's that? Noise in the shrine next door? That's queer.

(*The door of the temple flies open and Trachalio bursts out.*)

TRACHALIO (*at the top of his lungs—and at his oratorical best*) Citizens of Cyrene! Farmers! Anyone who lives in the area! In god's name, help for the helpless! Harm for the harmful! Are the merciless to be mightier than the meek who shrink at the very name of crime? Then help right a wrong, give the righteous their reward and the dastards their deserts. Fight the good fight to let us live by law and order and not by fists and force. Everyone here, everyone who hears my voice, in god's name, into this shrine of Venus as fast as you can! Help the poor souls who have

---

[1] A mythological princess of Athens.

entrusted life and limb to the protection of Venus and her priestess in accordance with our ancient custom! Wring the neck of wrong before it reaches *you!*

DAEMONES *(impatiently)* What's this all about?

TRACHALIO *(throwing himself on the ground and embracing Daemones' knees)* My dear sir, by these knees, I call upon you, whoever you are—

DAEMONES *(interrupting, as before)* Let go of my knees and tell me what this yelling's about. And make it short!

TRACHALIO *(not budging)* I beg you, I implore you! Do you want a good crop on your farm this year? Do you want to see it arrive at an overseas market safe and sound? Do you want to get rid of what ails you? Do you—

DAEMONES *(interrupting)* Are you in your right mind?

TRACHALIO *(unabashed)* Do you want an ample supply of seed for sowing? Then, my dear sir, please don't refuse to do what I'm asking you to.

DAEMONES *(testily)* And I call upon *you* by that back of yours and those legs and heels. Do you want a good harvest of birch-rod welts? Do you want a bumper crop of trouble this year? Then you'd better tell me what's going on here and what this shouting's all about.

TRACHALIO *(getting up, reproachfully)* You're not fair: I asked only for nice things for you.

DAEMONES *(promptly)* I am so fair: I asked only for what you deserve.

TRACHALIO Please! Listen to me!

DAEMONES What is it?

TRACHALIO There are two innocent girls in there. They need your help. The treatment they've had—and are getting this minute— is a blot on the escutcheon of justice and law. Right in the temple of Venus, too! Even the priestess is being manhandled.

DAEMONES *(finally aroused)* Who would have the gall to lay hands on a priestess? Who are these girls? How are they being mistreated?

TRACHALIO If you'll listen to me for a minute, I'll tell you. *(Breathlessly)* They ran to Venus' altar for safety. Now this fellow has the colossal nerve to want to pull them away. And both of them by rights ought to be free.

DAEMONES Who's the man who's so free and easy with priestesses and temples? And no speeches!

TRACHALIO A swindler, a crook, a murderer, a liar, a lawbreaker; a foul, filthy, unprincipled—in a word, a pimp. Need I say more?

DAEMONES You've said enough. Perfect material for a flogging.

TRACHALIO He even tried to strangle the priestess.

DAEMONES By god, he's going to pay for that, and pay plenty. (*Shouting to his servants inside*) Hey! Roughneck and Cutthroat! Come on out here! Where are you, anyway?

TRACHALIO Please, I beg you. Go in the temple and rescue them.

(*Two husky slaves rush out of the house and stand at attention before Daemones.*)

DAEMONES (*to Trachalio, reassuringly*) One word from me will be enough. (*To the slaves*) Follow me! (*They charge toward the temple.*)

TRACHALIO (*remaining prudently behind and calling to Daemones*) Give it to him! Tell those boys to make believe they're cooks scaling fish and have them scratch his eyes out!

DAEMONES (*to the slaves*) Drag him out here by the feet, like a stuck pig.

(*The three enter the temple. Trachalio stands near the door, listening intently.*)

TRACHALIO (*to the audience*) I hear a racket: the pimp's getting a going-over. I hope they knock every tooth out of the rascal's mouth. (*Stepping back as the door opens*) Here come the girls. They look scared to death.

(*Palaestra and Ampelisca come out and rush past Trachalio without noticing him.*)

SONG

PALAESTRA (*to the audience*)

The dread moment's at hand; now we're utterly helpless.
There's just no one to come to our aid or defense,
No release from our danger, no way to find safety.
And we're both so afraid we can't think where to run.
Oh, the vicious and brutal ordeal that that pimp
Put us through just a moment ago in the shrine!

Why, the monster attacked the old priestess, poor thing,
Shoved her this way and that—it was dreadful to see—
And then dragged us by force from the innermost altar.
In the state that we're in, we'd be better off dead.
In the depths of despair what is dearer than death?

TRACHALIO (*to himself*)

Hey, what's this? What a way for a young girl to talk!
I must swing into action—they need cheering up.

(*Calling*)

Hey, Palaestra!

PALAESTRA (*too frightened to turn around*)

Who's there?

TRACHALIO (*calling*)

Ampelisca!

AMPELISCA (*clutching Palaestra*)

Who wants me?

PALAESTRA (*as before*)

Who's that calling our names?

TRACHALIO

Turn around and you'll see.

PALAESTRA (*turning and seeing him, fervently*)

Oh, some hope for our safety at last!

TRACHALIO (*walking over to them, importantly*)

Now be calm.
Take it easy. Trust me.

PALAESTRA

Yes—if you'll give your word
We need fear no more violence and force. Otherwise
I'll be brought to a violent act on myself!

TRACHALIO (*as before*)

Now you're just being silly. No more of this talk.

PALAESTRA (*dully*) Don't try to console me in my misery with mere words. If you don't have some real help to offer, Trachalio, it's all over with us.

AMPELISCA (*wildly*) I've made up my mind to die rather than suffer at the hands of that pimp any longer. (*Hesitatingly*) But I'm just a woman, after all; every time I even think of death I get paralyzed with fright. Oh, what a nightmare this day is!

TRACHALIO (*heartily*) Courage, girls!

PALAESTRA (*dully*) Courage? Where am I going to find it?

TRACHALIO (*as before*) Take my word for it, there's no reason to be afraid. (*Pointing to the altar outside the shrine*) Come, sit down on this altar.

AMPELISCA Why should this one do us any more good than the one in the shrine? We were clutching it just now when they pulled us away by brute force.

TRACHALIO (*leading them to the altar and seating them on it*) You just sit down. I'll stand guard over here. See? The altar's your fort, here are the walls, and I'm the garrison. With Venus at my side I'm ready to counter the pimp's sneak attacks.

AMPELISCA All right, we'll do whatever you say. (*Falling on her knees and praying*) Dear Venus, here we are, both of us, on our knees, in tears, before your altar. We beg of you: guard us, watch over us. Give us our revenge on those criminals who had so little respect for your shrine. Be gracious and let us find safety by this altar. Thanks to Neptune we had a bath last night; please don't be offended or hold it against us if you feel such a washing isn't all that your ritual requires.

TRACHALIO (*looking up toward heaven, importantly*) Venus, if you ask me, that's a perfectly valid request and they deserve to have it granted. You should make allowances for them: the scare they had forced them into this informality. They tell me that you were born from a sea shell; don't leave these poor shells abandoned on the beach! (*As the door of the temple opens*) Look! Here's your savior and mine—the old man's coming out. He couldn't have picked a better time.

(*Daemones comes out followed by the two slaves, who are uncere-moniously shoving Labrax ahead of them.*)

DAEMONES (*to Labrax*) Get out of that shrine, you scum of the earth!

(*Turning to address the girls*) And you two sit down on the altar—where are they?

TRACHALIO   Over here.

DAEMONES   Perfect. Exactly what I wanted. Just let him try to get near them now. (*To Labrax*) So you thought you could get away with your lawbreaking inside a temple while we were around, eh? (*To one of the slaves*) Give him a sock on the jaw.

LABRAX (*blustering*)   This is an outrage—and you'll pay for it!

DAEMONES   What's that? You've got the nerve to make threats?

LABRAX (*as before*)   You're depriving me of my rights. These are my girls and you took them from me without my consent.

TRACHALIO   You go right down to City Hall here at Cyrene and pick yourself a judge—anyone you want, the most influential you can find. Let *him* decide whether these girls should be yours or should go free—and whether you shouldn't be clapped into jail and stay there until you wear the place out.

LABRAX (*turning on him*)   I'm in no mood today for conversation with a blasted slave. (*To Daemones*) It's you I want to talk to.

DAEMONES (*gesturing toward Trachalio*)   First you'll have it out with this fellow here. He knows you.

LABRAX (*curtly*)   My business is with you.

TRACHALIO   But you're going to take it up with me whether you like it or not. So these girls are yours, eh?

LABRAX   That's right.

TRACHALIO   Well, you just try touching either one of them with the tip of your little finger.

LABRAX (*belligerently*)   And what'll happen if I do?

TRACHALIO (*very brave with the odds four to one in his favor*)   So help me, I'll make a punching bag out of you, that's what'll happen. I'll tie you up and knock the stuffings out of you, you damned liar.

LABRAX (*to Daemones*)   You mean I can't take my own girls away from that altar?

DAEMONES   That's what I mean. That's the law around here.

LABRAX (*scornfully*)   Your laws have nothing to do with me. I'm taking both those girls out of here right now. (*Leering*) If you're so much in love with them, you old goat, you're going to have to come across with hard cash. And if they're such favorites with Venus, she's welcome to them—if she pays me.

DAEMONES   **Pay you!** There's something you'd better get straight: if you try the least bit of rough stuff, even as a joke, on these girls, I'll send you away from here in such a state you won't recognize yourself. (*To the slaves*) Listen, you two. The minute I give the signal, knock the eyes out of his head. If you don't, I'll wrap a whip around you like twine on a spool.

LABRAX   So you're going to use force on me, eh?

TRACHALIO (*exploding*)   Look who's talking about force! You stinking hypocrite!

LABRAX (*shouting*)   No blasted slave can talk to me like that!

TRACHALIO   Sure, I'm a blasted slave and you're a saint—but that doesn't change the fact that these girls should be free.

LABRAX   What do you mean, free?

TRACHALIO   What's more, damn it, you ought to be their slave. They come from the heart of Greece. (*Pointing to Palaestra*) This one was born in Athens. Her parents were respectable Athenians.

DAEMONES (*eagerly*)   What's that you say?

TRACHALIO   I said this girl is an Athenian and was no slave when she was born.

DAEMONES   You mean she's from my own city?

TRACHALIO (*surprised*)   You weren't born here in Cyrene?

DAEMONES   Oh, no. I'm a native Athenian, born and raised in Athens.

TRACHALIO   Then I implore you to defend your fellow citizens.

DAEMONES (*sighing*)   How I'm reminded of my own daughter when I look at this girl! The very thought stirs up old sorrows. Three years old she was, when I lost her, and if she's alive she'd be just that tall, I'm sure of it.

LABRAX   I paid their owner good money for both of them. What do I care whether they come from Athens or Thebes so long as I'm satisfied with the way they slave for me.

TRACHALIO (*confident enough now to assume his orator's manner*)   So, you sneaking cradle snatcher, you think you're going to get away with snatching infants from their mother's breast and grinding them to nothingness in your foul trade? I admit I don't know where this other girl comes from. But I know one thing: she's far above scum like you.

LABRAX (*sneering*)   I suppose they belong to you?

TRACHALIO   All right. Let's you and I take a back test to see which of us tells the truth. First I'll inspect you. And if that back of yours hasn't more corrugations from the whip than a ship's hull has nails, *I'm* the world's worst liar. Then you look at me. And if my hide isn't so smooth and unblemished that any leather-worker would classify it as absolutely top grade, give me one good reason why I shouldn't tan yours until I get tired of it. (*As Labrax glances toward the altar*) What are you staring at those girls for? You lay a hand on them and I'll gouge your eyes out!

LABRAX (*belligerently*) You know what? Just because you say I can't do it, I'm going to take them both away with me right now.

DAEMONES (*scornfully*) And just how do you propose to do that?

LABRAX You've got Venus on your side? I'll use Vulcan. (*Rushing toward the door of the cottage*) I'm going for fire.

TRACHALIO (*alarmed*) Where's he going?

LABRAX (*as he nears the door*) Hey! Anybody inside? Hey, there!

DAEMONES (*calling*) You touch that door and I'll fill that face of yours with fists for you. (*Nods to the two slaves, who run over and haul Labrax back.*)

SLAVE (*to Labrax, grinning*) We don't use fire. All we eat is dried figs.

TRACHALIO I'll give you fire all right—I'll light one on your head.

LABRAX Damn it, I'll get fire from somewhere else then.

DAEMONES And just what are you going to do with it when you get it?

LABRAX (*gesturing toward the altar*) I'll start a bonfire right here.

DAEMONES Funeral pyre for yourself, eh?

LABRAX No, sir. I'm going to burn the both of them alive right here on the altar, that's what I'm going to do.

TRACHALIO The minute you try it, I'll heave you in the fire by that beard of yours, haul you out just as you begin to brown, and feed you to the vultures.

DAEMONES (*to himself*) Now it comes to me! This is the ape I saw in my dream, the one I wanted to keep from pulling the swallows out of their nest.

TRACHALIO (*to Daemones*) Would you please do me a favor? Would you keep an eye on these girls and see that no harm comes to them while I go get my master?

DAEMONES Go ahead. Find him and bring him here.

TRACHALIO (*gesturing toward Labrax*) But don't let him—

DAEMONES (*interrupting*) If he lays a hand on them, or even tries to, he'll be sorry.

TRACHALIO Be careful now.

DAEMONES I'm being careful. You go along.

TRACHALIO But keep an eye on him too, so's he doesn't get away. We agreed to forfeit thirty thousand dollars to the hangman if we didn't produce him today.

DAEMONES Just run along. I'll take care of everything until you get back.

TRACHALIO I'll be back right away. (*Exits, stage right.*)

DAEMONES (*to Labrax*) Hey, pimp! I'll give you your choice: you prefer a beating to keep you quiet or will you stay still without one?

LABRAX I don't give a damn what you say. These girls are mine, and I'm going to drag them off this altar by the hair whether you or Venus or god almighty himself likes it or not.

DAEMONES Just try to touch them.

LABRAX Sure I'll touch them.

DAEMONES (*with elaborate cordiality*) Go right ahead. Step right this way. (*Points toward the altar.*)

LABRAX You just tell those boys of yours to step back that way. (*Points away from the altar.*)

DAEMONES Oh, no. Any stepping they do will be toward you.

LABRAX (*belligerently*) Oh, yeah? I don't think so.

DAEMONES What'll you do if they step closer? (*Nods to the slaves, who advance on Labrax.*)

LABRAX (*taking a hasty step backward*) I'll move back. Listen, you old goat, if I ever catch you back in town, believe me, I'll have my fun out of you before I let you go, or I'm no pimp.

DAEMONES (*grimly*) You do that. But, in the meantime, if you lay a hand on these girls I'll let you have it—and hard.

LABRAX Yeah? How hard?

DAEMONES Hard enough for a pimp.

LABRAX I don't give a damn for your threats. I'm dragging those girls out of here right now whether you like it or not.

DAEMONES Just try to touch them.

LABRAX Sure I'll touch them.

DAEMONES So you'll touch them, will you? And do you know what's going to happen? (*To one of the slaves*) Roughneck! Hurry into the house and bring out two clubs.

LABRAX (*taken aback*) Clubs?

DAEMONES (*to the slave*) Be sure they're thick ones. Quick! On the double! (*The slave dashes off. He turns back to Labrax.*) I'll see that you get the reception you deserve.

LABRAX (*to himself*)   And I had to lose my helmet in the wreck! If I still had it, now's the time I could use it. (*To Daemones*) Look, can't I at least talk to them?

DAEMONES   No, you can't. (*As the slave hurries back carrying two hefty clubs, jovially*) Look who's here—my clubman. Couldn't have come at a better time.

LABRAX (*to himself*)   Look what's here—an earache. Couldn't have come at a worse time.

DAEMONES (*to the slaves*)   Cutthroat, take one of those clubs. (*Pointing to either side of the altar*) Now one of you stand there, and one here. Take your positions. (*Nodding with satisfaction as they do*) That's the way. Now listen to me. If he lays a finger on them and you don't lay those clubs on him until he doesn't know which way is up, so help me, I'll murder you both. If he tries to talk to either one of them, stay just where you are and answer instead. And the minute he tries to get away from here, wrap those clubs around his shins as fast as you can.

LABRAX   You mean they're not even going to let me leave here?

DAEMONES (*distastefully*)   I've got no more to say to you. (*To the slaves*) And when that servant who went for his master gets back here with him, you come right home. Mind you—do exactly what I told you. (*Goes into the cottage.*)

LABRAX (*to himself*)   Amazing how quickly shrines change around here. A minute ago this one belonged to Venus; now it's Hercules'—that's what it looks like with these two statues, clubs and all, that the old man just set up. God almighty, I don't know where I can run to now. Storms everywhere: first on sea, and now on land. (*Calling*) Palaestra!

SLAVE   What do you want?

LABRAX   Hey, must be some mistake; this Palaestra isn't the one I know. (*Calling*) Ampelisca!

SLAVE   Watch yourself or I'll let you have it.

LABRAX (*to himself*)   Not bad advice, even though it comes from a pair of clods like this. (*To the slaves*) Hey, you two, I'm talking to you. No harm in my going a little closer to them, is there?

SLAVE   Not at all—for us.

LABRAX   How about for me?

SLAVE None for you either—if you can keep your eyes open.

LABRAX Keep my eyes open for what?

SLAVE (*brandishing the club*) See this? For a good hard wallop.

LABRAX For god's sake, please just let me get out of here! (*Takes a tentative step away.*)

SLAVE Go right ahead, if you want. (*The two take a step toward him.*)

LABRAX (*backing away in a hurry*) Very kind of you; thanks very much. No, I think I'll stick around—and you fellows can stand right where you are. (*To himself*) God damn it, I'm not doing well at all. (*Settling himself for a long wait*) Well, I'll get those girls yet. I'll stay put and starve them out.

(*Plesidippus and Trachalio enter, stage right, deep in conversation.*)

PLESIDIPPUS (*shocked*) You mean that pimp wanted to drag my girl away from Venus' altar by brute force?

TRACHALIO Exactly.

PLESIDIPPUS Why didn't you kill him on the spot?

TRACHALIO (*glibly*) I didn't have a sword.

PLESIDIPPUS You should have picked up a stick or a rock.

TRACHALIO (*as if appalled at the suggestion*) What? Chase a man with stones like a dog?

PLESIDIPPUS That scum? Of course!

LABRAX (*catching sight of them, to himself*) Oh, lord, now I'm in for it! Here comes Plesidippus. By the time he gets done, there won't be a speck of me left.

PLESIDIPPUS Were the girls still sitting on the altar when you left to get me?

TRACHALIO (*looking toward the altar*) They're there right now.

PLESIDIPPUS Who's minding them?

TRACHALIO Some old fellow who lives next door to the shrine. He gave us all the help you could ask for. He and his servants are standing guard. (*Importantly*) I ordered him to.

PLESIDIPPUS Take me right to that pimp. Where is he?

LABRAX (*ingratiatingly*) Good morning, Plesidippus.

PLESIDIPPUS Don't you good-morning me! You're getting a rope around your neck: do you prefer to be carried or dragged? Make up your mind while you still have the chance.

LABRAX (*gulping*) Neither, thanks.

PLESIDIPPUS (*to Trachalio*) Trachalio, get down to the beach on the

double. You know those fellows I brought out here with me to
help me hand this creature over to the hangman? Tell them to
go back to town and meet me down at the docks. Then come
back here and stand guard. I'm hauling this godforsaken good-
for-nothing into court. (*As Trachalio dashes off, stage right,
Plesidippus goes up to Labrax and ties a rope around his neck.*)
Come on, get moving. We're heading for the courthouse.

LABRAX (*with injured innocence*)   What did I do?

PLESIDIPPUS (*exploding*)   What did you do? I suppose you didn't take
a deposit from me for the girl and then carry her off?

LABRAX   I did *not* carry her off.

PLESIDIPPUS   How can you say a thing like that?

LABRAX   I only carried her on board. It was my damned luck that I
wasn't able to carry her off. Look—I told you I'd meet you at the
shrine of Venus. Didn't I do just what I said? I'm here, ain't I?

PLESIDIPPUS (*grimly*)   Tell it to the judge. There's been enough talk
around here. Follow me. (*Starts walking off, jerking Labrax after
him at the end of the rope.*)

LABRAX (*shouting*)   Charmides! Help! They've tied a rope around my
neck and they're hauling me off!

CHARMIDES (*appearing in the doorway of the temple*)   Who's calling
me?

LABRAX (*frantically*)   See the way they're hauling me off?

CHARMIDES (*coolly*)   I sure do. And I'm delighted to see it.

LABRAX (*unbelievingly*)   You mean to say you're not going to help me?

CHARMIDES (*disinterestedly*)   Who's hauling you off?

LABRAX   That young fellow Plesidippus.

CHARMIDES (*grinning*)   You were out to get him, now keep him. You
ought to creep into jail happy as a lark. You've just had happen
to you what most people in the world wish for.

LABRAX   What's that?

CHARMIDES (*as before*)   Getting what they've been looking for.

LABRAX (*desperately*)   Please, Charmides, stick with me! (*Grabs hold
of him.*)

CHARMIDES (*disgustedly*)   Just like you to ask a thing like that. You're
being hauled off to jail, so you want me to go along too. Come
on, let go of me! (*Brushes Labrax's arm away.*)

LABRAX   I'm sunk!

PLESIDIPPUS   I hope to god you're right. (*Turning to the girls*) Palaestra, dear, and you, Ampelisca, stay right here until I get back.

SLAVE I think they'd be better off in our house until you come back for them.

PLESIDIPPUS Good idea; thanks very much. (*The two slaves lead the girls into the cottage.*)

LABRAX (*shouting at them*) You're a bunch of robbers!

SLAVE What's that? Robbers? (*To Plesidippus*) Haul him out of here.

LABRAX (*calling*) Palaestra, please, I beg you—

PLESIDIPPUS (*jerking the rope*) Damn you, follow me!

LABRAX (*to Charmides*) My friend—

CHARMIDES (*distastefully*) I'm no friend of yours. You and I are quits.

LABRAX So you're throwing me over, eh?

CHARMIDES That's exactly what I'm doing. One drinking session with you was enough.

LABRAX (*as Plesidippus hauls him off, stage left*) God damn you to hell!

CHARMIDES (*calling after him*) Same to you! (*To the audience*) I'm a believer in the theory that men get turned into different kinds of animals. If you ask me, that pimp is being turned into a bird —a jailbird. He's going to build a nest in the town lockup right now. But I'm going to stand by him in court. Maybe I can help convince the judge to let him go—to jail. (*Exits, stage left.*)

ACT IV

(*Daemones comes out of the cottage.*)

DAEMONES (*to the audience*) That was a good turn I did today, helping those girls, and a very pleasant one to do. Now I have a pair of devoted followers—young ones, too, and not bad looking. But that shrew of a wife of mine is watching me like a hawk to make sure I don't start anything with either one of them. (*Looking off, stage right, toward the sea*) I wonder how my servant Gripus is doing? He took the boat out last night for some fishing. Believe me, he'd have shown more sense if he had stayed in bed. With the weather we had last night, and are having right now, he's wasting his time, his energy, and his nets. Look how rough that water is! I'll be able to fry what he catches on my fingers.

(*A call is heard from inside.*) There's my wife calling me for lunch. (*Heaving a sigh*) I'd better go in; it's time for my earful of her gabble.

(*Daemones goes into the cottage. A second later Gripus, "the fisherman," enters, stage right. He is hauling mightily at his net, dragging along in it a satchel that, to judge by the effort it takes to move it, is no light weight; a rope, tied to the satchel, trails loosely behind. Gripus is by nature sour and uncommunicative, very much like his fellow slave Sceparnio; at the moment, however, his face is wearing an expression that is almost beatific.*)

SONG

GRIPUS (*to the audience*)

> I'm sending thanks for this good luck
> To friendly Father Neptune in
> That salty, fishy house of his.
> I got a royal send-off when
> He let me leave his bailiwick:
> A load of loot, and my boat intact—
> Although it hit rough seas to reach
> A rich, new type of fishing ground.

(*Breathlessly*)

> It's a marvel, a freak to have made such a haul!
> See it here in the net? This is all that I got—
> Not an ounce more of fish did I pull in today.

(*Pauses, then resumes less excitedly*)

> I jumped from bed at 1:00 A.M.—
> I felt a chance to make some cash
> Was better than a good night's sleep.
> Despite the storm, I had in mind
> To see if I could somehow ease
> The weight of the family's poverty,
> As well as help my own poor lot.
> I didn't spare myself one bit.

(*Vehemently*)

> Any man who is lazy is not worth a damn,
> And I hate him like poison; I hate the whole breed.

If a man wants to finish his work in good time,
He should have enough sense to get up by himself
And not wait for his master to call him to work.
If a man likes to sleep, he'll get plenty of rest—
But he'll end up in trouble and not in the chips.

(*Jubilantly*)

> I, who haven't a lazy bone,
> Now have found the means for a
> Life of lazing if I want.
> Look at what my net picked up!
> Just what's in it I can't say,
> But it's heavy, that I know.

(*Excitedly*)

Do you know what I think? That there's gold inside this!
Not a soul in the world knows about it but me.
Now's your chance, Gripus boy, to be free as a bird.
All right, here's how I'll work it, my scheme goes like this:
I'll go up to the master, and, playing it smart,
Start by making a very low bid for my head.
I'll keep upping the price till he lets me go free.
And the moment that happens, I'll buy me a farm
And a house and some slaves. I'll invest next in ships,
Carry cargoes, make money, make a name for myself.
Then I'll build me a ship just for pleasure, not trade,
  And I'll do what the millionaires do—
  Take a round-the-world cruise in my yacht.
When I'm finally famous enough
I'll erect a big, fortified town.

(*Working himself up*)

> A metropolis named Gripopolis,
> A memorial to Gripus, hero renowned,
> Capital of a nation, one that I'll found!

(*Pauses a moment transfixed; then comes to*)

> My head's chock-full of big ideas
> About the things I plan to do.
> I'd better hide this satchel now.
> And then, King Gripus, prepare to munch
> The bread and beans you're getting for lunch.

(As he starts walking toward the cottage, Trachalio enters, stage left, sees him and his catch—and immediately becomes extremely interested.)

TRACHALIO *(calling)*

Hey, wait a minute, will you please?

GRIPUS *(suspiciously)*

What for?

TRACHALIO *(casually reaching down to pick up the trailing rope)*

You're dragging this rope. I'll coil it up for you.

GRIPUS *(curtly)*

Just let it be.

TRACHALIO *(holding on)*

No, let me help you, please.
To do good folks good turns is never a waste.

GRIPUS *(uneasily)*

The sea was rough last night, my friend, so don't
You get ideas: I don't have any fish.
Just take a look: this net I'm hauling back
Is wet, that's all; not a thing with scales inside.

TRACHALIO *(heartily)*

Lord, man, it's not your fish I'm looking for.
Your charming conversation's what I need.

GRIPUS *(pulling on the net and trying to walk away)*

You bore me to tears, whoever you are. Let go!

TRACHALIO *(pulling in the opposite direction and bringing him to a halt)*

I just won't let you leave this place. You'll wait.

GRIPUS

Hey, what's the big idea of holding me back?
Now you watch out or you'll get hurt. Let go!

TRACHALIO

You've got to listen—

GRIPUS

No, I won't.

TRACHALIO

You won't.
Right now, but later on you damn well will!

GRIPUS (*trying, without much success, to sound indifferent*).

Oh, speak your piece.

TRACHALIO

What I've in mind to tell,
My boy, you'll find well worth your while to hear.

GRIPUS (*as before*)

All right, let's have it. What's it all about?

TRACHALIO (*looking around warily*)

First look and see if anyone is near.

GRIPUS (*looks around and turns back; nervously*)

Is it something to do, say, with me?

TRACHALIO

Well, of course! But I've got to be sure
That you know how to keep your mouth shut.

GRIPUS

Come on, out with it. What's this about?

TRACHALIO

Just keep quiet. I'll tell you. But first,
Do you give me your word you'll play fair?

GRIPUS (*anxiously*)

Yes, I give you my word I'll play fair.

TRACHALIO

> Now then, listen. I happened to spot
> Someone just as he pilfered a purse
> From the pocket of someone I knew.
> So I later went up to the thief,
> And I offered a deal on these terms:
> "As it happens, I know whom you robbed.
> But I won't say a word to the man
> If you'll hand over half of the haul."
> Now, I've not heard a word from him yet.
> Well, how much of a share should I get?
> I expect you'll say half. Am I right?

GRIPUS (*blurting*)

> Oh, my god, I would ask even more!
> You're all set: if he won't come across,
> Turn him in to the owner, I say.

TRACHALIO (*promptly*)

> Good advice—and I'll use it right now.
> (*Pointing a finger at him*)
>   All right, you! Pay attention, you hear?
>   For my story not only is true,
>   But it all has to do—with you!

GRIPUS (*startled*)   What do you mean?

TRACHALIO   That satchel there—I've known all along whose it is—

GRIPUS (*interrupting, defensively*)   What are you talking about?

TRACHALIO   —and how it was lost.

GRIPUS (*heatedly*)   But *I* know how it was found and I know who
found it and I know who owns it now. What you know is none
of my business, no more than what I know is yours. You know
whose it used to be. I know whose it is now. (*Grimly*) There
isn't a man alive who can take it away from me, so don't get your
hopes up that you can.

TRACHALIO   You mean you won't give it up if the owner comes for
it?

GRIPUS   The owner? Make no mistake about it, my friend, there's only
one man in this world who owns this thing—me. I caught it
when I was fishing.

TRACHALIO You did, eh?

GRIPUS (*argumentatively*) You won't deny my right to the fish in the sea, will you? If, as, and when I catch any, they're mine. I keep them; they're my property. No one else lays a hand on them or puts in any claims for any share. They're my goods and I sell them as such in the fish market. The sea is absolutely public domain; everybody shares it in common.

TRACHALIO (*promptly*) Agreed. So then, my friend, why shouldn't I share this satchel in common? It came from the sea—public domain, you know.

GRIPUS Don't be a wise guy. If the law was the way you put it, fishermen would be finished. The minute any fish went up for sale in the market, everyone would start claiming a share; no one would buy a thing. Everyone'd say they were caught in the public domain.

TRACHALIO Who's the wise guy now? Compare a satchel to a fish? What a nerve! Are you trying to tell me you think they're the same?

GRIPUS (*shrugging*) That's no problem of mine. When I throw over a net or a line, whatever gets caught there I pull up. And what my nets or lines catch is mine, absolutely and positively mine.

TRACHALIO Oh, no, it isn't. Not if you pulled up some pot, say.

GRIPUS (*scornfully*) What are you, a lawyer?

TRACHALIO Listen, you stinker, did you ever in your life see a fisherman catch a satchel-fish or peddle one in the market? You can't take over just any trade you want, not by a long shot. Damn you, you want to be a fisherman and a satchel-maker all in one. Either you show me exactly how a satchel is a fish or you don't walk off with something that doesn't have scales and certainly wasn't born in salt water.

GRIPUS (*affecting incredulity*) What? You never heard of a satchel-fish before?

TRACHALIO Cut it out. There's no such thing.

GRIPUS (*assuming the air of an expert*) Oh, yes there is. I'm a fisherman, I know. But you don't often catch them. Isn't a fish around landed less often.

TRACHALIO You're wasting your time. You can't kid me, you crook. All right, what color is it?

GRIPUS (*as before, pointing to the satchel*)   Very few are like this one
here. Some of them have a dark red skin. Then there are some
that are big and black.

TRACHALIO   Oh, sure. (*Savagely*) If you want my opinion, you better
watch out or you'll turn into a satchel-fish yourself: that skin
of yours is going to get dark red, and then wind up black—and
blue.

GRIPUS (*half to himself*)   The god-damned trouble I had to run into
today!

TRACHALIO (*impatiently*)   This argument's getting us nowhere. We're
wasting time. Come on, my friend, who do you want to pick as
judge to settle this for us?

GRIPUS (*eyeing him balefully*)   Judge? The satchel.

TRACHALIO   Oh, yeah?

GRIPUS   Yeah.

TRACHALIO (*exasperated*)   God, you're stupid!

GRIPUS (*scornfully*)   Well, listen to the professor!

TRACHALIO (*getting a firm grip on the rope*)   You're not moving an
inch with this thing today—not unless you agree to a third party
to hold it or a judge to judge the matter.

GRIPUS   Look here, are you in your right mind?

TRACHALIO (*scornfully*)   I'm as mad as a hatter.

GRIPUS (*tightening his grip on the net*)   Then I'm as crazy as a loon
—but I'm not letting go.

TRACHALIO   You say one more word and I'll sink my fists in your skull.
You know what they do to a new sponge? If you don't let go,
that's the way I'll squeeze the juice out of you.

GRIPUS   You know how I slam the ink out of an octopus? You lay a
finger on me and that's what I'll do to you. (*Sticking his chin in
Trachalio's face*) So you want to fight, eh?

TRACHALIO (*abruptly losing his belligerence*)   Why do we have to
fight? Why don't you and I just split the swag?

GRIPUS   Don't get any ideas: the only thing you'll be able to get for
yourself out of all this is a sock on the jaw. (*Starts pulling the
net toward the cottage*) I'm getting out of here.

TRACHALIO (*running ahead and yanking the rope so that the net—and
Gripus—are spun about*)   No, you're not getting out of here—
I'm putting this ship about. You stay where you are.

GRIPUS (*between his teeth*) If you're going to play deck hand on this ship, I'll be skipper. (*Roaring*) Damn you, let go that rope!

TRACHALIO Sure I'll let go. You let go that satchel.

GRIPUS By god, you're not going to get one single solitary square inch of this satchel.

TRACHALIO (*standing his ground*) You can't get around me just by saying no. Either you cut me in, or you put up security, or you let a judge decide.

GRIPUS What do you mean? Something *I* caught in the sea—

TRACHALIO (*interrupting*) But *I* saw it from the shore.

GRIPUS (*disregarding him*) —with my own hands, my own net, and my own boat?

TRACHALIO I saw you get it from the shore, right? So, if the owner should come along, then I'm in this thing just as deep as you are, I'm an accomplice, right?

GRIPUS Right.

TRACHALIO All right, you stinker, you just prove to me how I can be an accomplice and not be entitled to a cut. Come on, show me how!

GRIPUS (*baffled and confused*) I don't know. I don't know anything about that legal stuff you city boys do. All I say is that this satchel is mine.

TRACHALIO And I say it's mine.

GRIPUS (*switching suddenly to affability*) Wait a second. I just figured out how you don't have to be an accomplice—or get a cut.

TRACHALIO Yeah? How?

GRIPUS First you let me leave here. Then you go your own way—and keep your mouth shut. You don't say a word about me to anybody—and I don't give you anything. You stay mum, and I keep my trap shut. That's the fairest and squarest way to do it.

TRACHALIO You mean you're not going to offer me a deal?

GRIPUS (*promptly*) I already did: that you let go that rope, go away, and stop bothering me.

TRACHALIO Wait a second. I've got a counteroffer to make.

GRIPUS Yeah? Well offer to get the hell out of here.

TRACHALIO (*disregarding the last remark, with elaborate casualness*) Do you know anybody hereabouts?

GRIPUS (*evasively*) My own neighbors, naturally.

TRACHALIO (*as before*) Whereabouts do you live?

GRIPUS (*waving vaguely*) Farther on. Lots farther on. 'Way off at
the end of those fields out there.

TRACHALIO (*concealing his satisfaction at the answer, even more casually than before*) How'd you like the fellow who lives in this
cottage to be judge?

GRIPUS (*concealing his satisfaction at the suggestion*) Suppose you
give me a little slack on that rope so I can step off to the side
and think it over?

TRACHALIO Sure. (*Slacks off the rope, letting Gripus lug the net a
few feet off to the side.*)

GRIPUS (*to the audience, jubilantly*) Hooray! I'm in! The swag's mine
for keeps. He's inviting me to call in my own master as judge,
right here on my own home grounds. Good old Daemones
wouldn't judge anyone in his household out of a penny. This
fellow here has no idea what kind of deal he's offering me. Sure
I'll take a judge!

TRACHALIO Well, what do you say?

GRIPUS (*as if grudgingly*) Even though I know for sure that by rights
this thing is mine, rather than have a fight with you, I'll do it
your way.

TRACHALIO (*heartily*) That's what I like to hear.

GRIPUS (*as before*) And even though you're bringing me up before a
judge I don't know, if he turns out honest, I may not know him
but I want to; if he doesn't, I may know him but he's the last
man in the world I want to. (*The door of the cottage opens and
Daemones and the two girls come out.*)

DAEMONES (*to the girls*) Much as I want to do what you want me to,
girls, I'm afraid that wife of mine will kick me out of the house
on account of you. She'll say I'm bringing in a pair of mistresses
right under her nose. I'd rather have you two running to that
altar for help than me.

PALAESTRA Oh, my god! This is the end!

DAEMONES (*reassuringly*) Don't be afraid. I'll make sure you're safe.
(*Noticing that the two slaves with the clubs are tagging along
after the girls*) What are you following them outside for? No
one's going to hurt them with me around. All right, guards, off
guard and into the house, both of you. (*They go back into the
cottage.*)

GRIPUS Hello, master.

DAEMONES   Why, Gripus! Hello! How did things go?

TRACHALIO (*startled, to Daemones*)   Is he your servant?

GRIPUS (*grinning*)   His servant, and proud of it.

TRACHALIO (*glaring at him*)   I've got nothing to say to you.

GRIPUS   Yeah? Then get out of here.

TRACHALIO (*to Daemones*)   Please, mister, tell me: is he your servant?

DAEMONES   Yes, he is.

TRACHALIO (*jubilantly*)   Oh, boy! If he's yours, that's the best thing that could have happened! I'll say it for the second time today: I'm mighty glad to meet you.

DAEMONES (*cordially*)   Glad to meet you too. Aren't you the one who left here to get your master a little while ago?

TRACHALIO   I'm the one.

DAEMONES   Well, what can we do for you?

TRACHALIO   So he's yours, eh?

DAEMONES   Yes, he is.

TRACHALIO (*grinning broadly*)   If he's yours, that's the best thing that could have happened.

DAEMONES   What's this all about?

TRACHALIO (*pointing to Gripus, vehemently*)   That devil there is a damned crook!

DAEMONES (*patiently*)   And just what has the "damned crook" done to you?

TRACHALIO   I want him drawn and quartered!

DAEMONES   Now what is this you two are making such a case about?

TRACHALIO   I'll tell you.

GRIPUS (*quickly*)   Oh, no you don't. I'll tell him.

TRACHALIO (*with elaborate formality*)   If I'm not mistaken, I have the right to open this action.

GRIPUS   If you had any decency, you'd get into action and get out of here.

DAEMONES (*sharply*)   Gripus! Shut up and listen.

GRIPUS (*unbelievingly*)   You mean he's going to speak first?

DAEMONES (*nodding curtly*)   You listen. (*To Trachalio*) And you start talking.

GRIPUS (*as before*)   You're going to let an outsider talk ahead of one of your own household?

TRACHALIO (*eying him balefully*)   Isn't there any way to handle this fellow? (*Turning to Daemones*) What I started to tell you was this. Remember that pimp you kicked out of the temple? Well, this fellow has his satchel. (*Pointing*) See? There it is.

GRIPUS (*trying to edge in front of the net*)   I haven't got it.

TRACHALIO   What do you mean you haven't got it? I'm not blind.

GRIPUS (*aside*)   I only wish you were! (*To Trachalio*) I have it, I don't have it—what are you sticking your nose into my affairs for?

TRACHALIO (*doggedly*)   What's more important is how you got it, whether legally or illegally.

GRIPUS (*to Daemones, heatedly*)   You can string me up by the neck this minute if I didn't find this satchel while I was fishing. (*To Trachalio*) And if I fished it up from the sea with my own net, how do you figure it's yours instead of mine?

TRACHALIO (*to Daemones*)   He's trying to pull the wool over your eyes. What I just told you are the facts.

GRIPUS (*menacingly*)   What did I hear you say?

TRACHALIO (*to Daemones*)   He's yours, isn't he? Can't you handle him somehow? Get him to shut up until his betters finish speaking?

GRIPUS (*leering and making an obscene gesture*)   So you want me to get what your master gives you, eh? Well, yours may "handle" you, all right, but ours doesn't pull that stuff with us.

DAEMONES (*to Trachalio, smiling*)   He got the better of you there, my boy. Now, what is it you want? Speak up.

TRACHALIO   For myself, nothing. I don't want any part of that satchel there, and I never once said it was mine. But there's a little jewel box in it that belongs to this girl here (*gesturing toward Palaestra*). She's the one I was telling you earlier was no slave.

DAEMONES (*nodding*)   You mean the one you said came from the same city I did?

TRACHALIO   Exactly. Well, the birth tokens she wore when she was a child are there in that box, and the box is there in that satchel. (*Nodding scornfully in Gripus' direction*) It's no earthly use to him, but he'll be doing this poor girl a real service if he gives her the only means she has for finding her parents.

DAEMONES   Say no more. I'll have him hand it over.

GRIPUS   So help me, I'm not giving him a thing!

TRACHALIO (*to Daemones*)   All I'm asking for is the jewel box and birth tokens.

GRIPUS   Oh, yeah? What if they're gold?

TRACHALIO What difference should that make to you? (*Loftily*) Any gold or silver will be bought and paid for in cash.

GRIPUS All right, my friend, you let me see that cash and I'll let you see the box.

DAEMONES Gripus, shut up or you'll be sorry. (*To Trachalio*) Finish what you started to say.

TRACHALIO (*earnestly*) I have just one favor to ask of you: have pity on this girl—I mean, if the satchel really is that pimp's, as I suspect it is. (*Pointedly*) You see, at this moment I can't say anything for sure, I can only guess.

GRIPUS (*to Daemones, excitedly*) Don't you see? That good-for-nothing's trying to lay a trap for us!

TRACHALIO (*to Gripus*) Will you let me finish talking? (*To Daemones*) I say the satchel belongs to that filthy pimp. Now, if it does, the girls will be able to recognize it. So will you please make him show it to them?

GRIPUS (*spluttering*) What's that? Show it to them?

DAEMONES (*mildly*) There's nothing wrong with his suggestion, is there, Gripus? Just to show it to them?

GRIPUS (*roaring*) I should say there is! A hell of a lot wrong!

DAEMONES How so?

GRIPUS Because the minute I show it to them, naturally they'll say they recognize it.

TRACHALIO (*heatedly*) Damn you, you think everybody's as big a liar as you are!

GRIPUS (*gesturing toward Daemones*) So long as he's on my side, you can say anything you like; it won't bother me in the least.

TRACHALIO He may be standing on your side, but he's going to take his testimony from this side (*pointing to the girls*).

DAEMONES (*sharply*) Gripus, you listen. (*To Trachalio*) And you explain what you want—and make it short.

TRACHALIO (*patiently*) I already did. But if you didn't follow me, I'll do it again. As I've already told you, neither of these girls should be slaves. (*Gesturing toward Palaestra*) This one here was kidnaped from Athens when she was a child.

GRIPUS Suppose you explain to me just what their being slaves or not has to do with this satchel?

TRACHALIO (*angrily*) Damn you, you want me to tell the story all over again just to waste the whole day.

DAEMONES (*to Trachalio, sharply*) Cut out the cursing and do what I
    asked you.

TRACHALIO It's just as I told you before. There should be a little jewel
    box in that satchel. It contains the birth tokens she can use to
    identify her parents. She was wearing them when she was
    snatched from Athens as a child.

GRIPUS (*savagely*) I wish to god someone'd put the snatch on you!
    What the hell's going on here? (*Gesturing angrily toward the
    girls*) What's the matter with them? Are they dumb? Can't they
    talk for themselves?

TRACHALIO Sure. But they're keeping quiet because they know that's
    what makes a good woman—knowing how to keep quiet and
    not talk.

GRIPUS So help me, by that token you don't make either a good man
    or a good woman.

TRACHALIO Why?

GRIPUS Because you're no good whether you talk or keep quiet. (*To
    Daemones*) Please! Am I going to get a chance to speak today?

DAEMONES (*turning on him*) One more word out of you today and
    I'll have your head!

TRACHALIO (*to Daemones*) As I was saying, would you please make
    him give the box back to the girls? If he insists on some sort of
    reward, he can have one: let him keep whatever else is in the
    satchel for himself.

GRIPUS Finally you said it! And you know why? Because you know
    very well what my rights in the matter are. A few minutes ago
    you were out to get half for yourself.

TRACHALIO You know what? I still am.

GRIPUS I once saw a vulture out to get something, and you know what?
    He didn't get away with a thing.

DAEMONES (*to Gripus, angrily*) Do you need a beating to keep you
    quiet?

GRIPUS (*stubbornly*) If he shuts up, I'll shut up. But if he's going to
    talk, let me talk too, and give my side of the story.

DAEMONES Gripus, hand me that satchel.

GRIPUS I'll trust you with it if you promise that, if there's nothing of
    theirs in it, I get it back.

DAEMONES You'll get it back.

GRIPUS (*taking the satchel out of the net and handing it over*)   Here it is.

DAEMONES   Now, Palaestra, and you too, Ampelisca, listen to me. Is this the satchel you say has your box in it?

PALAESTRA (*without hesitation*)   Yes, it is.

GRIPUS   Oh, my god in heaven, I haven't got a chance! She said it was hers before she even got a good look at it!

PALAESTRA (*earnestly*)   I know it's confusing, so let me clear things up for you. There should be a little wicker box in that satchel. Now, without your showing me a thing, I'll name every article that's in it. If I make a mistake, then I've wasted my breath and you people keep whatever's in there for yourselves. But if I don't, then please, please let me have my things back.

DAEMONES   Agreed. In my opinion, what you're asking for is plain and simple justice.

GRIPUS   And in mine, damn it all, plain and simple injustice. Supposing she's a witch or a fortune-teller and reels off the name of whatever's in there perfectly? Are we going to let some fortune-teller walk off with everything?

DAEMONES (*sharply*)   She's not walking off with a thing unless she names every item without a mistake. Fortune-telling won't get her anywhere. Now, unstrap that satchel so that I can find out who's right and who's wrong without wasting another minute.

TRACHALIO (*watching Gripus unstrap the satchel, aside with satisfaction*)   And that settles *his* hash.

GRIPUS (*to Daemones*)   The straps are off.

DAEMONES   Now open it.

PALAESTRA (*excitedly*)   I see the box!

DAEMONES (*taking it out and holding it*)   Is this it?

PALAESTRA   That's it! (*Extending her hand and touching it almost caressingly, to herself*) Dear parents, all I have of you I carry locked up here. Here are stored all my hopes, the only means I have of ever finding you.

GRIPUS (*to himself, growling*)   You deserve the wrath of god on your head, whoever you are, for squeezing your parents into something that small.

DAEMONES (*pointing to a spot at his side*)   Gripus, you stand here; this concerns you now. (*To Palaestra*) You stand over there and call off all the things in the box and tell us what each looks like. Mind you, don't leave anything out. And, believe me, if you make the slightest mistake, don't get any ideas about correcting it later. It'll be a sheer waste of time, my girl. (*Palaestra nods and steps a few paces away.*)

GRIPUS (*nodding approvingly*) You're asking only for what's fair.

TRACHALIO God knows he wouldn't ask anything like that of you. You don't know what it is to be fair.

DAEMONES (*to Palaestra*) All right, my girl, you can start now. (*As Gripus opens his mouth*) Gripus! Shut up and pay attention.

PALAESTRA (*with her back to Daemones and Gripus*) The box has my birth tokens.

DAEMONES (*holding the box open before him*) I see them.

GRIPUS (*to himself*) Knocked out in the first round! (*Grabbing Daemones' arm to bring the box closer to his chest*) Wait a second! Don't show them to her!

DAEMONES Now tell me what each one of them looks like.

PALAESTRA First there's a miniature gold sword. It's inscribed.

DAEMONES What's the inscription say?

PALAESTRA My father's name. Next, alongside the sword is a miniature two-headed ax, also of gold and inscribed; this time it's my mother's name.

DAEMONES Wait a second. What is your father's name? I mean the one on the sword?

PALAESTRA Daemones.

(*Daemones holds the trinket in his hand and stares at the letters in amazement. Slowly he lifts his head to look toward the sky.*)

DAEMONES (*to himself, hoarsely*) God in heaven! What is happening to all my hopes!

GRIPUS (*aside*) You mean what's happening to all mine!

TRACHALIO (*to Palaestra and Daemones, eagerly*) Please! Go on, don't stop!

GRIPUS (*turning on him*) Either you take it easy or go straight to hell!

DAEMONES (*in a voice so full of emotion it is barely audible*) Tell me, what's the name on the little ax, your mother's name?

PALAESTRA Daedalis.

DAEMONES (*to himself, choking with emotion*) It was heaven's will to rescue me!

GRIPUS (*aside*) And throw me overboard!

DAEMONES (*sotto voce to Gripus*) Gripus! This girl! She must be my daughter!

GRIPUS (*not exactly overcome by the news, sotto voce*) It's all right with me. (*Looking toward Trachalio, under his breath*) God damn you to hell for having gotten a look at me today—and me for being damned fool enough not to have looked around a hundred times to make sure no one was watching before I pulled that net out of the water!

PALAESTRA (*unaware of the excitement she is causing*) Next a miniature silver sickle, and two clasped hands, and a miniature windlass—

GRIPUS (*aside*) Windlass? I wish to hell you were windless.

PALAESTRA —and a gold medallion my father gave me on my birthday.

DAEMONES (*to himself, ecstatically*) It's she! I must take her in my arms! (*Rushing to her and taking her hands*) My daughter! I'm your own father! I'm Daemones! Daedalis—your mother—is right inside!

PALAESTRA (*throwing herself into his arms*) Oh, my father, my father! Who ever imagined this could happen!

DAEMONES (*holding her tightly*) What a joy it is to have you in my arms!

TRACHALIO (*beaming on them*) It's a joy to see how heaven has rewarded you both for being as good as you are.

DAEMONES Trachalio, pick up the satchel if you can and bring it inside. Hurry!

TRACHALIO (*to Gripus, grinning broadly*) See where all your dirty tricks got you? My heartiest congratulations on your bad luck.

DAEMONES (*to Palaestra*) Come, my daughter, let's go in to your mother. She'll be able to test you further about all this. She used to be with you more, and she's more familiar with these trinkets of yours.

PALAESTRA Let's all go in. Then we can do it all together. (*Turning to Ampelisca*) Follow me, Ampelisca.

AMPELISCA (*tearfully*) I'm so happy that god has been so good to you!

(*Daemones, Trachalio, and the two girls enter the cottage.*)

GRIPUS (*to himself*) Why the hell did I have to fish that satchel up today? Or, rather, why the hell didn't I stash it away in a safe spot after I fished it up? So help me, it was so rough out there when I found the thing, I knew I'd have a rough time with it. God, I'll bet that satchel's full of money. The best thing for me to do now is just sneak off and hang myself—at least for a while until the ache goes away! (*Exits, stage right.*)

(*The door of the cottage opens and Daemones emerges. He is radiant. He walks downstage and addresses the audience.*)

DAEMONES   I swear I'm the luckiest man in the world! Suddenly, like a bolt from the blue, I found my daughter. (*Shaking his head wonderingly*) You know, when heaven wants to do well by a man, somehow he ends up getting his fondest wish—if he's been decent and godfearing. Take me—today, like a bolt from the blue, I found my daughter, something I had given up hoping for, no longer believed could happen. And I'm going to marry her to a fine young fellow from one of the best families in Athens. What's more, I find that he's a cousin of mine. I want him to come out here and see me just as soon as possible, so I've told his servant to step outside; I want to send him to town right away. (*Looking toward the door*) He hasn't come out yet. I wonder what's keeping him? I think I'd better take a look inside. (*Walks back to the entrance and peers in.*) What's this? My wife hanging on to my daughter's neck? All this hugging and loving is getting to be a silly nuisance. (*Calling through the doorway*) My dear wife, it's time to stop the kissing and start getting things ready for me. As soon as I come in I want to give a thank offering to our guardian angel for having added to our family the way he has. The lambs and pigs for the sacrifice are all ready. (*Impatiently*) What are you women keeping Trachalio for? (*Stepping back from the door*) Good. He's coming out now.

TRACHALIO   (*as he hurries out the door, breathlessly*) I don't care where he is, I'll track him down and bring him back here with me. Plesidippus, I mean.

DAEMONES   (*nodding approval*) And tell him what happened about my daughter. Ask him to drop everything and come right out here.

TRACHALIO   Right.

DAEMONES   Tell him he has my permission to marry her.

TRACHALIO   Right.

DAEMONES   And that I know his father; he's a cousin of mine.

TRACHALIO Right.

DAEMONES And hurry.

TRACHALIO Right.

DAEMONES Bring him here right away, so we can start preparing dinner.

TRACHALIO Right.

DAEMONES (*somewhat irritated*) Everything I say is "right," eh?

TRACHALIO Right. But do you know what I'd like from you? That you remember the promise you made about my getting my freedom today.

DAEMONES Right.

TRACHALIO You get Plesidippus to agree to set me free.

DAEMONES Right.

TRACHALIO And get your daughter to ask him; she'll get it out of him without any trouble.

DAEMONES Right.

TRACHALIO And arrange to have Ampelisca marry me as soon as I'm free.

DAEMONES Right.

TRACHALIO I want to see some tangible appreciation for all I've done for you.

DAEMONES Right.

TRACHALIO Everything I say is "right," eh?

DAEMONES Right—I'm just returning the favor. Now, off to the city this minute, on the double, and then come back here.

TRACHALIO Right. I won't take long. In the meantime you get everything ready that we need.

DAEMONES Right. (*To himself as Trachalio dashes off, stage left*) The devil take him with his "rights"! My ears are ringing: whatever I said, it was nothing but "right," "right," "right."

(*Enter Gripus, stage right.*)

GRIPUS (*determinedly*) Daemones, when will it be all right to have a word with you?

DAEMONES (*wincing at still another "right"*) What's on your mind, Gripus?

GRIPUS It's about that satchel. If you've got any sense, you'll have the sense to hold onto something heaven's dropped right in your lap.

DAEMONES (*reproachfully*) Do you think it's right for me to claim somebody else's property as my own?

GRIPUS (*exasperated*) But it's something I found in the sea!

DAEMONES   So much the better for the man who lost it. But that doesn't make it any more your satchel.

GRIPUS (*disgustedly*)   That's why you're so poor. It's that sanctified goodness of yours.

DAEMONES (*gently*)   Gripus, Gripus, there are so many traps set for men during their lifetime to trick and fool them! What's more, the traps are often baited; if a man's avaricious and goes after the bait greedily, he gets trapped by his own greed. The man who's careful and experienced and astute in watching his step can live a long and honest life on what he's honestly earned. If you ask me, this prize you're so wedded to will fall prize to its owner—and the divorce will cost us money. (*In shocked tones*) I hide something brought to me that I know isn't mine? None of that for your old master Daemones, no, sir! The one thing any man of intelligence is always on guard against is consciously taking part in wrongdoing. I'll have nothing whatsoever to do with making any gains by collusion.

GRIPUS (*eying him pityingly*)   I've often seen actors in a play deliver themselves of gems of wisdom of this sort—and seen them get a round of applause for having mouthed for the audience all these rules of good behavior. Then, when the audience left and everybody was back in his own home, there wasn't a one who behaved the way he had been told to.

DAEMONES (*impatiently*)   Oh, go inside and stop bothering me. And watch that tongue of yours. Make no mistake about it—I'm not going to give you a thing.

(*Gripus, without a word, marches up to the door, opens it, then turns to deliver a parting shot.*)

GRIPUS (*bitterly*)   I hope to god whatever's in that satchel—gold or silver or what not—turns into ashes! (*Ducks into the cottage, slamming the door.*)

DAEMONES (*to the audience, shaking his head sadly*)   See that attitude? That's the reason we have such bad servants. Now if that Gripus of mine had gotten together with some other servant, he'd have involved the two of them in grand larceny. He'd have been thinking he had his hands on a prize, and he'd have turned out to be the prize himself. What he caught would have caught him. Well, I'll go in now and attend to the offering. And then I'll give orders to have dinner ready immediately.

(*Daemones goes into the cottage. A moment later Trachalio and Plesidippus enter, stage left. One glance at the latter is enough to reveal that he has gotten the news.*)

PLESIDIPPUS (*ecstatically*) Trachalio, my friend, my freedman-to-be, no, my patron—more than that, the founder of my household! Tell me that whole story over again. So Palaestra found her mother and father?

TRACHALIO (*smiling indulgently*) Yes, she did.

PLESIDIPPUS And she's an Athenian like me?

TRACHALIO I think so.

PLESIDIPPUS And she's going to marry me?

TRACHALIO I suspect so.

PLESIDIPPUS What do you think, will we become engaged today?

TRACHALIO (*pretending, indulgently, to be under formal interrogation*) Yes, Mr. Chairman.

PLESIDIPPUS What do you say, should I congratulate her father on having found her?

TRACHALIO Yes, Mr. Chairman.

PLESIDIPPUS How about her mother?

TRACHALIO Yes, Mr. Chairman.

PLESIDIPPUS Have you anything to tell the chair?

TRACHALIO Yes, Mr. Chairman: yes to whatever the chair asks.

PLESIDIPPUS (*slyly*) All right, can you estimate the chair's net worth?

TRACHALIO (*taken aback*) Me? (*Recovering*) Yes, Mr. Chairman—

PLESIDIPPUS (*interrupting*) Look, I'm standing; forget about this "chair" business.

TRACHALIO Yes, Mr. Chairman.

PLESIDIPPUS Should I rush up to her?

TRACHALIO Yes, Mr. Chairman.

PLESIDIPPUS Or should I go up to her quietly, like this? (*Demonstrates.*)

TRACHALIO Yes, Mr. Chairman.

PLESIDIPPUS Should I shake her hand when I go up to her?

TRACHALIO Yes, Mr. Chairman.

PLESIDIPPUS Her father's too?

TRACHALIO Yes, Mr. Chairman.

PLESIDIPPUS   And then her mother's?

TRACHALIO   Yes, Mr. Chairman.

PLESIDIPPUS   Should I embrace her father when I go up to him?

TRACHALIO   No, Mr. Chairman.

PLESIDIPPUS   How about her mother?

TRACHALIO   No, Mr. Chairman.

PLESIDIPPUS   (*eagerly*)   How about her?

TRACHALIO   No, Mr. Chairman. (*Starts walking toward the cottage.*)

PLESIDIPPUS   Oh, lord! He votes Nay just when I want Aye—and walks
out on the meeting.

TRACHALIO   (*calling*)   You're crazy. Come on!

PLESIDIPPUS   Lead on, my patron, whither thou will.

(*The two enter the cottage.*)

ACT V

(*Enter Labrax, stage left.*)

LABRAX   (*to the audience*)   Is there another man alive right now who's
worse off than I am? I've just come from court; Plesidippus got
them to condemn me, and they made me give Palaestra up. I'm
ruined! (*Bitterly*) If you ask me, pimps were put on this earth
just to make people laugh—that's the way it looks, judging from
the general hilarity whenever a poor pimp has to suffer. (*Turning
and walking toward the shrine*) I'm going to see to that other
girl of mine in the shrine here. At least I'll take her away with
me—the only remnant left of all my property.

(*The door of the cottage opens and Gripus comes out. He is holding
a spit encrusted with rust—eloquent testimony as to how long it's been
since Daemones last held a party. He turns to speak to those inside.*)

GRIPUS   (*through the doorway*)   By god, you're not going to lay eyes
on me alive after tonight—unless I get that satchel back!

LABRAX   (*to himself*)   Oh, god! Whenever I hear anyone mention a
satchel, it's like the stab of a sword through my heart.

GRIPUS   (*as before*)   That damned Trachalio gets his freedom and you
refuse to give a single thing to the man who fished the satchel
up in his net!

LABRAX (*his attention arrested, to himself*) So help me, what this fellow is saying sounds very, very interesting.

GRIPUS (*as before*) I'm going right out and post notices everywhere in letters a foot and a half high: "Found. One satchel full of gold and silver. For information see Gripus." You think you're going to get away with my satchel, don't you? Well, you're not.

LABRAX (*to himself*) By god, I think this fellow knows who has my satchel! I'd better have a talk with him. Lord in heaven, help me now!

GRIPUS (*as someone calls him to come back inside*) What are you calling me back for? I want to clean this outside here. (*Turns away from the door and starts scraping the spit; to himself*) My god! You'd think this spit's made of rust instead of iron. The more I scrape it, the redder and skinnier it gets. I think there's a curse on it: the thing's dying of old age right in my hands.

LABRAX (*in his most affable manner*) Hello there.

GRIPUS (*eying him distastefully*) Hello yourself, dirty face.

LABRAX (*as before*) What are you doing with yourself these days?

GRIPUS (*scraping away industriously*) Cleaning a spit.

LABRAX Business good around here?

GRIPUS What's it to you? You a broker?

LABRAX Oh, no. I'm one letter short of that.

GRIPUS Broke, eh?

LABRAX You hit the nail on the head.

GRIPUS I know. You look it. What happened to you?

LABRAX My ship was wrecked last night. Lost everything I had in it.

GRIPUS What did you lose?

LABRAX (*pointedly*) A satchel full of gold and silver.

GRIPUS (*his attention caught*) Do you remember any of the things in this satchel you lost?

LABRAX (*evasively*) What difference does it make? It's lost, isn't it? Forget it. Let's talk about something else.

GRIPUS What if I know who found it? I just want to see if you can prove it's your property.

LABRAX Well, there were eight hundred gold pieces in a pouch. Then another hundred gold eagles in a separate leather sack.

GRIPUS (*aside*) God almighty, what a haul! I'm in for a fat reward. There is a providence after all: I'm going to get a load of loot out of this fellow. It's his satchel, no question about it. (*To Labrax*) Go on, tell me what else was in it.

LABRAX   Thirty thousand dollars in silver in a sack, all good coin. And some silverware—a bowl, a bucket, a pitcher, a jug, and a cup.

GRIPUS   Wow! That's quite a fortune you had there.

LABRAX   I "had"; now I don't have a thing. Saddest and worst word in the language, "had."

GRIPUS (*eying him narrowly*)   What are you willing to pay the fellow who brings you information about its whereabouts? (*As Labrax hesitates*) Come on, speak up!

LABRAX   Three thousand dollars.

GRIPUS (*snorting*)   Stop kidding.

LABRAX   Four thousand.

GRIPUS   That's a laugh.

LABRAX   Five thousand.

GRIPUS   Peanuts.

LABRAX   Six thousand.

GRIPUS   Chicken feed.

LABRAX   I'll give you seven thousand.

GRIPUS   What's the matter? Your mouth hot and you want to air it out?

LABRAX   I'll give you ten thousand dollars.

GRIPUS   Wake up.

LABRAX   Not another cent.

GRIPUS   All right then, beat it!

LABRAX   Listen—

GRIPUS (*heading for the door*)   Once I leave here, my friend, I'm gone for good.

LABRAX   Will you take eleven thousand?

GRIPUS (*walking away*)   You're dreaming.

LABRAX (calling after him)   Name your price.

GRIPUS (*stopping*)   Thirty thousand dollars and you don't have to give me a penny more. But not a penny less! That's it; take it or leave it.

LABRAX (*shrugging*)   What can I say? I've got to take it. All right, I'll give you thirty thousand.

GRIPUS (*walking over to the altar*)   Come on over here; I want Venus to be a party to this deal.

LABRAX (*following him*)   Anything you want; just tell me what it is.

GRIPUS   Put your hand on this altar.

LABRAX It's on.

GRIPUS (*grimly*) You've got to swear by Venus here.

LABRAX What should I swear?

GRIPUS What I tell you to.

LABRAX You say it; I'll swear it. (*Aside, sardonically*) The old master being told what to swear!

GRIPUS Got hold of the altar?

LABRAX Right.

GRIPUS Give me your solemn oath you'll pay me the money the day you get your satchel back.

LABRAX So be it. (*Raising his eyes to heaven and intoning*) I solemnly swear in the name of Venus of Cyrene that, if I find the satchel I lost in the shipwreck and regain possession of it with the gold and silver safe inside, I will pay to this man—

GRIPUS (*interrupting*) Say "I will pay to this man Gripus" and touch me at the same time.

LABRAX (*sardonically*) To make it absolutely clear to you, Venus, I will pay to this man Gripus thirty thousand dollars on the spot.

GRIPUS Now say that, if you should welsh, Venus should ruin your body, your soul, and your business. (*Aside*) And once you've done swearing it, I hope she does it to you anyway.

LABRAX (*intoning*) If I go back on anything I have sworn, may all pimps suffer a life of misery.

GRIPUS Don't worry, that'll happen even if you keep your word. (*Walking toward the door*) You wait there. I'll bring the old man outside right away. As soon as I do, you ask him for your satchel. (*Hurries into the cottage.*)

LABRAX (*looking after him scornfully, to himself*) Even if he gets the satchel back for me, I don't owe him a dime. *I'm* the one who decides what I do about what I swear. (*The door opens and Gripus and Daemones come out lugging the satchel.*) Here he comes with the old man. I'd better shut up.

GRIPUS (*to Daemones*) Follow me. This way.

DAEMONES Where is that pimp of yours?

GRIPUS (*calling to Labrax*) Hey, you! (*Pointing to Daemones*) Here he is. This fellow's got your satchel.

DAEMONES (*to Labrax*) Yes, I have it and I don't mind telling you that I do. What's more, if it's yours, you're welcome to it. You'll find everything that was in it still there, safe and sound. Here, take it if it's yours.

LABRAX (*unable to believe his eyes*)   Well, what do you know! My satchel! (*Going up to it and fingering it lovingly*) Greetings, old satchel, greetings!

DAEMONES   Is it yours?

LABRAX (*Getting a firm grip on it*)   What a question! I don't care if it belonged to god almighty himself; it's mine now.

DAEMONES   Everything in it is safe and sound—with one exception: I took out a little box of trinkets I used in finding my daughter today.

LABRAX   Who's that?

DAEMONES   Palaestra, the girl you used to own. I found out she's my daughter.

LABRAX (*assuming his heartiest manner*)   Well, that's just fine! Things have turned out beautifully for you. Just what you hoped for. I'm delighted.

DAEMONES (*dryly*)   I find it a little hard to believe that.

LABRAX (*as before*)   It's the god's honest truth. (*Slyly*) And just to prove my feelings are genuine, you don't have to pay me a cent for her. She's a gift.

DAEMONES (*as before*)   So kind of you.

LABRAX   Oh, no, nothing at all, really.

GRIPUS (*pointedly*)   All right you, you have your satchel now.

LABRAX   That's right.

GRIPUS   Well, let's get on with it.

LABRAX (*producing his blankest look*)   Get on with what?

GRIPUS   Paying me my money.

LABRAX   I'm not paying you any money. I don't owe you a cent.

GRIPUS   Hey, what's going on here! (*Disbelievingly*) You don't owe me a cent?

LABRAX   That's right. Not a cent.

GRIPUS   But you gave me your oath.

LABRAX (*blandly*)   I know I did. I'll give you another right now if I feel like it. This oath business is strictly for holding on to property, not letting it go.

GRIPUS (*shouting*)   You hand over that thirty thousand dollars, you dirty liar!

DAEMONES (*to Gripus*) Gripus, what's this thirty thousand you're asking him for?

GRIPUS He gave me his oath he'd pay it to me.

LABRAX (*to Gripus, as before*) I get fun out of giving oaths. What are you, the chief justice? Going to try me for perjury?

DAEMONES (*to Gripus*) What did he promise you the money for?

GRIPUS He swore he'd give me thirty thousand dollars if I got his satchel back for him.

LABRAX (*to Gripus, scornfully*) Pick some free man to represent you and let's go to court. (*Grinning*) I'll prove you made me a party to a fraudulent contract, (*the grin widening*) and that I'm still a minor.

GRIPUS (*pointing to Daemones*) He'll represent me.

LABRAX (*losing his grin*) No. You'll have to get someone else.

DAEMONES (*to Labrax, firmly*) I'm not going to let you take a penny away from this boy—unless I find he's done something wrong. Now then, did you promise him the money?

LABRAX (*unabashed*) Sure I did.

DAEMONES (*promptly*) What you promised a servant of mine is by rights mine. (*As Labrax opens his mouth*) Don't get the idea you can pull any of your pimp's tricks on me; you won't get away with it.

GRIPUS (*to Labrax, jubilantly*) So you thought you had gotten your hands on some poor devil you could swindle, eh? You'll pay— and in good money, too. And the minute I get it I'm giving it to this man here (*pointing to Daemones*) to pay for my freedom.

DAEMONES (*to Labrax, reproachfully*) When you think of how well I've treated you and that it was all because of me this money was kept safe for you—

GRIPUS (*interrupting angrily*) None of that—all because of me, not you.

DAEMONES (*turning on him*) If you've got any brains, you'll keep your mouth shut! (*To Labrax*) —the least you could do is act decently and reciprocate for all I've done for you.

LABRAX (*softened by Daemones' conciliatory tone*) I take it you're asking me this because you recognize my rights?

DAEMONES I'm not exactly asking you to use them against me, you know.

GRIPUS (*his eyes fixed on Labrax' face, aside*) I'm in! The pimp's weakening! My freedom's just around the corner!

DAEMONES (*gesturing toward Gripus*) First of all, this boy who found that satchel of yours is my servant. Secondly, I kept it safe for you, money and all.

LABRAX (*nodding his head in agreement*) I'm really very grateful to you. About that thirty thousand I swore to give that boy of yours —I see no reason why you shouldn't have it.

GRIPUS (*to Labrax, shouting*) Hey, you! You give it to me, not him! Haven't you got any brains?

DAEMONES (*turning on him*) Will you please shut up!

GRIPUS (*wildly*) You're just pretending to be working for my interests; you're really out for yourself. I may have lost all the rest of the swag in that satchel, but, by god, you're not going to screw me out of this!

DAEMONES (*angrily*) If you say another word, I'll have you whipped!

GRIPUS (*as before*) Go on, kill me! I'll only keep quiet if you gag me with thirty thousand dollars. There's no other way to shut me up.

LABRAX (*to Gripus, disgustedly*) Oh, pipe down. He certainly is working for your best interests.

DAEMONES (*beckoning Labrax off to the side*) Step over here, will you?

LABRAX Sure.

GRIPUS (*calling to them as they move to one side*) Hey, let's keep it in the open! I don't want any of this whispering business.

DAEMONES (*sotto voce*) How much did you pay for that other girl? Ampelisca, I mean.

LABRAX (*sotto voce*) Ten thousand dollars.

DAEMONES (*sotto voce*) How'd you like me to make you a good offer for her?

LABRAX (*sotto voce*) I sure would.

DAEMONES (*sotto voce*) I'll split that thirty thousand with you.

LABRAX (*sotto voce, with pleased surprise*) Thanks!

DAEMONES (*sotto voce*) You take half for letting Ampelisca go free, and give me half.

LABRAX (*sotto voce*) It's a deal.

DAEMONES (*sotto voce*) The half I get will pay for Gripus' freedom. After all, it was because of him that you found your satchel and I my daughter.

LABRAX (*sotto voce*) Thanks very much. I'm much obliged to you.

GRIPUS (*calling*) Hey, how soon am I going to get my money?

DAEMONES It's all settled, Gripus. I've got it.

GRIPUS Damn it all, I want me to have it!

DAEMONES Well, damn it all, you're not getting it, so don't start getting your hopes up. And I want you to let him (*gesturing toward Labrax*) off his oath.

GRIPUS (*roaring*) Damn it all, that's the end of me. I'm a goner—unless I hang myself. And, damn it all, I'll do it right now—you won't get a second chance to swindle me, no, sir!

DAEMONES (*to Labrax*) How about joining us for dinner?

LABRAX Thanks. Be glad to.

DAEMONES Follow me in, both of you. (*Walks downstage and addresses the audience.*) Ladies and gentlemen, I'd invite you to dinner too —except that I'm not serving anything, and there's nothing decent to eat in the house anyway; besides, I know you've all got other invitations to eat out tonight. But, if you'd care to give a hearty round of applause to our play, you can all come to a big party at my house—sixteen years from now. (*Turning to Labrax and Gripus*) You two come to dinner.

LABRAX AND GRIPUS Thank you.

DAEMONES (*to the audience*) Your applause, please.

Terence (ca. 195–159 B.C.)

In the first half of the second century B.C. a rage for everything Greek infected Roman intellectuals. They made Greek their second language, bought Greek art enthusiastically, and read avidly in Greek literature. Among the leaders of the movement were two young nobles, Scipio and Laelius, the guiding spirits of a circle of admirers of Greek culture. When Publius Terentius Afer, a gifted young playwright whose work was unmistakably Greek in feeling, was brought to their attention, they took him up, made him their protégé, and encouraged him throughout his career. He fulfilled his sponsors' trust brilliantly.

Scipio and his friends were not interested in another Plautus, but in a Latin counterpart of the great writers of Greek New Comedy. Terence is precisely that. There is very little boisterous farce in his plays; it was uncongenial to him and his one attempt at it is not very good. There is no slapstick, few outright jokes, no passages to be delivered in song; the plots are carefully worked out, and the action flows smoothly and without interruption.

Like Plautus, Terence based his work on the plays of Greek New Comedy. But, since he was writing in the same vein as his models, what adapting he did is not nearly so apparent as his predecessor's wholesale revisions. As a matter of fact, Terence would have us believe he did very little: more than once he refers to himself as a mere translator. This has created something of a puzzle for literary critics. What sort of credit should be given him? Does he deserve the laurels we reserve for genuinely creative artists? Or merely the lesser recognition accorded gifted translators?

The opening words of every one of Terence's plays reveal that he was far more than a translator. Terence used the prologue for his own purposes, chiefly to answer his critics; what exposition was required he left for the dialogue of the initial scene. It follows that he must have radically recast the openings of his models since these had expository prologues. Nor was this all he recast. At least two of his plots contain elements that he took from two different Greek plays and interwove— something he could not have done without making major changes in the dialogue. Most illuminating of all is Terence's progress as a playwright. We happen to know the dates of the six plays he wrote in his short lifetime: his maiden effort was produced in 166 B.C., and his last two plays, generally considered his masterpieces, in 161 (*Phormio*) and 160 (*The Brothers*). They reveal a striking, steady improvement. Are we to conclude that, by some curious circumstance, he chose a succession of increasingly better plays to translate? A more logical explanation, surely, is to see in this the maturing of a creative artist.

Admittedly, Terence is not a fully original dramatist. The ideas for his plots, most of his characters, many of his comic situations, and whole segments of his dialogue derive from the plays he adapted. But much of the treatment is characteristically his, and the language and verse in which he clothed what he borrowed are among the best things Latin literature has to offer. With so little of Greek New Comedy preserved, we are supremely fortunate to have Terence's adaptations. And, for all we know, they might well be better than the originals.

To please his patrons was not enough for Terence; he wanted to be popular as well. He had his plays put on at the festivals—very likely the influence or money of his powerful backers helped get them a place on the program. They achieved, as might be expected in view of the make-up of Roman audiences, only moderate success. It took three attempts, for example, to present the whole of his *Mother-in-Law;* on the first two occasions, the announcement of some sideshow event stampeded the audience. His rivals, professional writers struggling to make a living, understandably resented such a privileged competitor and did what they could to discredit him, even going to the extent of insinuating that his plays were actually written by his sponsors and only presented under his name. The conflict is easily discernible in Terence's prologues, although you have to read between the lines to understand its nature.

If Terence didn't receive all the acclaim he deserved during his lifetime, the oversight has been more than made up for since. His influence on Western comedy has been second only to that of Plautus, and in reputation he stands even higher. Molière paid him the compliment of adapting his two masterpieces (*Les fourberies de Scapin* is based on the *Phormio* and *L'école des maris* on *The Brothers*); Congreve referred to him as "the most correct writer in the world;" and Meredith, in his *Essay on Comedy*, awarded him a place just below the pinnacle he assigned to his revered Molière.

For the act divisions in Terence's plays, see page 184.

Phormio

/

DRAMATIS PERSONAE

Davus, a servant (slave)

Geta, servant (slave) of Demipho

Antipho, a young man about town, son of Demipho, in love with
Phanium

Phaedria, a young man about town, son of Chremes and cousin of
Antipho

Demipho, an elderly, well-to-do Athenian

Phormio, a young, penniless adventurer who lives by his wits, friend of
Antipho and Phaedria

Hegio
Cratinus } elderly Athenians, advisers to Demipho
Crito

Dorio, a slave dealer

Chremes, Demipho's brother, an elderly Athenian married to a rich wife

Sophrona, Phanium's old nurse

Nausistrata, Chremes' wife

[*Phanium,* a beautiful young girl living in straitened circumstances]

SCENE. A street in Athens. Three houses front on it: Dorio's,
Demipho's, and Chremes'. The exit on stage left leads downtown, that
on stage right to the waterfront.

PROLOGUE

*(The Prologue addresses the audience. For his function in Terence's
plays, see p. 314. Unlike Menander and Plautus, who use the prologue
to introduce the play itself, Terence utilizes the opportunity to reply to
his critics, in particular an older contemporary named Lucius
Lanuvinus whom for some reason he avoids naming directly. The play
proper he introduces through the dialogue of the opening scene.)*

PROLOGUE   That Senior Member, of the playwrights' circle hasn't succeeded in driving your author from the field and forcing him
to retire, so now he's resorting to abuse to keep him from writing.
He goes around saying that, in everything your author has
turned out so far, the dialogue has been flat and the writing
undistinguished. *(Adopting a sarcastic tone as he proceeds to
cite one of the Senior Member's signally unsuccessful touches of
inspiration)* Granted, your author's pen has never produced a
scene in which a love-mad hero watches a doe fleeing before
the hounds and does nothing when it breaks into tears and begs
him for help. Well, if the Senior Member only realized that,
back in the days when his last play was a hit, this was more
because of what the leading man did for it than the author, he'd
be a lot less inclined to throw brickbats than he is.

Some of you may be thinking, "Oh, well, if the Senior Member hadn't cast the first stone, this young fellow, without anyone
to trade insults with, wouldn't have anything to say in his prologues." The answer to *that* is that, although the way to success
is open to anyone who makes a career of writing drama, the old
fellow was doing all he could to throw your author out of the
profession and into starvation, and your author just wanted to
answer him back, not hit him back. If he were interested in
trading compliments, he'd hear plenty of nice things about himself; just let him realize he's getting back simply what he's been
handing out. Well, I'm done with talking about him—although
he's not done with doing harm.

Now, what I really have to tell you is this—and please listen.
I have a new play for you. In Greek it's called *He Who Goes
to Court,* but your author has titled his Latin version *Phormio,*

since a scrounger by that name has the leading role and triggers most of the action—as you'll see if you'll do the author the favor of hearing it through. Please be good enough to listen in silence, and pay attention. I don't want to have happen what happened once before when, because of a disturbance, our company had to leave the stage—a stage we've returned to only because of the efforts of our leading man and the aid of your generosity and good will.

ACT I

(Davus, a fellow slave of Geta, enters stage left, wearing the traditional red wig of slaves in Roman Comedy and carrying a small purse. Actually, Davus is introduced simply to facilitate the exposition of the play; once the scene is over, he leaves the stage for good.)

DAVUS *(to the audience)* My best friend Geta came to me yesterday. He's had a little money out on loan to me for the longest while and there's still a bit of a balance outstanding, a few cents. He asked me to pay it up in full. Well, I'm paying it up in full and *(jingling the purse)* here's the money. I hear that his master's son got married; I guess he's collecting his pennies to buy the bride a gift. It's a crime the way the have-nots always have to be handing out to the haves. The poor devil scraped together a little nest egg, penny by penny, from his monthly allowance by denying himself everything his heart ever desired—and she's going to take it from him in one swoop without a thought for all the trouble it took him to get it. And, when she has a baby, Geta will be nicked for another gift, and then another on the child's birthday, and another when it gets confirmed. The mother's going to carry off everything he has; the child will be a steady excuse for gift collecting. *(The door of Demipho's house opens, and Geta emerges.)* Ah, here's Geta, I think.

(Geta is Demipho's personal slave, a young, able, resourceful chap, whom Demipho has enough confidence in to leave in charge of the household when he goes away on business trips. Geta is a tough-minded character who generally has no difficulty in facing up to emergencies; at

this moment, however, his whole demeanor reveals that something is very much on his mind.)

GETA *(talking through the open door to a servant inside)*   If some red-head comes looking for me—

DAVUS *(interrupting)*   Wait, he's right here.

GETA *(turning and seeing Davus)*   Oh, Davus. I've been trying to find you.

DAVUS *(handing him the purse)*   Here it is. No counterfeits, and the exact amount I owed.

GETA *(taking it)*   Thanks very much. Much obliged to you for not forgetting about this.

DAVUS   The way people are these days, it's got to the point where you've got to make a point of being grateful when someone pays you back what he owes you. *(Noticing that Geta is too pre-occupied to acknowledge this sally)* What are you so unhappy about?

GETA *(startled out of his preoccupation by the question)*   I? You have no idea of the fix I'm in, and the worries I've got.

DAVUS   What's the matter?

GETA *(lowering his voice and looking around guardedly)*   I'll tell you—provided you know how to keep a secret.

DAVUS   Use your head, will you? A man you found could be trusted with your money and you're afraid to trust him with a few words? There's no profit in absconding with words, you know.

GETA   All right then, listen.

DAVUS   I'm all ears.

GETA   Do you know Chremes, my master's older brother?

DAVUS   Of course.

GETA   And Phaedria his son?

DAVUS   As well as I know you.

GETA   Well, it so happened that both the old men went abroad at the same time, Chremes to Lemnos, and my master to Turkey. An old business associate got him out there by flooding him with letters promising him everything but the royal mint.

DAVUS   And he was interested? A man with all his money?

GETA   Never mind. That's the kind he is.

DAVUS *(bitterly)*   *I* should have been a millionaire!

GETA   When the two old men went away they left me as a sort of guardian for their sons.

DAVUS   That's a tough assignment they handed you, Geta.

GETA   Don't I know it! I've been through the mill. When I think it over I'm convinced I got the job because my guardian angel was sore at me. In the beginning I tried to make the boys toe the line. All I need tell you is that, so long as I did my duty by the old man, I kept losing the skin off my back.

DAVUS   I figured as much. There's no sense in fighting when you can't win.

GETA   So I began to yes them and do whatever they wanted.

DAVUS   You learned to play the game.

GETA   At first I had no trouble with Antipho—that's my master's boy —but right off that Phaedria picked up some chorus girl and fell madly in love with her. She belonged to the world's slimiest slave dealer, and we didn't have a dime to pay for her; the old men had seen to that. The only thing the poor fellow could do was feast his eyes, tag along after her, and escort her back and forth when she went for her dancing lessons. Antipho and I had nothing else to do so we used to go along to help him out. There was a barbershop right opposite the dancing school, and we used to hang out there until she was ready to go home. One day while we're sitting around in there, in comes a young fellow, all upset. We're curious. We ask him what's the matter. "Until this minute," says he, "I had no idea what a miserable burden poverty could really be. Just now, right near here, I passed a poor young girl mourning her mother's death. There she stood before the corpse, and there wasn't a friendly face, not a neighbor or relative, to stand by her during the funeral, except for one old woman. It was pitiful. And the girl was a beauty." All I need tell you is that it affected all of us. Right off Antipho said, "What do you say we pay her a visit?" Then someone else said, "Good idea. Let's go. Would you show us the way?" We leave, we walk over there, we see her. She *was* beautiful. And, what's more, there wasn't a thing to help out her natural good looks: there she was, hair hanging down, unkempt, crying, feet bare, clothes dirty—all the things that would have buried any beauty except that rare kind that comes from within. Phaedria, of course, was in love with his chorus girl, so he could only say, "Not bad," but Antipho—

DAVUS   (*interrupting*)   I know: he fell in love at first sight.

GETA Ah, but how! Listen to what happened. The very next day he goes up to the old woman. He begs her to arrange a rendezvous for him. But she refuses: tells him he's not behaving as he should; that this is a respectable girl, of respectable parents, an Athenian citizen as a matter of fact; that if he's willing to marry her he's perfectly free to do so legally but, as far as anything else goes, the answer is No. Well, Antipho didn't know what to do: he wanted to marry her, but he was afraid to while his father was away.

DAVUS Why? Wouldn't his father have agreed to the match when he got back?

GETA That man let his son marry some nobody without a dowry? Not a chance!

DAVUS What finally happened?

GETA What happened? There's a certain scrounger, Phormio's his name, and when it comes to sheer, unmitigated gall, this fellow —(*overwhelmed by the mere thought of Phormio*) god, do I wish he was in hell right now!

DAVUS What did he do?

GETA I'll tell you what he did. He thought up a scheme. "There's a law," he tells Antipho, "that female orphans have to marry their next of kin. The same law states that the next of kin must assume the obligation of such a marriage. Now, I'll pretend I used to be a friend of your girl's father. Then I'll claim that you're the next of kin and sue you to make you marry her. We'll go to court. I'll work up all the details: who her father was, who her mother was, how she's related to you—whatever will make a good story and hold water. And, since you're not going to deny any of it, I can't lose. Your father comes back, he sues me—so what? By that time we've got the girl."

DAVUS He's got so much nerve it's funny.

GETA He talks the boy into it, they set everything up, go to court, the court orders the marriage—and he marries her.

DAVUS What's that you say?

GETA You heard me.

DAVUS My god, Geta, what's going to happen to *you*?

GETA God knows. (*Theatrically*) One thing I do know: whatever Fate may bring, I'll bear the blow bravely.

DAVUS That's what I like to hear. That's acting like a man!

GETA (*resolutely, chin up*)   There's only one person I can count on—
myself.

DAVUS   Bravo!

GETA   I suppose I could get someone to plead my case for me, someone
who'll say, "Demipho, please, let him off just this once. But if
he tries anything like it hereafter, I won't lift a finger for him."
Which is the same as saying, "As soon as I leave, you can slit
his throat."

DAVUS   How about the boy who walks the girls home from school, the
one who's after that chorus girl? How's he doing?

GETA (*with a* comme ci comme ça *gesture of the hand*)   Not getting
very far.

DAVUS   Doesn't have much spot cash to offer for her, eh?

GETA   Spot cash? All he's got to offer is spot hope.

DAVUS   Has his father come back yet?

GETA   Not yet.

DAVUS   What about Demipho? When do you expect him?

GETA   I'm not sure. But I just heard that a letter from him is down at
the dock. I'm going now to pick it up.

DAVUS   Well, I've got to be getting along now; anything I can do for
you?

GETA   Take care of yourself. Goodbye. (*Davus exits, stage left. Geta
goes to the door of Demipho's house, opens it, and calls inside.*)
Boy! Hey, someone come out here! (*A servant appears, and Geta
hands him the purse he had gotten from Davus.*) Here, give this
to my wife. (*Exits, stage right.*)

ACT II

(*The door of Chremes' house opens, and the two cousins, Antipho
and Phaedria, come out.*

*Both are good-looking young fellows in their late teens. Their clothes
and bearing make immediately apparent that they come from well-to-do
families, that they have at their ready disposal whatever money can
provide. But it is equally apparent that the things money cannot provide are unequally divided between them. From Antipho's way of
talking, his guardedness, studied unobtrusiveness, and shifting glance,
one can tell he's a worrier and a weakling; in Phaedria's jaunty air, open*

face, and direct manner, one can read the direct opposite—a bold, devil-may-care youngster, afraid of nobody and nothing.

As they come through the door Antipho's nervous wringing of his hands and similar symptoms reveal a state of jitters even more highly charged than that which is usual with him.)

ANTIPHO   Things have gotten to the point, Phaedria, where every time I think of his coming home, I start getting scared of him—my own father, the very person who cares the most for me! (*Lapses into gloomy silence for a moment.*) And if I just hadn't acted so thoughtlessly, I could be looking forward to seeing him again as a son should.

PHAEDRIA   What are you talking about?

ANTIPHO   What a question! You know as well as I do what we had the nerve to do! If only Phormio hadn't gotten the bright idea to talk me into it! If only he hadn't pushed me, when I was so vulnerable, right into what started all my troubles! I wouldn't have gotten the girl. Oh, sure, I'd have had a few bad days at the time, but not this daily gnawing at my heart—

PHAEDRIA   (*interrupting impatiently*)   I know, I know.

ANTIPHO   (*disregarding the interruption*)   —while I'm waiting around for him to come back and take her away from me.

PHAEDRIA   Other people complain because they can't find love, and you're unhappy because you've got too much! (*Vehemently*) You're swimming in love, Antipho! My god, your life is what every man searches and hopes for. So help me, if I had the chance to enjoy my love affair even only as long as you have so far, I'm ready right now to offer my life as part of the deal. (*Bitterly*) Figure out for yourself which of us is better off: here you are with everything and here I am with nothing. To say nothing of the fact that you've got just what you wanted, not a slave who has to be bought, but a respectable girl, a wife, someone you're not ashamed to be seen with. You'd be in heaven if it weren't for just one thing: you don't have the sense to be satisfied with what you've got. If you had to deal with that pimp that I have to, you'd see what I mean. Well, that's the way most of us are, never happy with what we have.

ANTIPHO   It's the other way around, Phaedria; right now I think you're the one who's lucky. You're still in a position to make up your mind all over again about what you want to do—keep the girl, love her, or let her go. A poor devil like me is on the spot: I can't let her go and I'm not going to be able to keep her. (*Hears something and looks toward the wings.*) What's that? Is that Geta running this way? (*Peering hard*) It's Geta, all right. Oh, lord, he's got something to tell me and I'm scared to hear it.

(*Geta bursts in, stage right—he has run all the way from the waterfront—and stops abruptly at the side of the stage, away from the two boys.*)

GETA (*to himself, not noticing Antipho and Phaedria*) What a load of trouble I've got on my neck now! And so sudden! And me not ready for any of it! Geta, if you don't find a way out of this fast, your name is mud. (*Thinks a moment, then desperately*) I can't think of a way to bypass it or, once I'm in it, to get out of it. And we can't keep things under cover any longer—not what we had the nerve to do!

ANTIPHO (*not able to hear Geta but alarmed at his manner, to Phaedria*) What in the world's he so upset about?

GETA (*to himself*) Demipho's back. That means I've got just about sixty seconds flat to come up with an idea.

ANTIPHO (*still more alarmed, to Phaedria*) What's the matter with him?

GETA (*to himself*) When he hears what's happened he's going to hit the ceiling, and what in the world can I do to stop it? Explain things? He'll burn up. Keep my mouth shut? That'll just needle him. Try to clear myself? Sheer waste of energy. It's bad, it's real bad. It's not only myself I'm scared about; there's Antipho too. That's what's driving me out of my mind: poor devil, I'm worried sick about him. He's the one who's holding me back now. If it weren't for him, I could look after myself. If the old man took it out on me, I'd get even with him—I'd pick up some of the valuables around here and pack off, on the double.

ANTIPHO (*catching Geta's last words and now puzzled as well as alarmed, to Phaedria*) What's this talk about robbing and running?

GETA (*to himself*) But where's Antipho, anyway? I don't even know where to look for him.

PHAEDRIA (*finally catching what Geta said, to Antipho*) He's talking about you.

ANTIPHO (*his jitters getting steadily worse*)   From that messenger (*gesturing toward Geta*) I expect nothing but trouble, lots of it. (*Turns to run.*)

PHAEDRIA (*grabbing him*)   Are you out of your mind?

GETA (*turning and making for Demipho's door*)   I'll try him at the house; he's generally there.

PHAEDRIA (*to Antipho*)   Let's call him over here.

ANTIPHO (*raising his voice, to Geta*)   Stay where you are!

GETA (*stopping in his tracks and without turning around*)   Wow! You sound as if you mean it, whoever you are.

ANTIPHO   Geta!

GETA (*turning and finally seeing Antipho*)   Just the man I'm looking for!

ANTIPHO   Now, please say what you have to say and cut it short, if you can.

GETA   Right.

ANTIPHO (*nervously*)   Come on, out with it!

GETA   Just now, down at the dock—

ANTIPHO (*going white and sagging at the knees*)   You saw him!

GETA   You guessed it.

ANTIPHO   I'm sunk!

PHAEDRIA (*not quite following the cryptic interchange*)   What?

ANTIPHO (*to himself*)   What'll I do?

PHAEDRIA (*to Geta*)   What's this you say?

GETA (*to Phaedria*)   I just saw his father. Your uncle.

ANTIPHO (*holding his head in his hands, moaning*)   I'm lost. This is the end. There's no way out. And so sudden! (*Drawing himself up like a tragic figure and looking toward the house, where his wife is*) Phanium! If my fate has reached the point where I have to give you up—life for me won't be worth living!

GETA (*sharply*)   And since that's the situation, Antipho, now you've really got to be on your toes. (*Comes up to him and claps him on the shoulder.*) Faint heart ne'er won fair lady.

ANTIPHO (*wildly*)   I can't think straight!

GETA   I tell you, Antipho, now's the time you need your straightest thinking. If your father gets the idea you're scared, he's going to think you're guilty of something.

PHAEDRIA (*to Antipho*)   That's the truth.

ANTIPHO (*desperately*)   I can't change what I am!

GETA What would you do if you had to face up to something even harder?

ANTIPHO (*miserably*) Something harder? I can't even do anything about this!

GETA (*finally giving up the effort to inject some spirit into him*) We're getting nowhere, Phaedria. Let's go. What's the use of wasting our energy on him? I'm getting out of here.

PHAEDRIA Me too.

ANTIPHO (*in a funk*) No! Please! Look—what if I pretend? (*Making a pathetic attempt to assume a resolute expression*) How's this?

GETA (*turning on his heel in disgust*) Don't talk nonsense.

ANTIPHO (*making another attempt*) Here, look at my face. How about this?

GETA (*taking a look and wincing*) God, no!

ANTIPHO (*trying still another expression*) What about this one?

GETA (*takes a quick look, turns away, then does a double-take in surprise*) You've almost got it!

ANTIPHO (*trying an improvement*) How's this?

GETA That'll do—keep it just that way. Now, you've got to give him back word for word, tit for tat. He's going to work himself into a rage, but just don't let him shout you down.

ANTIPHO (*busy thinking over what he's let himself in for and only half listening*) Uh huh.

GETA Remember: you didn't want to get into this, you were forced into it.

PHAEDRIA The law was against you. The court made you do it.

GETA Got it? (*Hearing something, looks off into the wings.*) Who's that old man there at the end of the street? (*Peering hard*) It's Demipho!

ANTIPHO (*in a choking voice, panic-stricken*) I can't go through with it! (*Turns and makes a dash for the house.*)

GETA Hey! Antipho! What are you doing? Where are you going? Come on back, I tell you!

ANTIPHO (*as he goes through the door, whimpering*) I know what I'm like. I know I did wrong. My wife, my life—I'm leaving everything in your hands!

(*The door closes behind him. Phaedria and Geta look at each other in silence for a moment.*)

PHAEDRIA (*blankly*) Well, Geta, what happens now?

GETA Unless I'm very much mistaken, you're going to hear the riot act and I'm going to get hung up and horsewhipped. (*Thoughtfully*) You know the advice we just gave Antipho? Well, we ought to take it ourselves.

PHAEDRIA Forget about this "ought" business. Just tell me what you want me to do.

GETA Remember, when you went into this affair, what all of you kept saying when you were figuring how to keep yourselves clear of blame? That Phormio had a foolproof case against Antipho, easy to prove, sure to win, absolutely airtight?

PHAEDRIA I remember.

GETA All right. That's just the kind of talk we need now. Even better and smarter, if we can do it.

PHAEDRIA I'll give it everything I've got.

GETA You take the front line. I'll be the rear guard and (*falling in line behind Phaedria's broad back*) take up a concealed position in case the enemy breaks through.

PHAEDRIA Forward march! (*They march off to the side of the stage.*)

(*Phaedria and Geta station themselves in an unobtrusive spot where they can't easily be observed but can overhear whatever is said on stage. Demipho now enters, stage right. He is a hale, solid old fellow with a direct, no-nonsense manner. Clearly he's a man accustomed to giving orders and being obeyed without cavil, just the sort of father who would turn a son into a weakling like Antipho. His first words reveal that he already has a pretty fair idea of what has gone on during his absence—and doesn't like any of it.*)

DEMIPHO (*to himself*) So Antipho got married without my approval, did he? Didn't think twice about my rights in the matter. My rights? Wasn't even bothered that I'd get angry with him! What a way to act! The nerve of him! A fine guardian that Geta!

GETA (*aside*) Finally he got around to me.

DEMIPHO (*to himself*) I wonder what they're going to tell me—what excuse they'll think up.

GETA (*aside*) Don't worry, I'll think one up.

DEMIPHO (*to himself*) I suppose he'll tell me (*imitating Antipho in an access of contrition*), "I didn't want to do it but the court made me." All right, he's got a point there.

GETA (*aside*)   That's what I like to hear.

DEMIPHO (*to himself, ironically*)   And I suppose the court also made him keep his mouth shut and hand the case over to the other party when he knew the true facts all the time.

PHAEDRIA (*sotto voce, to Geta*)   Hey, he's got something there!

GETA (*sotto voce, to Phaedria*)   Leave it to me. I'll figure something out.

DEMIPHO (*to himself*)   I simply don't know what to do. I never expected anything like this to happen. It's incredible! It's got me so angry I can't collect my thoughts. (*Paces up and down agitatedly for a moment, then continues more calmly.*) Things like this make you realize that it's just when everything is going fine that you'd better start worrying about how to handle trouble when it comes—what to do if you get into an accident or go bankrupt or have to leave home. When you come back from a trip you've always got to keep in mind that your son may be in jail, your wife dead, or your daughter sick. If you remember that these things can happen, and to anybody, then you'll be ready for anything. So, then, whatever turns out better than you expect, you can count as absolutely pure profit.

GETA (*sotto voce, to Phaedria*)   Phaedria, I'm way ahead of him. I *did* worry about all the trouble I was in for when he got back from his trip: the ball and chain, the horsewhip, the rock pile, and hard labor on the farm. I *was* ready for all these. And whatever turns out better than I expect, I *am* going to count as absolutely pure profit. (*Giving Phaedria a push*) What are you waiting for? Go on up to him and start things off by giving him a big hello.

DEMIPHO (*noticing Phaedria, to himself*)   Ah, here's my nephew Phaedria coming to see me.

PHAEDRIA (*with a great air of being overjoyed at the meeting*)   Well, Uncle! How are you!

DEMIPHO (*curtly*)   Fine. Where's Antipho?

PHAEDRIA (*bypassing the question*)   What a pleasure to see you—

DEMIPHO (*interrupting*)   Sure, sure. Now answer my question.

PHAEDRIA   He's around. He's just fine. (*Rubbing his hands and beaming*) Well, did you find everything just the way you want?

DEMIPHO (*grimly*)   I wish I had!

PHAEDRIA (*putting on a convincing act of being surprised*) Why, what's the matter?

DEMIPHO What's the matter? That's quite a fine little marriage you fixed up here while I was away.

PHAEDRIA (*shifting from surprise to amused incredulity*) Are you mad at him about *that?*

GETA (*delighted with the performance, aside*) The boy's a professional!

DEMIPHO And why shouldn't I be? I'd like to have him right here in front of me this minute. I'd show him how that kind and gentle parent of his had to turn himself into a tyrant through nobody's fault but his.

PHAEDRIA Now, Uncle, he didn't do anything to get mad about.

DEMIPHO (*wearily, addressing the world in general*) Look at that! Always the same story. They're all alike. You know one of them, you know them all.

PHAEDRIA That's not true!

DEMIPHO (*still addressing the world in general*) If one of them gets into trouble, the other's right there to cover up for him, and vice versa. It's a mutual assistance pact.

GETA (*aside*) He doesn't know it but that's a perfect description. That's just what they do.

DEMIPHO Phaedria, if what I say wasn't true you wouldn't be taking his side right now.

PHAEDRIA (*as if speaking from deep conviction*) Uncle, if Antipho has really done something wrong, something that's going to make him less careful about his own good and his reputation than he should be, I wouldn't be on his side; let him get what's coming to him. But if someone who knows every crooked move in the book happened to hale a pair of green youngsters into court and put one over on them, is that our fault? How about the judges? They're always ready to hurt a rich man out of spite and help a poor one out of pity.

GETA (*shaking his head in admiration, aside*) If I hadn't been at the trial, I'd believe every word he says.

DEMIPHO And is there a judge who's going to know your rights in the case if you do what he did and don't open your mouth to answer?

PHAEDRIA (*glibly*) He simply reacted the way any decent young fellow would have. When he got before the court he just couldn't speak his piece. He was so scared and ashamed, he was tongue-tied.

GETA (*aside*) Good work, Phaedria! But what am I waiting for? I'd better speak up right away. (*Coming forward*) Well, Demipho, greetings! It's a pleasure to see you back!

DEMIPHO (*balefully*) Greetings to you, my keeper of the hearth, my vigilant overseer, my son's trusty guardian in my absence!

GETA (*playing the injured innocent to the hilt*) I've just been listening to these accusations you're making against us. None of us deserves it, and least of all myself. Just what did you want me to do under the circumstances? Slaves don't plead cases in court, you know; they can't even testify.

DEMIPHO (*taken a little aback*) Granted, granted. And I'll concede that he's just a boy and didn't know what was going to happen and got frightened; and, all right, you're just a slave. But I don't care how close a relative she was, he didn't have to go and marry her. You should have given her a dowry as the law says, and let her find someone else to marry. Didn't he have sense enough not to bring a penniless bride into the house?

GETA (*promptly*) He had the sense, all right. It's the money he didn't have.

DEMIPHO He could have gotten it somewhere—

GETA (*interrupting*) Somewhere? Easy enough to say!

DEMIPHO Then he should have borrowed it if there was no other way.

GETA (*snorting*) Hah! That's a good one. And just who'd give credit to a minor like him as long as you're alive?

DEMIPHO (*exploding with exasperation as each of his suggestions is neatly parried*) Well, it's just not going to be. It can't be! I'm not going to let him stay married to that girl one day longer. This calls for stern measures. I want you to let me see that fellow or let me know where he lives.

GETA You mean Phormio?

DEMIPHO (*sneering*) That defender of women's rights.

GETA I'll go get him.

DEMIPHO Where's Antipho now?

GETA He's out.

DEMIPHO Phaedria! Go find him and bring him here!

PHAEDRIA (*with alacrity*) I'll go right now. (*Exits, stage right.*)

GETA (*aside*) To his girl friend, he means. (*Exits, stage left.*)

DEMIPHO (*to himself*) First I'll go into the house to pay my respects
    there. Then I'll go downtown and round up a few friends to
    stand by me in this business. I want to be ready for that Phormio
    when he comes. (*Goes into his house.*)

ACT III

(*Enter Geta and Phormio, stage left, deep in conversation. Phormio
is a gaunt young fellow dressed sprucely and smartly in clothes that have
long since seen their best days. Officially he is a* parasitus, *that is, someone who keeps his belly filled and himself entertained by scrounging.
But you can see at a glance that he is no run-of-the-mine specimen.
There's an engaging openness of manner about him, an alertness, a
definite flair, that stamps him as someone special—in dress and looks
and attitude toward life an Alfred Jingle wearing a seedy mantle instead
of seedy jacket and trousers. As a matter of fact, in Phormio's case,
scrounging is merely the lowest level of his activity. He has raised the
technique of living by his wits to a fine art; he is a virtuoso at it. And,
like any true artist, he uses his talents not merely for the baser object
of getting enough to live on but creatively, for the sheer pleasure of
exercising a unique gift. It was Phormio the parasite who had, no doubt,
cadged many a meal and night's entertainment from Antipho—but it
was Phormio the artist who had paid him back by working out the
magnificent scheme of the phony trial.*)

PHORMIO So you say that Antipho was so scared of seeing his father
    that he cleared out?
GETA Exactly.
PHORMIO And left Phanium all alone?
GETA Right.
PHORMIO And the old man's in a state?
GETA Hopping mad.
PHORMIO (*thoughtfully, to himself*) Phormio, there's only one broad
    back to bear this burden—yours. You made this mess; you've got
    to clean it up, all of it. Phormio, strip for action!
GETA Yes, Phormio, please!

(*Phormio proceeds to go into a trancelike state of deep thought and,
oblivious of everything about him, conducts in dumb show an imaginary
harangue with Demipho.*)

PHORMIO (*struck by an idea disturbing enough to make him talk out loud*) Suppose he asks me . . . (*Goes off again into dumb show.*)

GETA You're our only hope.

PHORMIO (*disregarding Geta completely in his concentration*) Ah hah —what if he answers . . . (*Again goes off into dumb show.*)

GETA You got us into it.

PHORMIO (*abruptly coming out of his imaginary confrontation with Demipho*) I think I've got it.

GETA You've got to help us.

PHORMIO (*not hearing Geta, and beaming with self-satisfaction*) Bring on the old man. I've got my whole strategy worked out.

GETA What are you going to do?

PHORMIO If I clear Antipho, keep him married, and draw all the old man's fire on myself, you'll be satisfied, right?

GETA (*overwhelmed by the magnanimity of the offer*) Phormio! You're a real friend. And a brave man. But I get worried that a brave fellow like you will wind up walking right through a prison gate.

PHORMIO (*with the candor that comes from an objective appraisal of one's capabilities*) Oh, no. I've been over the ground. I know how to watch my step. Have you any idea how many people I've fleeced out of their last penny—I mean counting out-of-towners as well as locals? The better I get at it, the more I do it. Well, you never heard of anyone suing me for damages, did you?

GETA Why don't they?

PHORMIO (*confidentially*) A person doesn't go fishing for sharks. They're dangerous. He goes after what can't hurt him. There he stands to gain; going after sharks just means a lot of work with nothing to show for it. And another thing. People know I don't have a dime. It's the fellows who have something they can be skinned out of some way or other who have to watch out. I know what you're going to say: What if one of my dupes demands his dues and sues, and wins me to take home as a slave until I settle up? Oh, no, he doesn't want to bring a man with an appetite like mine into his house. And, if you ask me, he's using his head. Why should he pay me back for a bad turn I did him by doing me a good one three times a day?

GETA   Well, Antipho will never be able to pay you back for what you're doing for him.

PHORMIO   On the contrary, I'll always be in *his* debt. (*Earnestly*) The one person you can never pay back is the fellow who picks up the check. (*Gazing raptly in the distance, like a lover remembering some treasured moment*) You go to his club, have a swim, then a massage—and all on the cuff. There you are, nothing on your mind, and there he is, eating his heart out with worry at the expense. You're waited on hand and foot—and he has to go around barking at everybody. You have a fine time, get served your drink before he does, get a place at table before he does, sit down to a drive-you-crazy dinner—

GETA   What do you mean a "drive-you-crazy" dinner?

PHORMIO   Where the menu's so long it drives you crazy to make up your mind. Now, when you figure how very pleasant all this is and how much it all costs, what are you going to call the fellow who makes it possible? (*Emphatically*) An angel, that's what he is, an angel from heaven for us down here.

GETA   (*happening to glance toward the wings*)   The old man's coming! Watch your step. It's that first volley that's the hardest. Stand up under that and from then on *you* can call the shots.

(*Enter Demipho, stage left. He is deep in conversation with three cronies he has rounded up to stand by him and advise him. The three—Hegio, Cratinus, and Crito—are staid old fellows, pillars of society, sensible, serious, solid citizens.*)

DEMIPHO   (*to his advisory council*)   That's what he did to me. Did you ever hear of anything more outrageous in your whole life? You've got to stand by me.

GETA   (*sotto voce, to Phormio*)   He's sore, all right.

PHORMIO   (*sotto voce, to Geta*)   You haven't seen anything yet. Watch this—I'm going to get a rise out of him. (*Taking Geta's arm he walks to the center of the stage. At the same time he raises his voice to make sure that Demipho hears every word.*) God almighty, you mean to tell me Demipho has the nerve to say that Phanium isn't related to him? He actually said she wasn't his relative?

GETA   (*picking up the cue and raising his voice, too*)   That's what he said.

DEMIPHO (*pointing to Phormio, to the council*) Look! I think that's the fellow I was telling you about. Follow me! (*The four draw near.*)

PHORMIO He doesn't know who Stilpho was?

GETA That's what he said.

PHORMIO (*switching from incredulity to righteous indignation*) It's because the poor girl's been left without a penny. That's the reason for this never having heard of her father and this abandoning her. (*Shaking his head sorrowfully*) What greed will do to people!

GETA (*assuming the role of Demipho's defender*) If you're going to make nasty insinuations about my master, you're going to hear some nasty things about yourself!

DEMIPHO (*to the council*) Of all the unmitigated nerve! He's actually come here to accuse *me!*

PHORMIO Now, there's no sense in my getting angry with a youngster like Antipho for not knowing her father. After all, the man was much older. Besides, he was so poor he always had to work and hardly ever got into the city. My own father gave him a piece of land to farm. (*Reminiscently*) Back in those days the old fellow used to tell me time and again how this cousin of his would have nothing to do with him. What a grand old man! Never met anyone finer in my life.

GETA (*trying his hand at scorn*) Take a look at yourself alongside this man you're telling me about—(*Indicates by a gesture that the difference is too great for words.*)

PHORMIO You can go to the devil! Believe me, if I didn't think so highly of him I wouldn't have started a serious fight like this with your people. But I have an obligation to his daughter, and that master of yours has shut the door in her face. And he calls himself a gentleman!

GETA (*switching from scorn back to indignation*) Listen, you foulmouth, are you going to keep on saying nasty things about my master behind his back?

PHORMIO Certainly. He deserves it.

GETA Oh, he does, does he? (*Pretends to take a swing at Phormio.*)

DEMIPHO (*loudly*) Geta!

GETA (*pretending not to hear—and creating some synthetic words to go with his synthetic feelings*) Swindlerizer! Shysterizer!

DEMIPHO (*shouting*) GETA!

PHORMIO (*sotto voce*) Answer him!

GETA Who wants me? (*Turning and quickly assuming a look of astonishment*) Oh!

DEMIPHO Stop this!

GETA But he's been saying terrible things about you behind your back all day! Things he ought to be saying about himself.

DEMIPHO That's enough out of you! (*Turning to Phormio and speaking with frigid politeness*) Now, young man, first of all there's something I'd like to find out from you if you'll be so good as to answer me. Will you kindly make clear to me just who is this man you say was your friend and just how he claimed I was related to him?

PHORMIO (*assuming the expression of a man who's too smart to be trapped*) Fishing for information, eh? As if you don't know who he was!

DEMIPHO I know him?

PHORMIO That's what I said.

DEMIPHO (*still managing to be polite*) I tell you I don't. Since you say I do, you'd better refresh my memory.

PHORMIO What's this? You didn't know your own cousin?

DEMIPHO (*losing his carefully maintained composure*) You'll be the death of me! (*Controlling himself again*) Tell me the man's name.

PHORMIO (*suddenly losing his aplomb*) His name? Er—be glad to. (*Starts signaling surreptitiously to Geta.*)

DEMIPHO Come on, speak up.

PHORMIO (*aside*) My god, everything's ruined! I forgot the name!

DEMIPHO Eh? What did you say?

PHORMIO (*sotto voce, to Geta*) Geta! Do you remember that name she mentioned? Whisper it in my ear! (*Aloud, to Demipho*) Oh, no—I'm not going to tell you. As if you don't know it! You're just trying to test me.

DEMIPHO What do you mean, trying to test you?

GETA (*in a stage whisper*) Stilpho!

PHORMIO (*abruptly recovering his aplomb*) All right, I'll tell you. What do I care? It's Stilpho.

DEMIPHO (*genuinely puzzled*) Who?

PHORMIO Stilpho. You knew him, all right.

DEMIPHO (*emphatically*) I did not. And I never had a relative by that name.

PHORMIO Oh, is that so? (*Gesturing toward the advisory council whose three members have been blankly following the interchange*) Aren't you ashamed of yourself? In front of these good people? (*Shakes his head dolefully.*) Now, if he had left an estate of three hundred thousand—

DEMIPHO (*interrupting*) Oh, damn you!

PHORMIO (*continuing unruffled*) —you'd have been the first one to reel off from memory the family tree from the founding father down.

DEMIPHO (*grimly*) That's right. And if I had been there when the will was probated, I'd have stated exactly how his daughter was related to me. And that's just what you're going to do right now. Come on; how is she related to me?

GETA (*to Demipho*) Good work! (*Sotto voce, to Phormio*) Hey! Watch out!

PHORMIO (*truculently*) You'll find a clear and complete statement where it belongs—in the court records. And if I falsified any facts there, how come your son didn't enter a denial?

DEMIPHO (*exploding with exasperation*) Don't mention that son of mine to me! He's so stupid, it defies description!

PHORMIO And if you're so smart, why don't you go to court and have the case tried all over again? After all, Your Highness sits on the throne here alone; only you have the right to have the same case tried twice.

DEMIPHO (*throwing up his hands in despair*) It's an absolute outrage, but rather than go to court or listen to you any longer, let's make believe she is my relative. The law says I've got to provide a dowry; here's twenty-five hundred, take it, and get her out of here!

PHORMIO Ha ha ha! Pretty slick!

DEMIPHO (*surprised*) What's the matter? What's wrong with my proposition? Can't I even get what's common justice?

PHORMIO (*switching abruptly from the canny operator to the man of stern morality*) I ask you, just what do you think the law wants? To have her paid off and sent packing like some whore you're tired of? Or to have her married to her next of kin for the rest of her days so that a respectable woman like her will never be forced into a life of shame because of poverty? But that's what *you* don't want.

DEMIPHO (*sourly*)   All right, all right, to marry her to the next of kin. But just how and why do you figure that we—

PHORMIO (*interrupting*)   Now, now, you know what they say: a case decided is a case ended.

DEMIPHO (*snarling*)   Ended, is it? No, sir! I'm not going to quit until I settle this business!

PHORMIO (*patronizingly*)   You're being very silly, you know.

DEMIPHO   Never mind!

PHORMIO (*as if suddenly struck by a new idea*)   When you come right down to it, Demipho, you have nothing to do with me in this business at all. It's your son who lost the suit, not you. (*Archly*) You're a little too old by now for marriage, you know.

DEMIPHO (*grimly*)   You can take it for granted he'll say exactly what I've been saying—or I'll turn him out of the house along with that wife of his.

GETA (*aside*)   He's sore, all right.

PHORMIO   Better turn yourself out.

DEMIPHO (*baffled, seeing his last hope go glimmering*)   So that's it, damn you! Ready to cross me up whatever I do, aren't you?

PHORMIO (*sotto voce, to Geta*)   He's afraid of us even though he's doing all he can to cover it up.

GETA (*sotto voce, to Phormio*)   The first round goes to you.

PHORMIO (*in his best let-bygones-be-bygones manner*)   You can't get out of it, so why don't you put up with it? You'll be acting like the man you really are, and we can be friends.

DEMIPHO (*exploding*)   Me be your friend? I don't want to see you or hear that voice of yours ever again!

PHORMIO (*as before*)   You know, if you make up with her, you'll have someone to make you happy in your old age. Remember, you're getting along.

DEMIPHO (*snarling*)   You take her. Let her make you happy.

PHORMIO (*as before*)   Now, now, watch that temper!

DEMIPHO   Now, listen here. Enough of this talk. If you don't get that woman out of here, and right away, I'll throw her out. That's all I've got to say to you, Phormio.

PHORMIO   And if you don't treat her exactly as a respectable girl should be, I'll slap on you the biggest suit you ever heard of. That's all

I've got to say to *you*, Demipho. (*Sotto voce, to Geta*) Psst. If
you need me for anything, I'll be at my house.

GETA (*sotto voce, to Phormio*)   Right. (*Phormio exits, stage left.*)

DEMIPHO (*to himself*)   The trouble and worry that boy let me in for
when he got himself—and me—mixed up in this marriage! Why
doesn't he come to see me and let me at least find out what he
has to say for himself in all this? (*Turning to Geta*) Go and see
if he's come home yet.

GETA   Right. (*Goes into the house.*)

DEMIPHO (*to the advisory council*)   Well, you see how things stand.
What should I do? Hegio, what's your opinion?

HEGIO (*after a moment of deep thought*)   My opinion is that Cratinus
should tell us his, if it's all right with you.

DEMIPHO: Cratinus, what's your opinion?

CRATINUS (*sparring for time*)   You want my opinion?

DEMIPHO   Yes.

CRATINUS (*with great deliberation*)   I'd like to see you do what's best
for your interests. Now, this is the way I see it. What your son
did took place while you were away. Therefore it's only right
and fair to have the slate wiped clean—and you won't have any
trouble doing this. That's my opinion.

DEMIPHO   Tell us your opinion now, Hegio.

HEGIO (*with a deferential gesture in Cratinus' direction*)   I think
Cratinus here has given some very thoughtful advice. But you
know the human equation: number of men equals number of
opinions; each person has his own way of thinking. Now, as I
see it, you can't revoke something the law has decided, and it's
unethical to try.

DEMIPHO   What's your opinion, Crito?

CRITO (*after a moment of deep lucubration*)   I think the situation needs
more thought. (*Profoundly*) It's a very serious matter.

HEGIO   Well, we've got to be going; anything more we can do for you?

DEMIPHO   Thank you very much for your help. (*The council files out,
stage left. To himself*) I'm more up in the air than before.

(*Geta emerges from the house.*)

GETA   They say he's not back yet.

DEMIPHO (*with an air of finality*)   I have to wait for my brother. I'll
put it to him and I'll follow whatever he has to say—and I'll go

down to the dock right **now** to find out when he's expected. (*Exits, stage right.*)

GETA (*to himself*) And I'll go and find Antipho to tell him what's happened here. (*Starts walking off, stage left, and then stops.*) There he is! Couldn't have come at a better time.

ANTIPHO (*muttering to himself as he walks slowly on stage, buried in thought*) What a heel I am! I deserve to be called every name in the book. To run off like that and leave the girl who means everything to me for others to protect! What could I have been thinking of? That others would look after my own interests better than I? But all the other considerations don't matter—it was I who brought her into my house, and it was up to me not to run out on her and leave her in a position to be harmed just because she had put her trust in me. Poor girl, I'm the only hope she has; I'm everything to her.

GETA (*breaking in on the soliloquy, tartly*) As a matter of fact we've got our own complaints to make against you for running out on us the way you did.

ANTIPHO (*uneasily*) I went looking for you.

GETA (*disregarding the palpably false excuse and continuing his thought*) But, even so, we didn't let you down.

ANTIPHO (*screwing up his courage at this*) Tell me, how do things stand? What's going to happen to me? Does my father smell anything fishy?

GETA Nothing yet.

ANTIPHO You mean there's hope?

GETA I don't know.

ANTIPHO (*his courage becoming unscrewed*) Oh.

GETA But Phaedria was in there fighting for you every minute.

ANTIPHO (*warmly*) I knew he would.

GETA And Phormio too. He worked his head off for you, just as he's always done.

ANTIPHO What did he do?

GETA The old man was hopping mad but he talked him down. Did a perfect job.

ANTIPHO Bravo, Phormio!

GETA (*pointedly*) And I did what I could too.

ANTIPHO (*happily*) Geta, you're true friends, every one of you.

GETA Well, that's how the first round went. Right now things are quiet. Your father's waiting for your uncle to get back.

ANTIPHO (*the happiness draining out of him*) Why him?

GETA He said he was going to consult him and do whatever he advised.

ANTIPHO Oh, Geta, I can't tell you how scared I am now at the thought of my uncle's coming back! Don't you see? This is a matter of life or death for me, and, if you're right, everything's going to depend on what he decides.

GETA (*happening to look at Dorio's house*) There's Phaedria.

ANTIPHO Where?

GETA (*pointing to the door of Dorio's house, and sniggering*) There, coming out of the—er—playground.

(*Two figures emerge from Dorio's house, the owner himself with Phaedria tagging at his heels.*

Dorio is a slave dealer, a hardheaded businessman who owns a string of handsome girls carefully trained in all that is necessary to make a successful courtesan. Dorio either rents them out or sells them when he can find someone willing to pay the price—and the price was generally fairly stiff, since the girls were hand-picked to start with and had received an expensive education. Because of the nature of their occupation, dealers such as Dorio faced the same sort of problems that money-lenders do—and suffered the same sort of reputation.)

PHAEDRIA (*pleading*) Dorio! Please! Listen to me!

DORIO (*walking away*) No.

PHAEDRIA (*grabbing his arm*) Just for a minute.

DORIO Let go of me!

PHAEDRIA Listen to me. I've got something to tell you.

DORIO I've heard it a thousand times already. I'm sick and tired of it.

PHAEDRIA This time it's something you'll be glad to hear.

DORIO (*swiveling around at this*) All right, I'm listening. Let's have it.

PHAEDRIA I want you to do me a favor. Give me just three days more. Please! (*Dorio about-faces and starts walking again.*) Hey, where are you going?

DORIO (*disgusted with himself*) I should have known you wouldn't have anything new to tell me.

ANTIPHO (*sotto voce, to Geta*) I'm scared of that pimp! (*Catching a contemptuous glance from Geta*) I mean that he's going to get himself in trouble.

GETA (*sotto voce to Antipho, ironically*) Just what I'm afraid of too.

PHAEDRIA Don't you trust me?

DORIO About as much as a crooked fortune-teller.

PHAEDRIA   But I give you my word.

DORIO   Your word? Hot air!

PHAEDRIA   Just do me this one favor. It'll pay off for you, really pay off. You'll say so yourself.

DORIO   Don't give me that line.

PHAEDRIA   Believe me, you'll be glad you did it. It's the truth, I swear it.

DORIO   Wake up, will you!

PHAEDRIA   Give it a try. Just three days.

DORIO   (*wearily*)   The same old song and dance.

PHAEDRIA   (*working himself up*)   Dorio, you'll be more to me than my best friend. More than my own father, my own—

DORIO   (*interrupting*)   You're wasting your breath.

PHAEDRIA   (*desperately*)   What's the matter with you? Don't you have a heart? Here I am begging you, and you just can't feel pity for a fellow.

DORIO   (*mimicking him*)   What's the matter with *you*? Don't you have a brain? Here you are handing me a line and I'm supposed to hand you one of my girls free of charge!

ANTIPHO   (*sotto voce, to Geta*)   Poor Phaedria!

PHAEDRIA   (*to himself*)   He knows the score. I give up.

GETA   (*sotto voce, to Antipho*)   Acting just the way you'd expect, both of them.

PHAEDRIA   (*bitterly, to himself*)   And this had to happen now, just when Antipho's having troubles of his own!

ANTIPHO   (*coming forward with Geta*)   Phaedria, what's going on here?

PHAEDRIA   (*bitterly*)   Antipho, you don't know how lucky you are!

ANTIPHO   Who? Me?

PHAEDRIA   The girl you love is safe in your own home. You've been spared the experience of coming up against trouble like this (*gesturing toward Dorio*).

ANTIPHO   Safe in my own home? Oh, no! I'm like the fellow in the story—I've got a tiger by the tail: I can't hang on and I can't let go.

DORIO   (*to Antipho, gesturing toward Phaedria and dropping for the moment his harsh tone*)   My situation exactly with this fellow here.

ANTIPHO   (*to Dorio*)   Well, well, our pimp's getting soft. (*To Phaedria*) What's he done?

PHAEDRIA Done? Just about the most inhuman thing a human being could. He's sold my girl!

ANTIPHO Sold her?

GETA Sold her?

PHAEDRIA Sold her.

DORIO (*sarcastically*) Oh, sure, an absolute outrage—selling a girl I bought with my own money.

PHAEDRIA I've been begging him to break the agreement with the buyer and give me just three days more to collect the money my friends promised me, but he won't do it. (*To Dorio*) If I don't get it to you by then, you don't have to wait another minute.

DORIO You bore me.

ANTIPHO Dorio, he's only asking for three days. Come on, give in. Do him the favor and he'll pay you back for it twice over.

DORIO I want action, not words.

ANTIPHO (*working himself up*) Are you going to let that girl leave the city? They love each other—how can you sit back and see them be separated?

DORIO (*grimly*) Neither you nor I—

PHAEDRIA (*interrupting*) I hope to god you get what's coming to you!

DORIO (*to Phaedria*) Now, look here. Against my better judgment I've put up with your promises for months now. And all I've gotten is tears and no cash. Well, now I've found just the opposite, someone with cash and no tears. He goes to the head of the line.

ANTIPHO (*who, during Dorio's speech, has been in deep thought, to Phaedria*) By god, if I remember correctly, you agreed on a date with him for paying the money, didn't you?

PHAEDRIA We did.

DORIO (*unruffled*) That's right. I'm not denying it.

ANTIPHO Well, is it past yet?

DORIO (*blandly*) No. But today's offer beat the deadline.

ANTIPHO (*hotly*) You welsher! Aren't you ashamed of yourself?

DORIO (*scornfully*) When it means a profit? I should say not!

GETA You stinker!

PHAEDRIA Dorio! Is that any way to act?

DORIO (*genially*) That's the way I am. If you don't like it, take your business somewhere else.

ANTIPHO What do you mean by cheating this poor fellow that way!

DORIO (*losing a bit of his calm*)   Oh, no, Antipho. He's the one who's doing the cheating. He knew what I was like; I thought *he* was different. *He* lied to me; I treated him just the way I always treat everybody. But we'll forget about all that. Here's what I'm going to do. The colonel who wants to buy her said he'd bring the money tomorrow morning. You bring the money first, Phaedria, and I'll use my system with you—first come, first served. So long. (*Turns and goes into his house.*)

PHAEDRIA (*to himself, gazing after Dorio helplessly*)   What am I going to do? Where's a poor devil like me, without a dime to his name, going to get that kind of money overnight? And I could have raised it, my friends promised it to me, if I could only have talked him into giving me three days more. (*Stands distraught, oblivious for the moment to everything about him.*)

ANTIPHO (*to Geta*)   Geta! Are we going to stand by and let him suffer this way? After all, you told me how he stood up for me a little while ago. What do you say we try to return the favor? He could use it now.

GETA   I agree. That's the right thing to do.

ANTIPHO   Then do something. You're the only one who can save him.

GETA   What am I supposed to do?

ANTIPHO   Find the money.

GETA (*sarcastically*)   I'm willing. You just show me where.

ANTIPHO (*deliberately*)   My father's back home, you know.

GETA (*puzzled*)   I know. What about it?

ANTIPHO (*hesitating to put what he has in mind into words*)   Well . . . a word to the wise is sufficient.

GETA (*incredulously*)   Get it from *him*?

ANTIPHO   From him.

GETA (*exploding*)   God in heaven, what a thing to suggest! Great, oh, great. Leave me alone, will you! I deserve a medal if I just get out of *your* marriage with a whole skin. I don't need any orders now from you to go get myself drawn and quartered because of him (*gesturing toward Phaedria*).

(*Geta's explosion rouses Phaedria and, catching the drift of the conversation, he starts to listen avidly.*)

ANTIPHO (*despondently, to Phaedria*)   He's right.

PHAEDRIA (*flaring up*)   What's the matter, Geta? I'm a member of this family too, you know.

GETA I know, I know. But isn't it enough for you that the old man is mad at every one of us right now? Do you have to stick the needle in deeper and throw away every chance of ever talking him around?

PHAEDRIA (*dramatically*) To think that someone else will take her from my sight and lead her off to an unknown land! (*Striking a heroic pose and groaning*) Oh, Antipho! Look at me, speak to me, now while you still can, while I'm still before you!

ANTIPHO Why? What are you talking about? What are you going to do?

PHAEDRIA (*as before*) I don't care where in the world he carries her off to, my mind is made up: I'll follow her or die in the attempt!

GETA (*ironically*) God be with you whatever you do—but just take it easy, will you?

ANTIPHO (*to Geta*) Look, can't you do something for him?

GETA Something? What, for instance?

ANTIPHO Think, Geta, think! We don't want to let him do anything we'll be sorry for later.

GETA All right, I'll think. (*Paces up and down in deep thought. Finally, after several false starts, speaks.*) I think we can save him. But I'm afraid it means more trouble.

ANTIPHO Don't be afraid. We'll be right there with you to take whatever comes, good or bad.

GETA (*to Phaedria*) Tell me, how much money do you need?

PHAEDRIA Only fifteen thousand.

GETA (*gulping*) Whew! That's an expensive girl you have there, Phaedria. Fifteen thousand!

PHAEDRIA (*indignantly*) For a girl like her? It's dirt cheap!

GETA All right, all right. I'll dig it up for you.

PHAEDRIA Geta! You're terrific!

GETA (*looking around warily*) Now let's get you out of here.

PHAEDRIA (*not hearing the last remark in his excitement*) I need it right away.

GETA You'll have it right away. But you've got to let me have Phormio. I need him to help me.

ANTIPHO He's available. Don't be afraid to load anything you want on him. He'll handle it. He's the one man who knows how to be a friend in need.

GETA Let's go get him right now.

ANTIPHO You don't need me now for anything do you?

GETA No. Go in the house and cheer up that wife of yours. The poor
thing must be scared to death in there. (*Antipho, who had forgotten all about Phanium in the excitement, stands for a moment
conscience-stricken.*) Well, what are you waiting for?

ANTIPHO (*galvanized into action*) Nothing I'd rather do! (*Rushes into
the house.*)

PHAEDRIA How are you going to pull this off, anyway?

GETA (*taking him by the arm and leading him off, stage left*) Right
now let's get you out of here. I'll tell you on the way. (*They
leave.*)

ACT IV

(*Demipho and Chremes enter, stage right, deep in conversation.
There is much the same difference between the two brothers as there
is between their sons, although in this case the personalities are reversed.
Chremes, like his nephew Antipho, is the cautious sort, always harried
by worries and misgivings. That he has very little money of his own and
lives off the property and income of a rich wife, and that Nausistrata,
the lady in question, is a most formidable woman, accounts for this in
part. But another part, and by far the larger, has a much less prosaic
reason behind it. Chremes is a bigamist: he has a second wife and a
grown daughter on Lemnos. The very thought of Nausistrata's finding
out about his double life is enough to give him the shakes.*)

DEMIPHO Well, Chremes, the only reason you went to Lemnos was
to get your daughter and bring her back. Isn't she with you?

CHREMES No.

DEMIPHO Why not?

CHREMES From what I could gather, when her mother saw that I was
staying away longer than usual, she figured the girl was getting
too old to put up with this sort of treatment, so she packed up,
bag and baggage, and came here to find me.

DEMIPHO What kept you there so long once you found they had left?

CHREMES (*with an emphasis that is suspicious in view of the innocence
of the question*) God, was I sick! I couldn't get away.

DEMIPHO How come? Did you catch something?

CHREMES (*evasively*)   How come? I'm old. That's a sickness right there. (*Changing the subject*) Now, I've heard from the captain of their ship that they arrived safely.

DEMIPHO   Have you heard what happened to my son while I was away?

CHREMES   Yes! (*With even more of a worried air than usual*) And that's just the thing that's got me in a quandary. (*Throwing a glance at the house to make sure there's no sign of his wife, and dropping his voice*) You see, if I arrange a match for that daughter of mine with someone outside the family, I've got to tell him the whole story of where she came from, and so on. With your son there was no problem; I knew I could trust you as well as my own self. If some outsider really wants the match, he'll keep his mouth shut all right—but only so long as we're on good terms. There's always the chance he'll fall out with me, and then he's going to know more than he should—and I'm scared my wife would get wind of what's been going on. Once that happens, there's nothing left for me but to cut loose and clear out. After all, the only thing in the house I own is my own skin.

DEMIPHO   I know, I know, and this business has got me worried too. I gave you my word my boy would marry her and I'm not going to give up trying until I make good on it.

(*At this moment Geta, returning from his conference with Phormio, enters, stage left. He doesn't at first notice the two oldsters on stage, and they, deep in their conversation, don't notice him.*)

GETA (*to himself*)   That Phormio! What brains! Never saw anything like it! I go to see him to tell him we need money and start to explain how we can get it. Halfway through he cuts me short because he's caught on. Said he was glad to do it, was proud of me, was ready for the old man, and thanked heaven he had a chance to show he was as good a friend of Phaedria's as Antipho's. I told him to wait downtown; I'd bring the old man to him. (*Suddenly notices Demipho.*) Hey, there he is! Who's that back of him? Wow! Chremes has come back. (*Getting a grip on himself*) Dumbbell! What did you get so scared about? Because you've got two to take over the ropes instead of one? Use your head—two chances are better than one. (*Gesturing toward Demipho*) Go after the one you started with; if he comes across, fine. If not, tackle this new arrival.

(*At this moment Antipho emerges from the door of his house.*)

ANTIPHO (*to himself, as he comes out*)   I wonder how soon Geta's going to get back. (*Looks up and his jaw drops as he sees the two oldsters.*) My uncle! And my father with him! Now that he's back, what's he going to make my father do? Now I'm really scared! (*Sneaks over to a corner where he can hear without being observed.*)

GETA (*to himself*)   Here goes. (*Walks up to the two old men and puts on his best greetings-to-a-long-lost-friend manner.*) Well, well, Chremes!

CHREMES   Hello, Geta.

GETA   It's a pleasure to see you back.

CHREMES   Thanks.

GETA   How are things? A man always finds lots of changes when he comes back from a trip, doesn't he?

CHREMES (*pointedly*)   He certainly does.

GETA   That's right. Have you heard the news about Antipho?

CHREMES   The whole story.

GETA (*to Demipho*)   Did you tell him? (*To Chremes*) A downright outrage, Chremes, the way that boy was taken in!

CHREMES (*nodding vigorously*)   I was just going over it with Demipho here.

GETA (*earnestly*)   As a matter of fact, I've been going over it too, in my own mind. From every angle. And, you know, I think I've found the solution.

CHREMES (*eagerly*)   What, Geta?

DEMIPHO (*suspiciously*)   What kind of solution?

GETA (*directing his remarks principally at Demipho*)   When I left you a little while ago, I just happened to run into Phormio.

CHREMES   Phormio? Who's he?

GETA   The fellow that the girl—

CHREMES (*interrupting with a nod*)   I got you.

GETA   It looked to me like a good chance to sound him out. So I take him off to one side and I say to him: "Phormio, how about a little cooperation so that we can settle things between us in a friendly way without any friction? Now, my master's a gentleman; he likes to steer clear of courtrooms. I tell you this because all his friends have advised him, to a man, to throw the girl out. It's the god's honest truth."

ANTIPHO (*aside*)   What's he trying to pull now? Just where is he going to wind up anyway?

GETA (*continuing his imaginary discourse with Phormio*)   "I know you're going to tell me that if he throws her out you're going to hale him into court and make him pay through the nose. Well, he's already gone into that. Boy, you're going to sweat plenty once you start up with that man—he's a trained trial lawyer! But, let's just suppose he does lose the case: *he's* got the money to pay the fine and stay out of jail; but if you lose . . ." (*expressive gesture to indicate that such an event would be disastrous for the penniless Phormio.*)   When I figured I had softened him up with this sort of talk, I say to him: "Look, nobody can hear us now. Here's the proposition: my master gives up his case, the girl clears out, and you stop bothering us. All right, name your price."

ANTIPHO (*in a frenzy, aside*)   Has he gone stark raving mad?

GETA (*continuing the imaginary dialogue*)   "You give us a figure that comes anywhere near being fair and square and, believe me, with an honest man like my master, we'll settle things in three shakes."

DEMIPHO (*visibly repressing an urge to take Geta by the throat*)   And just who told you you could say that?

CHREMES (*sotto voce, to Demipho*)   Let him alone! It's the best possible way to wind up where we want to.

ANTIPHO (*aside*)   I'm sunk!

DEMIPHO (*to Geta*)   Go on, what did he say then?

GETA   At first he went wild.

CHREMES   How much did he ask for, anyway?

GETA   How much? Too much! The first figure that came into his head.

CHREMES   What was it?

GETA   Well, if you'll give him thirty thousand—

DEMIPHO (*exploding*)   I'll give him hell, that's what I'll give him! What a nerve!

GETA   Exactly what I told him. I said to him, "How much do you think he'd have given an only daughter of his own? A fat lot he's saving by not having one! Not when you turn up with a girl who's out to hold him up for a dowry!" Well, to cut it short and skip

all his ravings, this is what he wound up telling me: "This girl
was my friend's daughter, it was my duty to marry her, and I
wanted to right from the very first. After all, I had in mind all
along what the poor girl, without any dowry, would have to
put up with if she married a rich husband and had to spend her
life slaving for him. But I'll be frank with you. I need a wife
who'll bring me a little something I could use to pay off some
debts. Matter of fact, I'm engaged to a girl right now who can.
But, even so, if Demipho's willing to give me what I stand to
get from my fiancée, there isn't anyone I'd rather marry than
that girl.

ANTIPHO (*aside*) I don't know what to think! Why's he doing this?
Is he just plain stupid or just plain rotten? Is he blind or does
he know what he's doing?

DEMIPHO (*suspiciously*) Supposing he's up to his ears in debt?

GETA He mentioned a farm with a mortgage on it for five thousand.

DEMIPHO All right, all right. Let him marry her. I'll pay it.

GETA And a house for another five.

DEMIPHO (*shouting*) Whoa there! That's too much!

CHREMES (*throwing a worried glance at his house to make sure the noise
hasn't brought out his wife*) Pipe down! I'll pay that five.

GETA And he'd have to buy his wife a maid. And a few more pieces
of furniture. And the cost of the wedding. Another five, say, for
all this.

DEMIPHO (*at the top of his lungs*) I don't care if he brings a hundred
suits against me, I'm not giving him a dime. Let that godforsaken good-for-nothing have another laugh on me?

CHREMES (*throwing another anguished look toward the house*) Please!
Take it easy! I'll pay it. All you've got to do is get that boy of
yours to marry . . . (*checks himself from mentioning further
details, with a worried glance at the house*) the one we want
him to marry.

ANTIPHO (*aside*) Geta! You and your schemes! You've ruined me,
that's what you've done!

CHREMES (*sotto voce, to Demipho*) We're getting rid of her because
of me; it's only fair I take the loss.

GETA And he also said: "I want to know as soon as possible if they're
going to give me the girl, because I've got to know just where I
stand. I'll have to break off with my present fiancée and that
means giving up the dowry her parents agreed to pay me."

CHREMES (*panicked at the very thought of losing Phormio as the solution to his problems*) Tell him to tell them it's all off. Tell him he'll get the money right away. Tell him the marriage is all set.

DEMIPHO (*between his teeth*) And I hope it kills him!

CHREMES Luckily I happen to have some cash on me, the rents I collected for my wife from her property on Lemnos. I'll take it out of that. I'll tell my wife you needed it. (*The two go into Chremes' house.*)

ANTIPHO (*coming out of his corner*) Geta!

GETA (*turning around and seeing him for the first time*) You here?

ANTIPHO And just what was all that about?

GETA I was getting the old men to cough up the money.

ANTIPHO (*threateningly*) Is that all?

GETA (*deliberately misunderstanding the question*) God almighty, what do you want from me? That's all you told me to do!

ANTIPHO Listen, you double-crosser, answer my question!

GETA What are you driving at?

ANTIPHO (*wildly*) What am I driving at? Are you so blind you can't see what you've done? Set the stage for my suicide, that's what! Damn you, I hope you rot in hell! (*To the world at large*) Hey, everybody! If you've got a job you really want well done, here's your man! (*To Geta*) Why did you have to mention my wife and open up that wound again? I can't think of anything more senseless. Now you've filled my father full of hope that he can kick her out. Look at what's going to happen. As soon as Phormio gets the dowry, he's going to have to take her and marry her. What do we do then?

GETA (*quietly*) He's not going to marry her.

ANTIPHO (*sarcastically*) Oh, sure. And then, when they ask for their money back, I suppose he'll be ready to rot in jail just for me and Phaedria?

GETA (*still keeping calm*) Antipho, there isn't anything you can't spoil by stressing only what's bad about it. You're mentioning only the bad side of the picture and leaving out the good. Let's turn it the other way around. You say that once Phormio gets the money, he's got to marry the girl. Agreed. But he's got to arrange the wedding, send out the invitations, see to the clergyman—all this is going to take a little time. In the meanwhile, Phaedria'll collect the money his friends promised him and Phormio can use that to pay the old men back.

ANTIPHO   On what grounds pay them back? What's he going to tell them?

GETA   (*impatient at Antipho's sticking at what, for him, is a mere detail*)   Tell them? (*Launching into an imitation of Phormio in the imaginary act of reeling off excuses*) "After I left you, I can't tell you how much bad luck I ran into! A black cat crossed my path, I dropped a mirror in the house, walked under a ladder, my horoscope was terrible, my fortune-teller said absolutely no— and I knew I shouldn't have started this business until after Friday the thirteenth." Matter of fact, that's the best excuse of all. (*Comfortingly*) Everything will be all right.

ANTIPHO   Everything better be!

GETA   (*confidently*)   Everything will. Leave it to me. (*The door of Chremes' house opens.*) Your father's coming out. Run and tell Phaedria we've got the money. (*Antipho rushes off, stage left.*)

(*Demipho and Chremes emerge from the house. Demipho is carrying a well-filled purse.*)

DEMIPHO   Take it easy, will you? I'll see to it he doesn't try any tricks. You don't think I'd part with this money without witnesses present? What's more, I'll make it crystal clear to them who's getting it and for what.

GETA   (*aside*)   Look how careful he is. A lot of good it's going to do him!

CHREMES   Right. That's the way you've got to do it. But hurry, before he changes his mind. If that fiancée of his starts putting pressure on him, he may welsh on us.

GETA   (*aside*)   You hit the nail on the head!

DEMIPHO   (*turning to Geta*)   I'm ready. Take me to him.

GETA   I've been waiting for you.

CHREMES   (*to Demipho, struck by a last-minute idea*)   When you're done with him, drop in on my wife. Ask her to go see the girl before she leaves and explain the situation to her: that we're arranging for her to marry Phormio, but there's no reason for any hard feelings—he's from her own circle and will make her a much better husband, and we're giving him every penny of the dowry he asked for; we're not forgetting our obligations to her for one minute.

DEMIPHO   (*testily*)   What the devil do you care?

CHREMES A lot, Demipho. For a man to do the right thing isn't enough. People have to know about it and say he did right. I want the girl to go into this of her own free will so she won't go around saying we threw her out.

DEMIPHO But why your wife? I can do it myself.

CHREMES It takes a woman to handle a woman.

DEMIPHO All right, I'll ask her.

(He and Geta leave, stage left. Chremes watches them go off. He heaves a sigh of relief at the thought that this much of his trouble is apparently taken care of.)

CHREMES *(to himself)* And now I wonder where I can find that daughter of mine?

(At this moment the door of Demipho's house opens and Sophrona comes out. Sophrona is Phanium's nurse, the old woman Antipho had first approached and who had discouraged his dishonorable, and encouraged his honorable, advances. She walks toward the front of the stage, visibly agitated, without noticing Chremes who is standing near the door of his house.)

SOPHRONA *(to herself)* What am I to do? Dear, oh, dear, I don't have a single friend, not a soul to help me or talk things over with. My poor little girl! When I hear how terribly Antipho's father is taking what's happened I'm frightened to death for her. Something dreadful may happen to her and all because she listened to me!

CHREMES *(to himself)* An old woman coming out of my brother's house? And all upset? Who can she be?

SOPHRONA *(to herself)* I knew all along this marriage would be shaky but, without a penny to our name, there was no other way out. I only told her to do it so that, at least for the time being, she'd have a roof over her head.

CHREMES *(taking a long look, to himself)* God almighty! Unless I'm going crazy or my eyes are going bad, that's my daughter's old nurse!

SOPHRONA *(to herself)* And there's not a sign—

CHREMES *(in great agitation, to himself)* What do I do now?

SOPHRONA *(to herself)* —not a single sign of her father.

CHREMES (*as before*) Go up to her? Or wait here until I get a better idea of what she's talking about?

SOPHRONA (*to herself*) If I could only find him now, I'd have nothing to worry about.

CHREMES (*to himself*) It's Sophrona, all right. (*Letting his voice assume a natural pitch as he makes up his mind*) I'll call her.

SOPHRONA (*frightened at the sound of a voice*) Who's talking there?

CHREMES (*aloud*) Sophrona!

SOPHRONA (*dreading to turn around*) He knows my name!

CHREMES Look at me!

SOPHRONA (*with a start*) Oh, my god! Is that Stilpho? (*Walks toward him.*)

CHREMES (*dropping his voice*) No!

SOPHRONA (*confused and alarmed*) No?

CHREMES (*taking her by the arm and leading her away from the door of his house, with an anxious look over his shoulder as he does so*) Sophrona, please! Get a little further away from that door! This way, here. (*Leads her a safe distance away.*) Now, don't ever call me by that name again!

SOPHRONA (*utterly confused*) Why? Aren't you the person you always said you were?

CHREMES (*with an anguished look at the door*) Sh!

SOPHRONA What are you so scared of that door for?

CHREMES I've got a wild animal caged up in there—my wife. Now, about that name. It's an alias. I used it with you on Lemnos just to be on the safe side. Otherwise, if you people were careless and let the story leak out, there was always a chance it could get to my wife.

SOPHRONA My god! So that's why we poor women could never find you here!

CHREMES Tell me, what have you got to do with the family that lives here? (*Gesturing toward Demipho's house*) In that house you just came out of? (*Suddenly remembering something more important*) And where are the others?

SOPHRONA (*bursting into tears*) Oh, dear!

CHREMES What's the matter? Aren't they alive?

SOPHRONA Your daughter is. But her poor mother just pined away.

CHREMES (*not exactly laid prostrate by the news*) What a pity!

SOPHRONA There I was, left all by myself, an old woman without a
     penny and not knowing a soul. I did what I could. I arranged
     for your daughter to marry the boy who lives here.
CHREMES (*not believing his ears*) Antipho?
SOPHRONA Yes. That's the one.
CHREMES (*roaring*) What! Has he got two wives?
SOPHRONA (*puzzled*) He? Heavens, no. Only one, your daughter.
CHREMES (*puzzled himself now*) What about that other one who's
     supposed to be a cousin?
SOPHRONA (*catching on*) That's your daughter.
CHREMES (*incredulously*) What's that you say?
SOPHRONA We made that story up. The boy was in love with her, and
     that way he was able to marry her without a dowry.

*(Chremes stands stunned for a moment as this sinks in. When he
starts to talk it is half to himself.)*

CHREMES God in heaven! So many times things you wouldn't even
     dare hope for, happen by pure luck! I come home and run into
     my daughter married just the way I wanted, to just the man I
     wanted. Here we were, my brother and I, beating our brains
     out to arrange just this, and the boy did it all by himself with-
     out any worry on our part—but plenty on his!
SOPHRONA There's something you've got to take care of right away.
     Antipho's father's come back and they say he's simply furious at
     what's happened.
CHREMES It's nothing to worry about. (*Wagging his finger in her
     face*) Now, in the name of all that's holy, nobody's ever to find
     out that she's my daughter, understand?
SOPHRONA (*stoutly*) Nobody will from me.
CHREMES (*moving toward the door of Demipho's house*) Follow me.
     I'll tell you the rest inside.

ACT V

*(Demipho, followed by Geta, enters, stage left. He has just left
Phormio—and the experience of handing the money over has been
searing.)*

DEMIPHO (*to himself*) It's our own fault it pays people to be crooks.
We're so intent on getting a reputation for being good and kind,
we're pushovers. (*Clenching his fist as he thinks of the ordeal
he has just been through*) Talk about adding insult to injury!
Wasn't it enough I had to swallow the injury he did to me? Did
I have to throw money in the bargain to give him a living until
he could spring his next swindle?

GETA Right. Absolutely right.

DEMIPHO Turn right into wrong these days and you get a prize for it!

GETA True, absolutely true.

DEMIPHO So it shows that the way we handled this affair was idiotic,
absolutely idiotic.

GETA (*with affected casualness, watching Demipho narrowly*) I only
hope this plan of ours goes through and he marries her.

DEMIPHO (*starting*) You mean there's any question about it?

GETA (*pursing his lips and giving other indications of a considerable
state of dubiety*) Fellow like that? I wouldn't swear to it that
he's not going to change his mind.

DEMIPHO (*turning on him*) What! Change his mind?

GETA (*backing down in the face of the reaction he's stirred up*) I don't
say I know. I only say it could be.

DEMIPHO (*somewhat reassured*) I'll get going on my brother's idea and
have his wife come here and talk to the girl. Geta, go inside and
tell her Nausistrata's coming to see her. (*Enters Chremes' house
to fetch Nausistrata.*)

GETA (*to himself*) Phaedria's got his money, no word of a bawling out
for Antipho and me, and I've fixed it up so Phanium doesn't
have to leave for the time being. Now what? What's going to
happen next? Geta, my boy, you're stuck in the same rut; only
now you're in deeper. You didn't get out of your trouble, you
just delayed the day of reckoning. The cat-o'-nine-tails is going
to have kittens, if you don't watch out! Well, I'll go inside now
and explain to Phanium that she doesn't have to worry about
Phormio or anything he tells her. (*Goes into Demipho's house.*)

(*The door of Chremes' house opens, and Demipho and Nausistrata
come out. Nausistrata is all we have been lead to expect: an imposing
woman, with a no-nonsense air about her, who could, if need be, run
a business as efficiently as she does her household—and husband. She*

*is, in a way, a female counterpart of Demipho and, as a matter of fact,
he is clearly a favorite of hers. Nausistrata is, however, no old battle-ax;
beneath her businesslike exterior, she is actually quite warmhearted
and good-natured.)*

DEMIPHO You see, Nausistrata, I want you to talk her around. She's
    got to do it anyway, but make her want to. You're good at that
    sort of thing.

NAUSISTRATA I'll do it.

DEMIPHO You'll be doing me as much of a favor in this way as you
    did a little while ago with that loan.

NAUSISTRATA Glad to do it. I really don't do as much for you as I
    ought—and it's all the fault of that husband of mine!

DEMIPHO What about him?

NAUSISTRATA My dear man, the way he mismanages the hard-earned
    fortune my father left me! My father used to get sixty thousand
    a year from that property, regularly. How one man can be so
    much better than another!

DEMIPHO Sixty thousand? You don't say!

NAUSISTRATA And at a time when things didn't pay as well as today.
    Yes, sir, sixty thousand.

DEMIPHO Whew!

NAUSISTRATA What do you think of *that?*

DEMIPHO It certainly goes to show!

NAUSISTRATA I wish I had been born a man! I'd show him—

DEMIPHO *(interrupting a little impatiently)* I'm sure of it.

NAUSISTRATA *(disregarding him and continuing her thought)* —how
    to—

DEMIPHO *(interrupting again)* Now, Nausistrata, you've got to con-
    serve your energy to deal with the girl. She's a youngster; we
    don't want her to wear you down.

NAUSISTRATA I'll do exactly what you want. *(Goes toward Demipho's
    house but stops when she sees the door opening.)* There's
    Chremes! He's coming out of your house.

*(Chremes bursts out, in his excitement rushing right past his wife
without seeing her.)*

CHREMES Demipho! Did you pay him the money?

DEMIPHO *(with satisfaction)* Took care of it right away.

CHREMES (*taken aback*) I wish you hadn't. (*Suddenly noticing Nausistrata, to himself*) Wow! My wife! I almost said too much!

DEMIPHO (*testily*)   And just why do you wish I hadn't?

CHREMES (*making frantic signals to Demipho to drop the subject*) It's all right, it's all right.

DEMIPHO   What about you? Have you spoken to the girl and told her why we're sending Nausistrata?

CHREMES (*as before*)   I took care of it.

DEMIPHO   Well, what does she say?

CHREMES   We can't send her away.

DEMIPHO   And why can't we?

CHREMES (*hesitating as he searches for an excuse*) Because they're in love with each other.

DEMIPHO (*exasperated*)   What do we care?

CHREMES   A lot. Besides, I found out she's a relative of ours.

DEMIPHO   What! Are you crazy?

CHREMES   It's the truth. I mean it. I remembered; it all came back to me.

DEMIPHO   Are you in your right mind?

NAUSISTRATA   Now, Demipho, I don't want you mistreating any relatives!

DEMIPHO (*disgusted, to Nausistrata*)   She's no relative.

CHREMES   Don't say that. Her father went by a different name. That's what threw you off.

DEMIPHO (*getting more and more confused at both the conversation and Chremes' signals*) She didn't know her own father?

CHREMES (*disgusted at Demipho's lack of comprehension*) She knew him.

DEMIPHO   Then why did she give the wrong name?

CHREMES (*giving up trying to flag Demipho with signals, pointedly*) Why can't you leave this to me? Can't you understand?

DEMIPHO   Well, if you're going to talk utter nonsense—

CHREMES (*sotto voce*)   You're ruining me!

NAUSISTRATA (*bewildered*)   What's going on here, anyway?

DEMIPHO   I swear I don't know!

CHREMES (*throwing caution to the winds*)   All right, you want to know? So help me heaven if you and I aren't the closest relatives that girl's got!

DEMIPHO (*losing his patience and temper simultaneously*) God in heaven! Let's go see *her*. I want all of us to get to the bottom of this together.

CHREMES (*groaning*) Oh, lord!

DEMIPHO (*sotto voce*) What's the matter?

CHREMES (*sotto voce*) You! Can't you trust me?

DEMIPHO (*sotto voce*) Am I supposed to believe this? (*Chremes nods frantically.*) Should I stop asking questions? (*More frantic nods.*) All right, I will. But what about that (*noticing out of the corner of his eye that Nausistrata is straining her ears*)—er, daughter of "our friend"? What's going to happen to her?

CHREMES (*sotto voce*) It's all right!

DEMIPHO (*sotto voce*) Then should we get rid of her? (*nodding in Nausistrata's direction*)

CHREMES (*sotto voce*) Why not?

DEMIPHO (*aloud*) Then we'll let the girl stay?

CHREMES Yes.

DEMIPHO In that case, Nausistrata, we won't be needing you.

NAUSISTRATA I'm glad she's staying. I think it will be much better for all of us than what you were trying to do. She seemed like such a nice girl when I saw her. (*Enters her house.*)

DEMIPHO Now what's this all about?

CHREMES (*sotto voce*) Has she shut the door yet?

DEMIPHO Now she has.

CHREMES (*whooping*) Heavenly days! Lady Luck's looking after us! I found out that my daughter is married to your son!

DEMIPHO (*not believing his ears*) What! Now how could that—

CHREMES (*looking around warily*) I can't tell you here. It's not safe enough.

DEMIPHO Go inside then.

CHREMES (*as he follows Demipho into the latter's house*) Now, remember! I don't even want our own sons to find out about this!

(*Enter Antipho, stage left, back from having reported to Phaedria the success of their plan to raise the money. At this moment his morale is at low ebb.*)

ANTIPHO (*to himself*) No matter how things stand with me, I'm delighted Phaedria got what he wanted. (*Shaking his head rue-*

fully) That's the smart way: train your mind to go after only what can be fixed up without fuss if things go against you. In his case, the minute he got his money he got his release from worry. But I'm in a mess that just doesn't leave any way out: to keep my secret means mental torture, and if I divulge it I'm disgraced. I'm only going back home now because I still have hopes of holding on to her. But where can I find Geta? I want to ask him when he thinks would be the right moment to tackle my father.

(Enter Phormio, stage left. He doesn't notice Antipho, who is standing near the door of his house.)

PHORMIO *(to himself)* I took the money and paid the pimp. He set the girl free, but I carted her off and made sure Phaedria got her all for himself. There's only one thing left on the agenda: to get the old men to give me some time off so's I can throw a wild party. I'm taking a vacation the next few days.

ANTIPHO There's Phormio. Hi! What's new?

PHORMIO About what?

ANTIPHO About what Phaedria's going to do now. Did he tell you how he plans to drink up his well of love?

PHORMIO He's going to take his turn at playing your role.

ANTIPHO What's that?

PHORMIO Keeping away from his father. And he wants you to take your turn at his role. Wants you to plead his cause for him because he'll be away at a party at my house. I'm telling the old men I'm going to run down to the market at Sunium to buy that maid Geta gave them a story about. Otherwise, when they don't see me around here, they'll think I'm off somewhere throwing their money away. Hey, your door's opening.

ANTIPHO *(hastily going off to the side)* See who's coming.

PHORMIO It's Geta.

(Geta bursts out of the door carrying his coat. He's in a transport of joy, and, in his excitement, doesn't see either Antipho or Phormio.)

GETA *(to himself)* Oh, luck, Lady Luck! The favors you've loaded on Antipho today, all by yourself! And so sudden!

ANTIPHO *(sotto voce, to Phormio)* What in the world does he mean?

GETA (*to himself*) And all his friends can unload their worries now. But what am I wasting time for? Why don't I get into this coat and get going, find him, and tell him what's happened?

ANTIPHO (*sotto voce, to Phormio*) What's he talking about? Do you make any sense out of it?

PHORMIO (*sotto voce, to Antipho*) No. Do you?

ANTIPHO (*as before*) None at all.

PHORMIO (*as before*) Same here.

GETA (*to himself*) I'll go to Dorio's house; that's where they are. (*Starts off at a gallop.*)

ANTIPHO Hey, Geta!

GETA (*not recognizing the voice and thinking it's someone calling him back just for a joke, to himself*) There you are! The same old joke—call you back the minute you get under way!

ANTIPHO Geta!

GETA (*disregarding the command and moving off, to himself*) Still at it, by god! Go on, pester me; it's going to get you nowhere.

ANTIPHO Are you going to stop or aren't you?

GETA (*without turning around*) Go hang yourself!

ANTIPHO You little stinker, that's just what's going to happen to you if you don't stop this minute!

GETA (*to himself*) Wants to wallop me—must be one of the family. (*Turning around*) Here's the very man I was going after, in the flesh! Come here! Quick!

ANTIPHO What's up?

GETA Hail, mortal most favored of all mortals alive! Antipho, you're heaven's favorite son. It's beyond debate.

ANTIPHO I wouldn't mind. And I wouldn't mind being told just why I should believe it.

GETA Will you be satisfied if I drench you with joy?

ANTIPHO (*angrily*) Cut it out!

PHORMIO (*stepping forward to join them*) Just skip the promises and let's have the facts.

GETA (*surprised*) You here too, Phormio?

PHORMIO Yes, I'm here. Now stop wasting time.

GETA (*the words tumbling out in his excitement*) Listen to this! (*To Phormio*) After we gave you the money downtown just now, we came right home. (*To Antipho*) Then Demipho sent me to see your wife.

ANTIPHO (*suspiciously*) What for?

GETA Let's skip it; it has nothing to do with the case. I start to go
into her room when her slave boy runs up to me, grabs my coat
from behind, and hauls me back. I look around and ask him why
he's holding me back; he tells me no one's allowed to go in to
her. "Sophrona," says he, "took Chremes in there just now and
he's in there now with them." When I heard this, I got on tiptoe,
very quietly went up to the doorway, stood there, held my
breath, and stuck my ear against the door. Then I listened as
hard as I could, like this (*demonstrates*), to catch what they
were saying.

PHORMIO Good work, Geta.

GETA And I heard something that was absolutely sensational. By god,
I almost cheered out loud.

ANTIPHO What was it?

GETA (*keeping up the suspense as long as he possibly can*) What do
you think?

ANTIPHO I give up.

GETA It's a miracle. I found out that your uncle is—Phanium's father!

ANTIPHO (*totally unable to believe it*) What? What's that you say?

GETA He used to live with her mother in Lemnos. It was a secret.

PHORMIO (*not convinced*) You're dreaming! You mean the girl didn't
know her own father?

GETA Believe me, Phormio, there's some explanation for it. You think
I was able, standing outside that door, to catch everything that
went on between them inside?

ANTIPHO (*who had been deep in thought the past moment*) By god,
I remember hearing some story like that myself!

GETA Wait, I'll give you even more proof. Pretty soon your uncle
comes out of the house. Then, a little while later, he goes back
inside again with your father. Both of them now say you're
going to be allowed to keep the girl. Finally they sent me off to
find you and bring you back.

ANTIPHO Hey! Let's go! What are you waiting for!

GETA Right behind you!

ANTIPHO (*on the run*) Phormio! Goodbye!

PHORMIO Goodbye, Antipho! So help me, it's wonderful news! Congratulations! (*Standing, smiling at the departing figures, to himself*) What a stroke of luck for those boys! And right out of the

blue! (*The smile opens to a broad grin as inspiration seizes him.*)
This is the perfect time to blackmail the old men and relieve
Phaedria of his financial worries. Then he won't have to go
begging from his friends. That money—I made them give it
to me, and I'll make them give it to him. I found out how from
what I found out now. This calls for a new pose and a new look.
(*Tries out a posture or two, presumably typical of forthright men
of integrity and dignity.*) I'll hide in this little back street. Then
I'll show myself as soon as they come out. I won't be going on
that trip to Sunium I gave them a story about. (*Moves over far
to stage left.*)

(*Demipho and Chremes come out of the former's house. They are both
euphoric.*)

DEMIPHO   Chremes, the good lord deserves all my thanks, now that
things have turned out so well. But what we've got to do, and
right now, is see Phormio and get back our fifteen thousand
before he blows it all.

PHORMIO (*leaving his hiding place and walking toward Demipho's door,
loudly to himself*)   I'll see if Demipho's home. I want to—

DEMIPHO (*interrupting*)   Phormio! We were just going to see *you.*

PHORMIO (*affecting pleased surprise*)   Maybe about the very same
thing, eh?

DEMIPHO (*grimly*)   You're absolutely right.

PHORMIO (*innocently*)   That's what I thought. But what did you want
to come to my house for?

DEMIPHO (*testily*)   Don't be funny!

PHORMIO (*affecting incredulity*)   Were you afraid I wouldn't come
through once I got my hands on the money? (*Becoming the
injured innocent*)   Now, listen here: I don't care how poor I am,
there's one thing I always keep sacred, and that's my word.

DEMIPHO (*to Chremes*)   There! Didn't I tell you he was a gentleman?

CHREMES   Absolutely.

PHORMIO   That's just what I was coming to tell you, Demipho: I'm all
ready. Set the wedding date whenever you want. Once I saw
how you two had your hearts set on it, I thought it was only
fair to put everything else off.

DEMIPHO (*taken off balance, but thinking fast*)   Well, Chremes here
has talked me into not having you marry her. "What are people

going to say if you do a thing like that?" he says. "Back when you could have done it decently, you didn't; it would be a scandal to separate them and throw her out now." Just about the same objections you were throwing in my face a little while ago.

PHORMIO (*shifting into high dudgeon*)　You fellows are playing pretty fast and loose with me!

DEMIPHO　How so?

PHORMIO　What a question! I can't even marry my ex-fiancée now. How do you think I'd look going back to her after throwing her over the way I did?

CHREMES (*prompting Demipho, sotto voce*)　Say to him, "Besides, I see now that Antipho doesn't want to let her go."

DEMIPHO (*to Phormio, quickly, like a schoolboy reciting a lesson*)　Besides, I see now that my son doesn't want to let the girl go. (*In his usual manner*) So, if you don't mind, Phormio, we'll go downtown now and have that money turned back to me.

PHORMIO　But I've already turned it over to my creditors.

DEMIPHO (*ominously*)　What do we do now?

PHORMIO (*playing his role to the hilt*)　If you want me to go through with the marriage to that girl you promised me, I'm ready. But if you want her to stay there with you, Demipho, then the dowry stays here with me. After all, it was only to help out your family and its reputation that I broke off my engagement. My fiancée's dowry was just as big, and it's not fair for me to be cheated out of it just because of you.

DEMIPHO　You can go to hell, you and your big talk! You think we don't know the kind you are and what you've been carrying on?

PHORMIO　Now, don't make me lose my temper!

DEMIPHO　So you'd marry her if we let you, eh?

PHORMIO　Try it.

DEMIPHO　So my son could live with her at your house, eh? That was the plan, wasn't it?

PHORMIO (*ominously*)　Would you mind telling me just what you're talking about?

DEMIPHO (*realizing he's gone a bit too far*)　Never mind. Just you hand over the money.

PHORMIO　Oh, no. Just you hand over my wife.

DEMIPHO (*grabbing him by the arm*)　You're going straight to the courthouse.

PHORMIO (*breaking loose*) The courthouse, eh? All right, if you two are going to keep on annoying—

DEMIPHO (*interrupting truculently*) Just what are you going to do about it?

PHORMIO Do about it? Maybe you think I only look after women without dowries. I'm an old hand at taking care of the ones with money, too.

CHREMES What's that to us?

PHORMIO (*carelessly*) Oh, nothing. (*Turning and looking straight at Chremes*) Just that I happen to know a certain lady with money around here whose husband had another wife—

CHREMES (*startled*) Hah?

DEMIPHO (*to Chremes*) What's the matter?

PHORMIO (*calmly continuing*) —in Lemnos—

CHREMES (*aside*) That's the end of me!

PHORMIO —and a daughter. And he's brought the child up behind this certain lady's back.

CHHREMES (*aside*) You can start digging my grave!

PHORMIO And this is just what I'm going to tell her right now. The whole story. (*Makes as if to head for Chremes' house.*)

CHREMES No! Please! Don't!

PHORMIO Oh, so it was you, eh?

DEMIPHO (*gnashing his teeth*) He's making fools of us!

CHREMES (*desperately*) We give up. You just go on your way.

PHORMIO (*snorting*) That's a good one!

CHREMES What do you want, anyway? Keep the money. It's a gift.

PHORMIO (*to Chremes, whose face is full of shocked surprise that Phormio isn't grabbing at the chance and running*) I heard you. (*Swiftly he resumes his air of high dudgeon; though he has gotten what he was after, he is enjoying the situation too much to quit.*) What the devil do you mean by playing around with me, changing your minds like a pair of stupid kids? (*Imitating them*) "I won't, I will," then, all over again, "I will, I won't"; "Take it, give it back." You say something, you take it back; you make a deal, the next minute you break it.

CHREMES (*to Demipho*) How did he find out about it? Who told him?

DEMIPHO (*to Chremes*) I don't know! One thing I do know, though: I didn't tell a soul.

CHREMES (*to Demipho*) It's a miracle, so help me.

PHORMIO (*aside*) I've got him on pins and needles.

DEMIPHO (*to Chremes*) Listen here. Are we going to let him stand there with that grin on his face and do us out of all that money? God almighty, I'd rather die! Try to be a man; let's see a little spunk in you! Look, the story's already leaked out and you can't keep it from your wife now. She's going to hear it from others, so let's tell it to her ourselves. It'll have a much better effect. Then we can get even with this godforsaken good-for-nothing any way we want.

PHORMIO (*aside*) Oh, oh, I'm stuck unless I watch out. They're coming at me with no holds barred!

CHREMES (*in despair, to Demipho*) I'm afraid nothing will have a better effect on her!

DEMIPHO Don't worry, Chremes. I'll get you back in her good graces. I'm banking on the fact that the mother of this child of yours has passed away.

PHORMIO So that's what you're going to do, eh? Pretty smart tactics. By god, Demipho, you've been needling me and it's not going to do that brother of yours any good. (*To Chremes*) What do you mean? After playing around to your heart's content on Lemnos, not giving a second thought to that lovely wife of yours, even coming up with a new way to insult her, you're going to go up to her now and set everything straight by saying you're sorry, eh? Why, when I get done talking to her she'll be so burned up you're not going to put out the fire even if you squeeze out tears to throw on it.

DEMIPHO Oh, god damn him! To think that any man alive could have such gall! This crook ought to be run out of town to the nearest desert island for the public good.

CHREMES (*helplessly*) I'm at the point where I simply don't know what to do about him.

DEMIPHO (*savagely*) I do. Let's go to court.

PHORMIO (*brightly*) Court? Right this way, if you please. (*Starts walking toward the door of Chremes' house.*)

CHREMES (*frantically*) Follow him! Hold him until I get the servants out here!

DEMIPHO (*grabbing Phormio and struggling to hold him back*) I can't do it alone. Help me!

PHORMIO (*trying to pull himself free*) I'm suing you for assault and battery, Demipho!

DEMIPHO   Tell it to the judge!

PHORMIO   (*to Chremes as he joins in*)   You too, Chremes!

CHREMES   (*hauling away with Demipho*)   Get him out of here!

PHORMIO   So that's the idea, eh? That means I've got to use my lungs. (*Yelling*) Nausistrata! Come on out!

CHREMES   Shut his mouth! (*Tries to do so without success.*) Damn him! He's strong!

PHORMIO   Nausistrata!

DEMIPHO   So you're not going to shut up?

PHORMIO   Me shut up?

DEMIPHO   (*to Chremes*)   Punch him in the belly if he won't come!

PHORMIO   Poke my eye out while you're at it. But you'll pay for it. Both of you. Through the nose.

(*The door of Chremes' house opens and Nausistrata appears.*)

NAUSISTRATA   (*coming through the door*)   Who's calling me? (*Starting at the sight of the struggle*) Chremes! Please! What's this ruckus all about?

(*At the sound of her voice, the struggle ends abruptly. Phormio stands his ground coolly, Demipho remains alongside him still breathing fire— and Chremes attempts to make himself as inconspicuous as possible.*)

PHORMIO   (*to Chremes*)   Hey, what's the matter? Lost your tongue?

NAUSISTRATA   (*to Chremes*)   Who is this person? (*Waits a moment for a reply.*) Why don't you answer me?

PHORMIO   (*to Nausistrata*)   Answer you? How can he? He doesn't know he's alive.

CHREMES   (*to Nausistrata*)   Don't believe a word he says!

PHORMIO   (*to Nausistrata*)   Go and touch him; I'll stake my life he's stone cold.

CHREMES   (*to Nausistrata*)   It's nothing, nothing at all.

NAUSISTRATA   (*to Chremes*)   What's going on, then? What's this man talking about?

PHORMIO   (*to Nausistrata*)   You'll find out right away. Just listen.

CHREMES   (*to Nausistrata*)   Are you going to believe him?

NAUSISTRATA   (*to Chremes*)   My dear man, how can I believe him when he hasn't said anything?

PHORMIO   (*to Nausistrata*)   The poor devil's so scared he's out of his mind.

NAUSISTRATA (*to Chremes*)   It must be something special to make you sound so scared.

CHREMES   Me? Scared?

PHORMIO   All right, then, since you're not scared and what I have to say is just nothing at all, you tell her yourself.

DEMIPHO (*to Phormio*)   Damn you, he doesn't have to talk for you!

PHORMIO (*to Demipho*)   See here, you, you've done enough for your brother.

NAUSISTRATA   Chremes, my dear, aren't you going to tell me—

CHREMES   But—

NAUSISTRATA   What do you mean "but"?

CHREMES (*miserably*)   There's nothing to tell.

PHORMIO   Nothing for you to tell. But something for her to hear. (*To Nausistrata, slowly and deliberately*) In Lemnos—

DEMIPHO (*finally losing his nerve and deciding to affect ignorance*) What? What's that you say?

CHREMES (*frantically to Phormio*)   Shut up, will you!

PHORMIO (*continuing unperturbed*)   —behind your back—

CHREMES   Lord help me!

PHORMIO   —he got married.

NAUSISTRATA (*reeling back in shock*)   Oh, no! Oh, god forbid!

PHORMIO   That's what he did.

NAUSISTRATA (*bursting into tears*)   Oh, my god, my god! Oh, this will be the death of me!

PHORMIO   And he had a daughter. And you were fast asleep all the time.

CHREMES (*sotto voce, to Demipho*)   What are we going to do?

NAUSISTRATA   God in heaven! Oh, what a miserable, criminal thing to do!

PHORMIO   That's the story.

NAUSISTRATA   Did you ever hear anything worse in your life? Oh, those husbands! They're only old and feeble when it comes to their wives. Demipho, I appeal to you, since I can't stand talking to *him*. Tell me, is this what all those trips to Lemnos and those long stays there were all about? Is this the reason for the "bad business conditions" that cut down my rents from there?

DEMIPHO   Now, Nausistrata, I don't deny he deserves to be blamed in all this, but there are extenuating circumstances—

PHORMIO (*aside*)   We will now hear the funeral oration.

DEMIPHO   You see, he didn't do it because he didn't care for you or
because he wanted to hurt you. About fifteen years ago he got
drunk, violated some poor woman, and out of it came this
daughter. But he never touched the woman again. She was the
stumbling block in the whole business, and now she's dead,
she's passed on, she's passed away. And that's why I ask you,
please, just as you've always been, be reasonable now.

NAUSISTRATA   Why should I be reasonable? There's nothing I want
more than to be over and done with all this. But what's a poor
woman like me to expect? That he'll behave better because he's
getting older? He was no youngster back then—if getting old
has anything to do with a man's morals. Do you think *my* good
looks have improved with age, Demipho? What reason can you
give me to expect, or at least hope, that this won't happen again?
(*Demipho stands embarrassed and silent before these unanswer-
able objections.*)

PHORMIO   (*imitating an undertaker*)   The funeral procession for our
dear departed Chremes is about to begin. (*To the world at large*)
That's the way I do things. Come on, whoever wants, take a
swing at Phormio. I'll pay you back the same way I did this
poor devil. (*Waits a second to see if anyone will take up his
challenge. Then, to himself*) Oh, let's give him his return to
grace. I've had enough out of him to satisfy me. And she's got
something on him now that she can din into his ears every day
as long as he lives.

NAUSISTRATA   (*to Demipho, ironically*)   I suppose I deserved this.
Demipho, I don't have to give you a list of all the things I did
for this man.

DEMIPHO   (*hastily*)   I know them as well as you do.

NAUSISTRATA   Do you think I deserved what he did to me?

DEMIPHO   You most certainly did not. But look, what's done can't be
undone by recriminations. Forgive him: he's on his knees, he
confesses, he apologizes. What more do you want?

PHORMIO   (*aside*)   Before she starts issuing pardons, I'd better look out
for Phaedria and myself. (*Aloud*) Nausistrata, before you give
him any hasty answers, listen to me.

NAUSISTRATA   What is it?

PHORMIO   I swindled your husband out of fifteen thousand. I gave the
money to your son. He gave it to a slave dealer for his mistress.

CHREMES (*suddenly snapping out of his slough of despond*)   What? What's that you say?

NAUSISTRATA (*rounding on him*)   And what seems so terrible to you about that? If you can have two wives, a youngster like Phaedria can certainly have one mistress. You have absolutely no sense of shame. How do you think *you'd* look scolding *him?* Come on, answer me!

DEMIPHO (*soothingly*)   He'll do just as you want.

NAUSISTRATA   I'll tell you what I'm going to do. I'm not giving any pardons or making any promises or answering any questions until I've seen my son. I'll let him decide everything. I'll do whatever he says.

PHORMIO   You're a sensible woman, Nausistrata.

NAUSISTRATA (*to Chremes*)   Are you satisfied?

CHREMES (*hastily*)   Yes! Oh, yes! I never thought I'd get off so easy.

NAUSISTRATA (*to Phormio, taking him affectionately by the arm*)   Tell me, what's your name?

PHORMIO   Mine? Phormio. And, on my honor, ma'am, a friend of your whole family and the best friend of your son, Phaedria.

NAUSISTRATA   Phormio? Well, on my honor, sir, from now on if there's anything you want me to do or say for you, I'll be very glad to help out, as much as I can.

PHORMIO   That's very kind of you.

NAUSISTRATA (*glaring over her shoulder at her husband*)   Lord knows you deserve it.

PHORMIO   Nausistrata, do you want to start off by doing something right today that will make me very happy—and eat your husband's heart out?

NAUSISTRATA   I'd love to.

PHORMIO   Invite me to dinner.

NAUSISTRATA   You're invited.

PHORMIO   Let's go inside.

NAUSISTRATA   Let's. (*She takes his arm again and the two start to walk toward the house. Suddenly she stops.*) But where's Phaedria, our chief justice? .

PHORMIO   I'll have him here in a minute.

(*A supernumerary steps forward to the front of the stage.*)

SUPERNUMERARY   The play is over. May we please have your applause.

The Brothers

/

DRAMATIS PERSONAE

Micio, an elderly, well-to-do Athenian

Demea, Micio's brother; an elderly hardworking farmer, father of
  Aeschinus and Ctesipho

Sannio, a slave dealer

Aeschinus, a young man-about-town, adopted son of Micio

Syrus, his servant (slave)

Ctesipho, a young farmer, son of Demea and brother of Aeschinus

Sostrata, a poor but respectable widow, mother of a grown daughter,
  Pamphila, who is Aeschinus' sweetheart

Canthara, Pamphila's old nurse (slave) who has stayed on with the
  family

Geta, Sostrata's servant (slave)

Hegio, a poor but respectable elderly Athenian, an old family friend of
  Sostrata's

Dromo, a slave boy

[Pamphila, daughter of Sostrata]

SCENE   A street in Athens. Two houses, Micio's and Sostrata's, front
on it. The exit on stage left leads downtown, that on stage right to the
country where Demea's farm is.

371

PROLOGUE

(The prologue addresses the audience. For his function in Terence's plays, see p. 314.)

PROLOGUE Since the author is aware that his writings were being re-
viewed by unfair critics and that his enemies were running
down this play which we are about to present, he takes the stand
in his own behalf; and you are to judge whether what he has
done is a vice or a virtue.

Diphilus wrote a comedy, the *Synapothnescontes* [They Faced
Death Together]; Plautus turned it into his play the *Com-
morientes*. In the original Greek version, in the beginning of the
play, a young man steals a courtesan from the slave dealer who
owns her. Plautus left out this whole scene; your author availed
himself of it and, translating it word for word, incorporated it
into his *Adelphi*. This is the new piece we are about to present.
Examine it to see whether you think he has played the plagiarist
or whether he simply has salvaged a scene that another had
neglected and passed over.

Next, his detractors allege that certain eminent personages aid
him and are constantly at his side as he writes. They think this
is something to censure strongly; he considers it something to
praise highly. It is the mark of the favor of those who were
favored by every one of you and by all our people, men whose
services in war and peace and in public affairs on appropriate
occasions each one of you has availed yourself of, without reserve.

Don't look to me for the details of the plot. The old men who
come on stage in the beginning will describe some of it, and
reveal some of it through their actions. Let your good will encourage your author to go on with his writing.

ACT I

*(Micio comes out of the door of his house. He is a man just past the
prime of life. His immaculate tailoring and grooming, his whole air,
betoken someone accustomed to a comfortable and gracious way of life.*

Normally, he is urbanely genial in manner, more disposed to smile than to frown, to indulge in lighthearted banter than in serious talk. At this moment, however, he is obviously worried.)

MICIO *(through the door to some servant inside)* Storax! *(When no answer is forthcoming, he walks downstage and addresses the audience.)* Aeschinus didn't come home from his dinner party last night. Neither did any of the servants who went to get him. People say that if you stay out all night or come home late, you're better off if you've been doing what an angry wife imagines than what fond parents do. It's absolutely true. If you stay out late your wife imagines you're after some woman or some woman is after you, or that you're drinking and doing everything you want, having a good time while she's alone and miserable. But the thoughts that have been going through my head, the worries I've had because my son didn't come back! Maybe he caught pneumonia? Maybe he fell down somewhere and broke a leg? Bah! To think that anyone would plant in his heart or let grow there something dearer to him than his own self! And he's not even my own child, he's my brother's!

(He lapses for a moment into silence. Then, more calmly) Our ways of living have been different ever since we were boys. *(With a gesture at the rather elegant house he has come out of)* I took up this easygoing, leisurely life in the city and—some people regard this as a piece of luck—I never got married. He's just my opposite in everything: has his home in the country, got married, had two sons. I adopted the older. I've raised him from an infant; I've made him my own and loved him as my own. He's the apple of my eye; there's nothing I care for more. And I do everything I can to make him feel the same toward me. I'm lenient and indulgent; I don't insist that he has to do everything my way. On top of it all, while other boys hide their mischief from their fathers, I've trained my son to be open with me. Why? Because the boy who will dare to deceive or lie to a parent will certainly do the same to others. I'm convinced that a sense of shame and decency will do more to keep children in line than fear. My brother doesn't agree. He doesn't like my method. He's always coming to me to complain: *(mimicking his brother's tones)* "Micio! Why must you ruin that boy for us?

Look at the way he runs after women! Look at the way he drinks! Why do you give him money for such things? Why do you let him spend so much on clothes? The trouble with you is, you're too soft." But the trouble with him is, he's too strict; he goes beyond what's fair or good. And I believe he's all wrong in thinking that authority will last longer and work better based on force rather than affection. Here's how I see it, and I'm convinced I'm right: a man who does what he should because he's afraid of being punished will behave only when he's watched; as soon as he thinks he can get away with something, he reverts to character. But if you attach someone to yourself through kindness and understanding, he acts from the heart; he's anxious to reciprocate whether you're standing over him or not. A father's job is simply to train his boy to behave of his own free will and not because he's afraid of what someone may do to him. This is the difference between handling sons and slaves. And if you can't do it, then admit you don't know how to handle children.

(*He falls silent, and then happens to look toward stage right and notices someone coming.*) Isn't this the man I was talking about? (*As the person comes nearer*) None other. And he looks as if he's got something on his mind. I'm probably going to get my usual lecture. (*To Demea, who has now come up to him*) Hello, Demea! Glad to see you!

(*Demea is Micio's antithesis—a sour-visaged farmer in worn work clothes.*)

DEMEA (*with no acknowledgment of his brother's cheerful greeting, getting right to the point*) Just the man I want to see. I've been looking for you.

MICIO (*amiably*) What's on your mind?

DEMEA With someone like Aeschinus in the family do you have to ask what's on my mind?

MICIO (*to the world at large*) Didn't I say this would happen? (*To Demea*) What's he done?

DEMEA What's he done? A boy who's not ashamed of anything, not afraid of anybody, and thinks he's above the law? Forget what he's done before; this time he's gone too far!

MICIO (*worried, in spite of himself, at Demea's tone*) What in the world did he do?

DEMEA Smashed in a front door and broke into somebody's house; practically beat the owner and everyone in the household to death; and carried off a girl he's having an affair with. Everybody says it was an absolute outrage. I can't tell you, Micio, how many people stopped me on my way here to tell me about it. The whole town's talking! All right, if we must make comparisons, why doesn't he take after his brother? There's someone who keeps his mind on his business, a hard-working serious country boy. *He's* never done anything like that. (*As Micio turns away*) And I want you to hear about it as well as him, Micio. You're the one who's letting him be ruined.

MICIO (*with a knowing smile, a bit on the supercilious side*) When it comes to being unfair, you can't beat a provincial. He's convinced he's the only one who's ever done anything right.

DEMEA (*grimly*) And just what do you mean by that?

MICIO Simply that your judgment in these matters is poor. (*Earnestly*) Believe me, Demea, it's no crime for a young fellow to chase after women or get drunk. (*As Demea turns away in exasperation*) I tell you, it isn't. No, not even smashing in front doors. The only reason you and I didn't carry on like that was because we were too poor. Don't take credit now for what you didn't do then only because you didn't have the money. Be honest; admit that if we had had the same opportunities we'd have done the same things. And if you were only human, you'd let that boy of yours have his fling right now while he's the age for it. Your way, he'll have it at a time of life when he shouldn't, after he's waited for you to die off and he's hustled you into your grave.

DEMEA God almighty, you and your being human will drive me mad! What do you mean, it's not a crime for a youngster to carry on like that?

MICIO Now, listen to me once and for all so that you'll stop beating my brains out about all this. You gave me your son to adopt. He's mine now. Whatever mistakes he makes, Demea, are my responsibility, I'm the one who's most involved. He gives parties, gets drunk, dresses like a fop—I pay for it. He keeps a mistress—I'll give him the money so long as it suits me, and, when it doesn't, why, she'll probably kick him out. He smashed in somebody's front door—I'll have it repaired. He tore somebody's clothes—I'll have them mended. I've got the wherewithal, thank

god, and so far it hasn't been a drain. But here's my last word:
either shut up or pick any judge you like so that I can prove
that you're more at fault than I.

DEMEA *(impatiently)* Rubbish! Why don't you learn to act like a
father from people who really know how?

MICIO *(still maintaining his calm)* You may be his actual father, but
spiritually I am.

DEMEA *(sarcastically)* And just what have you done for him spiritually?

MICIO *(beginning to lose his calm)* If you're going to go on like that,
I'm leaving.

DEMEA *(realizing he's gone a bit too far, and softening his tone)* Come
now, that's no attitude to take.

MICIO   Well, how many times must I listen to the same old story?

DEMEA   I *care* about the boy.

MICIO   I do too. But Demea, let's divide up this care business. You
care for your boy, and I'll care for mine. Because, if you're going
to do the caring for both, that just about amounts to asking for
the boy back.

DEMEA   Micio! Come now!

MICIO *(somewhat mollified by Demea's tone)* Well, that's the way it
looks to me.

DEMEA   All right. If that's the way you want it, he can go to the dogs
or the devil and it won't make a damned bit of difference to
me. *(Warming up to the subject once again)* If I utter a single
syllable from now on—

MICIO   You're getting all worked up again, Demea!

DEMEA   You don't believe me, do you? I'm not asking for him back,
am I? But he *is* on my mind; after all, I'm not a stranger. If I
stand in his way—*(as Micio determinedly turns away)* all right,
I'll stop. You want me to take care of just one? Very well, I will.
Thank god he's a boy after my own heart. And that son of
yours will learn for himself later on that—no, I don't want to
be too hard on him. *(Shaking his head bitterly, Demea leaves,
stage right.)*

MICIO *(to the audience)* What he says isn't the whole story, but at
the same time it's something to think about. This business
bothers me—but I didn't want to let him see it. Let me tell you
the sort of person he is: even when I try to keep him calm, when

I use kid gloves in crossing him or talking him out of something,
he still can't take it like a human being; with that temper of
his, if I were to encourage him, or even just go along with him,
I'd end up as mad as he is, no question about it. (*Falls silent
for a moment.*) But Aeschinus hasn't done us any good in all
this. I can't name a call girl in town he hasn't chased after. Or
spent money on. But just the other day—I suppose he was tired
of them all—he told me he wanted to get married. I was glad
to hear it; I was hoping he was settling down. Now, lo and
behold, he's at it again. Well, whatever it is, I want to see him
and find out about it. I'll see if he's downtown. (*Exits, stage
left.*)

ACT II

(*Amid the sounds of a heated argument, four people enter, stage left.
In the lead is Aeschinus, grasping tightly a rather handsome, brassy,
heavily made-up girl, who is obviously scared out of her wits. On her
other side is Aeschinus' servant, Parmeno. And, chasing after the three,
is the slave dealer, Sannio.*

*Aeschinus is in his late teens, good looking, and dressed expensively
and fashionably, although perhaps a little on the flashy side. There's a
devil-may-careness about him that, under proper circumstances, could
be attractive, but at the moment has unfortunately degenerated, as it
so easily can, into irresponsibility and arrogance.*

*Sannio is a businessman. His business, a perfectly legitimate one, is
the providing of courtesans as entertainers. He owns a troupe of slave
girls whom he either rents out or sells when he can find someone willing
to pay the price. Since the girls were hand-picked to start with and had
to be given a long and careful training, they represent a considerable
investment. And it is clear that the girl Aeschinus has under his arm
is one of these extremely valuable pieces of property.*

*Sannio shows the signs of some rough treatment. He's not only angry,
but bewildered: Aeschinus, who to him was merely another young man
about town and potential customer, had just a few moments earlier
broken into his house and carried off one of his girls. As it turns out,
Aeschinus knew a great deal about Sannio; he had heard all about him
from his brother.*)

SANNIO (*at the top of his lungs*)   Help! I'm being robbed! Help, somebody, help!

AESCHINUS (*with elaborate calm, to the girl as they come abreast of
Micio's door*)   Just stand right here and take it easy. What do
you keep looking back at him for? Don't worry; he's not going
to touch you while I'm around.

SANNIO   I won't, eh? You just try and stop me, all of you.

AESCHINUS (*to the girl*)   Even a crook like that isn't going to risk another beating today.

SANNIO   Listen, Aeschinus, you're not going to get away with saying
you didn't know the kind of man I was. I'm a dealer in courtesans—

AESCHINUS (*ironically*)   I know.

SANNIO (*disregarding the comment*)   —as respectable a businessman
as you'll find anywhere. I know what you're going to do afterwards to get out of this: you're going to say you're sorry, you
didn't mean to do me any harm. Well, that doesn't cut any
ice with me. I'm going to court and get my rights, and I mean
it. You're not going to pay with a couple of words for all the
harm you've done me. I'm wise to your kind and their (*mimicking the man-about-town's accents*) "Terribly sorry! I'll take my
oath you absolutely didn't deserve such treatment." I didn't deserve it but I got it.

AESCHINUS (*deliberately disregarding him, to Parmeno*)   Run ahead
and open the door. Quick!

SANNIO   Hey! Didn't you hear what I said?

AESCHINUS (*still disregarding him, to the girl*)   Inside with you now.

SANNIO   Not if I can help it! (*He plants himself in front of the door
and grabs the girl's arm.*)

AESCHINUS (*blandly*)   Parmeno! Come over here. (*Points to a spot
right alongside Sannio.*) No, you're too far away. Here, right
alongside him. That's the spot. Now keep your eyes on mine
and don't take them off. I don't want even a split second lost
between the time I give you the signal and you connect with
the point of his jaw.

SANNIO   Just let him try.

AESCHINUS (*to Parmeno*)   Ready! (*Parmeno lets go a haymaker.*) Now
will you let go of her?

SANNIO (*nursing his jaw*)   Of all the lowdown criminal—

AESCHINUS You'll get a second dose if you don't watch out. (*Parmeno, in his zeal, takes this for an order and lets go another.*)

SANNIO Ow!

AESCHINUS (*to Parmeno*) I didn't give the signal, but it's all right; if you must make mistakes, that's the kind to make. (*To the girl*) Now, inside!

SANNIO (*infuriated, but helpless*) What's going on here? What do you think you are? A king or something?

AESCHINUS (*contemptuously*) If I were, I'd decorate you the way you deserve.

SANNIO What have you got against me, anyway?

AESCHINUS (*blandly*) Nothing.

SANNIO Do you know who I am?

AESCHINUS I don't want to.

SANNIO What did I ever take of yours?

AESCHINUS Nothing. If you had, you'd have been sorry for it.

SANNIO Just what do you figure gives you the right to take my property, something I paid good money for?

AESCHINUS Now, I don't want to have an argument out here in public. So if you're going to keep on being a nuisance, I'll have you hauled inside and beaten to within an inch of your life.

SANNIO What do you think I am? One of your slaves?

AESCHINUS You heard me.

SANNIO Of all the barefaced—and they call this a free country!

AESCHINUS Listen, pimp, do you want to go on with this raving nonsense, or are you ready to listen to me?

SANNIO Me? You're the one that's raving!

AESCHINUS Now, cut that out and let's get back to business.

SANNIO Get *back*? Business? What business?

AESCHINUS I've got something to tell you. Do you want to hear it?

SANNIO Sure. But it's got to be fair and square.

AESCHINUS (*sneering*) Pah! A pimp wants to be treated fair and square!

SANNIO (*bitterly*) All right, so I'm a pimp; (*mimicking the tones of a self-righteous citizen*) a liar, a plague on the community, a prime cause of juvenile delinquency. (*Abruptly looking Aeschinus in the eye*) But I never did you any harm!

AESCHINUS That doesn't mean you wouldn't, by god.

SANNIO (*clutching at the straw Aeschinus seemed to be offering a second ago*) Let's get back to what you were going to tell me, Aeschinus.

AESCHINUS   You paid ten thousand dollars for her, damn your hide.
I'll pay you what she cost you.

SANNIO   Suppose I don't want to sell. Are you going to make me?

AESCHINUS *(guilelessly)*   Nothing was further from my mind.

SANNIO *(relieved)*   I was afraid you would.

AESCHINUS *(maintaining his guileless air, without batting an eye)*   You
see, in my opinion, a free woman can't be bought or sold. *(Dropping the guileless air suddenly and resuming his former hard-
bitten tone)* And I'm ready to go to court to prove she's a free
woman. It's up to you: either take the money or hire yourself
a lawyer. Think it over, pimp, until I get back. *(Beckons to
Parmeno and takes the girl's hand. The three go into the house,
leaving Sannio alone on the stage.)*

SANNIO *(to himself, as he wipes off the blood on his face and straightens
out his clothes)*   God in heaven! No wonder people see red
when they get a raw deal. Here I've been hauled out of my
own house, pushed around, beaten to a pulp, had one of my girls
stolen—and in return for all this I'm to give up my profit and
practically make a present of her to him. *(With ponderous
sarcasm)* After all he's done for me, I'm glad to do it; he's only
asking for what he's entitled to. *(Heaving a sigh)* Just let him
pay me the money; that's all I ask. But I don't have to be a
fortune-teller to know what's going to happen. The minute I
tell him he can have her even at his price, he'll have a witness
on the spot to testify I was ready to sell—and there goes any
chance of suing him for stealing her. And expect any money out
of him? I must be dreaming! *(Mimicking Aeschinus' tones)*
"Very soon now—come back tomorrow." The whole thing's a
swindle, but I'd still put up with it if I could only get my money
back. *(Another sigh)* Let's face it: in my line of business you've
simply got to put up with being kicked around by these kids
and to keep your mouth shut. What am I kidding myself for?
I'm not going to get any money.

*(While Sannio is delivering his monologue, the door of Micio's house
opens and Syrus, Aeschinus' servant, steps out. In Greek New Comedy,
the young hero's servant must be, above all else, a quick and resourceful thinker, able to come up in a flash with some slick scheme for
settling a slower-witted master's predicaments. Syrus is a paragon of
this virtue.)*

SYRUS (*through the door to Aeschinus, inside*) Leave it to me. I'll handle him. I'll not only make him grab at your offer, but convince him he's getting a good deal. (*Walks downstage to Sannio, who is standing around moodily staring at the ground, and addresses him with an air of breezy friendship.*) Sannio, what's all this I hear about you and Aeschinus having a fight over something or other?

SANNIO We certainly did, just now. And I never was in one that was more one-sided in my life. We were both practically exhausted —he from handing it out and I from taking it.

SYRUS (*shaking his head with friendly consideration*) You brought it on yourself.

SANNIO (*looking up puzzled*) What could I do?

SYRUS (*blandly*) You should have humored the boy.

SANNIO I just about put my jaw on his fist. What more could I do?

SYRUS (*confidingly*) Listen. You know what I think? That sometimes knowing when not to take money is the best way to make it. Hah, hah, hah! Were you scared that, if you gave in even an inch to the boy and didn't stand on your rights, you wouldn't make any money on the deal? I never heard of anything so silly!

SANNIO (*sourly*) I don't pay spot cash for promises.

SYRUS You'll never make any real money, Sannio. Look, you don't know how to bait the hook for a customer.

SANNIO I admit it; your way is better. But I never was that smart. I always preferred to take whatever profits I could when I could.

SYRUS (*putting a friendly arm over Sannio's shoulder*) Look, I know the kind of fellow you are. As if you'd let ten thousand dollars keep you from doing the boy a good turn! (*Notes with satisfaction Sannio's jaw drop and then continues with studied casualness.*) Incidentally, they tell me that you're leaving for Cyprus—

SANNIO (*taken completely unawares*) Hah?

SYRUS (*going on with the same casualness*) —and that you've bought up a load of merchandise to ship there and that you've already chartered your vessel. (*Solicitously*) I understand; this is why it's hard for you to make up your mind what to do. Well, I just hope you'll finish up this business when you get back from there.

SANNIO I'm not budging an inch from this spot! (*Aside*) I'm sunk! So *that's* what they had in mind when they started all this!

SYRUS (*aside*) He's scared; I got under his skin there.

SANNIO (*aside*) Of all the dirty tricks! He's got me. What timing! Here I've got a cargo of girls bought and paid for and a lot of other goods to take to Cyprus, and unless I get there in time for the fair I stand to lose a fortune. If I drop this business now and take it up when I get back, I don't stand a chance; the thing's ancient history. (*Imitating the posture and tones of a judge*) "Now you come before me? Why did you put up with it so long? Where have you been all this time?" Sooner than hang around here or try to collect in court after I come back, I'll swallow the loss.

SYRUS (*who has been keeping his eye on Sannio every second*) Well, have you figured out how much you stand to make in Cyprus?

SANNIO (*baffled and beginning to weaken*) Is this the way for a gentleman like Aeschinus to behave? What a thing to do! Trying to take a girl away from me by brute force!

SYRUS (*aside*) I've got him on the run. (*To Sannio*) Here's the only thing I can offer; see if you like it. Sannio, rather than try to get all your money and run the risk of losing it all, cut the price in half. He can scrape up five thousand somewhere.

SANNIO (*exploding*) What's a poor devil like me to do? Now I've even got to worry about getting back what she cost me! Hasn't he got any feelings? He knocks every tooth in my mouth loose, clobbers me until my head's swollen the size of a pumpkin, and on top of it all wants to cheat me. I'm not budging from here!

SYRUS (*shrugging*) If that's the way you want it . . . I'm going now; anything more I can do for you?

SANNIO (*getting panicky as Syrus turns to leave*) God, yes! Look, Syrus, do me a favor. Let bygones be bygones. Rather than go to court, I'll sell him the girl. Just let him pay me what she cost me, Syrus. I know you haven't had any dealings with me before but, believe me, I won't forget it and you won't regret it. (*Slips an obviously well-filled purse in Syrus' hands.*)

SYRUS I'll do my best. (*Starts into the house but stops when someone comes in, stage left. To himself*) Look who's here— Ctesipho, happy as a lark about his new mistress.

SANNIO (*anxiously*) How about it?

SYRUS Wait a minute.

(Ctesipho, Aeschinus' brother, enters. He's near his brother in age and physique, but there all resemblance ends. For one thing, he clearly has been brought up not to waste any time on his general appearance: his clothes are not only plain but threadbare. More important, in place of the swagger and spirit that so mark his brother, he has a timid, furtive manner. Obviously Demea has done his work well: his boy is well broken in.)

CTESIPHO *(not noticing Syrus and Sannio, to himself)*   When you need a favor it's nice to get it, no matter who does it for you. But what a pleasure it is when the one who does it is just the person it should be. Aeschinus! My brother! I can't sing your praises loud enough. One thing I know for sure: no matter what superlatives I try to use, they still won't be enough to describe you. I'm convinced I have one advantage over everybody else: nobody else has a brother who, when it comes to the things that give a man class, is in a class by himself!

SYRUS   Ctesipho!

CTESIPHO *(with a frightened start at the sound of his name)*   Oh, Syrus. Where's Aeschinus?

SYRUS   Inside. He's waiting for you.

CTESIPHO   Oh, boy!

SYRUS   What's up?

CTESIPHO   You have to ask? Syrus, there's life in my veins today and it's all his doing. What a guy! What he could do for me he put first; everything else came second. The curses, the bad name, the trouble, the blame—it should have been mine but he took it all on himself. He couldn't have done more! *(The door of Micio's house starts to open. Ctesipho's ebullience suddenly departs, and he turns to Syrus, all worry.)* Who's that?

SYRUS   Stay where you are; Aeschinus is coming out.

AESCHINUS *(coming out of the door and not at first noticing Ctesipho)*   Where's that cheap crook?

SANNIO *(aside)*   He wants me. *(Looking closely to see whether Aeschinus has a purse.)* Isn't he carrying anything? Not a thing! That's the end of me!

AESCHINUS *(suddenly noticing his brother)*   Just the man I was looking for. *(Ctesipho, not yet recovered from his scare, is slow in greet-*

ing him.) What's the matter, Ctesipho? Everything's fine. Come
on, cheer up!

CTESIPHO   God knows, I really should cheer up with a brother like
you. Aeschinus, you're a real brother—aw, I'm afraid to go on
praising you to your face. You'll think I'm doing it to flatter you
instead of to show you how grateful I am.

AESCHINUS (*putting his arm over his brother's shoulders*) Come now,
enough of that nonsense. As if you and I don't know each other,
Ctesipho! I'm only sorry I heard about it so late and things almost
got to the point where nobody could have helped you even if
they wanted to.

CTESIPHO (*hanging his head and mumbling*) I was ashamed.

AESCHINUS   Stupid, you mean, not ashamed. Almost ready to skip town
for practically no reason at all! I won't even discuss it. God forbid
you should do anything like that!

CTESIPHO (*still mumbling, shamefaced*) I made a mistake.

AESCHINUS (*suddenly catches sight of Sannio. Turning to Syrus*)
Well, what's Sannio got to say to us?

SYRUS (*sotto voice, with satisfaction*) He's softened up now.

AESCHINUS (*to Ctesipho*) I'm going downtown to pay this one (*with
a contemptuous nod in the direction of Sannio*) off. You go on
inside, Ctesipho; she's waiting.

SANNIO (*surreptitiously plucking at Syrus' sleeve, sotto voce*) Syrus!
Come on now!

SYRUS (*pushing him away, to Aeschinus*) Let's go. (*Maliciously*)
This fellow's in a hurry to get to Cyprus.

SANNIO   Not as soon as you'd like. I've got time; I'm staying around a
while.

SYRUS   Stop worrying. You'll get your money.

SANNIO   But all of it!

SYRUS   Yes, all of it. Just shut up and follow me.

SANNIO   I'm right behind you. (*He follows as Aeschinus and Syrus
start to walk off.*)

CTESIPHO (*suddenly turning before he goes into the house, all worry
again*) Hey, Syrus!

SYRUS (*turning and walking back to Ctesipho*) What?

CTESIPHO   For god's take, do me a favor and pay this slimy creature
off as soon as you can. If he gets any more riled up, this whole
business may get to my father somehow and then I'm sunk.

SYRUS Buck up! It won't. Now, you go in and enjoy yourself with your girl friend while we're away. And have them set the table and get everything ready. As soon as we finish our transaction downtown, I'll do some marketing and come on home.

CTESIPHO Fine. Since everything's gone off so well, let's have an all-day party.

(Ctesipho enters Micio's house; Syrus with Sannio at his heels hurries after Aeschinus, stage left; and the stage is now empty.)

ACT III

(Two old women, Sostrata and Canthara, emerge from the door of the modest house next to Micio's. Sostrata is a respectable Athenian matron who had had the bad luck to lose her husband soon after marriage and has had to scrape and save to keep going ever since. Of the two servants—all she can afford—one is Canthara who was her nurse when she was a child; although rather on the decrepit side physically, Canthara hasn't lost any of her native good sense. The other is their man-of-all-work, Geta, a stolid and serious and dependable young fellow, passionately loyal to the family. The most important member of the little household is Sostrata's lovely daughter, Pamphila—and she at the moment is providing no joy but only grave concern, for she is on the verge of giving birth to an illegitimate child.)

SOSTRATA *(revealing, in the nervous twisting of her hands and similar actions, a state of extreme agitation)* Canthara, what's going to happen to her now?

CANTHARA What's the use of asking? God knows, I hope everything turns out all right. *(A cry of pain is heard from Pamphila inside, and Sostrata starts visibly.)* My dear, the pains are just beginning now. What are you so worried about? You act as if you never saw a child born or never had one yourself!

SOSTRATA *(wringing her hands)* Dear me, dear me, we're so alone; there's not a soul to help us. And Geta's not here and there's nobody to send for a midwife or to go call Aeschinus.

CANTHARA Oh, he'll be here any minute. You know he never lets a day go by without coming.

SOSTRATA   He's our only salvation in these troubles.

CANTHARA   (*consolingly*)   As it worked out, her getting seduced was the best thing that could have happened. I mean because it was by him and not anybody else. Such a fine boy, from such a good family—and that household he lives in! (*Shakes her head admiringly.*)

SOSTRATA   You're absolutely right. For our sake I pray heaven nothing happens to him. (*At this moment, Sostrata's man-of-all-work, Geta, bursts in, stage left. He's out of breath from running and tremendously upset.*)

GETA   (*to himself, barely able to gasp out the words*)   This is it. Even if everybody around lent a hand and tried every idea they could come up with, they couldn't help. Not with the trouble that faces me and my lady and her daughter now. Oh, my god, what a siege! We'll never get out from under! So many things and so sudden—violence, poverty, injustice, no friends, scandal. What a world! What crimes! What criminals! What a godforsaken scoundrel!

SOSTRATA   (*turning at the sound of Geta's voice to Canthara*)   Oh, dear, look at Geta! What's he running for? Why is he so scared?

GETA   (*to himself*)   His sense of trust, his sworn word, his feelings as a human being—nothing stood in his way. Not even that she was going to have a baby any minute—a poor innocent girl he took advantage of and seduced.

SOSTRATA   (*wildly*)   What's he saying? I don't understand.

CANTHARA   Let's go to him, Sostrata.

GETA   (*to himself, not noticing the women*)   My god, I'm so mad I'll go out of my mind! There's nothing I'd like better than to have that whole household meet me right now so I can give them a piece of my mind before I have time to cool off. Just give *me* the chance to even things up, that's all the punishment I ask from them. First I'd throttle that old man who begat this horror. Next that Syrus who put him up to it—gad, I'd tear him apart. First I'd grab him by the midriff, lift him good and high, and then bounce him on the ground head first and splash his brains on the sidewalk. And that Aeschinus—I'd gouge his eyes out and then heave him over a cliff. (*As he works himself up, he starts racing up and down, energetically clobbering imaginary victims.*) And the rest—I'd knock 'em and sock 'em, I'd wham 'em and slam 'em—(*Suddenly comes to an abrupt stop and stands stock-*

still.) What am I wasting time for? I've got to tell Sostrata, and quickly. (*Whirls about and makes for the door.*)

SOSTRATA (*to Canthara*) Let's call him back. Geta! (*She grabs him by his tunic.*)

GETA (*without turning around*) What is it? Let go of me, whoever you are!

SOSTRATA It's Sostrata!

GETA (*looking around in every direction but the right one*) Sostrata? Where? (*Finally seeing her*) I've been looking for you. You're just the person I want. You met me right at the right time. Sostrata—

SOSTRATA What's the matter? What are you trembling for?

GETA (*groaning*) Oh!

SOSTRATA Geta! Why have you been running? Catch your breath.

GETA It's all—

SOSTRATA "All" what?

GETA All over. We're done for.

SOSTRATA Please, please, tell me what this is all about.

GETA From now on—

SOSTRATA "From now on" what, Geta?

GETA Aeschinus—

SOSTRATA What about him?

GETA (*disregarding the interruption*) —is no friend of ours.

SOSTRATA What? Oh, no! Why?

GETA He's taken up with another woman.

SOSTRATA Heaven help me!

GETA (*bitterly*) And he's making no secret of it. He carried her off himself from her owner, right in public.

SOSTRATA Are you absolutely sure of this?

GETA Absolutely. I saw it with my own eyes, Sostrata.

SOSTRATA Oh, what's to become of me! Isn't there anything you can believe in these days, anybody you can trust? Our Aeschinus, our whole life, the man we pinned all our hopes on, depended on utterly! The man who swore he wouldn't live a day without her, who kept saying he was going to place the baby right in his father's arms and win him over that way into accepting Pamphila as a daughter-in-law!

GETA Sostrata, stop crying. It's more important to plan what we have to do about this. Should we just put up with it or should we tell somebody?

CANTHARA   Man dear, are you in your right mind? You really think
we ought to let this get out?

GETA   Personally, I don't like the idea. First of all, the facts show that
from now on he's no friend of ours. If we start talking about it,
he's going to deny everything, I'm sure of it. And that won't
do your reputation any good; it could even affect your daughter's
life. And even if he doesn't deny a thing, since he's taken up
with this other girl, it wouldn't help matters to let Pamphila
marry him. So, any way we look at it, I think we have to keep
our mouths shut.

SOSTRATA   (*hysterically*)   No! Not for the world! I won't do it!

GETA   What will you do?

SOSTRATA   I'm going to let the truth be known!

CANTHARA   Ah, Sostrata, my dear, think what you're doing!

SOSTRATA   (*now in control of herself, calmly*)   Things can't get any
worse than they are now. First of all, she never had a dowry.
On top of that, she's now lost her only substitute for one—she
can never be a virgin bride. But I have one last resort: if he's
going to deny what happened, I've got a ring he left behind
as evidence. So, since my conscience is completely clear in this
affair—no money was involved nor anything else that she or I
could be ashamed of—, Geta, I'm going to court!

GETA   All right, I'm convinced. You're right.

SOSTRATA   Now, you go as fast as you can and tell our Cousin Hegio
everything that's happened. After all, he was my husband's best
friend and he's very fond of us.

GETA   And, after all, god knows nobody else cares about us.

SOSTRATA   And Canthara, you hurry and call a midwife. I don't want
any delay when she's needed.

(*Sostrata enters her house, and Canthara and Geta leave, stage left.
A second later, Demea enters, stage right. He is greatly agitated.*)

DEMEA   (*to the audience*)   I'm ruined! I've just heard that Ctesipho
was in on that kidnaping with Aeschinus! After all the troubles
I've been through, this had to happen—to find out that that
Aeschinus was able to corrupt my son, a boy who still had some
good in him. I've got to find him—but where? If you ask me,
he's been lured to some low dive. That godforsaken Aeschinus
talked him into it, I'm sure of it. (*Looks up and notices Syrus*

coming in, stage left.) But here's Syrus. I'll find out from him where he is. Damn it all, though, he's one of their gang. If he gets the idea that I'm after my boy, the stinker won't tell me a thing. I just won't let him know that's what I'm after.

(*Syrus enters, stage left. He's returning from downtown and, as he had promised, he's done the marketing for the "all-day" party: two of the household's kitchen slaves are at his heels, loaded down with provisions. He catches sight of Demea and immediately launches into a monologue intended specifically and solely for that gentleman's ears.*)

SYRUS   Well, we told Micio the whole story. He was tickled pink.

DEMEA (*taking the bait, aside*)   Oh, my god! How stupid can a man be!

SYRUS (*continuing his monologue*)   He congratulated his son and then he thanked me for having given the boy the idea.

DEMEA (*aside*)   I'll burst a blood vessel!

SYRUS (*as before*)   He paid out the money on the spot and, on top of that, handed me two hundred and fifty dollars for our party. And I've already spent it, just the way *I* wanted.

DEMEA (*aside, caustically*)   Got a job you want well done? Here's just the man for it.

SYRUS (*deciding that this is the moment to acknowledge Demea's presence*)   Well, Demea! What a surprise to find you here! How are things?

DEMEA (*with a sour glance at Syrus' ostentatiously extravagant purchases*)   How are things? I can never cease marveling at the way you people do things around here.

SYRUS (*sighing, with a practiced deprecatory air*)   Lord knows it's one of our weaknesses. To be absolutely frank with you, it's downright silly. (*Whips around and, in tones that would do credit to a marine sergeant, addresses one of the slaves behind him, one eye at the same time cocked on Demea to note the effect.*) Dromo! I want the rest of the fish cleaned but keep that prize eel alive in water for a while. When I come inside I'll have it fileted. Not before, mind you.

DEMEA (*shaking his head and muttering to himself*)   Sinful. That's what it is, sinful.

SYRUS (*blandly*)   You're absolutely right. I'm always complaining about it. (*Addressing the other slave, again in his marine ser-*

geant's tones and again with an eye cocked on Demea) Stephanio! I want this salt fish made nice and tender.

DEMEA (*throwing his arms up in despair*)   God almighty, what does that brother of mine do it for? Does he find pleasure in ruining a child? Or does he think it's something to be proud of? This is terrible! If you ask me, the day's not too far off when that boy won't have a cent to his name and will run away and join a foreign legion somewhere.

SYRUS (*nodding his head vigorously in earnest agreement*)   Demea, that's what I call real brains—not seeing just what's in front of your nose, but looking ahead to the future.

DEMEA (*with a transparent attempt at being casual*)   Say, Syrus, is that chorus girl in your house now?

SYRUS   Right inside.

DEMEA   You think he's going to keep her there?

SYRUS   I'm afraid so. (*Confidentially*) He's out of his mind!

DEMEA (*shaking his head in doleful disapproval*)   What a way to act!

SYRUS (*shaking his head in doleful disapproval*)   It's because that father of his indulges him and gives in to him. It's stupid. It's immoral!

DEMEA   I'm ashamed of my brother. I'm disgusted with him.

SYRUS   Demea, there's such a difference, such a world of difference between you two. And I'm not saying this just because you're right here in front of me. You're a man of sense, from the top of your head to the tips of your toes. He's a dreamer. Now, would you ever have let that boy of yours do such a thing?

DEMEA   Let him! I'd have smelled it a mile away before he ever started anything like that!

SYRUS (*with feeling*)   You're telling *me* how you keep an eye on things?

DEMEA   All I ask is that my boy stay just as he is.

SYRUS (*sagely*)   As the twig is bent, you know.

DEMEA (*again with a transparent air of being casual*)   Speaking of Ctesipho, have you seen him today?

SYRUS   Your son? (*Aside*) I'll send this fellow packing back to his farm. (*To Demea*) He's probably been back working around the farm for some time now.

DEMEA (*suspiciously*)   Are you sure he's there?

SYRUS (*innocently*)   Sure? I saw him off myself.

DEMEA Fine. I was afraid he might be hanging around here.

SYRUS (*shaking his head admiringly, as if remembering something extraordinary he had just seen*) He was really sore.

DEMEA What about?

SYRUS He had it out with his brother about that chorus girl right in the middle of town.

DEMEA You don't say!

SYRUS He let him have it, all right. Just as we happened to be paying out the money, suddenly up comes your son. He pitched right into him: "Aeschinus! To think that you'd stoop to such things! To think that you'd disgrace the family this way!"

DEMEA I'm so happy, I could cry.

SYRUS (*continuing his histrionic rendition of Ctesipho's imaginary words*) "It's not this money you're throwing away. It's your life."

DEMEA God bless him. I've got hopes for him—he's a chip off the old block.

SYRUS Yes, sir!

DEMEA Syrus, that boy is a model of sensible behavior.

SYRUS Well, he's got someone right in his own home to learn from.

DEMEA (*proudly*) I do everything I can. I don't let him get away with a thing. I train him. On top of it all, I make him look into other people's lives, just as if he were looking into a mirror, to find a model for himself. "Do this," I tell him.

SYRUS (*nodding his assent vigorously*) Absolutely right.

DEMEA "Don't do that."

SYRUS (*tapping his brow admiringly*) Clever!

DEMEA "This will do you credit."

SYRUS (*enthusiastically*) That's the stuff!

DEMEA "This will bring you blame."

SYRUS Perfect!

DEMEA And furthermore—

SYRUS (*interrupting, having had all the Demea-isms he can take for the moment*) Oh, lord, I simply don't have the time right now to listen. I managed to buy just the kind of fish I wanted and I've got to watch out that they don't get ruined. We consider being lax in this sort of thing as much of a disgrace as you would in the things you just told me about. I use your system of training with my kitchen crew as much as I can. (*Mimicking*

Demea's tones and gestures) "This is too salty. This is too well done. This isn't clean enough. That's perfect; remember to do it that way next time." I do everything I can to teach them— *(with a deprecatory smirk)* as best I know how. On top of it all, I make them look into their pans, Demea, just as if they were looking into a mirror, and I warn them about what they have to do. I realize that our kind of work doesn't count for much, but what's a man to do? You've got to deal with people as you find them. *(Opening the door to go inside)* Well, anything I can do for you before I go?

DEMEA *(finally catching on, disgustedly)*   Yes! Get some sense in your heads, all of you!

SYRUS   Are you going back to the farm?

DEMEA   As quick as I can.

SYRUS *(maliciously)*   After all, what's the use of staying around here? You can give the best advice in the world and nobody here will listen. *(Enters Micio's house.)*

DEMEA *(to himself)*   I only came to find my son, and since he's left for the farm I'm going to get out of here. He's the only one I need worry about; he's my responsibility. Let my brother see to the other one, since that's the way he wants it. *(Starts walking off, then stops when he notices someone coming.)* Who's that I see off there? Hegio? My god, it is. Well, well. We've been friends ever since we were children. Now, there's a man of the old school, a man of character, someone you can put your trust in. God knows there's a mighty big shortage of his sort these days. You won't often find *him* involved in anything that'll hurt people around him. It's a pleasure to see that some of his kind are still with us. He makes life worth living, even now. I'll go up to him and pass the time of day.

(As Demea talks, Hegio and Geta enter, stage left. Hegio, about the same age as Demea, is an impressive old fellow. Like Demea, he is by nature grave and serious but, whereas the first impression Demea gives is one of dourness, Hegio's is of openheartedness and honesty. He is dressed decently but very plainly; obviously he has little money to spare. He and Geta are deep in conversation and don't at first notice Demea.)

HEGIO   To think that someone from that family could have done such a thing! *(Shaking his head sorrowfully)* Aeschinus, Aeschinus, you haven't done your father much credit in all this!

DEMEA *(aside)* He's heard about that chorus girl, all right. Here he is, a stranger, and he's all upset over it while that father doesn't give it a second thought. I wish he was here right now and could hear this.

HEGIO If they don't do what's right, they're not going to get away with it!

GETA Hegio, you're our only hope. You're the only friend we have. You're our protector. You're the father in the family. My old master on his deathbed put us in your care. If you abandon us, we're lost.

HEGIO Stop talking that way. I couldn't possibly. Not with the responsibility I have toward your family.

DEMEA *(aside)* I'll go up to him. *(To Hegio)* Hegio! It's a pleasure to see you.

HEGIO Why, hello, Demea. You're just the man I want.

DEMEA What about?

HEGIO That older boy of yours, Aeschinus, the one you gave your brother to adopt—he's done something no gentleman or man of honor would have done.

DEMEA What's that?

HEGIO You remember our old friend Simulus?

DEMEA Of course.

HEGIO *(slowly, emphasizing every word)* He seduced his daughter—

DEMEA What!

HEGIO Wait a minute—you haven't heard the worst yet.

DEMEA You mean there's more?

HEGIO Yes, more. This much somehow or other we might resign ourselves to. Youth, love, wine, the night—it all got the better of the boy. To err is human. As a matter of fact, when he realized what he had done, he himself went to her mother of his own accord and, in tears, got down on his knees, gave his word, and swore he'd marry the girl. He was believed, he was forgiven, the affair was hushed up. Well, the girl's pregnant because of him; she's already in her ninth month. And now, god help us, that soul of honor of ours has gone and gotten himself a tart to enjoy life with. He's deserted the girl!

DEMEA Are you absolutely sure of all this?

HEGIO Her mother is my witness, and so is the girl herself. And so is her condition. Geta here, too. He's a good man, as slaves go, and a hard worker. He's managed to support the family, and keep those women alive all by himself. Take him into court, put him in irons and cross-examine him.

GETA   Demea, you can even put me on the rack. It's the god's honest truth. What's more, Aeschinus himself won't deny it. Just bring him face to face with me.

DEMEA *(turning away and muttering to himself)* This is shameful. I don't know what to do. I don't know what to say to this man.

(A cry is heard from inside Sostrata's house. All three listen intently.)

PAMPHILA *(from inside the house)* Oh, the pain! God help me, help me, please!

HEGIO *(worriedly, to Geta)* What is *that?* She's not giving birth now, is she?

GETA *(gravely)* Yes, she is, Hegio.

HEGIO *(turning abruptly to Demea)* Demea! She's imploring all of you to keep faith with her! Don't make her force her rights from you; give them of your own free will. Above all, I pray god you'll act in this matter as you ought. But, if you decide differently, Demea, I'm going to stand by her and my dead friend with all my might. He was my relative. We were brought up together from the time we were children. We were always together, in the army, in civilian life. We went through hard times together. And that's why I'll work, I'll fight, I'll go to the courts —in the last resort, I'll give up my life sooner than desert these women. *(Pauses. Demea remains silent.)* Well, what have you got to say to me?

DEMEA *(muttering, eyes averted)* I'll go see my brother, Hegio.

HEGIO   But, Demea, there's something I want you to keep in mind. You and your family live a very comfortable life. You've been blessed with position, wealth, power, good fortune. If you want people to regard you as men of character, you've got to show that you're equally blessed with a sense of right and the will to do it.

DEMEA   You go on your way. Everything's going to be done that should be.

HEGIO   You'll only be doing your duty. Geta! Take me inside to Sostrata. *(Exits, with Geta, into Sostrata's house.)*

DEMEA *(to himself)* Didn't I say something like this would happen? If only it would go this far and no further! But that fool notion of leaving the boy completely on his own is bound to lead to a real disaster. I'm going to find that brother of mine and give him a piece of my mind.

(*Demea leaves, stage left. A second later, Sostrata's door opens and Hegio comes out. He stands by the open door speaking to Sostrata inside.*)

HEGIO   Be brave, Sostrata, and do what you can to cheer her up. I'm going to see if Micio is downtown. I want to tell him exactly what's happened. If he's going to do what he should, well and good. But if he has any other ideas in this matter, I want to hear them. I want to know as soon as I can what I've got to do next. (*Leaves, stage left. The stage is now empty.*)

ACT IV

(*The door of Micio's house opens and Ctesipho and Syrus come out. While inside, Syrus had begun to explain how he had gotten rid of Demea; the conversation continues as they come out.*)

CTESIPHO (*worriedly*)   And you say my father left here to go back home?

SYRUS   Some time ago.

CTESIPHO (*as before*)   Will you please tell me—

SYRUS (*interrupting, firmly*)   He's at the farm. Probably hard at work this very minute.

CTESIPHO   I sure hope so! I don't wish him any harm, but I'd like to see him get so fagged out he couldn't get out of bed for three days running.

SYRUS   Amen. (*Grimly*) Longer than that, if it could be arranged.

CTESIPHO (*missing the point of Syrus' crack, and taking it seriously*)   Right. I'm desperate to have today keep going and end as happily as it began. The one reason I hate that farm so much right now is because it's so near. If it was only farther away, he'd be stuck out there for the night and couldn't come back. This way, when he sees I'm not there, he'll come running right back, I'm sure of it. He's going to ask me where I've been: (*mimicking Demea*) "Well! I haven't seen *you* all day!" What'll I tell him?

SYRUS (*incredulously, never having had any trouble concocting excuses himself*) Can't you think of anything?

CTESIPHO Not a thing.

SYRUS You're worse than I thought. Don't you people have any friends or acquaintances or business associates?

CTESIPHO Sure. What about them?

SYRUS Tell him you had to go and do one of them a favor.

CTESIPHO You mean when I really didn't? I can't do it.

SYRUS You can so.

CTESIPHO (*his moral defenses easily breached*) That's only good for the daytime. What excuse will I give if I spend the night here?

SYRUS Damn, you're right. I only wish people would go around doing favors for friends all night too. (*Thinks a moment, then brightens.*) Listen, take it easy. I know him inside out. Even when he's ready to hit the ceiling, I know how to make him gentle as a lamb.

CTESIPHO (*wide-eyed*) How?

SYRUS He loves to hear people sing your praises. I'll make him think you're an angel. I'll tell him how wonderful you are—

CTESIPHO (*incredulously*) Me?

SYRUS Sure, you. I'll have him crying like a baby in no time—with joy. (*Suddenly notices somebody coming.*) Hey, look!

CTESIPHO What?

SYRUS Speak of the devil—

CTESIPHO (*in a funk*) My father!

SYRUS In person.

CTESIPHO Syrus! What are we going to do?

SYRUS Get inside, quick! I'll take care of him.

CTESIPHO Remember, if he asks, you haven't seen me anywhere, right?

SYRUS (*impatiently*) Can't you shut up?

(*Ctesipho hides behind Micio's door. Demea enters, stage left. His mood is clearly not improved. In addition to his normal sourness, he seems a bit stunned.*)

DEMEA (*to himself, not noticing Syrus*) What hard luck I have! First, I can't find Micio anywhere. Then while I'm busy looking for him, I run into one of the men from the farm and he tells me Ctesipho isn't there. (*Throwing up his hands in despair*) I don't know what to do!

CTESIPHO (*sotto voce, from his hiding place*)   Syrus!

SYRUS (*sotto voce*)   What?

CTESIPHO (*sotto voce*)   Is he after me?

SYRUS (*sotto voce*)   Yes.

CTESIPHO (*sotto voce*)   I'm sunk!

SYRUS (*sotto voce*)   Come on, keep your chin up.

DEMEA (*to himself*)   Why the devil am I so unlucky? I can't figure it out—unless, maybe, I was born for the sole purpose of being made miserable. If there's any trouble in the family, I'm the first to suffer, the first to find out about it, even the first to break the bad news. No matter what happens, I'm the only one who gets it in the neck.

SYRUS (*aside*)   That's a laugh. He says he's the first to find out; he's the only one that never finds out.

DEMEA (*to the audience*)   I'm here again to see whether my brother's home yet or not.

CTESIPHO (*sotto voce, from his hiding place*)   Syrus, please! Don't let him barge in here!

SYRUS (*sotto voce*)   Can't you keep your mouth shut? I'll keep him away.

CTESIPHO (*sotto voce*)   You mean I should leave myself in your hands? Not on your life! I'm going to take that girl and lock us both up somewhere in the cellar. That's the best way to play it safe.

SYRUS (*sotto voce*)   Go ahead. But I tell you I'll get rid of him. (*Ctesipho goes inside.*)

DEMEA (*aside, going toward the door*)   There's that damned Syrus.

SYRUS (*pretending not to see Demea, but carefully speaking loud enough to be overheard*)   How a person can stay alive around here if things go on this way, god only knows. How many bosses do I have, anyway? That's what I want to know. Oh, the trouble I've been through!

DEMEA (*aside*)   What's he griping about? What's he after? (*To Syrus*) Tell me, my fine fellow, is Micio home?

SYRUS   What the devil are you calling me? "Fine?" I feel terrible!

DEMEA   What happened to you?

SYRUS   What happened? Ctesipho beat me up. And that chorus girl too. He almost killed me.

DEMEA   What's that you say?

SYRUS   Here, look where he cut my lip.

DEMEA   Why did he do it?

SYRUS   He says I was the one who got Aeschinus to buy her.

DEMEA *(suspiciously, not ready to go for the bait so quickly this time)* Weren't you telling me you had just seen him off to the farm?

SYRUS   That's right. But he came back a little later, raving mad. He was a holy terror. Wasn't even ashamed to beat up a poor old man like me. *(Shaking his head sadly)* To think that not so long ago I used to carry him around in my arms when he was a little shaver, this high!

DEMEA *(exultant)*   Ctesipho! I'm proud of you. Just like your father. That's what I call being a man!

SYRUS   Proud of him? *(With carefully studied belligerence)* If he's got any sense, he'll keep his hands off me from now on.

DEMEA *(still apostrophizing his son)*   Good boy, Ctesipho!

SYRUS   He's good, all right. Beats up a poor woman and a miserable little slave who doesn't dare hit him back. Oh, good. Great.

DEMEA   Best thing he could have done. We both agree: you're at the bottom of the whole mess. Now, tell me, is Micio inside?

SYRUS   No, he isn't.

DEMEA   I wonder where I can find him?

SYRUS   I know where he is. *(Belligerently)* But I'm not going to tell you. Not on your life!

DEMEA *(this time falling right into Syrus' trap, menacingly)*   What's that you say?

SYRUS   You heard me.

DEMEA *(taking a threatening step toward him)*   I'll bash your head in!

SYRUS *(putting on a studied act of being terrified into talking)*   I don't know the name of the man he went to see; I only know the address.

DEMEA *(grimly)*   All right. Tell me where it is.

SYRUS   You know the arcade near the market down this way *(pointing)*? Well, you go past it, then straight up the street this way *(pointing)*, and when you get to the end there's a steep slope that goes straight down. *(Meaningfully)* Go straight down the slope. At the end there's a chapel on this side *(pointing)* and nearby is a little side street.

DEMEA   Which one?

SYRUS   The one where there's a big fig tree.

DEMEA I know the one.

SYRUS Well, you go down that street.

DEMEA (*puzzled*) That street's dead end.

SYRUS (*caught off balance by Demea's unexpected knowledge of the city*) By god, you're right! What's the matter with me, anyway? You'd think I'd lost my mind! I made a mistake. Let's get back to the arcade. Matter of fact, this way is lots nearer and there's less chance of going wrong. You know the house there (*pointing*), the one that belongs to Cratinus, the millionaire?

DEMEA Yes.

SYRUS All right. When you get past that house, go straight down the street there to the left (*pointing*), then when you get to the temple of Diana go right. Then just before you get to the town gate, right by the watering pond there, you'll find a little bakery, and opposite it, a carpenter's shop. That's where he is.

DEMEA What's he doing there?

SYRUS (*thinking fast*) He's having some benches made. Er—ah—for the garden. With oak legs.

DEMEA (*snorting*) For drinking parties, eh? Oh, fine. I'm going to see him right now. (*Leaves, stage right.*)

SYRUS (*sotto voce, to the departing figure*) Go ahead. I'm going to give you a workout today, you old fossil. And you deserve it. (*To himself, after a moment's thought*) Aeschinus is so late it's giving me a pain, dinner's going to be ruined, Ctesipho's busy making love—now's the time for me to look after myself. I'll go right inside, pick out the best the kitchen has to offer, get myself a glass and a bottle—and pass a very pleasant day.

(*Syrus enters Micio's house. A second later Micio and Hegio enter, stage left, deep in conversation.*)

MICIO (*earnestly*) I've done nothing in all this to deserve all these compliments, Hegio. I'm simply doing my duty. The family was to blame for doing something wrong; I'm righting it. There are, of course, people who, the minute you complain about a wrong they've done you, get the idea that you're going out of your way to wrong them, and promptly go out of *their* way to malign you. Are you thanking me because I'm not one of that sort?

HEGIO (*quickly*) Oh, no, not at all! I never for a moment thought you'd be the least bit different from what you are. But I'd very much like you to come with me to see the girl's mother, Micio, and tell her yourself just what you've told me, that it's his brother's affair with that chorus girl that's to blame for her suspicions.

MICIO Well, if you think it's necessary or the right thing to do, let's go.

HEGIO It's very good of you. You see, she's wasting away with worry and misery, and you'll not only set her mind at rest but you'll be fulfilling your obligations as well. However, if you think otherwise, I'll tell her what you told me, myself.

MICIO Oh, no, I'll go.

HEGIO It's very good of you. People who have a hard time making ends meet tend, for some reason or other, to be suspicious; they're ready to take offense at anything. Because they're so helpless, they always get the idea that they're being cheated. That's why, if you explain in person, it'll be more effective in placating her.

MICIO You're absolutely right.

HEGIO Follow me inside, then.

MICIO By all means.

(*They enter Sostrata's house. A moment later, Aeschinus bursts in, stage left. He is terribly upset.*)

AESCHINUS (*to the audience*) I'm going out of my mind! Out of the blue to have all this trouble dumped on me! I don't know what to do with myself, or where to turn. I'm so scared, I'm weak in the knees; my mind's a blank, I can't think straight. (*Groaning*) Oh, how am I ever going to get out of this mess? All the suspicion falls on me, and with good reason. Sostrata's convinced I bought that chorus girl for myself. That old nurse made this clear to me. They sent her to get a midwife and I happened to see her, so naturally I went right up to her and asked her how Pamphila was doing, whether she was about to have her baby, and was that the reason she was going for a midwife. She starts screaming at me: (*imitating Canthara*) "You get away from me this minute! We've had enough of your lies. You've broken enough of your promises to us already." "Hey! Please! What's going on here?" I say. (*Imitating her again*) "You've got the

girl to suit *you*. Keep her, and *goodbye*." I knew then and there
what they suspected, but I held myself in: I didn't want to tell
anything about my brother to that blabbermouth and have her
spread it all over town. But now what should I do? Tell them
the girl's my brother's? That's the last thing in the world I want
to let get out! So we'll skip that idea; I can see to it that the
story doesn't get out. But that's just the thing I'm afraid of—
then they'll never learn the truth! Everything fits in so plausibly:
I was the one who stole the girl, I paid out the money myself,
I carried her off to my own home. It was all my fault. I admit it.
      (*Paces agitatedly up and down a moment in silence.*) Why
didn't I tell my father about the affair I was carrying on with
Pamphila, bad as it was! I could have gotten him to let me
marry her. I've been stalling up to now. Aeschinus, from now on,
action! First item on the agenda: go up to them and clear yourself. All right, I will. (*Walks resolutely up to Sostrata's door,
and then hesitates.*) My god, it always makes me so nervous to
knock on this door! (*Knocking*) Hello! It's Aeschinus! Open
the door somebody! (*Listens for a moment.*) Wait—somebody's
coming out; I'll get out of the way, over here. (*Moves off to the
side where he can't be easily seen.*)

(*The door opens and Micio appears. He stands in the doorway speaking to Sostrata inside.*)

MICIO   You people do as I told you, Sostrata. I'll go find Aeschinus and
let him know the arrangements we've made. (*Comes out of the
door and, seeing no one, looks puzzled. To himself*) I thought I
heard someone knock.

AESCHINUS (*aside*)   Oh, god, it's my father! I'm sunk!

MICIO (*turning and noticing his son*)   Aeschinus!

AESCHINUS (*aside*)   Now, what's he been doing here?

MICIO   Did you just knock? (*As Aeschinus stands speechless and
stricken with embarrassment, aside*) He won't say. Why don't
I have a little fun with him? Not a bad idea—after all, he never
was willing to confide in me about this affair. (*To Aeschinus*)
Aren't you going to answer me?

AESCHINUS (*pathetically trying to be casual*)   Me? Knock? Not that I
know of.

MICIO   That's what I thought. I was wondering what business you could have had here. (*Aeschinus turns away and hangs his head, a picture of embarrassment and guilt. Micio, noting this with satisfaction, aside*) He's blushing—the country's saved!

AESCHINUS   Father, tell me please, what were you doing in there anyway?

MICIO   (*with an elaborately offhand air*)   Nothing to do with me personally. I met a friend downtown and he brought me here a little while ago to act as his legal representative.

AESCHINUS   What for?

MICIO   (*speaking with exasperating deliberation and dwelling maddeningly on details*)   I'll explain it to you. Some women live here who are not very well off. I don't think you know them. No, I'm sure you don't; they only moved in a short time ago.

AESCHINUS   (*impatiently*)   What about them?

MICIO   A mother and daughter.

AESCHINUS   Go on.

MICIO   Now this girl has no father. This friend of mine is her male next of kin. The law says she must marry him.

AESCHINUS   (*aside*)   I'm sunk!

MICIO   What's the matter?

AESCHINUS   Nothing. It's all right. Go on.

MICIO   Well, he's come to take her away. You see, he lives in Turkey.

AESCHINUS   What! Take the girl away?

MICIO   That's right.

AESCHINUS   All the way to Turkey, you say?

MICIO   Yes.

AESCHINUS   (*aside*)   I feel sick. (*To Micio*) What about the girl and her mother? What do they say?

MICIO   What do you think they'd say? Nothing worth repeating. Her mother gave me some story about the girl having a child by some other man but she doesn't mention any names. She says that he has the prior claim and that the girl shouldn't marry my friend.

AESCHINUS   Well? And don't you think that's right? Because afterwards—

MICIO   (*interrupting*)   No!

AESCHINUS   Please don't say No! (*As Micio remains ominously silent, falteringly*) Is he really going to take her away from here, Father?

MICIO   And just why shouldn't he take her away?

AESCHINUS *(at the end of his rope)* Father! You've acted harshly and without any human feelings and, what's more, if I must be frank, not like a man of honor!

MICIO *(calmly)* Why?

AESCHINUS   What a question! How about that poor fellow who was her lover first, who for all I know is desperately in love with her right now? How do you think he'll feel when he has to stand by and watch her carried off before his very eyes? What a terrible thing to do, Father!

MICIO   How do you figure that? Who betrothed her? Who gave the bride away? Whom did she marry anyway, and when? Who asked her guardian for his consent? Why did the boy pick a girl his family didn't know?

AESCHINUS   Is a girl her age supposed to sit around the house waiting for a relative from somewhere or other to come for her? Father, that's what you should have told your friend. That's the side of the case you should have been on.

MICIO *(blandly)* Ridiculous! Argue the case against the man I came to represent? But how does all this concern us, Aeschinus? What have we got to do with these people? Let's be on our way. *(At this moment Aeschinus breaks down.)* What's the matter? What are you crying about?

AESCHINUS   Father! Please, listen—

MICIO *(tenderly)* Aeschinus, I've heard the whole story. I know all about it. You see, I love you, so whatever you do concerns me very much.

AESCHINUS   I hope I can deserve that love as long as you live, Father. That's why I'm so terribly sorry to have done the wrong I did. *(Hanging his head)* I'm ashamed to look you in the eye.

MICIO   I believe you, I believe you. After all, I know your character; you're a decent boy. But I'm afraid you're too careless. Where in the world do you think you're living? You seduced a girl you had no right to lay a finger on. That was the first wrong you did; a serious one but, well, you're only human. Lots of others, good men at that, have done the same thing. But after it happened, tell me, didn't you think over the situation? Didn't you think ahead to what you were going to do and how you were going to do it? How was I to learn about it if you were ashamed to come to me and tell me yourself? And while you were making up your mind, nine months went by. So far as your part in it all is concerned, you've betrayed yourself, that poor girl, and your infant son. What did you think, anyway? That heaven would work wonders for you while you took it easy? That she'd be delivered right to your bedroom door without your lifting a finger? I shouldn't like to find you that careless with the rest of of your life! (*Stops talking and watches the boy sob broken-hearted for a moment. Then walks over to him and puts an arm about his shoulders.*) Cheer up! You're going to marry her.

AESCHINUS (*looking up, bewildered*) What?

MICIO (*smiling*) Cheer up, I said.

AESCHINUS (*still bewildered*) Father, please. You're not making fun of me now, are you?

MICIO I? Of you? Why should I?

AESCHINUS (*miserably*) I don't know. It's just that I'm afraid it can't be true. I want it too much!

MICIO Go on home and say your prayers before you go to get your wife. Go on now.

AESCHINUS What! My wife? Now?

MICIO Now.

AESCHINUS *Now?*

MICIO Right now, this minute.

AESCHINUS I swear to god, Father, I love you more than anyone in all the world.

MICIO What's that? More than her?

AESCHINUS Well—just as much.

MICIO (*dryly*) Very kind of you.

AESCHINUS (*turns to go, then, suddenly remembering something, stops*) Hey, what about that Turk?

MICIO He's dead—I mean he's left, got aboard ship. (*Noticing that Aeschinus has suddenly become thoughtful*) Well, what are you waiting for?

AESCHINUS Father, *you* say the prayers for me. You're so much better a man than I am, heaven will be that much more likely to listen to you, I'm sure of it.

MICIO (*smiling*) I'm going inside to get things ready. If you've got any sense at all, you'll do as I told you. (*Goes into his house.*)

AESCHINUS (*to himself*) What kind of relationship can you call this? Father and son? If he was my brother or my best friend, how

could he have done more for me? How can you help loving
him? How can you help losing your heart to him? Mmm. And
he's made me mightily concerned now not to slip and do anything he doesn't want—simply through his kindness and understanding. I've learned my lesson; I'll be on my guard. (*Suddenly
remembering what's in the offing*) What am I wasting time
here for? I don't want to be holding up my own wedding!

(*Aeschinus dashes into Micio's house. A moment later, Demea, foot-
sore and limping, enters, stage right.*)

DEMEA (*to himself*)   I've been walking till I'm exhausted. Syrus, you
can go straight to hell! You and your directions! I dragged myself
all over town, all the way to the town gate and the watering
pond—where haven't I been! There's no carpenter's shop there
and not a soul I talked to had seen my brother. My mind's made
up—I'm laying siege to this house until he gets back.

(*At this moment the door of Micio's house opens, and Micio appears
there. His first words are addressed to the people inside.*)

MICIO   I'm going next door to tell them we're all ready.
DEMEA (*surprised*)   There he is! Micio! I've been looking for you for
hours!
MICIO   What for?

(*As in the previous scene with Aeschinus, so now with Demea,
Micio maintains a bland imperturbability that strikes sparks off the other
in his highly wrought-up state.*)

DEMEA   I've got news for you—more major crimes of that fine young
man of yours.
MICIO (*in mock despair*)   Here we go again!
DEMEA   These are new ones. Capital offenses!
MICIO   Oh, come on now!
DEMEA   You simply don't know what kind of person he is.
MICIO   Yes, I do.
DEMEA   Wake up, you fool! I'm not talking about that chorus girl.
This time it's an offense against a respectable girl.
MICIO   I know.
DEMEA   You know and aren't doing anything about it?
MICIO   Why should I?

DEMEA   (*practically speechless*)   You're not raving mad? You're not
going to raise the roof? You're not—

MICIO   (*interrupting*)   I'd rather—

DEMEA   (*too carried away to listen*)   The girl's had a baby—

MICIO   (*interrupting*)   God bless it!

DEMEA   She hasn't a cent—

MICIO   So I've heard.

DEMEA   (*again too carried away to listen*)   —and the man who marries
her gets no dowry.

MICIO   Obviously.

DEMEA   What are we going to do now?

MICIO   What the situation calls for, of course. The girl will move
from there (*pointing to Sostrata's house*) to here (*pointing to
his own*).

DEMEA   God almighty, is that the way you ought—

MICIO   (*slyly affecting to misunderstand, and interrupting*)   What
more should I do?

DEMEA   What should you do? If you aren't really upset by it all, at
least act like a man should and pretend you are.

MICIO   (*with studied innocence*)   But I've already betrothed him to the
girl, everything's all set, the wedding is being arranged, I've
removed everybody's fears. That's what *I* call acting like a man.

DEMEA   (*pointedly*)   Are you pleased with what's happened, Micio?

MICIO   (*becoming serious for a moment*)   No—not if I could change it.
But I can't, so I'm taking it in stride. Life is like a card game:
if the card you really need doesn't turn up, you use your skill to
come out ahead with the one that does.

DEMEA   Oh, you're just great at coming out ahead. You and that skill
of yours threw away ten thousand dollars on a chorus girl that
you've got to get rid of as fast as you can whenever you can.
If you can't sell her, you'll have to give her away.

MICIO   I do not have to get rid of her nor am I at all anxious to sell
her.

DEMEA   What are you going to do with her, then?

MICIO   Keep her in the house.

DEMEA   In the name of heaven! A whore and a respectable married
woman together under the same roof?

MICIO   Why not?

DEMEA   And you think you're sane!

MICIO (*smiling*) I do.

DEMEA When I see how crazy you are, so help me, I'm convinced you're keeping that girl just to have someone to do a song and dance with.

MICIO Why not?

DEMEA And the new bride? She's going to learn these things too, eh?

MICIO Naturally.

DEMEA And you'll do the cancan with the two of them?

MICIO Good idea.

DEMEA Good idea?

MICIO And you can join us, if we need a fourth.

DEMEA My god, my god, aren't you ashamed?

MICIO (*smiling broadly now*) Demea! Your son's getting married— come on, forget about being angry now and put on a smile, to suit the occasion. (*Moves toward the door of Sostrata's house*) I'm going to speak to these people here. I'll be back later. (*Enters Sostrata's house.*)

DEMEA (*to himself*) God in heaven! What a way to live! What morals! Madness, that's what it is. A wife without a dowry coming into the house, a chorus girl already there, a household costing a fortune to run, a boy ruined by luxury, an old man off his rocker! I tell you, the good lord himself couldn't save this family if he wanted to.

(*As Demea stands in stage center buried in his thoughts, Syrus saunters out of Micio's house. He has just finished a good meal topped off by more than a few extra glasses. The effect of the latter is not exactly invisible.[1]*)

SYRUS (*to himself*) By god, Syrus old boy, you took mighty good care of yourself. Did your duty by yourself handsomely. Good work. Now since I've had all I wanted inside, I decided to take a little constitutional out here.

DEMEA (*aside*) Take a look, if you please, at *that* shining example of discipline.

SYRUS Well, well, our old man's come back. What's the matter? What are you so unhappy about?

DEMEA Damn you!

[1] Act V is traditionally indicated as beginning here, but such a division makes no dramatic sense.

SYRUS   Now, my fountainhead of wisdom, you're wasting your breath
around here!

DEMEA (*between his teeth*)   If you belonged to me—

SYRUS (*interrupting*)   You'd be a rich man, Demea. You'd have made
a million.

DEMEA (*disregarding the interruption*)   —I'd make an example of you
for every slave alive.

SYRUS   Why? What'd I do?

DEMEA   What did you do? In the middle of a mess involving a highly
serious crime, whose solution can hardly be called satisfactory,
damn you, you go and get drunk as if you had something to
celebrate.

SYRUS (*aside, with a longing look at the house*)   And I had to come out
here!

(*At this moment, one of Micio's slaves sticks his head out of the door
and calls to Syrus.*)

DROMO   Hey, Syrus! Ctesipho wants you inside.

SYRUS (*sotto voce*)   Beat it! (*The head pops back inside.*)

DEMEA (*his attention suddenly caught, to Syrus*)   Did he say Ctesipho?

SYRUS (*now sobered up*)   Oh, no.

DEMEA   Listen, you stinker, is Ctesipho inside?

SYRUS   No.

DEMEA   Then why did that fellow say his name?

SYRUS   Oh, that's a different Ctesipho. Chap who scrounges for a
living. Short fellow. Don't you know him?

DEMEA (*making for Micio's door*)   I'm going to find out right now.

SYRUS (*running after him and grabbing his cloak*)   What are you
going to do? Where do you think you're going?

DEMEA   Let go of me!

SYRUS   Don't go inside!

DEMEA   Take your hands off me, you cheap crook! Or do you prefer to
get your head bashed in right here and now? (*Syrus lets go, and
Demea rushes into Micio's house.*)

SYRUS (*to himself*)   There he goes. (*Shaking his head dolefully*) Not
exactly the most genial companion to have at a party, especially
for Ctesipho. (*Heaves a sigh*) Well, until this mess gets settled
the best thing I can do now is find me a quiet corner somewhere

and sleep off this jag. That's just what I'll do. (*Goes into Micio's house.*)

ACT V

(*The door of Sostrata's house opens and Micio comes out. His first words are spoken to Sostrata inside.*)

MICIO As I said, everything's ready on our side, Sostrata. Whenever you want, you—(*Stops suddenly on hearing a loud banging at his door.*) Who in the world is making that racket at my door? (*A second later the door flies open and Demea bursts out; obviously he has just had the unenviable experience of observing firsthand the present state of his beloved child's morals.*)

DEMEA What's to become of me? What can I do? What can I say? Where can I turn? Nowhere on earth, nor on the sea, nor in heaven!

MICIO (*aside*) Oh, oh. He's found out. That's what the shouting's about. That's the end: it's a fight to the finish now. To the rescue! (*Leaves Sostrata's door and walks over to Demea.*)

DEMEA Look who's here! The evil genius of both my sons!

MICIO Now, please get hold of yourself and try to be calm.

DEMEA I've got hold of myself, I am calm, and I'm skipping the recriminations. Let's examine just the facts. We agreed—as a matter of fact it was you who suggested it—that you would leave my son to me and I would leave yours to you. Right?

MICIO That was the agreement. I don't deny it.

DEMEA Then what's he doing in your house now? Why is he getting drunk there? Why did you buy him a mistress? Micio! Why isn't it fair for you to observe my rights the same as I do yours? I'm leaving your boy alone. You leave mine alone!

MICIO It's not right for you to speak that way.

DEMEA No?

MICIO No. After all, you know the old saying that friends have: "What's mine is yours and what's yours is mine."

DEMEA Very clever. But isn't it pretty late in the game for you to talk that way?

MICIO (*very seriously*) Demea, if you don't mind, just listen to me for a minute. In the first place, if this is what's eating you, that the boys are spending so much money, there's something I want you please to keep in mind. At the beginning you raised the two boys on the tight budget you did because you figured that your estate would be enough for the two of them that way, and because you naturally expected me to get married. Well, you just stick with the system you're used to—scrimp, scrape, save, slave to leave them as much as you can. This is your ambition in life; stick with it. But let them use my money which, after all, is a windfall for them that you never counted on. Your capital won't be diminished by one cent. Simply consider everything that comes from me as so much extra. If you'll just be willing to give this some real thought, Demea, you'll spare me and them and yourself a lot of trouble.

DEMEA   Forget about the money. It's their upbringing—

MICIO   (*interrupting*) Wait a second. I know. I was coming to that. Demea, every person provides enough clues to let you make a good guess about his character. Enough so that you can often say of two people who have done exactly the same thing, "This fellow we can let get by with it, but not that fellow." Not because what they've done is different, but because the ones who have done it are different. From what I've seen in our boys, I'm confident they'll turn out just as we want them. I see that they have sense, intelligence, self-control when it's needed, and are devoted to each other. You can recognize that in mind and character they're thoroughly decent boys. Any time you want, you can get them to fall right in line again. But you're probably worried that they're a little too careless where money's concerned. Demea, Demea, the older we get, the wiser we get about everything except one thing. There's only one vice that old age brings to men: we all think about money more than we should. Well, age will sharpen them up on this score.

DEMEA   I only hope this honor system and sweet reason of yours doesn't ruin us all.

MICIO   Enough of this talk. It won't. (*Ceasing to be serious and resuming his accustomed gay air*) Take orders from me today. Wipe that frown off!

DEMEA   Well, I suppose, considering the occasion, I have to. But tomorrow, at the crack of dawn, I take that boy back to the farm with me—

MICIO (*interrupting*) You can leave even earlier; it's all right with me. But until then I want to see a smile on your face.

DEMEA (*disregarding the interruption*) —and I'm taking that chorus girl with me out there too.

MICIO (*slyly*) That's half the battle won! That's the way to tie your boy down there for good. Just make sure you keep her there.

DEMEA (*grimly*) I'll see to that all right. I'll have her cooking and baking until she's one mass of ashes, soot, and flour. And when she's not doing that I'll have her outside clearing stubble at high noon. That white skin will look blacker than coal when I'm done with her.

MICIO Right. Now I'd say you're making sense. (*Mimicking Demea*) "And I'll make that son of mine sleep with her even when he doesn't want to."

DEMEA (*with ponderous sarcasm*) Very funny. What a blessing to have a disposition like yours. (*Taking a breath and pointing a finger at Micio*) My idea is—

MICIO (*interrupting*) Are you starting in again?

DEMEA I'm stopping. Right this minute.

MICIO Then come on inside. Let's spend this day the way it should be spent. (*He enters his house.*)

(*Demea starts to follow him, then stops and remains buried in deep thought for some moments. Two or three times he shakes his head and gives other signs of bewilderment. When he finally speaks, his usual irascibility is noticeably absent.*)

DEMEA (*to himself, thoughtfully*) When it comes to life, no one has ever worked out the perfect system. Time and experience and circumstances are always bringing something new, some warning to make you realize that you really don't know what you always thought you were sure of, and to make you give up, once you've tried them out, ideas you used to think were all-important.

This is what's happened to me today. I lived a hard-working life up to this minute; now, even though I'm this far along in years, I'm giving it up. Why? Because I've found out that, when you get down to cases, the best thing a man can do is be easygoing and good-natured. Anyone can see the truth of this by just comparing me and my brother. He's always led a life of leisure and dinner parties; he's the calm, amiable type, never hurt a soul, has a smile for everybody, lives for himself, spends his money on himself—and everybody has a kind word for him, everybody loves him. Me? I'm that yokel—mean, sour, stingy, nasty.

I got married. What a misery that was! I had children—more trouble. (*Heaving a sigh*) Well, while I was busy doing all I could for them, I frittered away the best years of my life in the struggle to make a living. Now, with most of my life behind me, what thanks do I get from them for all my hard work? They hate me. But he, without lifting a finger, enjoys all the pleasures of being a parent. They love him, and run away from me; they confide in him; they shower him with affection; they're both at his house—and I'm left alone. There's just no denying that they wish him a ripe old age and can't wait for me to die. So, the children that I worked all my life to bring up, he's made his own at hardly any expense. I get all the grief and he gets all the joy.

(*Pauses, paces up and down for a few moments, and then stops as if struck by a new thought. When he resumes, his attitude has changed visibly.*) All right. *All right.* Since he's asked for it, let's see how good *I* am at this business of smiling sweetly and doing favors. I want my children to love me too and to make a fuss over me. If giving things away and never saying No is the solution, I can play that game as well as the next man. (*Suddenly reverting to the old Demea for a moment, thinks of the cost*) Here goes the family fortune. . . . (*Brightening*) Why should I worry? I'm the oldest.

(*At this moment, Micio's door opens and Syrus comes out.*)

SYRUS (*sourly*) Hey, Demea, your brother says be sure and stay around.

DEMEA (*carefully adopting an air of cordiality as he turns*)   And whom have I the pleasure—(*seeing Syrus*) Well, Syrus, my old friend, hello! How are you? How are things going?

SYRUS (*puzzled and suspicious, guardedly*)   All right.

DEMEA (*rubbing his hands and beaming with cordiality*)   That's just fine. (*Aside*) Well, I just added three things I never would have said before: "my old friend," "how are you," "how are

things going." (*To Syrus*) Syrus, you don't act like a slave at all.
It would be a great pleasure for me to do you a good turn.

SYRUS (*more guardedly even than before*) Thanks.

DEMEA Ah, Syrus, it's true! You'll find out for yourself before very
long.

(*As Syrus stands flabbergasted, scratching his head and trying to
figure out what is going on, the door of Sostrata's house opens and Geta
comes out. His first words are addressed to Sostrata inside.*)

GETA I'll go next door and find out how soon they're coming for
Pamphila. (*Turning and seeing Demea*) Here's Demea. (*Addressing him*) Glad to see you, sir.

DEMEA (*all affability*) Hello, er—would you mind telling me your
name?

GETA Geta.

DEMEA Geta, I realized today that you are an extremely valuable man.
When a servant cares for his master, as I observed you do, Geta,
he's proved himself to the hilt so far as I'm concerned. So, if I
can ever be of any use to you, it would be a great pleasure for
me to do you a good turn. (*Aside*) I'm getting in some practice
on this business of being affable and it's going fine.

GETA It's very kind of you to think so, sir.

DEMEA (*aside, with satisfaction*) A modest start—the careful capture
of the kitchen crew.

(*Micio's door opens and Aeschinus bursts out.*)

AESCHINUS (*to himself*) They must be out to make this wedding the
holiest on record. They're wasting the whole day just getting
ready. It burns me up!

DEMEA What's the matter, Aeschinus?

AESCHINUS (*turning and noticing Demea*) Oh, hello, Father. I didn't
know you were here.

DEMEA Yes, my boy, I am your father, not only in actual fact, but,
by god, in spirit, too, and I love you more than anything else in
the world. But what's holding things up? Why aren't you bringing your bride home?

AESCHINUS (*despondently*) I want to. But I've got to wait. The
musicians and singers aren't here yet.

DEMEA Aeschinus, you want a word of advice from your old father?

AESCHINUS   What?

DEMEA   Forget the whole works—wedding march, procession, lights, musicians. You just have that fence that separates the back yards knocked down as fast as you can. Connect up the two houses and bring your bride in that way. Bring her mother. Bring the whole household.

AESCHINUS   What a wonderful idea! Father, you're the nicest guy alive!

DEMEA   *(aside)*   Hurray for me; now I'm called a "nice guy." My brother's going to have a house with a street running through it, he'll have a mob in the house, it'll cost him a fortune—what do I care? I'm a "nice guy" and people are beginning to like me. I'll just have that Croesus cough up another ten thousand. Syrus, What are you waiting for? Get going!

SYRUS   *(coming out of the daze he's been standing around in since his encounter with the new Demea)*   Get going on what?

DEMEA   On knocking down that fence! *(Syrus dashes into Micio's house. Demea turns to Geta.)* And you go and bring the women over.

GETA   *(his voice trembling with emotion)*   God bless you, Demea. I can see that you care for my people from the bottom of your heart.

DEMEA   *(allowing a bit of emotion to creep into his voice, too)*   You deserve it, you and your whole family. *(As Geta goes off into Sostrata's house, he turns to Aeschinus, who also has been watching the proceedings with mouth agape.)* Well, what have *you* got to say?

AESCHINUS   *(suddenly coming to)*   Oh, I'm all for it.

DEMEA   *(putting on an elaborate air of being concerned)*   It's much better than making the poor girl—in her condition—come around by the street here.

AESCHINUS   Father, that's the best idea I've heard in ages.

DEMEA   *(with a deprecatory wave of the hand)*   That's the way I am.

(There's a sudden clatter at Micio's door and, a second later, Micio himself bursts out.)

DEMEA   Ah, here comes Micio.

MICIO   *(to Syrus who is still inside)*   My brother's orders? Where is he? *(Turning and seeing Demea)* Demea! Did you give that order?

(The roles of the brothers are now reversed: it is Demea who is imperturbable and Micio who is all wrought up.)

DEMEA I did. *(Gazing upward, starry-eyed)* And what's more, I'm issuing orders that, in everything else as well, we're to join this family to us as closely as we can, cherish it, aid it, make it part of us.

AESCHINUS *(to Micio, earnestly)* Yes, Father; please!

MICIO *(taken aback)* Well—er—I think so too, of course.

DEMEA *(firmly)* As a matter of fact, it's our bounden duty. Now, in the first place, this boy's bride has a mother.

MICIO *(suspiciously)* That's right. What about her?

DEMEA *(emphatically)* A fine, respectable woman.

MICIO *(guardedly)* So they say.

DEMEA A little on the old side.

MICIO *(pointedly)* I know.

DEMEA Well past the age when she can have children. And she has no one to look after her. She's all alone.

MICIO *(aside)* What's he up to, anyway?

DEMEA *You* ought to do the right thing and marry her. *(Turning to Aeschinus)* And you ought to see to it that he does.

MICIO What? Me get married?

DEMEA You.

MICIO *Me?*

DEMEA Yes, you.

MICIO You're crazy!

DEMEA *(to Aeschinus)* If you'll stand up to him like a man, he'll do it.

AESCHINUS Father!

MICIO *(to Aeschinus)* What are you listening to him for? Don't be an ass!

DEMEA You're getting nowhere. You can't get out of it.

MICIO You're off your rocker.

AESCHINUS Father, please do it!

MICIO *(to Aeschinus)* You're mad. Leave me alone.

DEMEA Come on, do it for the boy's sake.

MICIO Are you in your right mind? At the age of sixty-five I'm suddenly to become a bridegroom and marry a broken-down old woman? Is that what you want me to do?

AESCHINUS   Please! (*Throwing a conspiratorial look at Demea*) I
promised them you would.

MICIO   Oh, you promised, did you? Listen, boy, you're pretty generous
with what's not yours.

DEMEA   Come on. What if he should ask for an even bigger favor?

MICIO (*exploding*)   There's no such thing!

DEMEA   Do it for the boy!

AESCHINUS   Don't spoil things!

DEMEA   Do it! Say the word!

MICIO (*retreating before this volley*)   Lay off, will you!

AESCHINUS   No, not until you say Yes.

MICIO (*weakening*)   This is downright compulsion!

DEMEA   Come on, Micio, be a sport.

MICIO (*sighing*)   If you ask me, it's a mistake, it's silly, it's ridiculous,
it's against my whole way of life. But if you two want it that
much, all right.

AESCHINUS   Thank you, thank you! It's things like this that make me
love you so.

DEMEA   Isn't it the truth? (*Aside*) What shall I ask for now? I don't
want to quit while the going's good. (*To Micio*) Well, now,
there's still another matter. Hegio is their nearest relative and
now he's an in-law of ours. He's not well off; it's only right
that we do something nice for him.

MICIO (*suspiciously*)   Such as?

DEMEA (*aglow with benevolence*)   You've got that little piece of
property in the suburbs that you lease out. Let's turn the income
from it over to him.

MICIO   *Little* piece did you say?

DEMEA   All right, it's a big piece, then. Even so, we should do it. He's
going to be a sort of father-in-law to Aeschinus here; he's a good
man; he's one of the family now—it's the right thing to do. After
all, Micio, it was you, not I, who said a while ago—and it was a
very good and wise thing to say—"When we get old we all share
one vice: we think about money more than we should." This is
one black mark you and I ought to avoid. You were right to
preach it and we ought to practice it.

AESCHINUS   Father, please!

MICIO   All right, all right. (*With a nod in Aeschinus' direction*) Since
he wants it that way, let Hegio have it.

DEMEA I congratulate you. (*Slyly*) Now you're my brother spiritually as well as actually. (*Aside*) He's had a good dose of his own medicine.

(*The door of Micio's house opens and Syrus comes out, rubbing his hands and dusting off his clothes.*)

SYRUS I've carried out your orders, Demea.

DEMEA You're a dependable man, Syrus. (*Turning to Micio*) You know, if you ask me, my considered judgment is that we ought to make Syrus a free man right away.

MICIO (*sourly*) Him? Free? And just what has he done?

DEMEA (*meaningfully*) Lots of things.

SYRUS Demea! My friend! So help me, you are a gentleman! I've worked hard taking care of your two boys ever since they were children. I gave them their lessons; I gave them their scoldings; I taught them all the rules of good behavior that I knew.

DEMEA (*despite his new role unable to resist this opportunity, to Micio*) We can see for ourselves. He's taught them even more things than that: to throw good parties, to pick up prostitutes, to serve drinks right in the middle of the day—this sort of education takes a very special sort of teacher.

SYRUS Demea, you *are* a nice guy!

DEMEA (*to Micio*) And, on top of it all, he was the one who put them up to buying that chorus girl. He took care of the whole busines and it's only right that he get his reward. It will set a fine example for the rest of the servants. (*Slyly*) And, finally, Aeschinus here wants it.

MICIO (*to Aeschinus*) Do you really want it?

AESCHINUS Oh, yes!

MICIO Well, if *you* want it—Syrus, come here. (*Strikes him with his hand, then releases him, the traditional informal method of manumission.*) All right—you're a free man.

SYRUS Thank you, thank you very much. I'm grateful to every one of you, but especially to you, Demea.

DEMEA My congratulations.

AESCHINUS Mine, too.

SYRUS Thank you very much. But how I would like to have the one thing that would make my happiness complete! If only Phrygia, my wife, could be free too!

DEMEA   She's a fine woman.

SYRUS   And today she was the first to nurse his (*nodding toward Aeschinus*) son. Your grandson.

DEMEA   (*slyly*)   God knows, this is a very important matter. If she was the first to nurse him, then there's absolutely no question about it; we're duty bound to set her free.

MICIO   Just for doing that?

DEMEA   Just for doing that. All right, you can charge me for what she's worth.

SYRUS   Demea! God bless you! And may all your prayers be answered always.

MICIO   Well, Syrus, you've done very well for yourself today.

DEMEA   Not quite. There's one more item, Micio, if you're to do your duty by him: give him a little something in cash to get started on in his new life. He'll pay it right back to you.

MICIO   There I draw the line.

AESCHINUS   He's a dependable man, Father.

SYRUS   Just give it to me; I swear I'll pay it back.

AESCHINUS   Come on, Father!

MICIO   I'll think it over.

DEMEA   (*to Syrus and Aeschinus, reassuringly*)   He'll do it.

SYRUS   Hurray for the best man in the world!

AESCHINUS   Hurray for the nicest father in the world!

MICIO   (*to Demea*)   What's going on? What's caused this sudden about-face? What's all this sweetness and light?

DEMEA   (*dropping his act, and speaking in dead earnest*)   I'll tell you. I just wanted to prove to you, Micio, that the reason people think you're so obliging and so nice is not because your way of life is the right one, certainly not because what you do is fair or good, but purely and simply because of your complaisance, your indulgence, your munificence. (*Turning to Aeschinus*) Now, Aeschinus, if my way of life is distasteful to you boys just because I don't say Yes indiscriminately to every request whether proper or improper, I wash my hands of you. Splurge, spend, do what your little hearts desire. If, however, you want me to help you—to watch for those moments when, because of your youth, you're going to be shortsighted or overeager or thoughtless, and to hold you back or set you right or, when the occasion calls for it, to encourage you—then here I am, ready to do the job for you.

AESCHINUS   Father, we put ourselves in your hands. You know what we need better than we do. But what are you going to do about my brother?

DEMEA   Oh, he can keep the girl. But let it be his last!

MICIO   Well done, Demea!

(The actors turn and face the audience. A supernumerary steps forward and addresses the audience.)

SUPERNUMERARY   Your applause, please!

Epilogue

The End of Ancient Comedy

Ancient comedy had three great periods, each about seventy-five years long: Old Comedy between roughly 475 and 400 B.C., New Comedy between 325 and 250, and Roman Comedy between 225 and 150. By 250 B.C. the creative spirit of Greek comedy and, a century later, that of Roman comedy were exhausted.

This does not mean that the producing or writing of comedies came to an abrupt halt. Aristophanes' works, because of their topicality, ceased to be part of the living stage shortly after his lifetime, but the plays of Greek New Comedy and of Plautus and Terence were favorites with theatergoers long after the authors had died. Writers continued to turn out comedies, but they were inferior stuff, unable to stand the test of time. In the Greek-speaking part of the ancient world, the producing of new plays went on, not only at Athens but at other centers as well, until the second century A.D.; after that the comic stage was limited to revivals, and these lingered on for another two centuries. In the Latin-speaking part, the end came more quickly. After the death of Plautus and Terence, the adapting of Greek models gave way to the writing of original comedies on purely Roman themes, but this had run its course by the end of the second century B.C. Revivals of Plautus and Terence went on all through this period and during the next century as well, but, soon after the close of the pre-Christian era, their works too ceased to interest audiences.

What delivered the *coup de grâce* to both Greek and Roman comedy was a growing taste for more popular fare. Ancient comedy did not so much die as get elbowed off the stage. The villains of the piece were the mime and the pantomime.

The ancient mime was a farcical skit acted out with much dancing and gesticulation. At its best it was capable of mordant political satire or shrewd social comment; at its worst it was guilty of the coarsest and lewdest buffoonery. Unfortunately, it was more often than not at its worst, and its effectiveness at this level was enhanced by having the actors play without masks and by using women in the female roles, two concessions the ancients accorded to no other type of dramatic offering. The mime was no newcomer to either the Greek or the Roman stage; it had existed side by side with legitimate comedy for centuries before it finally eclipsed its rival. A close runner-up in popularity was the pantomime. This was a solo ballet in which an actor, accompanied by music and a chorus singing a libretto, portrayed a series of scenes in dance and dumbshow. From the beginning of the Christian era onward, these two forms forged ahead of all others until, by the end of the second century A.D., they reigned supreme on the stage. The theater of Orange in southern France that so impresses sightseers today, the theater of Marcellus at Rome, the amazingly well-preserved theater at Aspendus deep in Asia Minor—all these great structures and dozens of others equally imposing were used for the most part to exhibit, not the charm of Menander or Terence or even the slapstick of Plautus, but the obscenities of the mime and the corporal appeal of the pantomime.

It was inevitable that the Church, once it had the power, would fight to ban such performances. By the end of the seventh century its victory was complete, and the curtain came down on the history of the ancient theater.